Music, Music Therapy and Refugees

"This insightful volume highlights the transformative power of music in healing trauma, especially for refugees. It explores historical perspectives and influences, offering culturally sensitive music therapy methods to support recovery. The book's emphasis on ethical practices and therapist self-care fosters inclusivity and reflexivity, enhancing health and well-being in diverse communities. Above all, this book is an inspirational and highly recommended resource that promotes hope and resilience, making it a valuable addition to therapeutic settings."

—Dr. Gro Trondalen, Professor of Music Therapy, Norwegian Academy of Music, Norway

"This book is as comprehensive as it is deep. Dr Alanne carefully situates the practice of music therapy within the broader context of music and trauma and offers sage advice about how music therapists design programs to meet the needs of refugees. He balances this optimism with a powerful and important chapter on music, violence and trauma, and also recognises the work of other musicians in promoting the health and wellbeing of refugees. A rich resource."

—Professor Katrina Skewes McFerran, The University of Melbourne, Australia

"This is an important, extensive and detailed book. Sami Alanne addresses the complexities of this subject with care and attention. In this way, the profoundly affecting and complex experiences he is referring to are given the space they need. I highly recommend this text and am certain it will be an invaluable resource for music therapists."

—Philippa Derrington, Senior Lecturer, Queen Margaret University Edinburgh, UK

"This book is a must read for all musicians, music therapists, psychotherapists and other caregivers working with Refugees and trauma. It offers a fluently comprehensive narrative of wide-ranging facts and information, carefully documented, on almost all aspects of understanding trauma, use of music including the negative aspects of using music as torture, music therapy, psychotherapy etc. The author is very knowledgeable and includes a multitude of international historical data. An ongoing issue is the importance of cultural dialoging. Further the author is a very experienced music-psychotherapist within the field, which is reflected in the dynamic of the text."

—Dr. Inge Nygaard Pedersen, Ass. Professor Emerita., Aalborg University, Denmark

Sami Alanne

Music, Music Therapy and Refugees

Aspects of Trauma

palgrave
macmillan

Sami Alanne
University of the Arts Helsinki
Helsinki, Finland

ISBN 978-3-031-94765-0 ISBN 978-3-031-94766-7 (eBook)
https://doi.org/10.1007/978-3-031-94766-7

Cover illustration: portishead1

This Palgrave Macmillan imprint is published by the registered company Springer Nature Switzerland AG.
The registered company address is: Gewerbestrasse 11, 6330 Cham, Switzerland

Acknowledgements

This book was supported by the Association of Finnish Nonfiction Writers with a grant for creative working for which I am grateful. I also owe gratitude to the University of the Arts Helsinki (Uniarts Helsinki), Uniarts Helsinki's Sibelius Academy, cERAda (the Educational Research in the Arts), especially university researcher Dr Kai Lehikoinen and Professor Heidi Westerlund, and Uniarts Helsinki's Research Institute, especially head, Professor Leena Rouhiainen, for their collaboration, support, and trust in my research and writing. I would also like to thank the anonymous referees of this book for their constructive feedback and comments that helped me a lot during the long writing process. My special thanks go to the Apollo Terapiapalvelut, and to clinical psychologist and training psychotherapist Riikka Porra, also to my loving spouse, for the collaboration, time, and warm support and understanding of the meaning of writing this book for me.

14th March 2025 Sami Alanne
Helsinki

Contents

Contents

Chapter 1
Introduction

This book is about refugees, their treatment, and encountering with music and music therapy. It is based on psychodynamic and psychoanalytic understanding of trauma, music, therapy, and refugees (e.g. Ahonen-Eerikäinen, 2007; Akhtar, 1995, 2018; Alanne, 2010, 2014, 2019, 2023; Alayarian, 2024; Bruscia, 1998; De Backer & Sutton, 2014; Lemma, 2006; Priestley, 1975; Salberg, 2024; Saraneva, 2002, 2018; Strehlow & Hannibal, 2019; Stubley, 2022; Volkan, 2018a, 2018b). However, it has an integrative approach of discussing also other current trauma and neuropsychiatric theories relating music, music therapy, and psychoanalysis (Beck, 2019: Castaneda et al., 2018; Rose, 2004; Sokira et al., 2023; Solms & Turnbull, 2002/2018; van der Kolk, 2014). Especially, the phase-oriented approach of trauma work by Judith Herman (1992/2022) that is often applied in music therapy and in psychodynamic psychotherapy like at the Tavistock Clinic, UK, is forming the ground for the clinical theory for the therapy and other music-related work in this book.

According to the United Nations High Commissioner for Refugees (UNHCR), a refugee is a person who has been forced to escape from his or her country because of persecution, violence, and war (Akhtar, 2018, p. 53). Asylum seeker is a person who is looking for sanctuary in another country and is recognised as a refugee to receive legal protection and material assistance. In the definition of National Institute for Health and Welfare in Finland, with a refugee, it is meant persons who have escaped from their home country or other country where they have lived regularly and they have permitted international protection outside their home country (Castaneda et al., 2018, p. 29). Refugees have escaped human rights violations, wars, turmoil and they have justified reasons to fear persecution because of their ethnicity, religion, nationality, political opinions, and belonging to a particular social group. Asylum seekers are persons who are applying protection and a permit for staying in the foreign country. When the asylum seekers are provided with an asylum in the host country, they are given a refugee status (ibid., p. 30).

S. Alanne, *Music, Music Therapy and Refugees*,
https://doi.org/10.1007/978-3-031-94766-7_1

There are global agreements for the treatment of refugees: The Universal Declaration of Human Rights (UDHR) in 1948 is the main legal instrument, which is underlining that every individual has right to a nationality (Akhtar, 2018, p. 53). The Geneva Convention (1951) is stipulating what kind of assistance, protection, and obligation refugees must achieve from the nations that have signed the Convention. Originally, the Convention concerned the post-WWII refugees; however, in the 1967 Protocol Geneva Convention was expanded for all the countries in the world. The Dublin Convention (1990) is stating that the first country a refugee is arriving after leaving his or her home country has the whole responsibility for the refugee. However, this international agreement is sometimes overruled because of the humanitarian reasons and the equitable distribution of refugees (ibid., pp. 53–54).

According to the earlier estimations of UNHCR, there are 65.3 million forcibly displaced people in the world (Akhtar, 2018, p. 54). About 10 million of them are "stateless people", and 21.3 million are refugees (ibid.). With a stateless person, it is meant a person who is not a citizen in any country because of the reasons like sovereign, legal, technical, or administrative reasons and oversights. In addition to stateless, and persons who have a refugee status, there are internally displaced persons who have been forced to escape from their country for similar reasons as refugees. However, they have not crossed the international border and have remained in their home country (ibid., p. 53). Music therapy and music activities have been provided also for the stateless and displaced persons like children in the camps suffering from wars and other catastrophes. Their situation can be quite similar to refugees in preventing them from traumatisation or further traumatisation, with trauma-informed music therapy discussed in this book for example.

Fifty-three per cent of the refugees have come from Somalia, Afghanistan, and Syria according to the earlier estimation of UNHCR (Akhtar, 2018, p. 54). However, refugees are in various parts of the world like in Europe, US, Australia, and many other countries in Asia and Africa. The more thorough analysis and study of the history and prevalence of refugeeism is out of the scope and limits of this book. However, clinical examples and research of music therapy and music projects provided in this book are from those areas of the world and countries like Finland, Norway, Netherlands, Germany, UK, US, and Canada. The current crises, wars, and catastrophes are influencing the number of refugees and dislocated people, so it may vary.

Refugeeism has a long history in the UDHR and other international agreements after WWII. However, it has longer history in the history of mankind as a phenomenon that seems durable from the wars between Attila the Hun and the Roman Empire to the post-WWII and current refugees from conflicts of Middle East, Africa, and Ukraine (Silove, 2004, pp. 14–15). People are fleeing natural catastrophes, wars, persecution, and violence of dictatorships constantly. Forced immigration may even increase because of the more developed technical possibilities for migration and the emerging crises like the climate change in the future (Kieseppä, 2022, p. 8).

The many examples of refugees, their traumatisation and torture, including music, are beginning from WWII and concerning the victims of Nazi Germany and holocaust survivors. Musical propaganda and violence continued in the post-WWII area in the cold war and against the communists in the Greek and South America, Chile. This happened at the same time with the development of academic music therapy in the US during and after WWII. In spite of the UDHR in 1948, the dehumanising use of music and interrogations in the prisons continued until recently. Examples from Balkan War, Iraq War and War on Terror after the 9/11 terrorist attacks of 2001 in US of how music was used as a weapon and torture are described. These wars and conflicts have contributed to the number and location of refugees that have been treated with music therapy, including their families and children who have participated in the music projects and activities.

Many of the refugees including their families and children of different age may suffer from trauma symptoms: 31.5% having Post-Traumatic Stress Disorder (PTSD), in addition to other mental health issues like depression 32% and anxiety disorders 11% estimated of them having, that are increased among refugees (Kieseppä, 2022, pp. 11, 13–14). Refugees are in high risk to develop mental disorders that can be caused by the lengthy asylum process and poor social integration including additional daily stressors like finding accommodation, work, or social relationships. The mental problems and social issues of the refugees are described in this book and how using music, music therapy, and psychotherapy are relevant for their helping. Music therapy and other music therapy practices described in this book may be used in preventing, ameliorating, and rehabilitating the pre-migration- and post-migration-caused mental and social problems refugees have encountered in their home country, during their journey, and while living in the host country.

In Chap. 2 "Traumas as a Phenomenon", the history and development of trauma as a concept and diagnosis will be introduced and discussed in the context of music therapy: How music and music therapy were a part of the treatment of trauma already during WWI. The concepts of Post-Traumatic Stress Disorder (PTSD) and the complex trauma, currently also known as C-PTSD, are defined, their symptoms and appearances discussed in the context of music therapy. Also, the concept of dissociation and its history as the central symptom and adaptation to trauma will be introduced and discussed relating to psychoanalysis and musical experiences.

Use of music and music therapy will be referred to and discussed frequently already in this chapter even though music therapy and its methods as a treatment will be generally introduced in their later own dedicated Chaps. 4 and 5. Introducing and discussing music and music therapy, including clinical experiences and vignettes, with the study of history relating to trauma diagnoses will help to follow, integrate, and understand also the history and development of academic music therapy developing at the same time. Interestingly, they both seem to have common roots in the treatment of traumatised soldiers of WWI and WWII.

In Chap. 2, also the impacts of trauma for people's lives and intergenerational traumas will be studied relating to refugees and their experiences of traumatisation and music. Last parts of the chapter will introduce psychodynamic understanding and concepts relating to trauma where transference developing between the therapist and clients is discussed with special attention paid to the therapy with refugees. In this context also developmental trauma disorder (DTD), developmental theory relating to cumulative traumatisation, C-PTSD, intergenerational trauma, and how issues may transfer over generations in refugees and their families will be discussed.

Towards the end of Chap. 2, which is forming the clinical theory part of this book, early development and music, attuning, separation-individuation development and refugeeism as a third individuation (Akhtar, 1995), holding environment, transitional experiences, containing of trauma, and mentalisation in a relationship with music will be explained. This is integrated with the earlier-discussed mind and body connections of neuropsychiatric theory of trauma and the dual coding system of the brain about how music may help the traumatised refugees to symbolise their traumatic experiences dissociated or split in their bodies. In the encountering of severely traumatised like refugees, the importance of the human relationship as a healing factor is emphasised (Herman, 1992/2022). In such a work with refugees, music and music therapy may become a part of the cultural dialoguing between refugees from different nationalities and ethnicities, which will be introduced as a method (Alanne, 2010, 2019; Saraneva, 2002, 2018).

Chapter 3, Music, Violence, and Trauma, is studying the music in torture experiences and how it has been used as a weapon in wars and in imprisonment. These possible traumatising events of refugees will be discussed in the context of modern time how music has been used as a non-touch method of interrogation in the Iraq War and the War on Terrorism that has continued as poisonous "re-education" of detainees until recently. The deceitful musical experiences in prisons and camps of Nazi concentration camps, Greek and Chilean camps, as well as prisons of Apartheid era South-Africa, and US interrogation centres will be discussed according to the former studies and experiences of detainees.

In the end of Chap. 3, transformed experiences of music after violence and trauma will be discussed and theoretically scrutinised: In the musical torture of detainees like in the Nazi concentration camps, music was representing the absolute power of perpetuators and their goals of exhausting and breaking the detainees (Brauer, 2016). Similar, breaking of the detainees' personalities with defying music and sounds was used at the US interrogation centres in the decade of 2000 (Cusick, 2013). Also, the therapeutic effects of music for the detainees are described how music provided them hope, empowerment, and comfort through their suffering.

Chapters 4 and 5 will introduce the music therapy work and methods with refugees of different age. Music therapy can use active or receptive methods like musical improvisations and music listening techniques of different kinds that can be used with refugees and other traumatised (Alanne, 2014, 2023; Beck, 2019; Bruscia, 1998, 2014; Grocke & Wigram, 2007; McFerran et al., 2020; Orth et al., 2004). These methods and techniques are described including clinical vignettes from research and work with refugee children, adolescents, and adults. Music therapy with refugees can be individual or group work including psychotherapeutic methods and discussions described with clients of different ages respectively. Music therapy is the use of music by the therapist and client to help the clients to improve or maintain their health (Bruscia, 2012). This work may include all facets like physical, emotional, mental, social, aesthetic, and spiritual aspects of clients, their relationships, and music. In music therapy, music can be used directly, music as therapy, or through the relationships, music in therapy, that have developed between music, therapist, client, and other participants like in a group (Bruscia, 1987, p. 9).

The first definition of music as therapy is referring to direct physiological effects of music in relaxing, reducing the pain, anxiety, and improving the sleep of traumatised refugees, for example (Alanne, 2010; Beck, 2019; Bruscia, 1987; Vibe Jespersen & Vuust, 2012). Music in therapy is referring to the relationship and transference between the therapist and client where the therapist can be a guide or a facilitator of psychic work with listened music for traumatised refugees like torture survivors. In such a way, techniques like guided imagery, projective music listening, and free association to music discussed in this book may help the clients to stabilise, work through, and integrate their traumatic experiences of PTSD often highly prevalent among refugees, asylum seekers, and torture survivors (Kieseppä, 2022, p. 13).

Similarly, psychodynamic music therapy discussed in this book can occur at four levels: Music as psychotherapy, music in psychotherapy, music-centred psychotherapy, and verbal psychotherapy with music (Alanne, 2014, 2023, pp. 239–244; Bruscia, 1998, p. 2). These levels are overlapping and can be used in single or multiple sessions, during one session, as one portion of session or phase of therapy, depending on the therapeutic process, and according to the needs of clients (Bruscia, 2014, pp. 171–172). When music is used as psychotherapy, it can be a part of the psychotherapeutic process of working through the traumatised issues and feelings (Alanne, 2014, p. 86). It can help in solving an unconscious conflict or a problem, discharge feelings, and provide catharsis like when improvising or playing music, musicking, with refugees. Then, music can be a psychotherapeutic object for the clients in helping them to do psychic work like when listening to music or communicating through music therapy improvisation techniques that are mirroring the client's emotions and experiences (Alanne, 2023, p. 239).

Using music in psychotherapy means that both musical and verbal techniques of psychotherapy are applied to therapy (Alanne, 2014, 2023, p. 241; Bruscia, 1998, 2014). The themes of therapy are worked through with verbal psychotherapeutic discussions and interventions like interpretation, clarification, confrontation, propping, empathic describing, and mentalising for the traumatised clients like refugees. Musical methods, techniques, and improvisation are used often in tandem with words for the same purposes and goals of treatment. Music has a specific role, advantage, and often unique meaning for the psychotherapeutic process with a client that is used alternatively or simultaneously with psychotherapeutic discussion like in the guided imagery or free association to music techniques with refugees (ibid., p. 241).

When music-centred psychotherapy is approached, with clients like refugees of different ages, music is created or listened, often improvised together like in a group. However, also psychotherapeutic discussions including guiding, interpreting, describing, and enhancing the meaning like with mentalisation of the music experience by the therapist are used (Alanne, 2014, 2023, pp. 240–241; Bruscia, 1998, 2014). Music is the main method in the music-centred music psychotherapy that is used to resolve and work through some specific issues, feelings, and conflicts relating to traumatic experiences in a client. They can relate to the client's life and personality as well as to client's interpersonal relationships and transference in therapy.

For example, guided imagery, thematic listening, and improvisation of music where a therapist is providing guidance on how to listen or play psychotherapeutically feelings involved and concentrating to a specific theme discussed in therapy may be a part of music-centred music psychotherapy approach (Priestley, 1975, pp. 130–134). Listening and playing of songs that may bring memories, feelings, and issues from the client's life and trauma may be shared and understood in the context of song with their lyrics. It may help the refugee clients in individual and group therapies to work through and integrate their traumatic experiences and a crisis of being a refugee and immigrant (Alanne, 2023, pp. 240–241).

In the verbal psychotherapy with music approach, therapy is mainly verbal psychotherapy with refugees and other traumatised (Alanne, 2014, 2023, pp. 242–243; Bruscia, 1998, 2014). Then, music is only applied in helping and enriching the verbal psychotherapeutic communication and discussion with a client. Music does not necessarily relate to a specific theme like traumas in clients' lives or discussed issues in therapy directly. In the verbal psychotherapy with music, the client's problems are encountered, worked through, and resolved with verbal psychotherapeutic methods. During the psychotherapeutic process of traumatised clients like refugee torture survivors, with this approach, non-referential music may be used to relax and stabilise their hyperarousal and anxiety or in activating their hypoarousal and depressive states for talking (Alanne, 2010). Also, different kinds of musical games like "guess the song and artist" with refugee children and other traumatised clients like adolescents with immigrant background can be used to increase the communication and participation in therapy, respectively (Alanne, 2023, p. 243).

Music psychotherapy has specific goals that are relating to psychic issues that can affect also the physical and social issues of clients (Alanne, 2014, 2023; Bruscia, 2012, 2014). In this way, it is different from music therapy in general that is approaching other than mental problems like physical handicaps, sensory impairments, communication disorders, development disabilities, and ageing. However, music therapy and psychotherapy may also overlap with these and other fields of practice that may include music education, music in hospitals, and schools where music therapists are also working (Bonde, 2019a, pp. 36–39; Bruscia, 2014, p. 172). In this book, there are described and discussed music therapy with refugees at schools and communities involving collaboration of music therapists with other professionals like teachers, social workers, and doctors. This is important because not all the refugees are necessarily traumatised when they arrive, but due to cultural stress of feeling otherness and racism, they may develop mental and social issues like behavioural problems at school where music therapy may help.

Practising music therapy or psychotherapy is requiring a specific professional training that is defining the goals and skills needed to treat clients adequately and ethically. This is making them different from other practices like music education or musical activities considered as hobbies that have other main goals for their practices than treatment and rehabilitation of refugees and traumatised, for example. Even though music therapy with therapeutic goals has similarities with special education, which has social-integrative goals, and music education, which has didactic and psychoprophylactic goals, in general, music teaching is a process of developing musical skills and acquiring knowledge of music. Music therapy work and goals are primarily non-musical and focused into the therapeutic needs of clients and their treatment (Bonde, 2019a, pp. 36–38).

Thus, in music therapy or psychotherapy, musical skills and their learning are not necessary for the clients like refugees. However, music therapy, music education, and special education, and other professional collaboration in health and social care where music therapists may work, can be the same continuum in developing services and supporting the mental health of refugees and immigrants with music. These projects and collaborations discussed in Chap. 6 with shared contributions including music, arts, and culture can increase equity and inclusion of refugees in the services (Bonde, 2019a; Castaneda et al., 2018; Fancourt & Saoirse, 2019; Ilmola-Sheppard et al., 2021).

According to recent estimation of the International Organization for Migration (IOM) in 2019, there are nearly 272 million immigrants around the world (Kieseppä, 2022, p. 11). They have migrated for family-, work-, or study-related reasons but also for similar reasons of conflicts, violence, economic, and political instability as the refugees and asylum seekers included in that number. Because of the similarities in problems, forced immigration relating to the conflicts, wars, and other catastrophes is also discussed in this book, even though most of immigrants do not have a refugee background or a legal status. However, immigrants may have similar problems in the host country because of their difficulties in adaptation to the new culture and society. This can have transgenerational and cumulative traumatising effect on immigrants and refugees relating to their status as there are many stress factors that can affect their mental health and homing in the host country. These include complete change of surroundings, family, relatives, and relationships left behind, high level of unemployment, unfamiliarity of language and culture of the host country that are increasing the burden of immigrants, their families, and children cumulatively (ibid.).

According to the Health Evidence Network Synthesis Report of the World Health Organization (WHO), the engagement with the arts and music after forced displacement helped the refugees and asylum seekers creating new support networks and developed their practical skills in finding work. In addition, music promoted cultural understanding, social inclusion in reducing prejudice, discrimination, and aggression between groups (Fancourt & Saoirse, 2019, p. 10). This makes music and arts in the lives of refugees and immigrants important as they increase the resilience against the traumatic and cultural stress in strengthening the sense of safety and belonging to a group of humans in their brains (van der Kolk, 2014, pp. 78, 122, 213–214). As described in the many examples of this book, the healing power of music can give hope, elevate, and synchronise the traumatised persons like refugees' body, brain, and mind, making them feel alive and connected with themselves and the others. This makes relationships including music and music therapy very usable for the health and wellbeing of immigrants and refugees in treating and preventing trauma.

References

Ahonen-Eerikäinen, H. (2007). *Group analytic music therapy*. Barcelona Publishers.

Akhtar, S. (1995). A third individuation: Immigration, identity, and the psychoanalytic process. *Journal of the American Psychoanalytic Association, 43*(4), 1051–1084.

Akhtar, S. (2018). *Mind, culture, and global unrest. Psychoanalytic reflections*. Routledge.

Alanne, S. (2010). *Music psychotherapy with refugee survivors of torture. Interpretations of three clinical case studies* (p. 44). Sibelius Academy. Studia Musica.

Alanne, S. (2014). *Musiikkipsykoterapia*. Teoria ja käytäntö. [Music psychotherapy. Theory and practice.] Acta Universitatis Ouluensis D Medica 1248.

Alanne, S. (2019). Musiikkipsykoterapia traumatisoituneiden pakolaisten ja maahanmuuttajien kuntoutuksessa. [Music psychotherapy in the rehabilitation of refugees and immigrants.]. *Psykoterapia, 38*(4), 306–318.

Alanne, S. (2023). *The theory and practice of psychodynamic music psychotherapy*. Barcelona Publishers.

Alayarian, A. (2024). *Group analysis for refugees experiencing trauma*. Routledge.

Beck, B. D. (2019). Music therapy for refugees. In S. Lindahl Jacobsen, I. Nygaard Pedersen, & L. O. Bonde (Eds.), *A comprehensive guide to music therapy. Theory, clinical practice, research and training* (2nd ed., pp. 342–352). Jessica Kingsley.

Bonde, L. O. (2019a). Definitions of music therapy. In S. Lindahl Jacobsen, I. Nygaard Pedersen, & L.O. Bonde (Eds.), *A comprehensive guide to music therapy. Theory, clinical practice, research and training* (2nd ed., pp. 29–36). Jessica Kingsley.

Brauer, J. (2016). How can music be torturous?: Music in Nazi concentration and extermination camps. *Music & Politics, 10*(1). https://doi.org/10.3998/mp.9460447.0010.103

Bruscia, K. E. (1987). *Improvisational models of Music therapy*. Charles C Thomas.

Bruscia, K. E. (1998). An introduction to music psychotherapy. In K. E. Bruscia (Ed.), *The dynamics of music psychotherapy* (pp. 1–15). Barcelona.

Bruscia, K. E. (2012). Introduction. In K. E. Bruscia (Comp.), *Case examples of music therapy for event trauma* (pp. 1–8). Barcelona.

Bruscia, K. E. (2014). *Defining music therapy* (3rd ed.). Barcelona.

Castaneda, A. E., Mäki-Opas, J., Jokela, S., Kivi, N., Lähteenmäki, M., Miettinen, T., Nieminen, S., Santalahti, P., & PALOMA Expert Group. (2018). *Pakolaisten mielenterveyden tukeminen Suomessa*. PALOMA käsikirja. [Supporting refugees' mental health in Finland. PALOMA handbook.] Guidance, May 2018. Publications of the National Institute for Health and Welfare.

Cusick, S. G. (2013). Towards an acoustemology of detention in the 'global war on terror'. In G. Born (Ed.), *Music, sound and space: Transformations of public and private experience*. Cambridge University Press.

De Backer, J., & Sutton, J. (2014). Introduction. The music in music therapy: Writing without a pen. In J. De Backer & J. Sutton (Eds.), *The Music in Music therapy. Psychodynamic music therapy in Europe: Clinical, theoretical and research approaches* (pp. 14–22). Jessica Kingsley.

Fancourt, D., & Saoirse, F. (2019). *What is the evidence on the role of the arts in improving health and well-being? A scoping review*. Health Evidence Network Synthesis Report 67. World Health Organization. Regional Office for Europe.

Grocke, D., & Wigram, T. (2007). *Receptive methods in music therapy. Techniques and clinical applications for music therapy clinicians, educators and students*. Jessica Kingsley.

Herman, J. L. (1992/2022). *Trauma and Recovery*. The Aftermath of Violence – From Domestic Abuse to Political Terror. Basic Books.

Ilmola-Sheppard, L., Rautiainen, P., Westerlund, H., Lehikoinen, K., Karttunen, S., Juntunen, M-L. & Anttila, E. (2021). *ArtsEqual*: Tasa-arvo taiteen ja taidekasvatuksen palveluiden suuntana. [ArtsEqual: Equality as the direction of the arts and the arts education services.]. University of the Arts Helsinki, CERADA.

Kieseppä, V. (2022). *Mental health service use among immigrants living in Finland.* Doctoral Dissertation. Finnish Institute for Health and Welfare, University of Helsinki, Faculty of Medicine.

Lemma, A. (2006). *Introduction to the practice of psychoanalytic psychotherapy.* Wiley.

McFerran, K. S., Lai, H. I. C., Chang, W.-H., Acquaro, D., Chin, T. C., Stokes, H., & Crooke, A. (2020). Music, rhythm, and trauma: A critical interpretive synthesis of research literature. *Frontiers in Psychology, 11*, 324. https://doi.org/10.3389/fpsyg.2020.00324

Orth, J., Doorschodt, L., Verburgt, J., & Drožđek, B. (2004). Sounds of trauma: An introduction to methodology in music therapy with traumatised refugees in clinical and outpatient settings. In J. P. Wilson & B. Drožđek (Eds.), *Broken spirits. The treatment of traumatised asylum seekers, refugees and torture victims* (pp. 443–480). Brunner–Routledge.

Priestley, M. (1975). *Music therapy in action.* Constable.

Rose, G. J. (2004). *Between couch and piano. Psychoanalysis, music, art and neuroscience.* Brunner–Routledge.

Salberg, J. (2024). Between silence and words: Attachment, trauma and the mode of transgenerational transmissions. In J. Salberg & S. Grand (Eds.), *Transgenerational trauma. A contemporary introduction* (pp. 27–44). Routledge.

Saraneva, K. (2002). Trauma ja pakolaisuus. Psykoanalyyttinen käsitys traumasta ja sen hoidosta pakolais- ja siirtolaiskohtaloissa. [Trauma and refugees. Psychoanalytic conception of trauma and its treatment in the destinies of refugees and immigrants.] In S. Haaramo & K. Palonen (Eds.), *Trauman monet kasvot.* Psyykkinen trauma sisäisenä kokemuksena (pp. 49–96). [Many faces of trauma. Psychic trauma as an inner experience.] Therapeia Foundation.

Saraneva, K. (2018). Vieraasta kulttuurista tulevan pakolaisen kohtaaminen ja hoitaminen—Haasteet terapeutille. [The encountering and treatment of refugee coming from foreign culture—Challenges for the therapist.] In A. Zonzi & N. Söderblom (Eds.), *Pakolaisuus.* Merkitykset ihmiselle ja yhteisölle (pp. 90–108). [Refugeeism. The meaning for individual and community.] Therapeia Foundation.

Silove, D. (2004). The global challenge of asylum. In J. P. Wilson & B. Drožđek (Eds.), *Broken spirits. The treatment of traumatised asylum seekers, refugees and torture victims* (pp. 13–31). Brunner–Routledge.

Sokira, J., Allen, J., & Wagner, H. (2023). The resilience framework for trauma-informed music therapy. In L. E. Beer & J. C. Birnbaum (Eds.), *Trauma-informed music therapy. Theory and practice* (pp. 9–18). Routledge.

Solms, M., & Turnbull, O. (2002/2018). *The brain and the inner world. An introduction to the neuroscience of subjective experience.* Routledge.

Strehlow, G., & Hannibal, N. (2019). Mentalizing in improvisational music therapy. *Nordic Journal of Music Therapy, 28*(4), 333–346.

Stubley, J. (2022). The Tavistock trauma service. In J. Stubley & L. Young (Eds.), *Complex trauma. The Tavistock model* (pp. 34–55). Routledge.

van der Kolk, B. (2014). *The body keeps score. Mind, brain and body in the transformation of trauma.* Allen Lane.

Vibe Jespersen, K., & Vuust, P. (2012). The effects of relaxation music listening on sleep quality in traumatized refugees: A pilot study. *Journal of Music Therapy, 49*(2), 205–229.

Volkan, V. D. (2018a). *Immigrants and refugees. Trauma, perennial mourning, prejudice, and border psychology.* Routledge.

Volkan, V.D. (2018b). Pakolaiskriisit, uhat ryhmäidentiteetille ja jaettu ennakkoluuloisuus. [Refugee crises, threats to the group identity, and the shared prejudice.] In A. Zonzi & N. Söderblom (Eds.), *Pakolaisuus.* Merkitykset ihmiselle ja yhteisölle (pp. 33–57). [Refugeeism. The meaning for individual and community.] Therapeia Foundation.

Chapter 2
Traumas as a Phenomenon

In this chapter, the current concept of trauma and the diagnoses of Post-Traumatic Stress Disorder (PTSD) and complex trauma (C-PTSD) are introduced (Bruscia, 2012; Herman, 1992/2022; Saraneva, 2018; Stubley, 2022a; Sutton, 2002; van der Kolk, 2014; van der Kolk & McFarlane, 1996/2007). In addition, traumas and how they may manifest in the people and client's life will be depicted, including the basic diagnostic trauma symptoms. The history of understanding traumas in the context of psychology, medicine, and psychoanalysis will be described from Janet and Freud to Herman and van der Kolk and other contemporary theorists, researchers, and therapists such as Mark Solms and Oliver Turnbull (2002/2018).

Psychodynamic understanding of traumas will be scrutinised in the light of the recent literature as well as from the classic psychoanalytic perspective of developmental traumas, object relation theories, and the relational intersubjective perspectives (BCPSG, 2010; Schulman, 2002; Stern, 1985/2004; 2010). The latest understanding of traumas as neuropsychiatric and neurochemical condition will be discussed and integrated into the concept of trauma (Alanne, 2010, 2023; Rose, 2004; Solms & Turnbull, 2002/2018; van der Kolk, 2014).

The concept of transfer in traumas and their anthropological burdens over generations and in families will be introduced in the light of current experiences of refugeeism (Castaneda et al., 2018; Saraneva, 2018; Siirala, 1966, 1983; van der Kolk, 2014; Volkan, 2018a, 2018b). The relationship of traumas to refugeeism in their encountering will be cleared what kind of traumatic experiences refugees may have in general. In the end of the chapter, more practical issues like interviewing a traumatised refugee, what things should be noticed, how to be in contact and approach their issues culturally sensitively are discussed.

In the encountering of a refugee, a method of "cultural dialoguing" will be introduced especially concerning using music and arts in creating a dialogue and therapeutic alliance (Alanne, 2010, 2019b; Saraneva, 2002, 2018). Finally, the possible counter-emotions and countertransference of a therapist towards refugees and their culture as well as traumatic experiences such as possible violence, war, torture,

S. Alanne, *Music, Music Therapy and Refugees*,
https://doi.org/10.1007/978-3-031-94766-7_2

rape, and hopelessness are identified. The work stress and resilience relating to the trauma work for the therapist and protection from being empathy fatigued, traumatised, burnt-out, or retraumatising the client is approached.

2.1 Post-Traumatic Stress Disorder (PTSD)

A Post-Traumatic Stress Disorder (PTSD) is common current diagnosis for the severely traumatised persons; however, not all who have traumatic experiences are diagnosed as having PTSD. The basic symptoms of PTSD are a persistent reliving of the trauma, persistent avoiding or responding with numbness to anything that could recall the trauma, and/or a tendency to experience increased arousal of various types. PTSD symptoms can severely disturb a person's social and occupational functioning, and they usually last more than one month (Alanne, 2023, p. 310; Bruscia, 2012, p. 5; Herman, 1992/2022; Stubley, 2022a; Sutton, 2002; van der Kolk, 2014; van der Kolk & McFarlane, 1996/2007). There are many kinds of specific trauma symptoms relating to the current diagnosis of PTSD that had its origins in the experiences and diagnoses of the Vietnam War veterans in the US during the mid-1980s (Stubley, 2022a, p. 11). In addition to the mentioned basic symptoms of PTSD, common PTSD symptoms include also reexperiencing of trauma as nightmares, flashbacks, intrusive thoughts, and images relating to trauma (ibid.).

In the language of traumas and their therapy, there are "triggers" that are activating symptoms like intense physiological distress as well as mentioned numbing and avoidance of experiences (Stubley, 2022a, pp. 11–12). Numbing and avoiding symptoms include anything associated with traumatic events that are also relating to the musical experiences of traumatised clients like torture survivors and refugees (Alanne, 2010, 2023). Numbing is usually emotional shutting down of feelings and thoughts associated with traumas. Numbing and avoidance behaviour relate to hyperarousal symptoms, hyper-vigilance, and exaggerated startle responses. Also, the moods of traumatised person may be lowering, there can be distorted thoughts, depression like feeling low, and experiencing one's life shortened in addition to negative thoughts about oneself and the world (Stubley, 2022a, p. 12).

Experiences associated with PTSD diagnosis are natural and man-made disasters like being a victim of violence, incarceration, and torture that may also include sexual assaults and experiences of war (Stubley, 2022a, p. 12). The traumatic events relating to PTSD also include experiences of being in a state of extreme terror, helplessness, and life threat. The most of PTSD diagnoses are responses to a single traumatising episode in the person's adult life (ibid.).

There are also responses to children's traumas that are often encountered in music therapy and psychotherapy that are fitting the symptoms of traumatised adults as well, especially clients with developmental traumas in their childhood (Alanne, 2023, pp. 309–310). They include the mentioned depression, anxiety, phobia, poor self-esteem, narcissism, socioemotional development problems, lack of trust in others, lack of emotional regulation, impulse control, tantrums, hyperactivity, and manic behaviour (van der Kolk, 2014, pp. 157–159). There may also be other trauma-related symptoms in diagnoses like personality disorders and psychotic illnesses where some traumatic experiences in childhood, adolescence, or adulthood can be found in the treatment (ibid.)

2.1.1 Complex Trauma

Currently, there is knowledge of cumulative traumas such as complex trauma that are long-term trauma experiences first depicted by Judith Herman (1992/2022). They are chronic, repetitive, or prolonged experiences of trauma. According to her, they are experiences involved in captivity like many of the victims described later in this book who were imprisoned by the Nazis in WWII, Cold War, or during the War on Terror. The persons having complex trauma have been unable to escape from the unbearable situations of helplessness, terror, and the threat that were overwhelming and uncontrollable for their defences. Herman built her view from her clinical work with adult survivors of sexual abuse, Vietnam War veterans, and victims of domestic violence (Stubley, 2022a, p. 12). This kind of severe traumatic events that are repeated is related especially to the torture and interrogations where the target of the interrogator is to break the identity, defences, and the whole personality of the victim.

In addition to the PTSD symptoms suggested by Herman (1992/2022), complex trauma is also including affect dysregulation, revictimisation, dissociation, somatisation, and identity disturbance (Stubley, 2022a, p. 12). In this client group, there are commonly developed personality changes as well as vulnerability to harm oneself and the others repeatedly according to Herman. This relates to the compulsive reexposure to the traumatic experiences already discussed by Freud (1920/1981) in repeating the trauma as a sort of unconscious mastering and acting it out experience (van der Kolk & McFarlane, 1996/2007, pp. 10–11).[1] However, this rarely happens because instead of remembering it, the trauma is enacted in the lives of traumatised persons. Reexposure often causes more suffering and trauma for the traumatised and their closest.

Currently, the diagnosis of complex trauma in *The International Classification of Diseases* (ICD-11) of the World Health Organization (WHO, 2025) is titled as the complex PTSD (C-PTSD) (Stubley, 2022a, p. 13). It is defined as exposure to the typically prolonged and extreme nature stressor that is difficult or impossible to escape. In addition to the mentioned three main issues of PTSD, the C-PTSD diagnosis must include disturbances of self-organisation that are disturbances in affects, disturbances in self-concept, and disturbances in relational functioning (pp. 13–14).

Disturbances in affects are difficulties of emotional regulations that can manifest as hyperactivation, deactivation, and behavioural problems in traumatised persons

---

[1] The psychoanalytic concept of repeated trauma will be discussed more thoroughly in Sect. 2.5 "Psychodynamic Understanding of Trauma".

(Stubley, 2022a, p. 13). Behavioural problems of traumatised may be self-destructive, reckless, and violent conduct as examples discussed earlier. *Disturbances in self-concepts* are including feelings like guilt, shame, and failure of oneself. Also, a traumatised person may have feelings and beliefs of being diminished, defeated, and worthless. *Disturbances in relational functioning* are difficulties of being with other persons and in relationships. For example, closeness with other people may be difficult to bear for traumatised; they can avoid contacts and lack personal engagements and interests with people (p. 14).

These relate to their own feelings and self-concepts they are trying to control with their defences like isolating oneself and restricting or hyperactivating their affects or relationships manically. For example, feelings of closeness may bring forth traumatic experiences unconsciously that are tried to distance in the relationships including therapy. In music therapy, in addition to the relationship between the therapist and client, also music may arise bad feelings relating to the underlying insecure attachment feelings and object losses (Austin, 2002, pp. 250–251, 254–256). These are often manifested in the tones, noises, and dynamics of the improvised music in therapy as well as in the song contents that relate to the traumatised experiences. Music as an activity may also be a possible acting-out of the difficult thoughts and feelings instead of discussing and experiencing them in therapy.

However, this defensive behaviour, often unconscious and a part of the dissociation of traumatic experiences, is still usually a way of communicating and building a relationship with traumatised refugees or their children as examples in my experiences. Psychotherapeutic discussion may come later in the therapeutic process with music (e.g. Sutton, 2002, pp. 29–31). Acting-out in music and therapy should be separated from the playing-out of feelings in clients, especially with children and adolescents, when playing games, toys, music, and so on, creative impulses, are considered as normal and useful activities in therapy (Alanne, 2023; Bruscia, 1987; Orth et al., 2004; Castaneda et al., 2018). The traumatic experiences of children may manifest themselves in the playing, music, narratives, and drawings of the refugee children where their experiences and stories from their escaping of home countries can be communicated and shared. Music, pictures, and arts as the functional non-lingual methods of psychotherapy may help in working with refugee clients (Castaneda et al., 2018, pp. 291–292).

2.1.2 Reexposure to the Trauma

In the noticed phenomenon related to trauma, however, not included in the PTSD diagnosis, persons like combat soldiers may seek danger and excitement by joining the police SWAT teams. Abused women, men, teenagers, and children may expose them to the situations where they are mistreated again. Traumatised sexually molested children may find themselves as prostitutes or in the relationships where they are abused again. This kind of reexposure to the trauma can be harm to others, self-destructiveness, and reenactment of trauma by revictimisation where the person may be a victimiser or victim (van der Kolk & McFarlane, 1996/2007, pp. 10–11).

In the *harm to others* reenactment of trauma, victimisation of traumatised is playing a major role in the violence of society (van der Kolk & McFarlane, 1996/2007, p. 11). According to multiple studies, a lot of violent criminals experienced physical or sexual abuse when they were children. There is also research showing a link between the drug abuse, juvenile delinquency, and criminal behaviour a few years after abuse. There can be also victimisation of others after childhood abuse according to research (ibid.).

The *self-destructiveness* reenactment of trauma is common behaviour of abused children (van der Kolk & McFarlane, 1996/2007, p. 11). Studies are showing high significance between the childhood abuse and variable self-harming behaviour later in life. These include suicide attempts, slashing, and starving of oneself. Another reason for self-destructive behaviour is relating to painful encounters with hostile caretakers during the first year of life that may cause the use of very early defensive patterns.

Many clients in music or psychotherapy, children, adolescents, and adults may have trauma experiences in their childhood, even though they do not have the PTSD or complex trauma diagnoses. For example, in child music therapy, especially with adopted children, there may have been hostile parenthood and some violence in their backgrounds (Gravestock, 2021, p. 25). In addition to the physical violence, there may have been also other kinds of abuse, sexual and emotional, and severe deprivation of the basic needs of these children. There have often been also rejection and abandonment experiences that these children and adults may suffer, act out, and repeat in their current relationships.

This can manifest as a destructive playing of games or instruments, and violent talk in music therapy, school, or with their peers who they may be threatening. Teenagers may also slash themselves, steal, be sexually overactive, binge-eat, use alcohol and drugs in addition to their violent behaviour and occasional tantrums. It is not so uncommon that this kind of symptoms is seen as a behavioural disorder and asocial or borderline traits in the client's personality. However, often they are related to trauma history, repeated abandonment experiences and lack of care in the client's background that is not always understood by the client or the clinician before therapy (van der Kolk & McFarlane, 1996/2007, p. 11). Currently this kind of traumatising events in childhood, like abuse, neglect, and household dysfunction, is considered as the adverse childhood experiences (ACEs) according to their research (Svedberg Yinger, 2023, p. 48).[2]

The *revictimisation* reenactment of trauma relates to this kind behaviour of adopted children in music or psychotherapy; these children as well as other traumatised clients may find themselves repeatedly from the same kind of situations where they are treated bad or abused as victims. Tragically, there is evidence and research that those who have been raped and traumatised often are raped again (van der Kolk

[2] See more about ACEs in Sect. 2.3 "Impacts of Trauma in People's Lives".

& McFarlane, 1996/2007, p. 11). Also, those women who have been physiologically or sexually abused in their childhood will be more often abused as adults than others. However, this may be totally unconscious reenactment of trauma, especially relating to severe trauma like concerning incest. In one study, those women seldom could connect their later drug use, prostitution, or suicide attempts to their earlier victimisation of trauma (ibid.).

Also, traumatised refugees and torture survivors may have described symptoms of PTSD and complex trauma where they are reenacting their traumatic experiences. They may also repeat their traumas by substance abuse and other kind of destructive behaviours that are challenging their life and health. This may sometimes remind a behaviour of borderline or asocial personality, but like with other traumas it may be unconscious reexposuring to their trauma and losses. Some torture survivors have a lot of physical symptoms and disorders because of their torture and violence experiences. Their bodies are changed, they have pains, and dysfunctions in their bodies that are affecting their daily life that can also be traumatising.

The self-destructiveness and self-harm may also relate to these symptoms and their development when they are not noticed, cared, or treated properly in time. In this way, traumatised clients may repeat their trauma, harm, and victimisation in their lives and treatments. Like with other traumas, a person may also see oneself as a victim again or a target of misbehaviour or racism. This may be a part of the negative transference and feelings like suspicion in the treatment that can be projected on a therapist or a clinician (Alayarian, 2024, pp. 139–140).[3] Sometimes this may be also true as the refugees and foreigners may easily encounter racism and threat. It may also be *avoiding of intrusions*, *reexperiencing their traumatic events*, and *feeling of excess threat* in the present as the three main issues of PTSD diagnosis (ICD-11) and their traumatised victimisation (Stubley, 2022a, p. 13).

2.1.3 Dissociation as an Adaptation to Trauma

Refugees may suffer from the described trauma symptoms that are dissociated in their bodies (Stubley, 2022a, van der Kolk, 2014). When the traumatic experiences are dissociated, they may be projected and transferred into their families and children, over next generation. Using music and arts as the communicative methods in trauma-informed care, therapy, treatment, and as a part of education may help to build alliance and dialogue with refugees and their families (Bernard & Dvorak, 2022). Their possible traumatic experiences, what they have seen, felt, and dissociated, split, or repressed from their consciousness can be shared and encountered with creative methods. Using music and creative functional methods like singing *I*

---

[3] The concept of transference in psychotherapy and psychoanalysis will be explained and discussed more in Sect. 2.5 "Psychodynamic Understanding of Trauma".

am safe song with a child in music therapy as an example may return safety, resilience, and support the recovery from trauma (Svedberg Yinger, 2023, pp. 49–50).

Dissociation is an essential concept in understanding trauma: how it is split off and fragmented as the uncontrollable experiences of the emotions, sounds, images, thoughts, and physical sensations in the mind and body (van der Kolk, 2014, pp. 66). It means that traumatic experiences are shut out from the consciousness as the separate psychic state (Stubley, 2022a, p. 25). Instead, these experiences may arise as bodily experiences that are associated with trauma but not always consciously. Their meaning and contents cannot be necessarily understood as they are often unavailable to the rest of personality and seem to be coming "out of the blue" with anxiety and bodily experiences (ibid.). In dissociation a person is reliving the trauma that is often worse than the traumatic event itself that has starting and ending points (van der Kolk, 2014, pp. 66–67). However, the dissociations and flashbacks of the people with PTSD may occur at any time, day or night, in wake or sleep. One cannot know beforehand when intrusive experiences are coming which increases the suffering of traumatised (ibid.).

Dissociations may occur as intrusive images, so-called flashbacks, that relate to the trauma but cannot be necessarily recognised or understood as such otherwise (Stubley, 2022a, p. 25). Dissociation may also be earlier described kind of violent behaviour and symbolic acting-out of the traumatic experience without a reason or knowledge of its origins. Often dissociations are experienced and felt as somatic sensations that cannot be controlled or understood why they occur. A person coming in therapy and suffering from dissociation may not even know that one has a traumatic experience, which is the reason for such bodily reactions (van der Kolk, 2014, p. 66).

Dissociated traumatic experiences may also manifest unconsciously as inexplicable anxiety and repeating nightmares that are often combined (Stubley, 2022a, pp. 24–25). For example, a traumatised may see strange dreams and wake up in terror too early. Dissociations may also occur as unexplained medical symptoms and somatisations. There can be even hallucinations, trance, mystical states, sleepwalks mixed with other trauma symptoms in the dissociative states of a person. A person may experience altered states of awareness, daydreams, meditative, hypnagogic, and hypnopompic experiences like with drugs or in sleep.

Also, musical experience may be compared to the dissociative state when a person is enjoying music in the altered state of mind that is bringing imagery and associations like in a dream. In music psychotherapy, like guided imagery and music (GIM) and its applications adapted for traumatised refugees, for example, mind's capability to process trauma with music is used for the benefit of clients (Alanne, 2010, 2023; Beck, 2019; Beck et al., 2018; Beck et al., 2021). In spite of that dissociation is a symptom of trauma that a person is suffering even as a disorder, psychologically it can be understood as a defence of the mind for the overwhelming traumatic experience (Stubley, 2022a, p. 24). It can also be understood as adaptive strategies and states of mind like in the mentioned daydreaming, meditating, or listening to and playing music over fear and psychic pain. Thus, it is more than a medical symptom but a transient and often continuing psychic process (ibid.).

Dissociation is affecting the cognitions of traumatised as a discontinuity of experience and memory which is sometimes explaining their weird behaviour, medical symptoms, and over/underreacting in social relationships (Stubley, 2022a, p. 24). The traumatised may feel this as shameful when they are easily triggered and stressed because of the annoying sounds, smells, or bumps in the road as the signs of possible threat like in the war zone (van der Kolk, 2014, p. 67). They may come easily excited, enraged, and numb their bodily feelings associated with trauma like childhood sexual abuse. These reactions may seem irrational even to themselves as they cannot control them. They may feel ashamed because they are numbing their feelings in the birthday party of their own children or in the funeral of loved ones. This is alienating them even more of their experiences where the therapy like music therapy can help them to feel, have control, and names over their emotions and bodily experiences (pp. 67–68).

It is important to understand for the recovery of trauma that dissociation and reliving of trauma has an adaptive purpose in maintaining the psychic balance. This may sound as paradoxical because of the symptoms, suffering, and all the tragedies and consequences relating to trauma. However, in the dissociation, there is knowing and not knowing, detachment and attachment by compartmentalising of memories, thoughts, and feelings from their experiences (Stubley, 2022a, pp. 24–25). There can be separate "lockers" for everything where the things are put and stored like one client described the dissociative process and strategy of ego to survive.

With such isolations and compartmentalisations of experiences, there is no reflection in between the thoughts and experiences that are separated as the different structures of mind. This increases the fragmentation of self-experiences and development of dissociated self-states as the pathological process where there is no connection between the self and experiences, the subject and object. Another way of coping trauma or unconscious strategy of ego is to separate or have a connection with one's experiences and self-states to feel alive in acting out behaviours like compulsively seeking excitement, danger, or pleasure from obsessive sports exercising, overspeeding in the traffic, sex, and substances as examples (van der Kolk, 2014, p. 67).

Musical activities may also have dissociative purposes to shut out or act out the split self-states like in one child's music psychotherapy with an immigrant background where musical activity of playing and composing in therapy was a mean to separate oneself with musical acting-out from talking and feeling of trauma experiences in therapy. In the longer process of therapy, it became possible, even though it was difficult and manifested as interruptions and cancellations of appointments during the process. In and outside the therapy there seemed to be a different boy who was playing and doing music in good mood and positive contact with a music psychotherapist, but who elsewhere experienced that he does not like music therapy.

Thus, there seemed to be different self-states occurring in and outside of therapy, which manifested as a positive musical creativity, capability to concentrate and create a social relationship with a therapist but also as asocial and narcissistic behavioural problems outside the therapy. During the longer music therapy, his thoughts and feelings were integrated, discussed, and expressed in music. Also, the child's behaviour and capability for schoolwork and relationships improved. He did not feel so bored easily anymore which in the beginning felt so "horrible" that he could not bear it, he told in therapy. For this he needed acting-out with music or other things in his life, which he explained later in therapy.

There is normal and pathological dissociation when it is understood as an adaptation to the trauma (Stubley, 2022a, pp. 24–25). In this boy's music psychotherapy, music seemed to be both: He used music and other activities, especially mobile phone, in therapy and foster home as the means of acting-out, shutting-off, and forgetting experiences. However, he also used music and mobile technologies as the means for structured creativity by himself that capability of concentrating and containing experiences in his personality was further developed and integrated with music in music psychotherapy. In such a way, music and music therapy may be a part of dissociative process as an adaptation and recovery from trauma.

2.2 Historical Perspectives of Trauma

The concepts of trauma and dissociation began to develop in the late nineteenth century from the works of researchers like neurologists James J. Putnam, Jean-Martin Charcot, and Pierre Janet (van der Kolk et al., 1996/2007, pp. 49–50, 52). Also, Sigmund Freud, neurologist, and the founder of psychoanalysis, was the first one to develop an understanding of trauma and dissociation in his studies on hysteria with Joseph Breuer (pp. 53–54). In 1881, American neurologist Putman developed a theory that traumatisation is regression towards the earlier, simple, reflexive, and automatised functionality. Janet had developed similar ideas and in his doctoral study of 1889 had documented relationships between psychological automatisms and trauma (p. 49).

In 1887, French neurologist Charcot first proposed that the symptoms of hysterical patients had their origins in the traumatic history of patients (van der Kolk et al., 1996/2007, p. 52). Another French neurologist Janet documented 591 patients in his first book and reported that 257 of them had traumatic origins in their mental disorders. Janet was the first to use the concept of subconscious that he invented for his theory of traumatic memories. According to him, subconscious was a collection of memories and mental schemes that are guiding the interaction of a person in environment. Janet thought that if the person is in contact with one's experiences in the past and has clear perceptions of the current situations, the person can adapt oneself with the stress adequately. He also argued that if a person can develop and integrate one's mental schemes, s/he is better in coping with the future challenges (ibid.).

These were major contributions to the theory of mind that paved a way for the Austrian neurologist Freud, who developed his theory of mind and treatment named as psychoanalysis on the dynamic changes between the unconsciousness and consciousness. However, as Janet was considering trauma as the result of outer traumatising events, Freud considered in his theory that a traumatising event was a result of an inner force and a conflict within the person's ego (van der Kolk et al.,

1996/2007, pp. 52–54). Even though in the beginning Freud was referring to Janet and considered that hysterical reminiscences are coming from subconscious, he ended up developing a theory that emphasised inner world of psyche as a source of trauma.

First Freud thought that many traumatic experiences of patients had incest origins as traumatising events (van der Kolk et al., 1996/2007, pp. 52–54). However, later he considered that they were patients' unconscious fantasies from their childhood towards their parents that were repressed from the consciousness that had not happened as actual events. This led him to develop his own theory of Oedipus complex, which means the rival of son with his father from the love of a mother that provoked fear, guilty, and anxiousness in the child (Freud, 1905a/1981, pp. 56–57). Daughters developed a similar Electra complex and rival towards their mothers. The development of these complexes led to the penis envy and punishment and castration fears in children that were repressed and fixed into the phallic phase of psychosexual development according to Freud (1905b/1981, pp. 195, 233).

Currently, this view of Freud is criticised, and psychoanalysis has long admitted the existence of external traumatic experiences and their treatment as real events (Salberg, 2024, pp. 5–10).[4] However, already Freud and psychoanalysis in his time took seriously the sexual abuse of children and not denied its existence. Like van der Kolk et al. (1996/2007, p. 56) are arguing, maybe sexual abuse of children was too "awful" and embarrassing for Freud and his civilised associates to seriously consider. Sandor Ferenczi discussed and wrote about outer realities of trauma like war for soldiers and interpersonal violence affecting the children to respond with "identification of the aggressor" trauma reaction (ibid., Salberg, 2024, p. 7). However, Ferenczi's contributions of traumatised children and describing among the first in 1916/1917 PTSD symptoms like tremors, tics, paralyses, phobias in the soldiers of WWI trauma were supressed in psychoanalysis for decades (Salberg, 2024, pp. 7,9–10). His writings put him in an opposite position and disagreement with Freud and his theory of unconscious fantasies. It is also known that Freud did not write and study about much very early preverbal and preoedipal experiences that, maybe, were also too much for him. He referred to "oceanic feelings" of musical and religious experiences that he could not understand and relate to (Freud, 1930/1981, pp. 64–65).

This suggests that he had similar embarrassment towards them as the rational personnel who could not fully enjoy and explain them for his personal reasons like not knowing why music moved him (1914b/1981, p. 211). It has been speculated how he might have considered music and arts of the era in 1890–1910 in Vienna representing "musicomania" (Reik, 1953/1960, p. 6), and barbaristic regressive forces like arising of the Nazism that he was afraid to admit enjoying and understanding them as the rational man of science and Enlightenment (Alanne, 2014a, 2021; Kohut, 1977/1980; Lehtonen, 2007; Reik, 1953/1960). From the current perspective of considering his already older age at that time and new music genres like

[4] See Sect. 2.5 "Psychodynamic Understanding of Trauma".

jazz evolving, it may have been difficult for him to identify with such new music and era. Instead, it seems that he was seeing the music and culture through the glasses of normality and his own theories that distanced and excluded him from taking a part of such lived experiences.

It is important to understand the influence of Freud's view in the context of history in psychiatry and trauma that had many followers. In addition to the suppression of Ferenczi's pioneering understanding of outer and interpersonal effects of trauma, also the theories of Janet were forgotten for decades until 1980s and the developing of modern understanding of PTSD (van der Kolk et al., 1996/2007, p. 53). In spite of the strong influences of Freud, other psychoanalysts after him, especially Abram Kardiner, developed the understanding of trauma and PTSD including actual war events, disasters, and childhood abusing and other mistreatment (van der Kolk et al., 1996/2007). In the beginning, also other medical doctors and researchers than Freud were sceptical and did not believe that trauma had outer origins from a war as an example. The patients suffering from traumatic fears, stress, and reactions after a war, or a battle, were thought to be simulating their symptoms. Also, the reason for their reactions was seen as hysterical and cowardliness that had origins in the vulnerability and weaknesses of their personalities (ibid., pp. 48–51).

For example, during WWI, the understanding of the mind–body connections in traumatic experiences and their symptoms was not still developed (van der Kolk et al., 1996/2007, pp. 48–49). Before trauma and battle neuroses were concerned, doctors did not know how to discern between cowardliness and breakdowns of brave men, poor morale, and poor leadership in units. In the late nineteenth century, there were descriptions like "railroad spines", "irritable hearts", or "soldiers' heart" referring to the organic conditions separated from the psychological origins of trauma (p. 48). In 1915, a British military psychiatrist Charles Samuel Myers used the term "shell-shock", and it was accepted widely even though it was noticed that men who were not directly exposed to gunfire could experience it too (ibid., pp. 48–49).

In 1919, Janet argued that traumatic experiences were relating to the cognitive schemes how the frightening experiences are incapable to match the earlier schemes (van der Kolk et al., 1996/2007, p. 52). Thus, they could not come to awareness as they were split off from the consciousness and could not be controlled voluntarily. This was the original idea of dissociation in traumatic experiences that was explained with cognitive psychology. In my opinion, it is a psychodynamic theory of the conflicting psychic representations that cannot be integrated. As such, it may be understood as a neurotic constellation where the frightening experiences cannot be thought, verbalised, or adapted adequately. Janet noticed that the reactions of the traumatised were relevant responses for the trauma event, but they could not adapt with new responses to the situations that reminded their trauma currently. He proposed that because of the extreme emotional arousal people were "unable to make a recital which we call narrative memory, and yet they remain confronted by [the] difficult situation" (Janet cited in van der Kolk et al., 1996/2007, p. 52).

Janet argued that because of the "phobia of memory" that is split off, there cannot be a synthesis of traumatic events into the ordinary consciousness (van der Kolk et al., 1996/2007, p. 52). These are early formulations of dissociation and the need for integration of traumatic experiences as we currently know them. Janet explained that traumatic experiences remain as "fixed ideas" in the mind if they are not "liquidated" and translated into a personal narrative (ibid.). Otherwise, they will continue to be reexperienced as intrusive thoughts, terrifying perceptions, obsessional behaviour, and bodily experiences like anxiety reactions. This is the current clinical theory how trauma experiences are manifested and represented as symptoms that are treated with free association, reexposure, narrative, or grounding techniques in psychotherapy. However, it would still take many decades before there was even a consensus of psychic trauma, diagnostic agreements, or its treatment (ibid., p. 53).

Freud's ideas and theory were very close to Janet's theory of unconscious fixed ideas that patients are unable to integrate the trauma and seem to be "attached" to it (van der Kolk et al., 1996/2007, p. 53). In Freud's theory, there are also fixation points of childhood conflicts and trauma that are manifested as symptoms or repeating of trauma. However, the early Freud's psychoanalysis pointed fixations and repeating of trauma rising from the Eros and Thanatos, the sexual and death instincts, and their driving energies seeking to restore the earlier state of things (Freud, 1920/1981, pp. 44, 62). Janet's theory was more at the cognitive level of schemas how traumatised were unable to assimilate new experiences as they are loose psychological energies in their efforts to keep the fragmented trauma contents out of their awareness (van der Kolk et al., 1996/2007, pp. 53–54).

Later, Freud did not accept the idea of dissociation as the hypnoid states even though he first believed that dissociation and splitting off the contents of consciousness and fixation in the trauma memories were the essential explanation of hysteria (van der Kolk et al., 1996/2007, p. 53). As discussed, Freud rejected the idea of true events as the explanation of childhood trauma and thought they were repressed unacceptable sexual and aggressive wishes of children. Freud explained the amnesia of childhood and trauma with psychic defences of ego in favour of his own theory and doctrine of psychoanalysis that compelled the competition in thinking of trauma for a long time.

However, there were other psychoanalysts that were interested in war traumas, like Wilfred Bion at the Tavistock Clinic, in United Kingdom, who trained and treated soldiers during WWII after her his own experiences in WWI. Later, he published a well-known study of the topic *Experiences in Groups* (Bion, 1961/2004), which was a ground-breaking reference book in group therapy including music therapy. The Tavistock Clinic was founded in 1920 by Chrichton-Miller and his colleagues, who had a lot of experiences from WWI in treating traumatised soldiers (Temple & Waddell, 1998/2002). By founding the Tavistock, they wanted to provide psychological treatment for all traumatised, not only from war. This knowledge of the clinic was used in WWII. However, during WWII there was still no proper diagnosis and treatment for the trauma outside or in the battlefield other than shell-shock (van der Kolk et al., 1996/2007, p. 49). Therefore, it was very difficult to separate the trauma from cowardliness for the doctors at the time. For example, over

200 British soldiers were executed because of cowardliness during WWII. This was 11% of those who were accused and convicted to death for cowardliness. Thus, it seems that there had developed some understanding and empathy for trauma from the earlier studies.

2.2.1 Treating Traumas with Music and Music Therapy in WWII

Because of the growing understanding of trauma and its relationships with emotions, the military forces became more concerned about emotional wellbeing and spirits of the groups. Here also music and music therapy came in during WWII to increase the wellbeing of soldiers. This can be seen as a preventive trauma work and therapy in a time when the military forces and medicine officially denied the existence of a war trauma or post-stress-related syndrome. Music was recommended in the US War Department document during WWII as "one of the most effective vehicles for bringing a group together, for releasing the emotions, and for creating a spirit of fellowship and spirit de corps—if he simply listens to music, his interest are broadened and his sense of well-being is generally increased" (Sullivan, 2007, p. 288).

Music therapy as a profession and education developed during WWII as the therapeutic effects of music had been recognised in the US War Department (AMTA, 2014, p. 6). Most usually music was used to increase the spirits of the troops, but music therapy was also included in the physical and emotional rehabilitations. For some reason, this was not told to the public or media. The military officers were interested in developing promising music-based interventions for the injured who needed long-term medical or psychological services. In 1945, the Office of the Surgeon General created a detailed programme for the use of music in rehabilitating soldiers in Army hospitals. In this programme, published in the *Technical Bulletin 187* of the same year, music was included in the recreation, education, occupational therapy, and physical reconditioning therapy services.

There were 122 VA hospitals where this therapy service including music was provided and 80,000 service members were participating in one or more music programmes according to the report of US War Department published in the *Technical Bulletin 187* of 1945. There were 7538 patients who received medically referred or recommended music services. Over 276,000 service members participated in recreational and music programmes. This is often considered to be the beginning of modern music therapy and its study when it was also noticed that there was a need of more studies to prove the therapeutic value of music (AMTA, 2014, pp. 6–7).

However, already in WWI there were amateur and professional musicians who went to veteran hospitals performing for the thousands who had physical or emotional traumas. As a result of patients' consistent positive physical and emotional responses to music, physicians and nurses requested to hire more musicians. At the same time, it was noticed that musicians would need a training to be able to work adequately in healthcare hospital conditions. In 1919, at the Columbia University there was the first music therapy course by Margaret Anderton. Anderton had experience of providing music-adapting services during WWI for the wounded Canadian soldiers (AMTA, 2014, p. 6).

The first US musicians performing in Veteran hospitals during WWII included women like Anderton in WWI playing in bands as their military service (Sullivan, 2007). However, performing music in hospital was not new in US either as it had been already done during the American Civil War in nineteenth century (ibid., p. 284). Already, in the Civil War hospitals there were permanent civilian or regimental bands playing for the injured. Also, the boosting effects for the moral of soldiers, motivation, healing, and surviving from the war were noticed by the interviewed volunteer following one band's performance at that time. In this regard using music to alleviate physical or psychological pain was not a new discovery in the veteran hospitals of US.

Also, other kinds of military strategies of using music developed during the 1930s and 1940s, not just for the spirits and therapy, but also for increasing physiological and emotional exhaustion and pain (Brauer, 2016; John, 1991/2001; Moreno, 1999; Naliwajek-Mazurek, 2013). Before, during, and after the WWII music was used in Nazi concentration camps as well as for the political detainees in Greek influenced by US and NATO, using these positive effects of music to torment prisoners (Papaeti, 2013a & b).[5] Maybe this is one of the reasons, using music in the army, even as a part of rehabilitation or providing spirits and empowerment for the troops, was not publicly addressed.

Nazis in Germany used music and other arts to camouflage their crimes and murdering for the media and public in the Theresienstadt concentration camp (John, 1991/2001). In wars, actual goals, missions, forces, and capabilities are often hided from the public and enemy for strategical reasons. It is conflictual in this context that the trauma related to violence, war, and other disasters was denied during these times, especially in 1940s and afterwards, when music was used to exhaust detainees psychologically and physically, to give up their spirits. Also, other kinds of brainwash and torture techniques using sounds and sensory deprivation to manipulate the mind and break the will and ego of the detainees emerged in the Cold War after WWII where US and Central Intelligence Agency (CIA) were involved.[6] This nonethical use of music as a weapon and torture seemed to begin to develop around WWII as the therapeutic use of music. Interestingly, they were both studied and used by the military forces first and they have continued to be used until present.

This denying of trauma in medicine may relate to politics of military forces and their governments that allowed violence, torture, and other activities that produced trauma for the soldiers and other people. In this way, they did not have to take

[5] See Chap. 3 for the study and discussion of music as a weapon as a part of violence in wars, interrogations, and prisons.

[6] See Chap. 3 for the discussion of Cold War methods, music, and sounds in causing trauma.

responsibility for trauma as there did not exist one. As discussed by van der Kolk et al. (1996/2007), psychiatry is a mirror of the society, culture, and "the spirit of age" (p. 66). Cultural values are affecting psychiatry and psychology of how the situation of women and children, sexuality, or refugees, and trauma are discussed and diagnosed in the society. For example, trauma was long seen as a traumatic neurosis and episodic illness. Similarly, different sexual expression and identity from the public were seen as perversion, illness, or even as a crime like homosexualism. So, public accepting trauma and other clinical diagnostics requires and involves financial consideration, legal processes, economic and political processing, as well as questions concerning their compensation for the soldiers and workers (pp. 66–67).

2.2.2 Development of PTSD Diagnosis

As already told, the acceptance of PTSD diagnosis took until 1980s finally. It was a long process that required a work of many pioneers mentioned. Abram Kardiner had a special contribution in developing and integrating trauma work and study beginning from the 1920s when he treated traumatised US war veterans (van der Kolk et al., 1996/2007, p. 56). First, in 1923, he failed to build his theory of war neuroses on early psychoanalytic theory. However, during WWII, in 1941, he re-evaluated and published his careful clinical observations and detailed descriptions of complex and not ordinary symptoms of his patients. In these cases, he showed how these patients had many diagnoses in their backgrounds before it was understood that there was a connection between their trauma and current symptoms. The symptoms of patients with trauma included hysteria, malingering, and epileptiform disorders. These findings already demonstrated the diagnosis of PTSD that was finally officially defined and included in 1980 to the DSM-III of the American Psychiatric Association (APA) (ibid., pp. 57, 61).

Like Janet and Freud, Kardiner understood that the symptom of trauma was relived in the experiences of traumatised (van der Kolk et al., 1996/2007, pp. 57–58). These patients often had vague dissociative states where they were easily triggered by some sensory stimuli. Suddenly, these traumatised patients could hit and defend themselves like being assaulted in a war. Also, they could have flashbacks of being in a trench when they were riding a metro and going to a tunnel. Others had panic attacks triggered from the stimulus that reminded somehow of their trauma. They could not understand that their unordinary conscious experiences and emotional states were responses of their earlier unconscious trauma (p. 58). Kardiner also noticed that these patients suffered and reacted from sensitivity to pain, temperature, and other sudden stimuli like a slap in their back or sudden misstep as examples. They were stuck in their trauma as they easily felt useless to any activity and became withdrawn and detached (p. 57).

In addition to the treatment and study of WWII veterans, there were also studies of concentrations camp survivors (van der Kolk et al., 1996/2007, pp. 58–60). Their traumatic experiences relating to the use of music in the camps will be studied in the next chapter of this book. During WWII, there was a lot of interest to treat military personnel with groups as there were pioneering group stress debriefing treatment in US Army, for example. Also, hypnosis and narcosynthesis were tried, so that the patients would remember and abreact their trauma. It confirmed Janet's view that abreaction in not enough without transformation and substitute for the treatment of trauma. Also, Freud (1914a/1981, pp. 150–151) and psychoanalysis had in this point changed their earlier view of the abreaction as the curative factor in psychoanalysis. Instead, the durable change from traumatic experiences and their compulsory repetition in transference between the therapist and client would need remembering and working through obstacles in the mind identified as psychic resistance. British Bion and his colleagues started using group psychotherapy and therapeutic community because of their war experiences (van der Kolk et al., 1996/2007, p. 59). However, the work and experiences of war trauma were soon forgotten for decades as well as the pioneering discoveries of Janet and Kardiner (ibid.).

After WWII, the researchers of concentration camp survivors followed the long-term effects of trauma in the Holocaust survivors as well as other war-related traumas (van der Kolk et al., 1996/2007, pp. 59–60). The researchers came up with the term of "concentration camp syndrome" (p. 59). It already included the symptoms of the later PTSD diagnosis as well as durable personality changes of the traumatised. One of the most important findings was the extreme and long-lasting stress these survivors suffered that affected their health in later life (p. 60). Another psychoanalyst Henry Krystal wrote about long-term effects of massive traumatisation in concentration camps. These traumatised had a core experience of "giving up" when they accepted their death and destruction as unavoidable (ibid.).

Also, Krystal already referred to the hyperalert anxiety, progressed blocking of emotions, and behavioural inhibitions in the Holocaust survivors (van der Kolk et al., 1996/2007, p. 60). According to him, they also seemed to experience their feelings as somatic states and could not describe their meaning. Instead of adaptive responses, they were prone to undifferentiated affect storms and psychosomatic reactions. Krystal emphasised that the development of "alexithymia" as this phenomenon is still known is in the core of the psychosomatic symptoms typically occurring in chronically traumatised persons (ibid.).

These were important observations and findings as many of the traumatised clients, like refugees, may not have words for their feelings; instead they may have sudden headaches, feelings in their stomach, etc., that they cannot explain. These may arise at stressful situations or triggered by some stimuli or feeling even during the psychotherapy or music therapy sessions like in the earlier-referred young boy's music therapy who had sometimes sudden headaches and stomach issues during improvisations. Then, they can be explored and contained verbally or musically. Sometimes they will pass quite quickly during the session like this boy who needed a bit of concentration and a pause before continuing his improvisation. With self-made music this boy could represent his feelings in music during his music therapy.

2.2.3 *Contextualising Traumatic Experiences and Their Treatment*

Interestingly from the modern gender and sexual discourse point of view, the study of trauma included mainly white males from 1895 to 1974 (van der Kolk et al., 1996/2007, pp. 60–61). In 1970s began the study of abused children and family violence, and the "rape trauma syndrome" was described in 1974 by Ann Burgess and Linda Holmstrom working at Boston City Hospital. They noticed that victims of rape suffered from the similar symptoms like terrifying flashbacks, nightmares, insomnia, nausea, startle responses, dissociation, and numbing symptoms as those suffering from traumatic neuroses of war (see also Herman, 1992/2022, pp. 44–45). However, even in 1980 the incest was still belittled to be very rare among women and causing no particular damage in the leading textbook of psychiatry in the US (van der Kolk et al., 1996/2007, p. 61).

In 1981, a pioneering researcher of trauma, psychiatrist Judith Herman from the US began to document the evidence of widely spread sexual abuse of children and its devastating effects on them. Herman (1992/2022, p. 46) compared the neuroses of war with the "war of sexes" where the raped victims, beaten women, and sexually molested children are casualties. She referred to the "battered women syndrome" of the women who had to escape to the shelter (ibid.). It came from psychologist Lenore Walker and her discovery of psychological trauma of the abused women and children after 1980. This development was partly a result of the feminist movement for women's rights and rape victims beginning in 1970s (ibid., pp. 44–47). As a result of the Boston study of the raped and abused women and children looking for shelter by Burges and Holmstrom in 1974, the children's sexual abuse was rediscovered according to Herman (p. 45). Herman also sees the war of sexes as the "recapitulated hysteria" of the nineteenth-century combat neurosis where women and children are maintained in the "hidden violence of men" (ibid.). It is fair enough to say that there are also women who are violent and toxic psychologically to their children and families contributing to the traumatising family dynamics. The reason for this may be that a parent like a refugee is traumatised him/herself and is projecting/transferring the trauma into the family and producing a vicious circle of traumatisation.

However, it was a historical turn, even a paradigm shift, in addition to the emerging of PTSD diagnosis, documenting and understanding the trauma experiences of abused women and children. For example, Freud (1900/1981) had rejected his original theory that patients had experienced sexual abuse and incest in their childhood that was causing their traumatisation. He considered that they seem to be so common experiences that they cannot be true but instead he believed that they were patients' unconscious fantasies and early sexual interests and rivalry towards their parents that were repressed (pp. 256–258, 260–264). Currently, the adverse impacts on children and their development are better understood as the ACEs, but still the developmental traumas of children and adolescents are not necessarily noticed and understood properly (van der Kolk, 2014, pp. 149–151).[7] Even though there are a lot of documentation and research from the 1980s, there is still not an official recognition and diagnosis of developmental trauma (van der Kolk et al., 1996/2007, p. 64).

In spite of the pioneering works of Herman (1992/2022) and Bessel van der Kolk (2014), another US psychiatrist and psychotherapist, who has contributed significantly to understanding and treating trauma globally from the 1980s until present, adverse effects in development are still not often necessarily considered and recognised as traumas. Even though ACEs and childhood maltreatment are causing in people many kinds of symptoms like dissociation, depression, anxiety, substance abusing, self-harm, and suicide attempts (Grummitt et al., 2024; van der Kolk, 2014). In my experiences of adult and child clients in music therapy and psychotherapy, it is common that causes of depression, rage, anxiety, hyperactivity, incapability to concentrate, numbness, even psychotic episodes, panic attacks, substance abuse, and other addictions as examples are not understood as traumatic reactions or dissociation resulting from often harsh experiences of deprivation, negligence, and abusing in their life history (van der Kolk, 2014, pp. 157–59). This can be unclear for the client, parents, teachers, and the treating staff as also noticed by van der Kolk (ibid., pp. 149–151). As a result, many clients come to therapy without a trauma diagnosis.

Traumatised refugees, war veterans, including Vietnam War, war children, sexually abused children, and women have been treated with music therapy and studied since 1980s (Orth et al., 2004, pp. 443, 449). In 1982, a pioneering Dutch music therapist Jaap Orth began to work with traumatised refugees in the Netherlands. He used music therapy methods like improvisational music therapy, for example singing and discussion used with children of Balkan War in 1990s and Guided Imagery and Music (GIM), which was also used with Vietnam veterans. GIM is a method of producing mental imagery and narratives in a client with music that are psychotherapeutically guided and discussed during the listening of prechosen musical programme and reflected after the experience (ibid., pp. 445–449).

In addition to the music therapy methods used with other traumatised, he had to adapt and develop new kinds of approaches in his music therapy practice at the Phoenix-centre, a part of the De Gelderse Roos health organisation in the Netherlands (Orth et al., 2004, p. 449). This was because there were cultural differences in his clients like how they understood music and "being ill" (ibid.). He noticed that clients were dealing their unhealthiness differently depending on their culture. In the Western world, people are discussing their mental issues and complaints directly, but people from the other parts of the world, even three-quarters of world population, are experiencing their health complaints in a physical way.

This somatisation relating to mental issues in clients from other than the Western culture—adult and children—in music therapy including torture survivors I have noticed myself too (Alanne, 2010). Clients from different cultures like from Middle

[7] See Sect. 2.3 "Impacts of Trauma in People's Lives" for the description and discussion of Adverse Childhood Experiences (ACEs).

East may talk about headaches instead of their depression and anxiety as mental concepts. This is different than the earlier-mentioned alexithymia relating to trauma, whilst they can relate to each other as an incapability to speak about feelings. However, I think they are also important to understand separately and not to medicalise or judge culture differences and norms according to the Western ideologies.

This relates also to the developed discussion and criticism towards PTSD diagnosis and trauma treatment when other than white males were began to be studied in the 1990 and early 2000 decades. Researchers were interested in how people from other parts of the world and different societies like Uganda managed with their social functioning, mental issues, and traumas (Bracken, 2003, p. 75). In Uganda, intrusive and avoidance symptoms were found in people that had suffered from war if they were asked specifically. However, this was not necessarily related to their level of social functioning that was maybe better even though they had highest scores on PTSD symptoms.

In 1991, similar results and discussion relating to the cultural differences arose from the study in Nicaragua of war-displaced people who were survivors of atrocities (Bracken, 2003, p. 75). They had psychosomatic complaints when they asked for help; however, they were active and effective in maintaining their social life even though they had PTSD symptoms commonly. Also, in 1987, one earlier study of Cambodian war refugees in the US was reported with similar results that the same intrusive–avoidance symptom complex does not have necessarily the same significance in other cultures and settings.

Also, people from different cultures may understand dreams like nightmares differently because they may be considered the same as the waking reality (Bracken, 2003, p. 76). There are also different understandings of deity and spiritually how illnesses and effects of treatment like music therapy are understood. One torture survivor, described later in this book, from Africa wondered whether I am some kind of medicine man because I could bring him so clear imagery with music from his home country in a music psychotherapy session (Alanne, 2010). In addition to the positive experiences, dreams and imagery relating to them may be very frightening and having special significance in the lives and behaviours of some people from other cultures. In other cultures, dreams are considered as irrational and insignificant, and it may be difficult to understand nightmares as intrusive symptoms of trauma, for example (Bracken, 2003, p. 76).

In music therapy with traumatised refugees, especially working with Vietnamese refugees, Orth began to develop new ideas to approach clients and music from the cultural point of view (Orth et al., 2004, pp. 449–451). He noticed that clients from different cultures perceived, interpreted, and expressed music differently. Orth began to develop and build musical instruments that could be played and improvised in pentatonic scales and quarter tones that enabled the clients to produce music easier. According to him, in this way they could tune their music into their own culture and overcome the obstacles with other music that they could join now (p. 450).

It seems that in this way clients as well as the therapist could speak the same musical language and understand each other. This enabled the helping of clients with music as a sort of universal language when the therapist or a client could not speak the same language verbally. Music, music therapy, and other creative forms of therapy are still used and recommended as non-verbal methods of treatment and study with refugees. Especially, they are used with children who have long-lasting symptoms, lingual problems, and difficulties to express themselves because of their traumatic experiences (Castaneda et al., 2018. p. 291).

In 1994, another development in contextualising the trauma was the adding of acute stress syndrome (ASD) to the DSM-IV (Solomon et al., 1996/2007, p. 103). It included short-term elevated reactions like PTSD symptoms of intrusiveness, hyperarousal, anxiety, and avoidance from two days to one month after traumatising event (p. 110). Also, there had to be noticeable interferences in social and occupational functioning or difficulties to perform a necessary task for the person. Many professionals thought that pathologising possibly normal adaptation to the stressful situation could prevent the recovery. Also, in a combat situation, it could be a part of normal functionality. Therefore, it was suggested that it is the intensity and the extensity of stress reactions and their interference with the functioning that are distinguishing the dysfunctional and functional anxiety and stress from the normal (ibid.).

Sutton (2002, pp. 22–24) is considering the ASD diagnosis as helpful in understanding how people may suffer from more acute and distressing symptoms of traumas in the first 48 hours. After that they usually are lessening, and not all of them are developing to a PTSD. Even though there may have been symptoms like numbing, detachment, derealisation, and depersonalisation, they will lessen after one month. According to Sutton, separation of the ASD and PTSD diagnoses enables the seeing of the trauma from the immediate high level of distress to the long-lasting effects and symptoms. In this sense, trauma is not a single event produced by the external factor like it is often verbalised and understood. Instead, it continues to repeat itself as an internal process and an attempt to assimilate what a person has seen or experienced. This can be an accident, natural disaster, acts of war, the death of close one, violence, and torture that anyone or especially refugees may have experienced and witnessed as a traumatic experience that is continuing to affect their lives.

In music therapy, this may be a traumatised child whose father has been in local army and in danger because of surrounding troubles in Northern Ireland (Sutton, 2002, p. 29). They had affected his mind and manifested as increasingly aggressive and chaotic behaviour in the schoolroom and playground when he came to music therapy. He was in the place for the children with complex speech and language impairment. Under stress he was unable to produce words. First, his music was chaotic and unformed in music therapy, and there were fragments of "attacks" on the instruments (ibid.). However, as the therapy progressed, he was able improvise a story, The Trap, during six sessions. He told many scenarios in which occurred monsters, something lurking in a wood, an army, bombs, and bullets. For the therapist, they revealed the fears of the boy towards his father who was fighting in a local army. Narratives also seemed to represent the fears of the population at the time when few months later a big bomb killed and wounded several people. Violence, murder, and bombs were happening also during the music therapy sessions (ibid.)

It seems that in music therapy of 40 sessions this eight-year-old boy could tell and express his inner conflict that was intensified to the scream and rage (Sutton, 2002, pp. 29–32). After this cathartic point, he was relaxed and playful in the therapy. As a result of music therapy, the boy's non-fluency in speech vanished, and he could leave the specialist school and integrate into normal education. I think this is a good example of music therapy process where adverse childhood and traumatising experiences are encountered first non-verbally with music and then with storytelling where the language skills are developed. Also, the trauma itself seemed to be working through emotionally and verbally with a music therapist. It possibly finally decreased the anxiety relating to the secret in a family and community. Working through of trauma with music opened the boy's capability to speak instead of numbing and silencing himself (pp. 31–32).

The traumatic events in childhood may cumulate to a developmental trauma and even a complex trauma, or a dissociative identity disorder (DID).[8] The complex trauma, or the complex PTSD (C-PTSD), was finally included as a diagnosis on the ICD-11 in 2022 as described earlier (Stubley, 2022a, p. 13). This happened 30 years after Herman (1992/2022) first published her *Trauma and Recovery* book in 1992, where the basic symptoms and characters of complex trauma were described (pp. 176–178). However, it was still not included in the latest DSM-V (2013) of the APA because it was considered to overlap with other diagnostic categories like depression, anxiety, somatisation disorder, borderline personality disorder, and the dissociative disorders (Herman, 1992/2022, pp. 386–387).

As commented by Herman (1992/2022, pp. 386–387) in the 2022 new epilogue of her already classic study, in life symptoms and disorders do not always meet the neat categories of medicine. I think it is a general dilemma in medicine that the diagnoses are overlapping with each other. Trauma as a phenomenon affects people in many ways, their feelings, relationships, bodies, and societies. Some may question should it be labelled as a disorder because it is an adaptive and in some degree normal physiological and psychological response to an overwhelming situation where people can find ways of helping themselves respectively (van der Kolk, 2014, p. 38). The diagnosis of C-PTSD may be understood including the PTSD and the personality characters of borderline personality, which is also relating to the traumatising events in the development (Herman, 1992/2022, p. 388).

Originally, the complex trauma, or the C-PTSD, as it is currently diagnosed according to the ICD-11 (2025) worldwide, was considered to be with a trauma history from months to years where the victim was subjected under totalitarian control (Herman, 1992/2022, pp. 174–176). Herman referred to the hostages, prisoners of war, survivors of concentration camps, some religious cults, and refugees who had experienced a massive trauma and fears noticed by several clinicians earlier. They

[8] See Sect. 2.3 "Impacts of Trauma in People's Lives" for more discussion of ACEs and developmental traumas.

did not seem to fit the already accepted PTSD diagnosis in 1980s. In the complex trauma were also included the victims of totalitarian system of childhood physical and sexual abuse, domestic beatings, and organised sexual exploitation. They are not single-event traumas but include several prolonged and repeated traumatising events that are affecting the development of personality harmfully (p. 174).

In the DID, which is another currently recognised trauma-related diagnosis, also referred to as the complex form PTSD, severe childhood traumatisation like adverse childhood experiences and maltreatment are thought to produce separate ego states and feelings that people are suffering (Stubley, 2022b, pp. 38, 52; van der Kolk, 1996/2007a, p. 192). This is called tertiary or secondary dissociation in the literature that is caused by repeated childhood exposure to extreme stress. Formerly, in 1980, DID was called as multiple personality disorder (MPD), which has also been treated with music therapy (Duey, 1991/1996).

In the DID, as it is currently known, a person has dissociated separate states of mind that are triggered by the traumatised element of that mind. In this kind of structural dissociation, a person may function well in some parts of his/her life but has totally dissociated some aspects of self like feelings relating to intimacy and aggression. In their lives, they are unaware of their system of separate functioning of mind after their trauma has passed. Their daily life is interfered with a feeling of deadness from a protective detachment and overwhelming affects which are making them feel disconnected from others (van der Kolk, 1996/2007a, p. 192). In adult psychotherapy, the separated ego states and the "splitting of personality" of the client already described by Ferenczi may appear as feelings of authenticity, confusion, disorientation, and uncertainty in a therapist (Stubley, 2022b, p. 52).

When traumatic experiences are contained in the separate ego states, they can be understood as fixations and exaggerations in a normal development (van der Kolk, 1996/2007b, p. 193). In the object constancy of psychological development, school-age children normally understand that things are not always as they appear. Children like to play different roles and games where they can be fantasy characters, cowboys, Indians, and policemen, and they try different identities. When children are exposed to stress, they may use this capability of fantasying and creating different identities and self-states to protect themselves. In children's behaviour, this may relate to the alterations of mind from agitated and dysphoric to the calming and contending oneself by rocking, verbalising, stroking, singing, etc. (ibid.).

I have observed this kind of behaviour also with adolescent and adult clients frequently, where clients are unaware of their rocking, stroking, singing, or have sometimes noticed themselves what they are doing in music and psychotherapy (Alanne, 2016b). This seemed to relate to the early non-verbal development like moving and shaking feet as a sort of acting-out in therapy. A common feature of these clients has been some kind of adverse experiences in their childhood not depending on their age. Often these clients may have difficulties in remembering their childhood experiences and things in their life. In addition, many clients in music therapy have difficulties in expressing and verbalising themselves. They often just say that they "don't know", what they are thinking or feeling, or how music sounds or feels when they are asked. Instead, they may explain themselves with somatic complaints of headache, feeling bad, or tired (Alanne, 2010). This may be related to their traumatic backgrounds, dissociations, and developmental traumas as the reasons why they cannot symbolise, express themselves with words, and communicate with themselves and others (Stubley, 2022a, pp. 22–24; van der Kolk, 1996/2007a, p. 193; 2014).

2.2.4 *Trauma, Body, and Brain*

Recently, beginning from the 1990s and continuing in the first 2000 decades, the physiological explanations have emphasised how trauma affects the body and brain (Crenshaw, 2006; Rose, 2004; van der Kolk, 2014). This relates to better understanding of the brain and their functioning because of the development in the brain research methods and technologies. In addition, it seems that the general scientific attention of the era has been more interested in brain research sometimes as a sort of new thing. In fact, it is an old thing that is a part of the medical history as a general gold standard of Hermann von Helmholtz from nineteenth century to derive its treatments and theory from the physiological principles like Janet or Freud earlier.

Therefore, it seems that scientists in medicine, psychology, and music therapy have gone into their roots in finding somatic answers for the psychological issues including trauma sometimes more preferable.

However, quite recently the cultural and sociological aspects of trauma have been raised again in the contexts of sexual harassments and differences as well as from the perspective of women's and black people's rights also in music therapy (Bruce, 2022; Gombert, 2022; Myerscough & Wong, 2022; Pickard, 2022; Scrine & Koike, 2023). They are the same issues that Herman (1992/2022) already studied and emphasised but from a different angle of ableism, disablism, cultural and social colonialism of certain groups of people because of their gender, sexuality, race, class, nationality, and culture. They will be discussed towards the end of this book.[9]

Van der Kolk (2014, pp. 213–214) has studied the embodied experiences of trauma. He is referring to the rhythms and relationships of faces, gestures, and touches beginning from the moment of birth. The mother and her child are in synchrony but because of trauma this physical synchrony is broken according to him. He refers to frozen eyes and collapsed bodies of PTSD clients as examples. In 1997, he noticed the healing power of community through music and rhythms that people in South Africa joined. They were a group of rape survivors who gathered even though there were bullet sounds, smoke, and smell of tear gas around them. In the atmosphere of fear, 40 people were killed at the same time; frozen and collapsed women could join the hum and rhythm of moving their bodies forth and back. Soon they got up and were singing and dancing. Their faces became attuned, and their

[9] See Sect. 6.3 "Challenging the Oppressive Practices of Music".

bodies vitalised. Van der Kolk was amazed to see and study how music, rhythms, singing, and movement were healing trauma in his opinion.

Understanding the brain and specifically mirror neuron functioning in humans has changed the view of trauma, therapy, and the child development (Alanne, 2010, 2023; Elliot & Silverman, 2013; Gallese, 2011; Mukamel et al., 2010; Stern, 2004; van der Kolk, 2014). In 1994, mirror neurons were found accidentally in monkeys by the researchers Giacomo Rizzolatti, Leonardo Fogassi, and Vittorio Gallese, who noticed that the monkey's brain reacted when it saw the researcher taking food (Christensen, 2019). After that similar cells were found in the human brain (Mukamel et al., 2010). This capability of understanding other humans or living beings does not seem to be related to seeing but also with feeling and imaging. For example, it has been noticed that mirror neurons reacted to the sounds of tearing a paper without seeing it, and there was a similar response by only imaging it happening (Stern, 2010, p. 47).

Many studies after the first finding have followed around the world showing that mirror neurons are explaining empathy, imitation, synchrony, and development of language in a new way (van der Kolk, 2014, pp. 58–59). Mirror neurons enable people to better understand other people as they can synchronise their actions with each other. This includes the positions of body like standing, sitting, relaxing, or the way of using their voices in the same sound or rhythm. Also, the feelings of others may be understood with the help of mirror neurons, including negative feelings and experiences. The frontal lobes are important in adjusting the empathy and how to "feel into someone else" (p. 58). They are making possible to "play out" things, which is important for the creativity as well as for the therapy of traumatised (ibid.). In therapy, it is an important capability to develop where music can help to feel safe and mirror the other. Many traumatised clients and refugees have experiences of not being seen, mirrored, or taken account which may provide corrective experiences in the relationship with a therapist and music (p. 59).

In therapy, client may also learn new ways of being in a relationship where they are also not affected or triggered by the negative feelings of the others (van der Kolk, 2014, p. 59). In music or psychotherapy, this understanding of neurons, body, and brain enables synchronising with a client through the body of therapist. Also, the client's brain functioning may synchronise with other parts of brain when discussing or listening to music, or playing music with a therapist (Rose, 2004, pp. 78–80, 119). Music and arts, and particularly music, have been compared to prosthetic devices in brain because they can integrate different information and help in psychological orientation to speak, feel, move, and memorise like in Parkinson's, aphasia, and the sundown syndrome. Music can orient the confused dementia clients with time and help them to momentarily function and be in the present moment (ibid.). As such, there seems to be concordance between the neurophysiological structures of brain and the psychological functions of mind when working with music (Alanne, 2014a, 2023; Rose, 2004).

In music therapy, it has been known for long time that the music and sounds affect the emotions, and in the brain music increases the production of endogenic morphine endorphin as an example (Alanne, 2010, 2014a, 2023; Christensen, 2019;

Crenshaw, 2006; Swallow, 2002). Music also inhibits the production of the adreno-corticotropic (ACTH) stress hormones that the amygdala triggers in survival reactions like hyper-vigilance (Rose, 2004, p. 121). This is important for the treatment and rehabilitation of traumatised because thalamus is an input of sounds, sights, smells, and kinaesthetic experiences in the brain (van der Kolk, 2014, p. 61). Thalamus sends its information to amygdala, which is controlling the significance of emotions. If threat occurs, amygdala sends a message to the hypothalamus to activate stress hormones and defend against this threat. This is the so-called *low road to consciousness* in the brain named by the neuroscientist Joseph LeDoux. Many traumatised like PTSD clients have a damaged amygdala, which is responding to threats too intensively. Also, music with traumatised refugees and survivors of torture may trigger such confusing experiences in the beginning or some parts of the treatment when the clients may not want to listen music because they are feeling bad and cannot control their experiences (Alanne, 2010).

Another reason may be that their filtering/controlling systems in the higher areas of brain are too weak, so that they cannot always control their experiences and mind which is making the music listening disturbing for them. In PTSD, as well as with other traumas, when the filtering systems of brain are weak, this often results in losing control of oneself emotionally (van der Kolk, 2014, p. 61). Then, the automatised emergency reactions like prolonged startle and aggressive outbursts activate. According to LeDoux, this is the *high road to conscious* that is running from the thalamus through the hippocampus and anterior cingulate to the prefrontal cortex. The prefrontal cortex is a part of the rational brain that is regulating, refining, and interpreting thoughts and feelings (ibid.).

If this regulating system is weak, severely traumatised like torture survivors may not want to talk about their traumatic experiences because they are afraid of their activation and feel they cannot control it. I assume that the experience in the brain and mind of traumatised is similar when music is experienced as a disturbing and chaotic bad object (Alanne, 2010, 2023). Frequently, as discussed earlier, the traumatised experience is mixed with physical and psychological issues, and the client cannot differentiate or name what they are feeling or thinking. They may simply feel headache, for example, as an explanation and somatisation, how they are feeling themselves or the music in music therapy.

The lower core structures of brain, the limbic brain and the mentioned thalamus and amygdala, are regulating the emotional experiences of pleasure and pain that music can affect. Another important nervous system is the vagus nerve, which is regulating the safety, relaxation, and fight-or-flight responses (Crenshaw, 2006; van der Kolk, 2014). Because of the unsafety our physiological sympathetic system reacts mobilising our muscles tightening, heart beating, and lungs breathing faster as the fight/flight response activates in our body (van der Kolk, 2014, p. 81). Finally, we are freezing in danger, we cannot breathe, heartbeat drops, and our bowels stop working or are emptying. As a result of threat, our body signals defeat, withdrawal, and it collapses.

When the threat increases the oldest part of the human brain, the reptilian brain, automatically activates the fight-or-flight response with a parasympathetic nervous system that cannot be controlled (van der Kolk, 2014, p. 83). Then, people may be raging and not responding to human voices anymore. They may also be oversensitive to threatening sounds. As the body prepares for the fight traumatised, other people as well, feel energised and alive as their senses become more active. However, in the safe situations, like at social dinners and birthday parties, traumatised and abused may feel numb and cannot relate with other people because their brain cannot regulate or interpret the situation as normal.

Music and music therapy may help to relax, lose stress, anxiety, pain, and panic attacks as music is affecting the limbic brain and the nervous system positively and increasing the production of endorphins (Alanne, 2014a, 2023; Bernatzky et al., 2013; Hole et al., 2015; Lee, 2016; Pitkäniemi et al., 2020; Standley, 1996). However, with severely traumatised clients like refugee survivors of torture, the sounds of music may trigger feelings of unsafety and dissociation because of the damaged amygdala that the therapist should be aware of when using music. The traumatised brain cannot necessarily regulate the relaxation anymore, seeking pleasure or threat, and withdrawal reactions in their minds and bodies. The feeling of threat and the fight/flight reaction may trigger too easily even in the normal safe situations. This is why the therapist should be aware of such triggering things in the consulting room or in the music as a part of the trauma-informed practice developed in music therapy (Else & González, 2023; Scrine & Koike, 2023). This can help in creating a safe experience for the traumatised client with discussion, negation, or suitable music that enables them to regulate their responses in therapy.

Recently, there has developed a resilience-orientated framework for trauma-informed practice in music therapy (Sokira et al., 2023). It is based on Herman's (1992/2022, p. 224) three-stage recovery process, where in stage 1, the goal of the therapy is the *establishing of safety*, in stage 2, *remembrance and mourning*, and in stage 3, *reconnection* (Sokira et al., 2023, p. 12). Also, another kind of approach has been developed in accordance with the current trauma therapy theory and its connections to the mind, body, and dissociation, which are influenced by pioneers such as Janet, Freud, Kardiner, Herman, van der Kolk, and others (McFerran et al., 2020).

The stage-recovery process is also called as the phase-orientated approach in psychodynamic psychotherapy used at the Tavistock Clinic in the UK currently (Stubley, 2022b, pp. 40–41). In the first phase of the treatment, the goal is the *stabilisation* of client's situation and developing a basic trust/safety, in phase 2, it is the *trauma processing* (working through), and in phase 3, it is the *reintegration* of trauma (Wolf, 2007, p. 18). They are also following the guidelines of International Society for Traumatic Stress Studies (ISTSS) for treating C-PTSD.

These phases of treatment are not linear necessarily, or should not be taken literally, as originally emphasised by Herman (1992/2022, pp. 223–225). They may be used or needed at any phase of the treatment or session, depending on the clients and techniques used (Sokira et al., 2023, p. 12; Stubley, 2022b, p. 41). However, the treatment of trauma needs to stand on safety, and the goals of treatment are showing the way for the recovery process and what kind of phases it usually includes in the treatment (Herman, 1992/2022, pp. 223–225). This approach has been used in music psychotherapy with traumatised refugees and torture survivors, and it is forming the clinical-theoretical basic frame of this book (Alanne, 2010, 2013, 2019b; Beck et al., 2018, 2021; McFerran et al., 2020).

2.3 Impacts of Trauma in People's Lives

A trauma may affect in many ways a person's life whilst it is not even recognised as such. For example, a developmental or relational trauma may appear as an incapability to recognise and understand one's feelings. A person may want to please others because s/he is afraid of one's own feelings that may lead to guilt or shame unnecessarily (Music, 2022, pp. 84–85). Because of the lack of contact in their formative relationships and needed care, including abuse and neglect of their basic needs like emotional being there, containing, holding of feelings, these people are confused with their own feelings, needs, and responsibilities with other people. They may try to adapt perfectly to the others' needs and worldviews according to mother's or spouse's moods as examples (p, 84).

However, in their experiences, they may feel that they have not been heard or seen by the parents because they have been unstable, inconsistent, and absent from their lives (Hoi Yan Fu, 2023, p. 114). The relationships and the family dynamics in their childhood have often been insecure and stressful. They may be desperately looking for the acceptance of others in school or work. They are always doing more than what is needed or required of them, which is burning them up eventually. Often in their minds, only grades of "A", "10", or not even that is not enough to satisfy the needs of their highly demanding self-experience and low self-esteem. If that is not possible, they may easily feel worthless and depressed (Music, 2022, p. 85).

This has to do with many children and other clients in music psychotherapy who have narcissistic wounds, which is making them easily feel that they are poor in music (Alanne, 2023, p. 86). They are anticipating playing perfectly immediately even though musical skills and capabilities are not requisite for participating in music therapy. These often deprived narcissistically injured and severely traumatised clients cannot tolerate low moods and dependence on others in their experiences. They are trying to control and reject the moods if they are getting too threatful, anxious, and painful in music, therapy, and relationships, respectively (p. 88).

With traumatised adopted children as well as with refugees, music may be in a "window of tolerance" where they can feel, think, play, and regulate their feelings instead of being in hyperarousal, numbness, depressive, and dissociative states (Gravestock, 2021, p. 150). Music and even positive relationships, including therapist, may activate embodied experiences relating to development trauma, physical abuse, abandonment, and insecure attachments. However, within safe musical and therapeutic relationships, these experiences may be experienced, contained, and regulated in a new reparative way (pp. 150–151).

The more there is a lack of care, deprivation, possible violence, poverty, or threats in childhood, the deeper the wounds that are causing trauma. This kind of traumatisation is continuing exposure to the multiple types of traumatisation, which is why it affects the development of the personality. Adverse childhood experiences

(ACEs) were already introduced and discussed in the earlier paragraph how they may affect the lives of children and young people long afterwards. Many of the traumatised refugees may suffer from such experiences relating to the war and oppression in their home countries. Also, the escape, often long, demanding, and even dangerous escape from the home country, leaves frightening memories that may have been dissociated.

The parents of the refugee children and adolescents may not be available for them during the journey normally, and there may be separations from the family as well as fear of dying, violence, and losing of parents and relatives as ACEs. Their internalised representations of parents and close ones may have become weak, and they may appear as vague shadows, present but distant at the same time. In their minds they are carrying the terror, destruction, and death as the war outside has transferred to internal war like depicted by one child psychotherapist treating refugee children (Castaneda et al., 2018, p. 291). With such traumatic experiences that may slow and arrest the emotional development of refugee, music and other creative methods may help in symbolising, communicating, and integrating such experiences in psychotherapy (ibid.).

2.3.1 Adverse Childhood Experiences (ACEs)

The adverse childhood experiences and traumatisation they produce affect not only the personality and the mental health of people, but also the physical health of traumatised. ACEs may have long impact on the bodies of traumatised as they can produce a greater risk of respiratory and cardiovascular diseases, and, for example, diabetes mellitus according to research in adults (Stubley, 2022a, p. 28). ACEs mean potentially traumatising events for the person that have occurred before 18 years of age (Svedberg Yinger, 2023, pp. 48–49). They are referring to the childhood *abusing*, physical, sexual, and emotional, *neglecting*, physical and emotional, and *family/household dysfunctioning* relating to the substance abuse, mental illness, incarceration of someone in the household, and divorce/separation of parents. According to the survey of the 17,000 adults in 1998 and more research after that, they are so stressful or disruptive situations that they are causing medical, mental, and social problems later in life (p. 48).

Currently, childhood maltreatments like exposure to physical or verbal violence at home and spanking are also considered as ACEs. In addition, challenges in household like poverty, parental/sibling deaths, sibling violence and foster care, childhood illnesses, and longer separations of the family because of deployment and immigration are considered as ACEs (Svedberg Yinger, 2023, p. 48). These are possible traumatising events that many of the refugees are encountering in their lives. They are also common among children in music and psychotherapy.

Other recommended ACEs are peer victimisation by bullying physically, verbally, or in the cyberworld, sexual dating violence, and peer rejection as examples. Also, community violence is included in the recommended ACEs that can be seeing and hearing of violence like stabbing, shooting, or experienced threat of them and physical fighting (Svedberg Yinger, 2023, p. 48). Many of the refugee children may have exposure to such happenings that may even include seeing the deaths of their relatives, parents, and other people, or their dead bodies. Refugees, including torture survivors, and their families may have also seen violence and torture of their close ones, their raping, arresting, and disappearing (Alayarian, 2024, pp. 35–36). Many of the refugees' families and children may still be in their home countries after they had to leave the country to survive.

According to one recent meta-analysis, where genetic and environmental causes were controlled, childhood maltreatment prior to 18 years explained for 21% to 41% of common mental health conditions in Australia, including highest amounts of self-harm and suicide attempts (Grummitt et al., 2024). Effects of childhood maltreatment, physical abuse, sexual abuse, emotional abuse, or neglect were found in more than 1.8 million cases of depression, anxiety, and substance abuse disorders, which could be prevented by eradicating childhood maltreatment. Childhood maltreatment caused 66,143 years of life lost and 184,636 disability-adjusted life-years, which could be also saved, respectively (ibid.).

In the light of the research of ACEs, it would be wise to pay attention and do early interventions in the life of children and their families who have social problems. As also suggested by van der Kolk (2014, pp. 350–351), things that could help children feel that their life is safe and meaningful could prevent them from using substances, doing crimes, or developing mental disorders like depression, or physical illnesses leading to death such as heart disease, cancer, stroke, or diabetes. Many traumatised refugees, including torture survivors, suffer from physical disorders in addition to their PTSD or C-PTSD diagnoses because they have not taken care of their health as a part of their traumatisation and reexposuring to it.

This is also concerning refugees, immigrants, torture survivors, and their children if their parents cannot adapt to a new society and look for help because of their traumas and fears, their children will suffer too. Earlier when I was treating adult torture survivors with music psychotherapy in the beginning of 2000s, then there was not much paid attention to their children and families in Finland. This worried me and made me later suggest that their treatment and rehabilitation should also be included in the national guidelines of supporting refugees' mental health in Finland (Castaneda et al., 2018). It is possible that severe traumatisation of parents after torture and their often very difficult situation and treatment take all the attention of treating staff and parents. Then, the children of the family and their wellbeing may be forgotten. It is very important to pay attention to them as a preventive mental health work and to avoid their possible secondary or intergenerational traumatisation.[10]

I had already seen the possible consequences of ACEs for immigrants' and other children's mental health in my music therapy practice. Traumatised adults and parents, especially those suffering from PTSD or PTSD-C, may be emotionally numb,

[10] Intergenerational traumatisation will be discussed more thoroughly in Sect. 2.4 "Intergenerational Trauma".

dissociating, in their own thoughts, violent, working constantly, or having substance abuse problems. When they are in treatment they may be absorbed in their own mind and maybe do not have time and attention for their children. Also, a parent who is socially isolated and fearful cannot necessarily help their children much to adapt to a new society and culture. In addition, because of their own traumas, they may easily lose their tempers, be violent, and rude to their close ones as well as withdraw from their company. This may lead to the secondary traumatisation of their children and families if they are not paid attention in the health and social care as well as in schools.

2.3.2 *Oppression and Traumatisation*

Developmental traumas may also be or lead to relational traumas where the relationship between the self and others is distorted. As discussed earlier there may be many reasons for this, like somehow failed parental mirroring of child's feelings and basic needs. Also, child abusing and physical punishments and their threats as a continuous stressful situation and toxic climate in a family or parent–child dynamics may lead to the traumatisation of a child or other family members.

Developmental traumas may show in children as pervasive dysregulation patterns, attention and concentration problems, and difficulties of being with others and oneself (van der Kolk, 2014, p. 158). Children in developmental trauma profile are suffering from rapidly changing moods and feelings; they easily have tantrums and panics related to the feeling of being detached. Their feelings may go from one extreme to another very fast and they have major difficulties in calming themselves when they are upset that is a typical state of being for most of their time. They also cannot describe their feelings.

These children are very stressed and have symptoms like headaches, sleep disturbances, and unexplained pains (van der Kolk, 2014, p. 158). Often, they are oversensitive to the touches, sounds, and lights. They cannot concentrate or pay attention because they are easily agitated or withdrawn, shut down in their experiences. To reduce their tension and anxiety, they are masturbating, rocking, or self-harming themselves chronically with biting, cutting, burning, and hitting themselves. They may also pick their skin until they are bleeding and pull their head out. Many of these children, often referred to music psychotherapy, have difficulties in language skills and schoolwork. Their energy and attention go to the controlling of their environment hyperactively and therefore they are easily distracted, and they cannot concentrate to other things than survival.

These children or later adults have a background of been ignored and abandoned frequently in their lives (van der Kolk, 2014, p. 158). As a result, they are very needy and clinging in their relationships. This concerns also the relationships where they have been abused, molested, or otherwise mistreated. Because of the continued mistreating, they are feeling self-loath and defining themselves as defective and worthless in their lives. This affects their relationships so that they cannot trust people, which is no wonder after all they have experienced. They have difficulties in making friends because they are feeling themselves despicable and are therefore easily frustrated and overreacting to disappointments.

In the psychodynamic understanding, this is the transference of a client how s/he is responding with certain unconscious or conscious feelings to situations according to their traumatic feelings and experiences. Many clients in music and psychotherapy have developmental traumas that they are unaware. Often, they come to therapy with other diagnoses like depression, generalised anxiety, somatoformic anxiety, childhood emotional problems, ADHD, adverse childhood experience, even a psychosis, even though when studied closer they have a developmental trauma. A developmental trauma is like the current official diagnosis of C-PTSD diagnosis and its symptomss earlier described (Stubley, 2022a, p. 14).

However, the developmental trauma disorder (DTD) does not have such an official diagnosis status yet, even though it was proposed already in 2009 by van der Kolk and his colleagues according to their studies (van der Kolk, 2014, pp. 157–159). In the beginning, the purpose was to have one diagnosis for a database of 20,000 abused and neglect children and adolescents discovered worldwide instead of many diagnoses. In my own clinical experiences, the situation for children and adolescents referred to music psychotherapy is still the same that that they often do not have any kind of trauma diagnosis. However, it can be questioned would one diagnosis for many symptoms be a part of medicalisation of traumatic experiences that have different backgrounds in the lives of our clients without fully understanding their circumstances.

Also, C-PTSD can develop through time from chronic and repetitive traumatic experiences in adulthood (Stubley, 2022a, pp. 14–15). However, many of the traumatised adult clients referred to rehabilitative psychotherapy do not have any trauma diagnosis in my experiences. Instead, finding and understanding their often-cumulative traumatisation may very well be resulting from their psychotherapeutic processes. Many adult refugees, asylum seekers, and torture survivors, or other adult survivors of relational violence, develop a C-PTSD. According to the growing evidence, a history of childhood trauma or a trauma in the family increases the possibility of PTSD in adults. It also seems that a secure attachment figure in childhood protects from traumatisation as the children's resilience increases (p. 15).

Alice Miller (1979, 1980) was a pioneer of studying the history and psychology of poisonous education how the child learns to fear consciously and unconsciously the physical punishments of parents and adults. This leads to the kind of earlier-described false self-identity and narcissistically injured personality wounds where a person is afraid of showing feelings, expressing one's own needs, or using his/her skills and talents but is instead rejecting them in favour of pleasing others. Sometimes persons are manically using their skills to keep up the feeling of safety, family together, and others happy in their relationships, thus avoiding conflicts. The traumatised child has learnt that his/her feelings and needs are not important, or may even consider them as bad, judging, ignoring, silencing, and denying them. Then, a part of the person's self that has not been nurtured and cared is not internalised and is therefore left undeveloped and dissociated (Hoi Yan Fu, 2023, p. 114).

This may be the reason why the expression of own sounds, voice, and music in therapy may be difficult and threatening when music and sounds are reverberating with the dissociated parts of the self and the oppressor. For example, the music or the singing of the client may be unauthentic because there is no connection between the music, own needs, feelings, and the body. Even though music and musical performances may seem proper but instead of expressing music according to own experiences, a person is adapting to the needs of the others and outside world in a relationship with music and the therapist (Hoi Yan Fu, 2023, pp. 114–115).

This is the client's transference discussed more later in this book towards the music and the therapist that is repeating of the trauma in the musical relationship. Then, a client may not actually always enjoy what s/he is doing in life, work, hobbies, or relationships, because it is not satisfying his/her own needs. The narcissistically injured part of the self is not developed and integrated into the other parts the self, so that the needs could be even recognised and fulfilled. This may cause experiences of meaninglessness and depression in life, because a person is stressing situations where s/he should always succeed even perfectly. Then, only instant sensual responses, pleasure and pain of games, sex, sports, often combative, and other actions in general, drugs and alcohol, may provide pleasure and self-esteem for a while as acting out of the feelings for a traumatised (van der Kolk, 2014, pp. 32, 158). Eventually, this will cause a burn-out and freezing as the consequences of traumatisation because a person cannot control environment constantly to feel safe from the triggering of bad objects and accomplish in everything successfully.

In music and psychoanalytic psychotherapy, these own needs of a client and how to be with an object in a new way can be studied and recognised. What comes from the needs of the client and what is adapting and matching to the possible threats and needs of others can be discussed in therapy. In music with traumatised and refugees, this would mean how to express own feelings, sounds, and music instead of adapting to the needs of parents, teachers, or therapists. Music and music therapy may be such methods that can help in rebuilding and integrating development with ACEs and developmental traumas with refugee and immigrant children and adolescents who may be also adopted and living with foster parents or in institutions (Gravestock, 2021).

In addition to the oppressive systems and poisonous education of adults and parents, refugees have suffered from similar oppressive regimes and fear in their home countries that are causing a relational trauma for them (Nathanson, 2022, pp. 130–132). Often, their freedom to express themselves in their lives has been taken. They have been arrested, interrogated, or tortured because of their ethnicity, culture, or political opinions. Frequently, there are very strict rules in the totalitarian countries where the slightest breaking of them may cause harsh penalties like going to prison. These can result from the criticism of government, their politics, or rules.

For this, and the fear of the perpetrator, who is often a representative of oppressive government, from police or army, they may try to hide and live in a constant fear in their home countries. There may also be war or other violence, a lack of food and other things, or why they need to flee from their countries eventually. In this kind of oppression, there are similarities with the victims of other kinds of violence or sexual abuse where there is a grooming phase of the perpetrator where the victim's capacity to freedom and to say no is robbed (Nathanson, 2022, p. 133). This is a part of the oppressor's corrupted policies and culture that have been developing for a long time where a passive resistance works no longer but is considered as agreement by the oppressor.

In this grooming, there is often building trust with victims, and good experiences, which are a part of the manipulating for the next phase of oppressor (Nathanson, 2022, pp. 131–132). This grooming phase may also begin with fear and be "toxic" like with the oppressive governments when the victims are afraid to close the door and say no to the perpetrators before it is too late (p. 132). A part of the refugees' traumatisation has occurred while living under the oppressive government and trying to survive without fully resisting it. In many cases, this reminds of situations of sexually or physically abused who are afraid of saying no and cannot escape from the perpetrator who is often an admired adult, friend, or a parent.

For this reason, the traumatisation from such abusing and corrupted trust is similar when the representatives of home country, its regime, authorities, police, army, etc., turn against you and your family. It is an object loss psychologically, like the experience when you lose someone close and whom you have trusted. Instead, it has betrayed you and is threatening your safety and wellbeing like an enemy. In addition, the symbols of country and nationality, including music and other culture, are now associated with dictators and tormentors as a part of their losses in the new culture (Akhtar, 1995; Alanne, 2014b, 2023; Volkan, 2018a).

One example of this happened to the music of Chilean Nueva Canción movement folk songs that raised from the socialistic cultural protesting towards exploitation of workers (Neustadt, 2004, pp. 128–129). These songs were banned and silenced in Chile from the day one of coup in 1973, and over the time this music that gave hope and identity under oppression was forgotten in people's minds, even though musicians continued protesting the dictatorship of Pinochet from the exile. In the late 1990s, a socialistic march *Venceremos* was played instrumentally first time publicly after over 23 years in the centre of Santiago. Even though there was the amnesia relating to Nueva Canción, it immediately triggered emotions from anger and fear to jubilee depending on people as this music was still remembered and associated with the era of dictatorship, coup, and the disappeared ones (p. 132).[11]

The manipulation, propaganda using also music and other arts that is often combined with arrests and sudden attacks of violence and control, makes you feel insecure and stressed for the safety of you and your family. For most of all, this is all

[11] The role of music as a weapon and torture in the detainee camps and interrogation centres in Chile during the dictatorship will be studied and described in Chap. 3, and especially in Sect. 3.5 "Deceitful Musical Experiences in Prisons and Camps". Interestingly, earlier the period of Chile's and Argentina's history relating to music and musical torture during the dictatorships has been a part of the fictional literature's themes as a way of remembering and recovering them (Neustadt, 2004).

done with the purpose to control and break you, so that there would be no own will, freedom, and resistance. For this reason, also music and arts may be silenced, because like in Chile they give hope and identity for the people. This often leaves wounds, including fear, anxiety, and amnesia, that will follow to the next generations if they are not understood and worked with refugees and asylum seekers.

2.4 Intergenerational Trauma

A trauma in the family or traumatic experience in the childhood or adolescence is affecting the mental health, global health, and wellbeing in adulthood (Alayarian, 2024, pp. 21–23). Often, in music or psychotherapy, when the clients or their families are interviewed and assessed, there are adverse childhood experiences (ACEs) in their family background that have roots in the earlier generations like parents' and grandparents' families. There may be alcoholism, substance abuse, violence like physical punishing, mental disorders like depression, and psychotic disorders in the parents or their parents, including suicides. There are also social problems like poverty, unemployment, and other financial issues, as well as divorces that have affected the families in many generations.

According to research, for parents who have been tortured or experienced atrocity like many of the refugees have, their children have symptoms of anxiety, depression, post-traumatic stress, attention deficits, as well as behavioural disorders (Abrams, 2021, p. 198). There is also evidence from parental linking of PTSD and secondary traumatisation, depressive symptoms, parentification of the child's role, and self-harming coping mechanisms like substance abuse and eating disorders. Like other ACEs, transmitted transgenerational trauma may have many physiological consequences like cardiovascular disease producing heart attacks and strokes as well as metabolic disorders like diabetes. There is also evidence of epigenetic biological changes transmitting trauma with atrocity-related PTSD (p. 199).

Intergenerational traumas, also called transgenerational traumas, are traumas where certain traumatic experiences like genocide, colonisation, epidemics, natural disasters, and other catastrophic events are transmitted over generations (Abrams, 2021, p. 198). According to current understanding, research, and theories, the mechanisms of intergenerational trauma can be interpersonal (relational), social, and genetic. Often it is in the form of historical trauma related to collective experiences of wars, genocides, oppression, slavery, violence, and racism towards other ethnic, political, or social groups of people.

This kind of traumatisation may occur in personal, family, communal, or even international level when Holocaust victims and their relatives are considered as examples (Abrams, 2021; Alayarian, 2024; Volkan, 2018a). However, the intergenerational trauma does not affect all the family or community members evenly: Some of them can be more severely traumatised compared to others who may have some traumatic feelings or memories but who are not clinically suffering from mental disorders or post-traumatic stress that can be diagnosed. They may appear as normal and fully functional in their lives because they may have more resilience than others in the community (Alayarian, 2024, pp. 21–22).

A part of the difficulty in understanding and treating intergenerational traumas is that what seems normal can be splitting, dissociation, repression, and enacting of hurtful feelings and painful experiences in a family. They may be internalised by the other family member, often a child, where the trauma is transferred or deposited, consciously or unconsciously (Abrams, 2021, Siirala, 1966/1969; Volkan, 2018a). Other different psychological ways of transmitting intergenerational trauma in the relationships over generations are symbiosis, empathy, attachment, enmeshment, personal or collective identifications, projective identification, introjection, dependency, co-dependency, interdependency, parenting, compensation, and acculturation (Alayarian, 2024, p. 21).

A Finnish psychiatrist and psychoanalyst Martti Siirala wrote the about the "transfer" or "vicarious illness" in the family and over generations where another person becomes the carrier of the burden in the family dynamics (Siirala, 1966/1969, pp. 94–95). In such circumstances, a person, often a child, develops psychic symptoms. For example, when traumatic experiences and overwhelming anxiety, losses, or suffering that are not or a part of them are not encountered, this is left for another person to carry (Siirala, 1983, pp. 137–138; Uurtimo, 2000, pp. 25–30).

Siirala described this human situation where the experiences are repressed or split from the consciousness and out of experiences as primary objectification or split in his conceptualisation of transfer (Siirala, 1983, pp. 24, 137). They are not shared like in transference that Siirala sees as a possibility of sharing and encountering suffering and a way of recovering and redistribution of burden (p. 138). This shows the direction towards hope, light, and togetherness, and away from anonymity according to him. In the split situation of transfer, a suffering individual becomes a placement where the family, culture, nation, or society has transferred the split part of experiences or resigned from noticing and knowing them. A society or a community can also destroy the person's creativity and possibilities in life with its vicious and pressing attitudes that are causing frustration, anxiety, and eventually illnesses (Siirala, 1966/1969, pp. 37–39; Uurtimo, 2000, pp. 11–14, 22–23).

Bullying at school, home, or work, racism, a totalitarian system of nation, community, or parents in their poisonous education, can be a part of placing of the pressure on the individual if s/he does accept, follow, or practise the rules or norms of the community (Uurtimo, 2000, 11–14, 22–23). This situation Siirala called as "social pathology" where in medicalisation, a person is studied in isolation of his/her environment, or in totalitarianism, where there are very tight and broad control systems and regulations for differences or distortions, respectively (Siirala, 1966/1969, p. 39 Uurtimo, 2000, pp. 13, 30–34). This kind of oppressive systems and social pathology occurred in the racisms of South Africa, Nazi Germany, Soviet Union, and Chile according to Siirala. Similar pathology occurred also during the Greek Junta when people were thought to carry communist "viruses" and how "music therapy" was used to educate and cure communists from such a disease like shown later in this book (Papaeti, 2013a, pp. 38–39).[12]

In this light, trauma may occur in one person, group of people, or the whole community where it affects their relationships and identities (Alayarian, 2024, p. 21). Even though one person or all the people are not necessarily traumatised, still there can be a trauma in the collective identity of community or a nation. In the family system, for example, not everyone is necessarily delusional or psychotic if one family member is; however, there is a possibility of shared psychotic disorder and delusion within the close relationships of family. In society, wars, genocide, and ethnic cleansings, for example, are significant events where the group identity can be traumatised. ACEs, childhood deprivation, maltreatment like domestic or physical abuse, and incest make people vulnerable for traumatisation, and for repeating their experiences indirectly to next generations as their children may become violent and perpetuators. There is also a possibility of reexposuring to a victim's or perpetuator's role in the cycle of transmitting the traumatisation over generations (p. 22).

Many refugees, asylum seekers, torture survivors, and their families have exposed to ongoing and chronic threats in their lives that have already began in their home country with oppression, interrogations, torture, and racism (Alayarian, 2024, pp. 21–22). Even though not all of them have necessarily been an object of violence themselves, there has been an ongoing threat which has affected their sense of secure life. This insecurity has already affected their one or all psychological functioning when there was a transmission of trauma. Furthermore, as the resilience of refugees has already been decreased, they are encountering the stress of immigration, application of asylum, and achieving a citizenship.

Refugees may have come from poverty, or they may have needed to leave most of their belongings in their home countries. In addition, they may have paid a big money for their escape for those who have arranged their long journey that may be a part of the human trafficking. The escape from their home country may be dangerous and life threatening because of the poor and unhealthy conditions in human trafficking where people have died. In their host country, they may have to face poor conditions of refugee camps or stay in crowded refugee centres waiting for their asylum seeker status and permission to stay. Frequently, a part of the family or the whole family may be still in the home country, and they must apply permission for uniting their family and children.

All this affects the situation of refugees and asylum seekers that can further traumatise them, affect their socioeconomic status, and lower their level of achievement (Alayarian, 2024, pp. 22–23). As a result, there may be many kinds of socio-psychological problems that are affecting also their children and young people like arresting their intellectual and educational development. This may also concern those families and their children who are not specifically refugees, but immigrants from far away and very different cultures. Their children that come to music therapy

---

[12] See Sect. 3.5 "Deceitful Musical Experiences in Prisons and Camps" for more through the discussion of music and oppression during the Greek Junta.

may also have socioemotional problems, depression, and phobias. Their parent or parents may suffer from similar issues and fears like it could have been very difficult for them to learn a new language, function and move in the new culture and environment, even though they may have been living there for a decade. Their fears and attitudes as well as difficulties in learning and adapting to society may transfer to the problems in their children. This is including the deteriorated capability to use health and social services available, or achieve therapy for their children, or themselves.

This is a vicious circle if the refugees' health and social wellbeing are not concerned in the society. If the adult refugees are not able to take care of their families, children and adolescents will suffer next, which is continuing of the transmission of trauma over generations. This will affect negatively to their homing and adapting to a new society and increasing the possibilities of social isolation, deprivation, mental and physical disorders, violence, substance abuse, and criminal activities. This will create new kinds of problems of being the Other in the society, an outsider and not a part of large group, who is often targeted with racist projections of hate, insults, prejudices, and politics that is resisting the immigration and refugees (Volkan, 2018b, pp., 52–53).

This is also a part of the transmitting of trauma with negative attitudes and psychological projections where the bad, the strange, is transferred to the refugees, immigrants, and people from other culture, who are suddenly responsible for the problems in society and causing economic issues, unemployment, and increasing criminality. Such attitudes in the society or a nation that can objectify and treat other people as not humans but like preys, filth, or animals, not belonging to us can be deposited in the minds of children and people (Volkan, 2018a, 2018b).

The fears, anxiety, and other emotions of refugees are deposited unconsciously in the minds of their children during the war, war-like situations, and forced migrations (Volkan, 2018a, pp. 47–48). During this their children does not necessarily have a possibility to integrate their own experiences and feelings of what happened, but they are confused with their own fantasies and parents' experiences. They have become "living statues" where adult's images and ego and superego functions of idealising values of country or war horrors as examples have been taken in by the child without knowledge and understanding where these adult's experiences came from (ibid.). The child may try to be perfect in everything trying to safe him/herself or the family from catastrophe. A child or an adult may see or experience nightmares during the day or night like in a war. In such a situation, an adult has been using unconsciously the child as a retainer of traumatised memories of their families, grandparents, their backgrounds, and prejudices (Volkan, 2018b, p. 44).

Examples of such deposits, or transfers, are how some animals like pigs are considered as filthy in some cultures: Turkish children may not be allowed to play with pigs and touch them even though the child is thinking that the pig is lovely (Volkan, 2018b, pp. 45–46). This may cause the child to think that pigs belong to others, only to Greeks, and not, for example, to the Turkish large group identity. In the child's mind, this may become a retainer of bad where further experiences from Greeks as the Other, who play with pigs and even eat them, become a part of the internalised experiences of bad, and therefore possible enemies. This is because the child has not integrated the self and object experiences relating to pigs how they were adorable according to his/her own experiences. Instead, they were told to be bad, filthy, and not to be eaten or played with by the adults. This kind of very early prejudices and dispositions relating to animals; ethnicities like Jews, Romans, black people, gender, sexuality, nationality, and so on; and how to respond to them may become the Other in a child's mind who then transmits them over generations.

This may be a part of the collective trauma where a specific group of people, nationality, or ethnicity have been oppressed that is affecting their group identity (Alayarian, 2024, p. 22). A traumatisation and its transmission over generations may also relate to the colour, religion, political beliefs, and the culture of person. Cultural artefacts, music, and arts are part of the group and personal identity of people. They can bring such memories and imagery that are supporting their identity, but they are also targets of oppression and racism in totalitarian systems (Dimitrijević & Buchholz, 2024, pp. xxiv–xxv). Therefore, the music and the culture of refugees, a right to education, may have been forbidden and silenced like in Nazi German, Soviet Union, or Chile during their dictatorships (Moreno, 1999; Neustadt, 2004). For refugees, the music and the culture of homeland may have also become the Other representing something bad that happened and was silenced. It may not be wanted to talk about or experienced because it reminds about the oppressor and the old times that is therefore repressed from the living memories.

For young people, it may mean something sad and strange because their parents have silenced it and possibly have transferred or deposited their feelings of it into their children as something bad and avoidable. This may also relate to the Other in different cultures, ethnicities, and their music that have been conceived as bad, filthy, or sinful, "devil's music". This psychological threat of such deposits has been used as a weapon and in manipulation of detainees and refugees in the prisons and interrogation centres. This may have further traumatised them and confirm their feeling of being outsider, without rights, their own voice, and not being a human (Alanne, 2010; Brauer, 2016; Cusick, 2013; Papaeti, 2020).[13]

The concept of depositing of trauma is close to the concept of transfer where somebody, usually a child, is the carrying the burden of trauma. It is something that is dissociated away from the consciousness of parents and cannot be integrated and understood by the child or adults. Then, it is possible that a child becomes also the object who is suffering and who have problems. Instead, problems of the family, or a parent, are not recognised or discussed even though they are sometimes evident. This may become an obstacle for the treatment and therapy. However, psychological understanding of such intergenerational traumas, their developing, and effects to a person from his/her cultural background helps in encountering and solving them.

---

[13] See Chap. 3 for the full discussion and study of musical violence and oppression.

2.5 Psychodynamic Understanding of Trauma

In psychodynamic theory and psychoanalysis, traumas are considered in broader context than in the earlier-described medical diagnoses of PTSD and C-PTSD or DID that are representing severe traumatisation that have changed the personality and identity of a person. However, like described their nature is psychodynamic including the current brain theories relating to traumatisation. Also, psychodynamic psychotherapy and psychoanalysis are considering the brain structures and looking equivalents in the brains for psychoanalytic theory of consciousness, unconsciousness, ego, id, superego, emotions, as well as music (Rose, 2004; Solms, 2017, 2018, 2021; Solms & Turnbull, 2002/2018). As described earlier, Freud and other psychoanalysts were in important roles in understanding human mind and traumatisation from the psychological perspective that led a way to current understanding of traumas and their treatment.[14]

Psychoanalysis is not only considering the childhood development and the inner experiences in developing personality and their traumatisation. For a long time, as discussed earlier, also the meaning of outer experiences of wars, disasters, violence, sexual abuse, oppression, and transgenerational traumas has been understood as injuring the mind (Alayarian, 2024; Salberg, 2024). Also, the earlier concepts and theories in psychoanalysis relating to sexuality, gender, and race have been critically reviewed recently. However, still at the bottom of psychodynamic understanding, including traumatisation, are the personal experiences, emotions, memories, the life history, and the meanings relating to oneself, the others, and their interpersonal relationships.

2.5.1 *Early Object Relations and Their Traumatisation*

Current psychodynamic theories developed after the classical psychoanalysis of Freud like object relational, interpersonal, or relational, attachment, and mentalisation theories are emphasising the role of relationships in the development of personality. They are all studying the early relationships, between a mother and her baby, as well as other caretakers. Object relation theories include works of authors like Klein, Bion, Winnicott, Mahler, Kernberg, Ogden, Volkan, and Bollas in psychoanalysis where the development from the beginning is understood in the light of the developing self-experiences of infant. In such object relation theories and their vocabularies of current psychoanalysis, it is considered that the mind of an infant is internalised as "internal objects" or "representations" (Lemma, 2006, pp. 32–33).

With object relations in psychoanalytic theories, it is thought that the infant internalises his/her experiences of oneself and the other as the representations that are linked with affects (Yeomans et al., 2015, pp. 4, 8–12). These object representations

[14] See Sect. 2.2 "Historical Perspectives of Trauma".

are divided into the all-good and all-bad objects in the early development of self-organisation that in the beginning relate to the basic needs of being hungry, satisfied, loved, and deprived. In the object relation dyads of infant–caregiver, these experiences fulfil the positive needs of pleasure and idealised image of object in contrast to the totally negative image of object in the experiences of frustration that provoke neediness, helplessness, anxiousness, discomfort, and pain in the self, if these needs are not met (pp. 9–10).

Disruptions between the infant and caregivers, such as caregivers' neglect, indifference, and emphatic failure, may have adverse effects to the development that are interfering the organisation of self/other dyads and their internalising (Yeomans et al., 2015, p. 10). Early sexual abuse and the presence of other traumatic experiences are adding the possibilities of deviation from the normal development. However, also the infant's temperament is affecting the development of internalised object relationships that become building blocks for all the later self and the other experiences as well as for functioning within the external world. The early object relationships are including internalised affect arousal and cognitive-perceptual elements as a part of the development (p. 8).

With pleasurable and joyful experiences of the infant–caretaker dyad an infant begins to collect a coherent sense of self and the others, and their internalised narrative (Yeomans et al., 2015, p. 8). This develops safe attachment if the infant experiences the caregiver as loving and thoroughly understanding and rhythmically satisfying the infant's needs. In these early experiences, an infant internalises that s/he is safe, loved, and cared for. These internalisations help the infant to cope with frustration, fear, and anxiety that are a part of the normal development path. However, if the basic needs of infants are deprived and there are a lack of care, abuse, adverse experiences, and disturbed environments in the life of infant, they form insecure attachments with their primary caregivers (p. 10).

These adverse object relationships interfere with the normal development path and weaken the child's capacities for control and self-regulation. As a result, the internalised conceptions of self and other may be loaded with negative affects and defensive reactions and functioning that are distorting their information system in avoiding the pain (Yeomans et al., 2015, p. 10). This fits the disorganised and sometimes chaotic experiences of severely traumatised clients and borderline personality disorders and their core fear of rejection. Also, children and young people in music psychotherapy may be disorganised when the music and sounds they are producing may be a part of externalising or internalising their object relationships in the therapeutic dyad with music (Ahonen-Eerikäinen, 2007; Alanne, 2023). Then, music and sounds as well as the therapist may have functions and representations transferred from former internalised good and bad objects in the client's early development and other object relationships.

In the early development, experiences are divided into good and bad object experiences in the infant and still young child before they mature to more organised, differentiated, and individual understanding of the self and the others. According to Melanie Klein (1946, 1952), these experiences were originally internalised object relationships of the good and bad mother from the physical experiences of her feeding breast that is the first object relationship of an infant (Alanne, 2023, pp. 57, 102–103). Initially, the infant experiences the breasts of mother either gratifying or denying the oral pleasure. The unpleasurable and too frustrating object experiences are split from the consciousness and externalised as the bad breast and other partial objects.

In these early experiences, the splitting occurs according to unconscious fantasies of love and hate towards the breast (Klein, 1946; Alanne, 2023, pp. 102–103). Because of the frustrations, the intolerable feelings of an infant, oral sadistic and destroying urges, are projected onto the bad breast. At the same time, they arise internalised fears of attacking and retaliating in an infant. This can be considered as early traumatisation where the early internalised object relationships and situation are introjected and projected as good and bad objects according to Klein. This kind of experiences may also relate to the later experiences of music where music as a bad object is producing frustration, anxiety, irritation, or fear.

Klein (1946, 1952) called this as the paranoid–schizoid (PS) position where the experience of infant has split the mother's breasts to good, comforting, breast, and bad, frustrating, breast. This is a developmental stage and organisation where the early object relationships are divided to good (love) and bad (hate) objects instead of chaotic and disorganised experiences. The infant experiences the bad objects as persecuting because of the projection and projective identification where the parts of the self are placed outside the self. However, as this developmental position is not yet fully differentiated self-experience, the bad objects appear as frightening and persecuting to an infant (Alanne, 2023, p. 103, Volkan, 2018a, p. 8).

Klein called the later developmental position as the depressive (D) position, where the whole object relationships of good and bad are possible (Alanne, 2023, p. 103). In D position, experiences may have different aspects and values integrated like love and hate towards a person and still a relationship is possible (Alayarian, 2024, p. 101). In this position, sorrowing of a lost object becomes possible and there is a sense of guiltiness and willingness to repair without splitting as a defence (p. 102). These feelings have very early origins in the envy of an infant of a good breast that turns to hate towards the other breast where these feelings are projected to. Losing an "all good" object raises sorrow and unconscious fantasies in an infant (Volkan, 2018a, p. 8).

This development of PS position begins around the age of four to six months in its rudimentary forms and continues through life (Volkan, 2018a, p. 8). There is some fluctuation between the PS and D positions like in stressful situations according to current post-Kleinian theories as a part of the normal development and personality (Lemma, 2006, p. 38). In an infant, this may also cause early sense of guilty that may be internalised as very harsh and sadistic ego or destructive superego in the personality if the infant becomes too frustrated and deprived from the basic needs. In the good-enough development, the splitting of PS position will be worked through to the D position, where different feelings can be felt and recognised in oneself and the others (Alanne, 2023, p. 103).

If the person is struggling between the PS and D positions and cannot handle depressive anxieties, there may develop manic defences, urges, and fantasies to control the bad objects and remain the "all good" object representations (Volkan, 2018a,

p. 8). As a result, a person may also regress from the D position to an earlier PS position like in traumatic experiences and fight/flight stress reactions. Another specific defence relating to the PS position of ego in addition to splitting is projective identification where fantasies and feelings are projected onto objects and then identified with controlling them as appearing outside the self. There may also be omnipotent denial and idealisation in trying to retain the image of all-good objects with splitting (ibid.).

In the traumatic experiences, the feelings and memories relating to trauma are split and dissociated from the experience. As a result, a person may regress from the D position to the PS position where there are experiences like nightmares, flashbacks, somatic pains, illusions, and so on, as the traumatised may also feel like s/he is attacked and persecuted by the oppressors. This is also concerning the sense stimuli of sights, sounds, kinaesthetics, and other somatic experiences that the traumatised may be oversensitive. Then, also beautiful music may be experienced as stressful and causing annoying alertness in a traumatised refugee like a torture survivor (Alanne, 2010, 2023).

2.5.2 Separation-Individuation Development

In the psychoanalytic theories of trauma, this phase in infancy and traumatisation is also referred as the separation-individuation phase of development from the undifferentiated experiences in the age of around 4–5 to 36 months (Mahler et al., 1975/1991, pp. 52, 109–110). In a good-enough development, an infant develops more differentiated sense of self and the emotional object constancy after that period. However, the differentiation of self-experiences is also considered to continue and develop throughout the life as a mourning of loss in music and songs, for example (Handler Spitz, 1987, p. 541). There may also be arrested development and regression into the earlier stages of undifferentiated states of self-experience like with psychoses and borderline and other personality disorders (Akhtar, 1995; Blos, 1967; Tähkä, 1993/1997; Volkan, 2018a; Yeomans et al., 2015).

In addition, there may be "perennial mourning" in dislocated and refugees who are traumatised in a way that they are stuck in their past (Volkan, 2004, 2018a). They cannot deal with their losses, family, land, identity, and move on in their mourning; instead they may suffer from long-term depression because they are still living with their memories and internalised representations in the presence. They cannot experience their loss of objects as "futureless", which would mean accepting and internalising the reality of loss when mourning comes to its normal end according to psychoanalysts Veikko Tähkä (1993/1997) and Vamik D. Volkan (2018a, pp. 12, 17).

In the therapeutic process with music, mourning and working through may become possible for the asylum seekers and torture survivors who are stuck in their memories of death parents, family, and old countries (Alanne, 2010). As a result, more adaptive and creative capabilities may develop instead of maladaptive strategies, defences, and strategies of isolation, restricted life with fears, somatic illnesses, substance abuse, workaholism, inability to join and function in a new society and learn its language. For example, music therapy groups and other group work with music and arts may help refugees to deal and mourn with their many losses.

As perennial mourners they may not be clinically depressed because they are still in contact with their old mental representations like they were still living. However, the natural melancholia relation to losses may come out as anger and other maladaptive attitudes, as they are not feeling comfortable with their lives. This may continue for the rest of their lives and until their own deaths (Volkan, 2018a, pp. 17–19).

These traumatised people may live with an unassimilated "foreign body" inside of them as they cannot identify with the love and hate aspects relating to their losses (Volkan, 2018a, p. 18). Instead, they are assimilating the lost object (introject) into their self-representation as an illusion of choice and wish that the life could continue, which is reducing their anxiety. However, at the same time, they are struggling with ambivalent feelings of yearning and a wish that their suffering would end, and they could mourn their losses to their practical ending as futureless.

These traumatised cannot deal with their losses and they are arrested in the separation-individuation phase of development (Volkan, 2018a, pp. 10–11). Peter Blos (1967) has written about the second individuation during the adolescence after the childhood, and Salman Akhtar (1995) has proposed the third individuation for the immigrants' adaptation to a new society. In the second individuation, there is regression in the service of development and ego where adolescents process their earlier development, infantile needs, drive positions, and self-images that are loosened. According to Blos (ibid.), this contact with earlier object relationships, narcissistic formations, conflicts, and their solutions enables their repairing and continuing of development in adolescence. This natural development phase in adolescence with new identification role models, objects, and sexuality makes the difference between the teenagers and younger children's interests in their personality functioning according to Blos.

The third individuation of the immigrants and refugees proposed by Akhtar (1995) is an identity transformation relating to an immigrant situation in life (Volkan, 2018a, pp. 11–12). Akhtar is an immigrant himself as well as Volkan, and many other psychoanalysts who studied first the psychology and psychodynamics of immigrants in psychoanalysis (ibid.). Whereas the second individuation is continuing of the first childhood separation-individuation, Akhtar's (ibid.) third individuation is not reformation of childhood psychology and development like the mentioned childhood object relationships, solutions of conflicts, and arrested development. According to him, there is already an adult-like personality, sexuality, and re-established superego formation of adolescence in the third individuation. Rather, Akhtar is considering the third individuation as more phenomenological relating to the changes in identity and how to live and adapt into a new society, environment, and culture as a challenge for immigrant (Akhtar, 1995, pp. 1051–1053).

Akhtar (1995, p. 1052) writes about the challenges of immigration of how leaving own country is a "culture shock" that is causing many losses for an immigrant. As discussed earlier, immigrants leave their culture, familiar food, native music, social customs, and language when they are moving or fleeing into a new country of new songs, strange tasting food, and sounding language. There are also new and different political concerns, pale festivals, unknown heroes, and history without own connection or experience relating to them. Even the landscapes and climates are different than an immigrant is used to.

However, in spite of the challenges of settling down and homing in the new country, there is also a chance of psychological development for the immigrant according to Akhtar (1995, p. 1052). An immigrant may find new superego role models and objects for reorganising identifications from the culture shock that is truly shaking the identity of immigrant and mourning of it. Akhtar emphasises that this is more of adult adapting to an immigration than replication of the childhood and adolescence developmental phases even though they cannot be fully discerned. This adaptation and individuation are concerning more moral, aesthetical, temporal, lingual, and social aspects of life and identity according to him (p. 1053).

I think that the similar development may happen also in psychotherapy and in the therapeutic process with music (Alanne, 2016a, 2023). A child, adolescent, or adult may identify with the feelings of music. Music and songs are referring to the experiences in life, how it feels to be in love or hate someone, for example. They are also relating to the core experience of how it feels to be human or, more specifically, how it feels to be me. Thus, with music young people are learning from their emotional world and sexuality as well as from the experiences, cultures, social aspects, and psychologies of the others.

This is psychic working and development of identity with music in childhood and especially in adolescence where it provides new possibilities for the superego identifications and dealing with sexuality. In adolescence, this may be a part of the second individuation, and later in life a part of third individuation where new things are learnt from the culture like in adult education as the new ways of seeing life, work, and oneself differently. This is a part of growing in life that takes time where an immigrant or a refugee may be in a middle of crisis and very stressful situation in adapting to the new environment and roles.

Also, musical experiences have their origins in the separation-individuation and early development between the infant, mother, and other caregivers. They are providing a safe holding environment and affect attunement that is a sort of a "dance of wellbeing" for the infant's development (Alanne, 2023; Gratier & Trevarthen, 2007; Monaci et al., 2021; Stern, 1985/2004, 2010; Trevarthen, 2011; Trevarthen & Malloch, 2000; Winnicott, 1971/1997). The research of early development has findings that music and language have similar backgrounds in the early non-verbal reciprocity and communication.

This kind of research and knowledge of early interaction and its musicality have already been considered in psychoanalysis and psychotherapy on how their discussions may include musical elements like rhythms, intonations, dynamics, silences, and so on (Alanne, 2023; Blum et al., 2023; Grassi, 2021; Kennedy, 2020; Knoblauch, 2000). Thus, music and sounds in psychotherapeutic encountering are providing a window to study the early non-verbal experiences as the signs of possible traumatisation that are not on the verbal level of consciousness.

This development can be seen as a part of the "relational turn" in psychotherapy and psychoanalysis where the intersubjective experiences and their meaning between the therapist and client are emphasised (Alanne, 2023). Earlier more psychoanalyst/therapist-orientated interventions and interpretations of the clients' unconscious experiences were preferred and considered as clinically objective. Similar development towards relational aspects has happened in music therapy that has been influenced by the research of Daniel Stern (1985/2004; 2010) and his conceptions of affect attunements, vitality affects, and their musicality in the early development.

2.5.3 Early Development and Musical Experiences

It is assumed that the very early experiences of pleasure relating to the oral phase of development, a mother rocking an infant, holding and feeding her baby, feeling a warmth of mother's body and breast, are associated with later musical experiences, how they are felt enjoyable (Alanne, 2023, pp. 46–47). Often these early experiences also include musical elements in swaying and singing a lullaby for a child as examples. In these experiences, an infant is in close connection with a mother enjoyably and safely which later are associated with similar emerging and floating experiences with music and its oceanic feelings.

The early self-development relates to the bodily experiences of pleasure and frustration if the infant's basic needs like mother's milk is not filled quite immediately (Alanne, 2023, p. 103; Tähkä, 1993/1997). These experiences are disorganised and undifferentiated until the infant learns to control and wait for the fulfilment of basic needs. Undifferentiated experiences and affects of physical pain, grief, and suffering are caused by the frustration of infant when they come intolerable. From this undifferentiated sense of self-experiences relating to the mother and other caretakers, the first object relationships are internalised as the presence of good and bad objects. Later, they will become more mature and symbolic representations like in arts, music, and language.

The first sounds of an infant come meaningful to an infant when the infant learns to recognise the mother's voice and other familiar voices (Alanne, 2023, p. 103). These sounds may have become familiar already in the womb where they were associated with the tactile experiences and senses of being connected with a mother as some possibly earliest object relationships and the sense of self as "being here" (Siltala, 2014). After the birth, the infant's own voices, making sounds, and bodily rhythms are probably the first games and good objects for the infant. From these rudimental sensorial good objects, known as transitional objects after Donald W. Winnicott, the infant is developing the separateness between objects. It means learning to control reality and what is absent with fantasies which in the beginning is the presence of the mother and her gratifying breast (Fisher & Gilboa, 2016, p. 1231; Lehtonen, 1996; Rechardt, 1987; Winnicott, 1971/1997).

The disturbing sounds in the environment cause stress for the infant, especially loud sudden noises may trigger a Moro reflex, a startle reaction with pulling hands in, spreading arms out, and crying in the infant (Alanne, 2023, pp. 46–47). According to psychoanalyst Heinz Kohut and musicologist Siegmund Levarie (Kohut & Levarie, 1950/1978), loud noises are causing annihilation anxiety and fear in addition to the emergency of Moro reflex for survival. Thus, it seems that the loud noises and sounds are causing a threat of annihilation, as an early traumatic experience of a possibility and sense of "not being here" anymore. In this very early phase of ego development, a newborn cannot have an idea or a representation of death yet, which as a concept develops years later in a child.

The frightening sounds are alerting and appear as bad objects for the infant (Alanne, 2023, pp. 103–104). For the traumatised, especially for a refugee survivor of torture who may have been interrogated or tortured with music and sounds, music may trigger similar uncontrollable psychic experiences. From the psychoanalytic perspective of Freud's (1920/1981, pp. 62–63) drive theory, they are representing unbound psychic energies of libido and Thanatos, which is why they are felt as chaotic and stressful (Lehtonen, 1996, pp. 80–81).

From the Kleinian perspective, this can be considered as regression to disorganised psychic state where a person may also temporally be in a PS position and using splitting as a defence. Very loud music, sounds, and sudden noises like sirens or crashing sounds can pass through the defences of ego harmfully. The music's capability to violently perpetuate inside the mind without a control has been used as a weapon in interrogations and torture as well as in manipulating with sounds and music refugees and dislocated people (Alanne, 2010; Chornik, 2013; Cusick, 2006, 2013; Papaeti, 2020).

This capability seems to relate to the early undifferentiated state of being where the object experiences of an infant are still without clear boundaries. Music and sounds may represent the oral pleasures, relaxing and soothing experiences with a mother (Alanne, 2023, pp. 46–47). At the same time, music and sounds are connected with frustration, stress, and fear of annihilation in the core experiences of ego and in the emerging sense of subjective self. For this reason, in stressful situations and traumatic experiences, music and sounds may felt as disturbing because a person or a client in therapy cannot control them (p. 104). A client like a refugee survivor of torture may not want to listen or play music at home or in therapy because music and sounds are activating and reverberating with the bad objects of traumatic experiences and their memories (Alanne, 2010).

Then, music and sounds appear as threats for the ego control of unconscious experiences and repression (Alanne, 2023, p. 104). This need of controlling experiences and bad objects relates to the early experiences internalised in the childhood during the first separation-individuation phase before achieving the object constancy. As described, music and sounds are also reverberating with the earliest experiences of being life or destroyed as assimilated experiences of bad objects. In this sense, further regression and depression anxiety would lead to the undifferentiated state of being which is tried to avoid in PS position. Losing this achievement of differentiation would mean the losing of boundaries and the control of all object relationships like in a psychotic state that is representing an unconscious threat of annihilation and psychic death (Tähkä, 1993/1997, pp. 105–107).

These kinds of experiences and unconscious fears of bad objects are not only relating to severe traumas caused by accidents, violence, death, abuse, or when music and sounds have been a part of the violence in wars or interrogations, like explained and studied more in the next chapter (Alanne, 2023, p. 104). They are also a part of the normal experiences and innate bodily reactions in surviving psychologically in stressful and conflictual situations temporally where early developmental traumas, losses, and frustrations may activate and trigger bad object experiences and feelings.

As such, they are normal dynamics and fluctuations between the D and PS positions when a person has mainly achieved the D position, the capability to mourn the lost object as good and bad, and the object constancy (Alayarian, 2024, p. 102). In the D position, the feelings of love, hate, envy, and gratitude are integrated that appears as a willingness to repair instead of omnipotent denying and destroying the bad objects internally. This is also affecting the other object relationships because of the various splitting that results as a fragmentation of ego and a kind of disintegration and total disturbance of traumatised refugee like in dissociative disorder and depersonalisation (ibid.). A severely traumatised person or a refugee with C-PTSD, or a client with a BPD, may be easily alerted and reacting to stressful situations, including music and sounds, with dissociation. As a result, s/he may also be constantly in the PS position as a part of the traumatisation.

According to Kohut and Levarie (1950/1978), the enjoyment of music is in the satisfaction that it is bringing for the ego control of sounds that develops when an infant can cope with the noises and the sound environment (Alanne, 2023, p. 46). Sounds become an early game for the infant which unconsciously means a controlling of annihilation anxiety relating to sounds. Thus, it is playing with the early traumatic and threatful experiences of sounds as bad objects that is strengthening the ego and its functions of internalising experiences instead of dissociation or splitting. However, if these experiences were too chaotic and felt as unsafe, they would lessen the emerging ego control respectively.

In music therapy with traumatised refugees, it is therefore important to consider the safety of the environment, including sounds and music, so that there would be a possibility for ego control of the client. Because of the severe traumatisation, there may be sleep deprivation, flashbacks, depression, anxiety, and even hallucinations as a part of the dissociation that are already weakening the functioning of ego and its capability of controlling sounds. The fear of losing control of experiences and falling into disorganised self-experiences where unconscious flooding may be a part of avoiding, numbing, and dissociation of traumatic experiences. In such cases, a therapist should be aware of the situation, when the client feels unsafe and cannot cope with the sound environment, so that there would not be any unnecessary harm done to a client with music and sounds in treatment.[15]

---

[15] This will be discussed more in Chap. 4 how to deal with such situations with clients.

With the traumatic experiences, flooding of consciousness, flashbacks, and possible hallucinations, and other dissociative states, it is important to understand their differences to the psychotic states, even though they sometimes may appear as similar (Volkan, 2018a, p. 19). With the traumatic experiences and dissociations, the general reality testing of a person is usually mainly functioning whilst a person may have occasional hallucinations during the nights and strange bodily symptoms, and nightmares. Sometimes a traumatised person may be talking with a dead person like a mother or a friend who was killed by the oppressors. As a part of their trauma and mourning process, they may experience their presence as an internalised mental representation very alive (Tähkä, 1993/1997; Volkan, 2018a, p. 17).

These experiences may feel very frightening and uncanny for the traumatised as they may experience guilt and wonder are they going mad or having a psychic illness. These kinds of repeating dissociations are regression from the ego's D position to the PS position as the traumatised may wake alerted during the night ready to defend him/herself from perpetrators. These hallucinations remind dream experiences and musical imagery where a person is in the altered state of mind. When working with guided imagery and music in music psychotherapy, in a client's imagery and free associations to music, there may arise traumatic memories of being in home country, prisoned and mock-executed like in a dream and a clinical vignette of Ben described later (Alanne, 2010).

Freud noticed the hallucinations, dream experiences, and their relationship to music in his famous *Interpretation of Dreams* (1900/1981) book that meant the beginning of psychoanalytic era in understanding the human mind and trauma. Even though he discussed music very scarcely in his studies, in his founding book, he noticed how visual and acoustical presentations, including music, are mixed with memories and their thoughts are replaced as hallucinations in dreams. Freud wrote:

> *— in asserting that dreams hallucinate—that they replace thoughts by hallucinations. In this respect, there is no distinction between visual and acoustic presentations: It has been observed that if one falls asleep with the memories of a series of musical notes in one's mind, the memory becomes transformed into an hallucination of the same melody; while, if one then wakes up again—and the two states may alternate more than once during the process of dropping asleep—the hallucination gives way in turn to the mnemic presentation, which is at once fainter and qualitatively different from it.* (Freud, 1900/1981, p. 50)

Because the dissociative and dream states may be very similar and a person does not necessarily understand s/he is hallucinating, dreaming, or awake, there should be some caution in treatment with traumatised refugees, even though they should not be considered as psychotic states but as a psychic adaptation to traumatic experience. Even temporal psychotic symptoms and defences may also be considered as such psychic defences with traumatised where clients sometimes need fantasy, projection, splitting, and omnipotent thoughts to maintain their psychic integrity and ego functions.

2.5.4 Containing of Trauma in a Relationship with Music

In these kinds of experiences, a traumatised person, like many refugees and torture survivors, is in between bodily experiences of pain, insomnia, headaches, and those of more mental experiences like dreams, imagery, conscious and unconscious thoughts and feelings, even spiritual. Also, in musical experiences, our bodily, emotional, psychic, and spiritual experiences may be mingled respectively with more conscious and analytic stances. Wilfred Bion (1897–1979) who continued object relation theories and the work of Melanie Klein (1882–1960) conceptualised in a new way with his "attacks on linking" that means projecting of envy to cut off the problematic object relationships (Alayarian, 2024, pp. 101–102). However, this also leads to a destroying of all-good objects as well and to a disorganised and fragmented self-experience.

In musical experience, this would mean the loss of music as a good object and cutting off the contacts with music in avoiding envy and bad object experiences. This sometimes happens in music therapy relationships and transference where music may be suddenly away from the sessions because it is targeted with the experiences of being "bad" in music compared to a therapist or other musicians. The feeling of unconscious envy and ungratified experiences in childhood development may feel so bad that a client wants to cut the links totally between music and sounds during the sessions. There may also be unconscious fear of losing the idealised good object, including music and the therapist, that is therefore experienced as too close, "hot", in a relationship with a narcissistic injured client who is unconsciously fearing the rejection of therapist. Unfortunately, sometimes this leads to the interruptions in therapy, and a client is not showing up to a session or is cancelling them or is totally leaving the therapy without the agreed ending period and working through such transference issues.

Bion (1959, 1961/2004) discussed about the containing of such painful and traumatic experiences with a client in his theory (Alayarian, 2024, pp. 102–103). According to him, in the early relationship a mother is containing the chaotic and undifferentiated self-experiences of an infant. The mother is a container, when breast feeding the infant, for example, of infant's feelings, pleasure, gratitude, anxiety, frustration, anger, grief, and pain. Then, these experiences may become digested and contained in the infant's self-experience. A similar process occurs also in therapy where the therapist sometimes must be the container of the traumatised client's projected painful and intolerable experiences. In such a way, like in infancy, a client may identify and integrate these experiences and become a container him/herself of trauma. This is an important internalising of an object relationship and a capability for container-contained function using a defence projective identification according to Bion.

In music, there is a possibility that music is an object where the unbearable feelings of traumatised client can be contained (Alanne, 2020, 2023; De Backer & Sutton, 2014b; Robarts, 2003). With music and therapist as containers, the client's dissociated unbearable and undifferentiated experiences may transform from the non-organised state of affects and other sensomotorial experiences that are between the mind and body to beta elements. These experiences that Bion (1961/2004) called as the beta elements are a part of the primary process thinking in unconsciousness. With music and other art forms, the unconscious primary process of traumatic experience may become conscious thinking of emotions, symbols, language, dreams, imagery, and music, Bion called as alpha elements. They belong to the secondary process of thinking (Alanne, 2023, p. 54).

2.5.5 Mentalisation and Trauma

In music psychotherapy, there is a specific method called *sensorial playing* when the client cannot necessarily feel the music and is detached from it (De Backer & Van Camp, 2014, p. 75). Then, the music of traumatised client may be chaotic and there is no clear melody, rhythm, or harmony. Music may also be very mechanical or patterned in a way that it appears as some kind of imitation of playing an instrument. It may appear like there are no feelings that are identified in the expression of sounds. This may be a part of the client's traumatisation and dissociation as well as a sign of undeveloped capacity for mentalising that occurs in a psychic equivalence, teleological, and a pretend mode (Alanne, 2023, pp. 62, 135–136; Strehlow & Hannibal, 2019, pp. 335–336).

The mentalisation concept was developed by Peter Fonagy with his colleagues including Jon G. Allen and Anthony W. Bateman. It is adding neurobiological understanding to psychoanalytic theory, childhood development, and traumatisation as mentalisation is partly considered as an innate sociobiological capability between the mind and the body (Allen et al., 2008; Fonagy et al., 2004). Difficulties in mentalising are like the problems often occurring with the childhood trauma and failures in the attachment if there has been a lack of emotional marked mirroring by the early caretakers (Strehlow, 2009, p. 173). Then, the child may develop an experience of unintentional being. The phases of mentalising are referring to the age of child before six years and it relates to the child developing a psychic idea of feelings and thoughts (Alanne, 2023, pp. 134–135).

Even though mentalisation is considered as having innate biosocial prerequisites in early development, it may also be developed and learned in life and therapy (Alanne, 2023, pp. 135–136; Allen et al., 2008; Fonagy et al., 2004). From the three modes of mentalisation, a *psychic equivalence* is appearing as very concrete thinking that is undifferentiated from the objects (Strehlow & Hannibal, 2019, pp. 335–336). As a result, clients may be thinking automatically that the therapist is thinking and feeling similarly with themselves. Their thoughts may have very concrete meanings, which are experienced as real and happening when they are discussed. Thus, in the psychic equivalence mode, clients cannot necessarily see other points of view than their own. This may make them easily irritated and leads to conflicts in their lives.

In the *teleological mode*, a child is still in the world of concreteness and is understanding self and the others by their actions, behaviours, and physical appearances (Alanne, 2023, pp. 135–136). In this kind of thinking, what the other is doing is an indicator of their intensions. The language of action is observed like clients, younger or older, who are moving their bodies and hands in playing music and keyboards without actual skills or feelings related to it. However, this is already participating in music, music therapy, and a form of musicality, like the mentioned sensorial playing with psychotic or deprived child clients. It is only being in the different mode of thinking in music that can be developed in music therapy with traumatised refugees or immigrants when listening to music as an example.

When there are issues in the teleological mode of mentalisation, a person cannot necessarily understand the emotional contents and gestures in musical expressions or in the behaviours of others. A therapist can help the client to understand and mentalise them by describing the situation in the present moment empathically, however, not teaching like a caretaker to a child but describing how the therapist hears and sees the client's situation in the present moment (Laitinen, 2017, pp. 76–77). This is done in personal and reflective way studying together by the therapist who is asking questions why the client or therapist said and felt so. Also, music may develop a capability to mentalise with identifications to its emotional contents as well as according to the experiences and questions of therapist in psychotherapeutic discussions (Alanne, 2023; Hannibal, 2014; Strehlow, 2009; Strehlow & Lindner, 2016).

Mentalising as a psychotherapeutic technique is close to transference interpretations of here and now and especially the *empathic describing* of Tähkä (1993/1997) in psychoanalysis (Laitinen, 2017; Lemma, 2006; Yeomans et al., 2015). Tähkä recommended empathic describing for the borderline clients and their situations to help in their separation-individuation development. In music therapy, mentalisation and emphatic describing, or portraying, reflecting, clients' experiences and feelings through music or words may have similar goals and they can be used with traumatised clients like refugees respectively (Alanne, 2010, 2023). This may help in the third individuation of immigrant where music can be a part of the process in communicating and adapting into a new culture, its customs, culture, and society (Akhtar, 1995).

In the *pretend mode*, there may also be verbalisations but other than black or white, concrete thinking (Alanne, 2023, pp. 135–136; Strehlow & Hannibal, 2019, pp. 335–336). It is the opposite of the psychic equivalence mode as the feelings are dissociated from the experiences with words and narratives. There may also be intellectualising and externalising of the experiences as a pseudomentalisation because of avoiding trauma and not working through it. In the pretend mode, there is no connection between the inner and outer realities of client (Keinänen, 2017, p. 89). It relates to the emptiness, meaningfulness, and dissociation after the person's psychic capability has been surpassed. Then, a client may talk endlessly without meaning in therapy, and what s/he says may be contradictory. Also, the feelings expressed may be different to what is said.

In the pretend mode, there is superficiality of how things are told, explained, or felt because there is no true connection with these experiences (Laitinen, 2017, pp. 66–67). In fact, they may even seem as false, or client having a false self-identity, because true feelings relating to traumatisation are avoided and there is no contact with the traumatised experiences anymore. As a result, a therapist may have a countertransference feeling of emptiness and a lot of questions after sessions (ibid.). This may also concern talking about music and other experiences, feelings, memories relating to them that are tried to hide with superficial, trivial, or technical comments where the purpose is the detachment from feelings, experiences, and relationships. Similarly, a client's music may feel empty without meaning when the client is in the pretend mode. However, it may be a part of the transference and resistance of client where the links of the object experiences are attacked, and the connections of ego have already been destroyed according to Bion's (1959) view.

The incapabilities in mentalisation are normal development, especially under stress, but major difficulties in understanding and identifying with the feelings of oneself and the others, "keeping mind in mind", are signs of developmental trauma (Allen et al., 2008, p. 312). The difficulties in mentalising may show as incapability to understand the feelings of the others' faces like when continuing criticisms in social discussions that feels embarrassing and insulting for others. Mentalisation is in connection with other socioemotional development and issues relating to the separation-individuation phase. The ideas of mentalisation are close to the object relationship theories and are adding to their understanding for the meaning of intersubjective experiences and their traumatisation in childhood development (Alanne, 2023, pp. 135–136; Strehlow & Hannibal, 2019, pp. 335–336).

Many severely and chronically traumatised have difficulties in understanding the expressed emotions of faces and meeting their gazes (van der Kolk, 2014, p, 102). They are easily interpreting themselves as disgusting and despicable as a part of their traumatisation and felt shame that is projected into Other's eyes as a bad object experience. In fact, mentalisation as a method of therapy was developed for the BPD clients who often have major difficulties understanding their own and other's feelings (Alanne, 2023; Strehlow & Hannibal, 2019). They are easily projecting and splitting their own negative feelings and self-experiences to others (Yeomans et al., 2015). BPD clients also have difficulties in emotional regulating because they are externalising and acting out their feelings and negative thoughts as bodily symptoms and/or self-abusing behaviour patterns.

Playing music and improvising in the present moment with a therapist may help the client to mentalise, contain, and integrate the chaotic, sometimes fragmented pieces of music, to coherent sounds and experiences. The therapist is also a container in such dissociative and disorganised experiences who is attuning to the client's experiences, sounds, and music together. There are also elements of musical holding and being present with music like the holding of a mother and her gratifying good breast when listening to or improvising music (Alanne, 2010, 2023; De Backer & Sutton, 2014b; Hannibal, 2014; Klein, 1946; Levinge, 2015; Priestley, 1975; Strehlow, 2009; Strehlow & Lindner, 2016; Winnicott, 1971/1997).

2.5.6 Holding Environment and Transitional Experiences for Refugees

Winnicott (1971/1997) described a holding environment as the safe and caring place that is created for the infant by the caretakers. Then, music may be a transitional object for a client that feels safe to play with and project feelings, images, and memories relating to the homeland when listening to one's native music (Akhtar, 1995, p. 1062). Music, songs, and particular instruments may also be transitional objects for the clients like for the Holocaust survivor musicians who carried positive imagery, fantasies, normality, and identity with music through their lives that seemed to be an integral part of their survival from the camps (Fisher & Gilboa, 2016, pp. 1231–1232). For the immigrants, the long phone call or listening to music is helping in adapting to external realities of being far from "the mother" that the home country is unconsciously symbolising and feeling it being close internally. Respectively, in the minds of immigrant, the new country may unconsciously symbolise the father according to Akhtar (ibid., pp. 1058–1059).

As an example, for immigrants from East, the old home country may be idealised as a good object and the new country and culture in West may be devalued and characterised as greedy, violent, and representing sexual promiscuity where the bad object experiences are split (Akhtar, 1995, pp. 1058–1059). As a part of the third separation-individuation working through and identity change for an immigrant, movies, music, literature, and games of new country may become enjoyable and "transitional area" of Winnicott where the split is no longer needed between "mine" and "yours" as food, customs, and language become "ours" (pp. 1067–1068).

As a result of traumatisation and stressful situation of being a refugee and immigrant, the client's capacity for symbolisation and mentalisation may be disturbed. Then, the thinking and musical improvisations may regress into the non-organised and concrete functioning of the symbolic equation state of mind like with psychotic clients (Alanne, 2023, p. 62). This makes it difficult for the traumatised clients to produce imagery, associations, and feelings towards music and verbalise them to the therapist. However, with music it is possible to approach the subjective experiences of client as a sonorous object and "structuring sound" that can be felt and participated even if client would not understand the words and style of music or cannot play it (Grassi, 2021, pp. 15–16).

Music can be shared and felt together that may help in creating contact with a traumatised refugee who may be "frozen" and confused in dissociative experiences. Then, music may be a "good enough holding environment" for an immigrant, dislocated, and a refugee in a new country that they are needing for their transforming identity (Akhtar, 1995, p. 1077). The holding and containing experience by the music and therapist in the present moment may help in integrating the disorganised experiences of traumatised to beta and alpha elements of thinking and being together in a relationship (Alanne, 2019b, 2020, 2023; Grassi, 2021; Robarts, 2003; Schulman, 2002). In psychotherapy, like in the early relationship of mother and infant, there are also the structuring sounds, rhythms, dynamics, and music in moving along with the feelings experienced and shared between the therapist as a container and the clients and their experiences as contained (Grassi, 2021, pp. 52–53).

2.5.7 *Musical Interaction, Attunement, and Trauma in Transference*

Musical experience and interaction seem to be at the same level with trauma because it is resonating through sounds within our body and mind, respectively (De Backer & Sutton, 2014a, pp. 16–18). Music as a sounding object begins to feel immediately for a child as something that is sensed coming from outside as well as being in relationship with oneself. A person influenced by the music is "caught up in it" (p. 17). This seems to happen quite automatically how music and sounds are received with pleasure, chills, or as stressful and annoying through our body and brain. Music and sounds pass the psychic defences and penetrate deep into the structures of brain, limbic system, amygdala, and brain stem. They are the same brain structures that are activating and reacting in stressful situations that make us alerted and vigilant. A severely traumatised person may constantly be in such a dissociative state as discussed earlier (van der Kolk, 2014).

The penetrating powers of music and sound was already understood at the Nazi concentration camps during WWII where music and singing were systematically used as sounding objects to psychologically torment and physically exhaust detainees and their will to live (Alanne, 2010; Brauer, 2016; John, 1991/2001; Moreno, 1999; Naliwajek-Mazurek, 2013). After WWII, in Cold War era, as well as in the twenty-first century during the Iraq War, and War on Terror, music was continued to use in penetrating the body and mind of the detainees to similarly exhaust and break their ego down (Alanne, 2010; Cloonan & Johnson, 2002, 2008; Cusick, 2006, 2008, 2013; Grant, 2013; Papaeti, 2020).[16] The energising and deactivating effects of music have a long history in detainee camps and interrogation centres where music has been used to entertain as a sort of therapy, to keep up the work, and often at the same time to torment and exhaust, destroy the body, with a betraying energising positive spirit of music. The same positive effect was noticed and recommended by the US army for their troops already in 1945 (Alanne, 2023; AMTA, 2014; Sullivan, 2007).

In the core of such holistic effects of music there seem to be already discussed relationships with mother and other early caretakers. The pleasure and stress relating to music and sounds seem to be in these early holding and containing experiences where the secure attachment and the capability to mentalise are developing. Insecure and stressful situations, ACEs, in the early development and relationships are traumatising and resulting arrested development and incapability of containing

---

[16] See Chap. 4 for more discussion and study of music, violence, and manipulation.

and mentalising experiences. Music and sounds seem to resonate with these early good and bad object relationships that are at the same time experienced as coming outside and identified and mirrored as the Other (De Backer & Sutton, 2014b, p. 18). In this sense, we are responding and reflecting our experiences through ourselves and our pasts in the present moment.

Our bodies are already sensing and attuning with pleasure (love), stress, disquiet, pain, anger (hate), and so on to the situations that relate to our development and life history. This autoaffectionality, like I have called it, seems to have origins in the early interpersonal relationships (Alanne, 2023). They have affected the neurobiological development and mirror neurons of how people pick up other people's emotions and intentions (van der Kolk, 2014, pp. 58–59). At the physiological level, people seem to even synchronise their movements unconsciously, how they are sitting and standing, or using their voices with the same volumes and rhythms (p. 59).

Similarly, in the negative experiences of traumatised development, the neurobiological mirroring system of traumatised clients may be distorted, and the client cannot recognise or separate inner experiences from the experiences of the Other, or the bad from the friendly contact (van der Kolk, 2014 p. 102). According to neurobiological evidence, the insecure attachment and losses are inducing traumatic stress (Alanne, 2023; Crenshaw, 2006; Fonagy, 2004; Glaser, 2000; Solms & Turnbull, 2002/2018). Because of the prolonged intimidation or abuse, the development of child's prefrontal cortex and limbic system of the brain may be inhibited, and they cannot manage with their feelings. Instead, they are reacting to them according to their traumatic experiences (van der Kolk, 2014, pp. 59–60). This is because their interpersonal neurobiological experiences relating to the attachment and feelings of being safe or unsecure mirror the nerve system that is responding automatically. For the traumatised, feelings of being ignored or dismissed may cause rage and mental collapse when the person is not feeling safe and calm (Alanne, 2023).

In music psychotherapy, especially psychiatric children suffering from the disorders in the socioemotional development and attention regulation may find it difficult or even impossible to regulate their impulses. Neurobiologically, including the vagus nerve, which is explained to adjust and transmit bodily experiences such as perceiving of a danger, the empathic attuning with one's face and voice as well as movement and music is soothing (Crenshaw, 2006). In therapy, the safe relationship and the gaze of therapist are communicating encountering, hearing, and caring, which are activating the mirror neurons and the embodied understanding of the other (van der Kolk, 2014, p. 78). Thus, human brains seem to attune for the safe that the gazes, sounds, and music of other people are representing for them (Alanne, 2023; van der Kolk, 2014).

Therefore, it is important to create a holding environment with music in a therapeutic relationship that supports creativity and therapy as a *potential space* like Winnicott (1971/1997, p. 41) has described as the mutual relational area between the infant and the caretaker. In a potential space, where there are parts from minds of both the infant and the mother, symbolic play and illusions become possible for the infant as the intermediate "me" and "not me" possessions of reality and social world (Alanne, 2023, p. 95). Winnicott considered psychotherapy as a highly specialised play between an analyst and a client that is universal and a sign of health according to him.

In psychotherapy, like in the early development of separation-individuation, clients have the possibility to develop their sense of differences from the Other that the discussions with the therapist are providing (Alanne, 2023, pp. 95–96). Shared intersubjective experiences with a therapist that may include music in music therapy are strengthening the ego in tolerating the experiences and feelings of the other. Also, as discussed, the sharing of emotions, affects, and experiences is helping in the development of language and social skills. As a part of the emotional recognition and marking, it is also developing the child's capability of mentalisation in addition to the emotional regulation. For an immigrant or a refugee, this would mean a new third individuation from the homeland symbolising the mother with the help of a therapist (Akhtar, 1995).

According to Winnicott (1971/1997, pp. 107–110), when the capability of symbolic play and thinking lessens, the need to use violence and behave aggressively increases. I have observed this in my music psychotherapy work with adopted, deprived, and traumatised children who have an immigration background. They do not necessarily play as they do not have a potential or a capability for it anymore. They have difficulties in controlling their emotions and attentions as they are losing their interest fast and having aggressive outbursts (Alanne, 2023, p. 96).

In addition, they seek pleasure and feel easily bored. They withdraw, others are stuck, passive, quiet, and they often need some help from the therapist to activate them and play music or games in therapy. These children also have difficulties in learning, social relationships, and mentalising as a part of their traumatisation and resulting incapability of symbolic play. This withdrawal from play, including listening or improvising music, in psychotherapy concerns also severely traumatised adults who may be quiet, nervous, anxious, and restless in their physical appearances and cannot concentrate.

For the thinking and creativity, the prefrontal cortex and the frontal lobes are important because they able planning, reflecting, imagining, and "playing out" things (van der Kolk, 2014, p. 58). They are the ground for the great human capability of creativity in the brain, and they also contribute importantly to the control of behaviour and adjusting of emotions (p. 60). As discussed earlier, traumatised person's prefrontal cortex cannot anymore control such cognitive functions that are needed for playing in a broad sense, to think, imagine, and reflect symbolically. This can make their rehabilitation and psychotherapy in music psychotherapy more difficult. Severely traumatised clients may also have an alexithymia, so they cannot talk about their feelings and traumas because they are dissociated and somatised from their experiences.

However, in therapy like music therapy and psychodynamic psychotherapy, there is a possibility for recovering in the positive therapeutic relationship and transference between the therapist and client. Many elements of music psychotherapy like music, sounds, voices, gazes, words, movements, and games convey emotion, playfulness, and positive intersubjective experiences. Music and arts as the cultural forms are symbolising the other people, and such activities as listening to music and singing songs may strengthen their feeling of belonging to the social group of people, a tribe, in the brains (van der Kolk, 2014, p. 78).

Music and sounds may prevent from the stress of isolation and trauma as music is decreasing anxiety and the amount of adrenocorticotropic stress hormone (ACTH) that is producing stress in the system (Alanne, 2014a, 2023; Christensen, 2019; Kreutz et al., 2013; Lehtonen, 1996; Solms & Turnbull, 2002/2018). Music may have corrective effects for the traumatised clients in music psychotherapy as their endorphin production increases which may calm the traumatised brains that are hyperactive, vigilant, and stressed (Alanne, 2023; Christensen, 2019; Swallow, 2002; van der Kolk, 2014).

Trevarthen (2011) has found music and dance from the early interaction between a mother and infant, which are essential for the emotional and brain development of child—it has been described as the "dance of wellbeing" by Trevarthen and Malloch (2000). In the positive relationship and transference of therapy, the brain is transmitting pleasure and attachment with good responsiveness and social caring, mutual gazing, and facial mirroring (Rose, 2004; Solms & Turnbull, 2002/2018). Like in the early interaction, the positive attuning, containing, holding, and mentalising in therapy are enabling the recovering of the affect regulation and the trauma in the brain (Rose, 2004, pp. 123–126).

Stern (1985, 2010) and Alvarez (1992/1999) have pointed out the meaning of early development and non-verbal musicality for the psychotherapy relationship of how there are moments of meeting and aliveness in the psychotherapy sessions between the therapist and client. Stern (2010) together with his colleagues in the Boston Change Process Study Group (BCPSG, 2010) emphasised the non-verbal meeting, vitality affects, and attuning for the psychotherapeutic process between the therapist and client. According to them, in the psychotherapeutic relationship a therapist can be moving along with the client's feelings that can add something more for the interpretation of client's experiences. This kind of interpretations that are confronting or reflecting the present moment in a therapeutic relationship is called as the here-and-now or transference interpretations in psychodynamic psychotherapy and psychoanalysis (Alanne, 2023; Lemma, 2006).

James Strachey (1934/1969) emphasised the meaning of alive moments for transformative experiences in psychoanalysis, so that the client could identify and internalise with the hot feelings and issues discussed in therapy. Similarly, music and songs can be used as emotional "something more" interpretations to address issues in a child's or adult's play and support the change and development in addition to language in psychotherapy (Stern, 2010; Alanne, 2020, 2023). This relates to the procedural implicit knowing of unconscious experiences and their corrections in traumas in addition to the discursive experiences and verbal interventions in psychotherapy (Lemma, 2006, pp. 78–79).

With the implicit knowledge of client's feelings in the moments of meetings, therapists may provide non-verbal interpretations from their meaning with expressions of words, gestures, and silences according to their counter-emotions (Stern, 2004, pp. 150–151). In the traumatised experiences, implicit knowing is relating to the dissociations, emotional memories, and affects. They are mediated by the amygdala and the brain stem, the lower brain structures, that have been recently considered as the location of primary consciousness, the unconsciousness, and the repressed by Solms (Lemma, 2006; Solms, 2017/2019, 2021). Before, the consciousness was thought to be in the upper parts of brain, like the cortex, in psychoanalysis (Alanne, 2023, pp. 155–156).

When the consciousness, repressed memories, and dissociations of traumatic experiences are considered this seems to be correct. In the emergency situations, including loud sounds and music, in the brain fight-or-flight alarm responses are activated. Also, emotional experiences and memories, especially fears, can be sensitised and conditioned in the brain as unconscious behaviour (Lemma, 2006, p. 79). This affects our different object relationships and seems to be repressed, internalised, and automatised, like the avoiding behaviour and observing the dangers in environment, of the traumatised experience (Alanne, 2023, p. 156).

The problem in often compulsive and neurotic behaviours of controlling traumatised bad objects is that they are felt immediately with strong anxiety and stress, so that a client does not have an idea where these experiences came from. In that sense, they do not seem to be "indirect" and "completely out of conscious awareness" in the procedural unconsciousness like argued by Lemma (2006, p. 80). In fact, they seem to be direct experiences of something that a traumatised client is not aware of as I have argued before (Alanne, 2023, p. 157). This seems to be also in accordance with Solms (2017/2019, 2021), who is arguing that the consciousness/unconsciousness are in the lower parts of the brain. This relates to the development of species where being aware and alert are crucial skills of survival in the natural environment. This development of species can be seen from the structures of human brain where the lower parts and the small brains are like those of other animals. Therefore, the traumatic hyper-vigilance, fear, and the flight/fight or freeze can be seen as adapting to the environment (van der Kolk, 2014).

In addition, for the traumatised, the capability to verbalise, reflect, and control their experiences seems to be diminished as they are responding with unnecessary anxiety and stress like a catastrophe happening to their normal situations in life. At the brain level, the hippocampus is a structure where the affective material in the brain is processed to thinking and symbolic communication (Schulman, 2002, p. 172). It is connected to the prefrontal cortex of the large brain, and nerve impulses are going through it from the amygdala (van der Kolk, 1996/2007b, pp. 294–295). In the high arousal experience of trauma, the passing of nerve impulses from amygdala to hippocampus is disrupted which is why the traumatic experiences do not store in the discursive memory. As a result of this, traumatic experiences and feelings cannot be integrated, nor remembered or verbalised necessarily. Instead, they are stored as the elements and fragments of information including sensory experiences like visual images, somatic sensations, arousal, and relationship configurations (Schulman, 2002; van der Kolk, 1996/2007b).

From the psychoanalytical point of view, the non-integrated fragments of trauma memories and experiences may be considered as beta elements that are functioning between the mind and the body (Bion, 1962/1967; Schulman, 2002, p. 172). However, psychobiologically, they cannot integrate into alpha elements, unified whole of representations in the brain because of the less functional hippocampus of traumatised (van der Kolk, 1996/2007a, van der Kolk et al., 1997). The reason for this may also be that the emotional overarousal and stress is causing the amygdala produce an overdose of endorphins (van der Kolk, 1996/2007b, 2014; van der Kolk et al., 1997). Instead of thinking and learning from experiences, severely traumatised person may be aggressive and function in a fight/flight mode with their muscles or withdraw depending on the personality before traumatisation. Also, non-organised traumatised memories, psychologically chaotic and undifferentiated part-object experiences, seemed to remain as timeless and ego-alien for the traumatised (van der Kolk, 1996/2007b, p. 295).

In the psychodynamic point of view, trauma occurs when the experience is unbearable and cannot be processed by the ego anymore (Schulman, 2002, p. 162). Then, the capabilities of ego for thinking and creating symbols have been broken because of the overwhelming floods of affects and hyperarousal. As a result, there are unconscious needs and pressure for ego defences like dissociation and splitting. Finally, this leads also to the fragmentation of ego and a PTSD, and symptoms related to it. In psychological sense, there has not been enough container-contained functioning for the ego and its self-experiences that could have bear the unbearable and integrate the traumatic experiences into alpha elements of thinking.

Therefore, in the treatment of trauma, creating a holding environment for clients in a therapeutic relationship supports the therapy as a potential space for it (Winnicott, 1971/1997). In music therapy, feelings can be played out into the art with the techniques of music psychotherapy that are developing their capabilities for playing and symbolic functioning. Neuropsychologically, a client has a possibility to internalise the embodied meaning of tactile, kinaesthetic, respiratory, and rhythmical interaction of music in therapy (Rose, 2004, pp. 126–127). They are the intersubjective sensorimotor and affectomotor experiences of being together in music as the internalised caretaker and mother in the brain and the psychological functioning (Alanne, 2023; Rose, 2004). In such a biopsychological understanding of trauma, music and songs can be used as emotional "something more" interpretations and interventions to address issues and support the change and development in addition to language (Stern, 2010; Alanne, 2020, 2023).

2.5.8 Dual Coding System of Brain, Trauma, and Music

According to Gilbert J. Rose (2004), a pioneer of psychoanalytic study of arts and music, mental representations are coded in the verbal and non-verbal system of the brain. The verbal system is associated and stored as the linguistic forms of words that include their semantic and phonological coding. The non-verbal system is coding the kinaesthetic, visceral, and other sensory representations in the brain, and it is "directly activated by pictures, sounds, tastes, smells and feelings" (p. 6). Rose suggested the rethinking of insights in psychoanalysis and how the verbalisations and arts should have equal status because of their capability to modulate feelings in embodied experiences (ibid., pp. xxix). He further argued that there should be stronger links between words and experiences in psychoanalysis that is important considering traumas and their treatment where the trauma is dissociated from the body, or the body is remembering the trauma. More recently, similar arguments relating to music and words, and their equal value in transmitting and modulating experiences, have been also proposed by other authors (Alanne, 2010, 2020, 2023; Grassi, 2021; Kennedy, 2020).

This is important knowledge relating to music therapy and treating traumas as the dual system of brain can be integrated even simultaneously as the therapist and client are moving along with the emotions of music. Then, music "acts as an external auxiliary ego" in understanding the time and place, memories, feelings, and language relating to the singing songs, for example (Rose, 2004, p. 121). In this regard, music can be a part of mentalisation and verbalisation in music psychotherapy with traumatised refugees when listening and discussing about the music, for example (Alanne, 2010, 2023; Strehlow & Hannibal, 2019).

According to Rose (2004, p. 121), the dynamic unconscious may be located into the areas of limbic system, amygdala, and the brain stem. In this area strong feelings and stress reactions like panic, rage, and fear are experienced (Alanne, 2023, p. 140). The amygdala is responsible for the control of feelings, including stress reactions. It also relates to the relaxation, pleasure, and the feelings of attachment music may provide as a love object. Traumatic experiences with strong feelings and reactions relating to them are processed in the same non-verbal area and system of brain. They are not necessarily connected and coded in the verbal memory at all because they are repressed or dissociated (Alanne, 2023; Rose, 2004; Solms & Turnbull, 2002/2018; van der Kolk, 2014).

The non-verbal area of the brain is related to the procedural memory where there are the bodily experiences of music and trauma (Alanne, 2010, 2019a, 2023; Schulman, 2002, Solms & Turnbull, 2002; Rose, 2004). There are also processed, internalised experiences of the containing and holding of emotions as well as the here-and-now interactions, transference interpretations, and functional directiveness relating to music and the therapeutic relationship. In the procedural knowing, music is experienced as good or bad like some other sensory stimuli and experiences, feelings, and tastes that are coded non-verbally in the brain. This is presentational knowledge of traumatic experiences and bad objects, knowing before knowing them verbally according to the instant feelings like disgust, pain, anger in the bodily knowledge. As such, traumatic experiences are resonating with these primary sensory experiences and their internalised non-verbal memories in the development.

In the discursive memory relating to the verbal coding of memories, there is processed integration of traumatic experiences, collecting a life story and verbalising them in therapy. Thus, this is the focus of the historical/genetic interpretations in psychoanalysis, psychodynamic psychotherapy, and music therapy. Within the discursive memory, music may also be a conscious coping strategy and emotional regulator of self-experiences and the reflexive thinking. In this regard, corrective experiences of trauma may occur as the verbal and bodily experiences that are linked in the psychological processing of trauma in the brain (Rose, 2004).

Rose (2004, p. 119) has presented well-known examples of the music's capabilities of being a "prosthetic device" for the functioning of brain and clients suffering from neurological syndromes. They include Parkinson's disease, aphasia, autism, and traumatic stress. It seems that music can synchronise psychic and neurological structures of the brain that are responsible for the processing and understanding of the time and place, memories, feelings, and language. There seems to be concordance between the structures of the self in the mind and body that enables the Parkinson clients to walk, aphasia clients to sing, and dementia and autistic clients to be in a present time, memorise and verbalise themselves temporally with music and songs. In the severely traumatised clients, music may arise fear, pain, and alertness as music is reverberating with their traumatic experiences that are split and disorganised in the lower brain structures (Alanne, 2010, 2023, pp. 140, 142).

Freud (1923/1981, p. 26) as a neurologist considered that "the ego is first and foremost a bodily ego…" and that "the ego is ultimately derived from bodily sensations". He already noticed the concordance between the conscious mind and brain structures as he was thinking that conscious verbal memories are primarily residues of auditory perceptions (p. 20). According to Freud, visual thinking was more linked with the unconscious processes than words (p. 21). In Freud's structural theory of the ego and the id, Freud is describing the ego as wearing a "cap of hearing" in the auditory lobe (pp. 24–25). Freud's theory is in accordance with the current thinking of connections between perceptions, unconsciousness, and the lower brain structures for the traumatic stress reactions (Alanne, 2023, p. 116; van der Kolk, 2014; Schulman, 2002; Solms, 2017/2019, 2018).

In the traumatic reactions, music and sound as well as other sensory perceptions seem to perpetuate into ego and consciousness directly and surpass its capabilities to process them verbally. This psychological knowledge seems to be used in interrogations and their sensory "ego down" manipulating tactics of prisoners in concentration camps, during the Cold War and the War on Terror (Alanne, 2010; Brauer, 2016; Cusick, 2006, 2013). In the neuropsychoanalytic point of view, traumatised experiences become automatised patterns of behaviour in the procedural memory and the neural systems of the brain (Solms, 2017/2019, 2018). They are painful to modulate and are therefore slow and difficult to treat. This is concerning also traumatic experiences and transferences relating to music and music therapy with refugees where music may naturally cause resistance as an embodied bad object (Alanne, 2023, p. 143).

Roger Kennedy (2020, p. 76) has written that "music and affect share the common dynamic of tension and release", which relates to the innate capability of music to reverberate within self-experiences. As already mentioned, these emotional interactions are internalised very early in the development between the infant, mother, and other caretakers. According to Rose (2004, p. 130), music is transformation of the interpersonal system of affect regulation to an intrapsychic and abstract level with rhythmic sensorimotor stimulation. Similarly, there are possibilities of internalising and externalising the emotional contents in a therapeutic relationship and music, which enables the internalising of a new relationship with music and a therapist (Ahonen-Eerikäinen, 2007, pp. 94–95; Alanne, 2023, p. 161).

This transformation can also be understood as development from traumatic non-organised bad object experiences and bodily beta elements to more symbolic thinking of alpha elements in music (Alanne, 2019b, 2020, 2023; Robarts, 2003; Schulman, 2002). This processing of traumatised experiences also means new modulations and internalisations in the neural systems of brain, where they may transform from the non-verbal coding of dissociated elements to the verbal coding. In the therapeutic relationship with music, clients like traumatised have a possibility to reflect their transferences verbally and musically. For example, free improvisation in music therapy that is like the free association in psychoanalysis allows clients to externalise their experiences and object relationships in music. With the containment and holding of a therapist, clients may internalise new corrective experiences and object representations within the music (Alanne, 2023, p. 162).

There is also similarity in musical and lingual processes and their development in relation to time that can be understood with Freud's (1915) concepts of unconscious and deferred action (Nachträglichkeit) (Kennedy, 2020, pp. 24–25): In linear consciousness and timeless unconsciousness feelings are condensed as meanings in the minds of client and therapist. These are intersubjective parallel processes like in dreams where daily thoughts are mingled with unconscious dream thoughts, hopes, and fears, memories of traumatic experiences. Thus, in the therapeutic process like dreams there may occur reorganisation of traumatic experiences from non-lingual to lingual experiences and memories like in the human development (ibid.).

The split and dissociated experiences of the early childhood do not have lingual contents as these experiences come to the area of verbal coding much later (Grassi, 2021; Kennedy, 2020; Schulman, 2002). Similarly to the cognitive and language development of infant, where earlier non-verbal coded experiences develop and condense into words that have abstract symbolic meaning, the meanings of music and words are transforming in a therapeutic process.

Language and music have common roots in the sounds, rhythms, vibrations, and their communication (Grassi, 2021, pp. 4–5): In the early object relationships between the mother and the infant, there are dynamic polarities, tensions, and affects like in music and the verbal working of psychotherapy. There are waiting–delay, gone–present, continuity–interruptions, satisfaction–displeasure, progression–regression, and other non-verbal ambient and knowing of the present oscillating in the life of an infant that are internalised.

Many of these dynamics and affect attunements are already present in the feeding situation of an infant where the infant anticipates the breast and enjoys the oral holistic pleasure of being fed and nurtured when the mother or other caretaker comes finally (Alanne, 2014a, 2023, Sinkkonen, 1997; Stern, 1985/2004, 2010). In language or music, there may be similar pleasure of oceanic feelings being hold and contained in the peaceful, "rippling" and "floating", tones of the words or melodies, "flowing" of speech, silences, changing intensities, and rhythms respectively that a therapist is listening with a third ear (Alanne, 2023, p. 44; Reik, 1948/1998).

There is musical reverie between the therapist and client in the psychoanalytic work where a therapist is listening to the client's inner experiences through his/her own counter-emotions, rhythm, feeling, being, and the inner music of how unconscious experiences are flowing in the relationship (Erel-Brodsky, 2016; Kennedy, 2020; Lombardi, 2008). These mutually lived self-experiences and the affects of interaction can be sounds from unconsciousness that can include musical forms like rhythms, melodies, and expression of voice in the dynamics of verbal analytical encountering of psychotherapy (Alanne, 2016a, 2016b, 2023; Grassi, 2021).

The sounds and music may also be sounds of trauma when they are expressing the internalised early interaction and development in therapy. In the dynamics of therapeutic process and transference between the therapist and client, the silences, interruptions, strong reactions and feelings, and withdrawals may express how the person was seen or heard or was not encountered but instead ignored as a part of the traumatisation. In a work with traumatised refugees, these early internalised object relationships and their generalised interactive biosocial models relating to the Other, the therapist and music, come to the play.

In a psychodynamic point of view, it means the transference and the deferred action, reexposure and repeating of the traumatic experiences that come to therapy, relationship, and music. It may also be therapeutic regression and mourning for the traumatised refugee in a repairing relationship including identifications and internalisations with a therapist and music. As a result, from the rudiments of human encountering and trauma may emerge new meaning, representations, symbolism, transformed experiences, and growing in psychotherapy as a part of the revisited separation-individuation development in life (Akhtar, 1995; Alanne, 2010, 2014a, 2023, Erel-Brodsky, 2016; Grassi, 2021 Gravestock, 2021; Kennedy, 2020).

2.5.9 Cultural Dialoguing in Psychotherapy and Music

Psychotherapy can be a form of cultural dialoguing with a refugee that can also include music (Alanne, 2010, 2019a; Saraneva, 2002, 2018). It is a method where things from the new and old country may be discussed and shared together with a therapist, a client, or a group. It may help the psychic turmoil and stress of the refugee in adapting to a new country and situation as a part of the third individuation and developing a new identity as an immigrant (Akhtar, 1995; Saraneva, 2002).

Kristiina Saraneva (2002, p. 74) has written that a therapist should have some knowledge of the culture of his/her client. However, theoretical knowledge of different cultures may also lead to generalisation that is usually not enough. Instead, therapists should have a genuine belief in the similarity of people at the ground of their work. In spite of the different cultures and their subcultures, people have similar basic needs, feelings, and sufferings even though their expressions may be culturally related according to her.

At the same time, therapists should absolutely be aware of their own cultural relatedness as the second principle in treating refugees or immigrants (Saraneva, 2002, p. 74). However, this may not always be so easy and possible because the cultural views may present themselves in many conscious and unconscious attitudes of things that are a part of the society or the religion of the therapist. There may also be life values, social and religious norms, as well as diagnostic and treatment views that are belonging to the Western ideology and culture that therapists should be aware of. Without awareness, they may affect the therapeutic work even though therapists have studied their “inner culture” like their childhood family dynamics in their own therapies (ibid.).

According to Saraneva (2002, p. 74), a therapist may keep the cultural dialogue in his/her mind while meeting clients from different cultures. This helps to discern and notice the differences between cultures before making conclusions and interventions for the client’s reactions. In the beginning, this may require explaining for the client how the treatment and other things happen in the new culture. This helps the client in understanding the concept of trauma and its treatment. Also, in music therapy, it may be good to explain for the client something about music therapy and its methods before using them. This may take some time and require the use of metaphors in helping the client to understand the treatment of trauma.

The objective of cultural dialoguing with refugees and other immigrants of different age is also the equality in the treatment relationship (Saraneva, 2002, pp. 74–75). In psychodynamic therapy, a therapist is trying to understand the client’s experience, unconsciousness, and the culture, and not to explain and analyse them from the therapist’s own points of view. The whole treatment of traumas is depending on the understanding of client’s experiences and narratives.

With a method of cultural dialoguing, a therapist may also make this objective of understanding transparent for a client and ask questions about the client’s culture (Saraneva, 2002, pp. 74–75). These questions may continue in the form of how is this in your country? In our country, it is like this, and so on. This enables the client to express him/herself verbally and build trust towards the therapist and treatment. Music and other art forms can be a part of such dialogues when listening to music in music psychotherapy, for example (Alanne, 2010, 2019b). What kind of music is sung or listened in your country? What kinds of movies are made there, and how do you like music or movies here?

A therapist can be more open in discussions with refugees and immigrants than usual, which is making the situation more holding and containing for the clients. Winnicott (1971/1997, p. 109) has written: “Playing and cultural experience are things that we do value in a special way; these link the past, the present, and the future; they take up time and space.” In this regard, a refugee has a possibility to integrate his/her experiences with cultural dialoguing. A therapist and the new country may become as new meaningful objects with cultural phenomena like music, food, and movies that can be discussed and identified as a part of the recovery from traumas and adapting into a new society (Akhtar, 1995; Saraneva, 2002; Volkan, 2018a).

Many refugees and immigrants have experienced violence and racism in their lives and during their staying in the new country (Saraneva, 2002, p. 75). Because of this and other traumatisation they may easily feel insulted or feel themselves worthless to others as a part of their negative transference. The cultural dialoguing may help in such situations where a refugee may experience hate and disappointments towards his/her old country that are projected into the new country and the therapist as the Other. Then, music and the cultural dialogue in therapy may become a sort of transitional spaces where the difficult memories and feelings of a refugee can be worked through (Akhtar, 1995; Saraneva, 2002).

When a refugee or an immigrant has been tortured with music or it has been a part of the oppressors' propaganda, manipulation, or the violence machinery, a therapist or other caretaker must consider this possibility in cultural dialoguing with a client. Before using music actively, a therapist can first discuss about the client's former experiences of music to provide a safe place for the client. In the beginning, a therapist may interview politely and ask if music has been used in interrogation, torture, or imprisonment of the client. It is also good that a therapist would have some knowledge how music has been used in violence and as an object of bad. This will help in attuning and understanding of the traumatised clients' experiences of sounds and music in and outside of the therapy sessions.[17]

2.5.10 Transference Phenomena of Trauma in Treatment

The understanding of traumatised clients and how they may transfer and project their experiences into the music and therapist is important, so that a therapist would not be traumatised him/herself. As a result of listening to horrible experiences of traumatised refugees and violence, torture, war, and other cruelties, a therapist may lose the capability for empathy and suffer from *empathy fatigue*. This is already a sign of the work overload and stress that may lead to a burn-out if the therapist sees the clients having no hope anymore or feels powerless him/herself to care and help the traumatised in their often very difficult situations. A therapist should be aware of the counter-emotions and countertransference like the mentioned hopelessness, powerlessness, and cynicisms that may be a part of the client's transference in the treatment.

Also, the culture of refugees may be strange for the therapist, and their politics and religions may differ from the therapist's views that may bring feelings of anger and resentment as negative cultural countertransference (Saraneva, 2002, pp. 76–77; 2018, pp. 104–106). There may also be colonial countertransference when there are no common language, values, and customs between the therapist and client. Then, a client may feel and appear as uneducated and not clever enough. Even racist feelings and thoughts may arise where the clients are appearing as primitive people. This kind of feelings and thoughts are signs of empathy fatigue and burn-out.

Another type of countertransference recognised is the ethnological identification of the therapist with a client (Saraneva, 2002, 2018, pp. 106–107). Then, a therapist may feel to be the same group of "us" when the therapist belongs to the same people

[17] See Chap. 5, and especially Sect. 5.2 "A Culturally Sensitive Approach to Music and Arts with Clients from Different Nationalities" and Sect. 5.3 "Building an Alliance and Trust with Refugees: Cultural Dialoguing" for more on how to encounter refugees with music.

and culture with a client. Then, the therapist and client ally against "them" of the other culture. This slows the adaptation to the new home country and may hinder working with some issues needed in therapy. It may be also projection of the client's split and trauma that the therapist is enacting in my opinion.

As a result of countertransference, a therapist may be traumatised if s/he cannot any longer separate between the life and work in the client's situation. A therapist may become a "wounded healer" because of the work and the potential personal vulnerability and traumatisation (Alanne, 2023; Austin, 2002). Then, a therapist may enact and feel the need to be a saviour for all the clients, which is eventually causing a burn-out. Clients may also project their idealised wishes and desperate needs for rescuer to the therapist. The dynamics of wounded healer countertransference may be a need to treat the therapist's own trauma with over-identification or projective identification to the client's situation that is experienced too personally or close (McWilliams, 2021, pp. 173–174). When countertransference issues are occurring frequently in the treatment, or there is empathy fatigue, stress, and burn-out, the risk of retraumatising client unintentionally increases. Then, a client and therapist may have become the carriers of the vicarious trauma that needs to be understood and encountered by the therapist.

Therefore, therapists should be aware how much they can bear the unbearable themselves that has already traumatised their clients (Schulman, 2002, pp. 162, 179). Therapists should be able to monitor their own possible tiredness, withdrawal, dissociation, feelings of indifference, and other counter-emotions that may relate to their clients' traumatic experiences, but which can also be signs of their own defences and traumatisation of the things that are surpassing their limits of resilience. In therapy and life, therapists need to take care of their own resilience so that they can help in developing their clients' resilience and limits for the psychic stress. This will decrease the possibility of retraumatising the clients, or the therapist and client being the objects of vicarious traumatisation.[18]

When using music in therapy or treatment, it can be a part of developing the client's resilience and emotional regulation as positive and empowering experiences (Sokira et al., 2023, pp. 10–11). However, it is important to know about the stressful sounds and music for the traumatised experiences and the therapeutic process. As discussed earlier, some refugees may have been tortured with music, or they may have been forced to listen to music in the prison that has increased their traumatisation. Also, music and sounds are capable of penetrating forcefully into the ego and its capability for controlling feelings, thoughts, unconscious impulses, and memories. As a result, they may flood into consciousness violently if the therapist is not careful. This would be a repeating of the traumatic experiences how music and sounds have been used against the clients in breaking their personalities unethically, which should be avoided in the treatment with music.

[18] See the clinical discussion of the topics in Sect. 5.5 "The Self-Care and Empathy Fatigue of Therapist", Sect. 5.5.1 "Working with the Transference and Countertransference Issues", and Sect. 5.5.2 "Supervision and Training".

References

Abrams, B. (2021). Encountering transgenerational trauma through analytical music therapy. *Nordic Journal of Music Therapy, 30*(3), 197–218. https://doi.org/10.1080/08098131.2020.1853801

Ahonen-Eerikäinen, H. (2007). *Group analytic music therapy*. Barcelona Publishers.

Akhtar, S. (1995). A third individuation: Immigration, identity, and the psychoanalytic process. *Journal of the American Psychoanalytic Association, 43*(4), 1051–1084.

Alanne, S. (2010). *Music psychotherapy with refugee survivors of torture. Interpretations of three clinical case studies*. Sibelius Academy. Studia Musica.

Alanne, S. (2013). Psykodynaaminen musiikkipsykoterapia kidutuksesta traumatisoituneiden pakolaisten kanssa: Kliininen näkökulma. [Psychodynamic music psychotherapy with the refugees traumatised from the torture: A clinical point of view.]. *Psykoterapia, 32*(4), 264–276.

Alanne, S. (2014a). *Musiikkipsykoterapia*. Teoria ja käytäntö. [Music psychotherapy. Theory and practice.] Acta Universitatis Ouluensis D Medica 1248.

Alanne, S. (2014b). The ethnocultural and psychodynamic meaning of music for traumatised refugees. *Music Therapy Today*, 10(1), 48–49. Special issue: Proceedings of the 14th World Congress of Music Therapy Vienna/Krems, Austria, July 7–12, 2014.

Alanne, S. (2016a). Music as psychotherapy and the structure of personal identity. In M. Degli Stefani & F. Facchin (Eds.), *PerSona. Voce e identità. Opportunità musicali per la salute e il benessere* (pp. 131–137). CLEUP—Cooperativa Libraria Editrice Università di Padova.

Alanne, S. (2016b). Musiikki ja äänet tienä varhaislapsuuden kokemusmaailmaan—Kokemuksia mutismin psykoterapiasta. [Music and sounds as the road into the experience world of early childhood—Experiences of mutism's psychotherapy.]. *Psykoterapia, 35*(3), 186–195.

Alanne, S. (2019a). Musiikki, vuorovaikutus ja sisäinen kokemus psykoterapiassa. [Music, interaction, and the inner experience in psychotherapy.]. *Psykoterapia, 38*(1), 39–49.

Alanne, S. (2019b). Musiikkipsykoterapia traumatisoituneiden pakolaisten ja maahanmuuttajien kuntoutuksessa. [Music psychotherapy in the rehabilitation of refugees and immigrants.]. *Psykoterapia, 38*(4), 306–318.

Alanne, S. (2020). Musiikin ja kielen suhteesta—sekä psykoterapeuttisesta arvosta. [About the relationship of music and language—And their psychotherapeutic value.]. *Psykoanalyyttinen Psykoterapia, 16*, 6–15.

Alanne, S. (2021). *Väärän tiedon puu*. Mallintava tieto ja kulttuurin elämästä vieraantuneisuus. [The three of ignorance. Modeling knowledge and the estrangement of culture from life.] BoD.

Alanne, S. (2023). *The theory and practice of psychodynamic music psychotherapy*. Barcelona Publishers.

Alayarian, A. (2024). *Group analysis for refugees experiencing trauma*. Routledge.

Allen, J. G., Fonagy, P., & Bateman, A. W. (2008). *Mentalizing in clinical practice*. American Psychiatric Publishing.

Alvarez, A. (1992/1999). *Live Company*. Psychoanalytic Psychotherapy with Autistic, Borderline, Deprived and Abused Children. Routledge.

American Music Therapy Association (AMTA). (2014). *Music therapy and the military populations*. A Status Report and Recommendations on Music Therapy Treatment, Programs, Research, and Practice Policy. Silver Spring: American Music Therapy Association.

Austin, D. (2002). The wounded healer. The voice of trauma: A wounded healer's perspective. In J. P. Sutton (Ed.), *Music, music therapy, and trauma. International perspectives* (pp. 231–259). Jessica Kingsley.

Beck, B. D. (2019). Music therapy for refugees. In S. Lindahl Jacobsen, I. Nygaard Pedersen, & L. O. Bonde (Eds.), *A comprehensive guide to music therapy. Theory, clinical practice, research and training* (2nd ed., pp. 342–352). Jessica Kingsley.

Beck, B. D., Messel, C., Lund Meyer, S., Cordtz, T. O., Søgaard, U., Simonsen, E., & Moe, T. (2018). Feasibility of trauma-focused guided imagery and music with adult refugees diagnosed with PTSD: A pilot study. *Nordic Journal of Music Therapy, 27*(1), 67–86.

Beck, B. D., Meyer, S. L., Simonsen, E., Søgaard, U., Petersen, I., Arnfred, S. M. H., Tellier, T., & Moe, T. (2021). Music therapy was noninferior to verbal standard treatment of traumatised refugees in mental healthcare: Results from a randomized clinical trial. *European Journal of Psychotraumatology, 12*(1), 1930960. https://doi.org/10.1080/20008198.2021.1930960

Bernard, G., & Dvorak, A. L. (2022). Using music to address trauma with refugees: A systematic review and recommendations. *Music Therapy Perspectives, 41*(1), 30–43. https://doi.org/10.1093/mtp/miac013

Bernatzky, G., Strickner, S., Presch, M., Wendtner, F., & Kullich, W. (2013). Music as non-pharmacological pain management in clinics. In R. Macdonald, G. Kreutz, & L. Mitchell (Eds.), *Music, health, and wellbeing* (pp. 257–275). Oxford University Press.

Bion, W. R. (1959). Attacks on linking. *International Journal of Psycho-Analysis, 40*, 308–315.

Bion, W. R. (1961/2004). *Experiences in groups and other papers*. Routledge.

Bion, W. R. (1962). A theory of thinking. In W. R. Bion (Ed.), *Second thoughts* (pp. 110–119). William Heinemann.

Blos, P. (1967). The second individuation process of adolescence. *Psychoanalytic Study of the Child, 22*, 162–186.

Blum, A., Goldberg, P., & Levin, M. (2023). *Here I'm alive. The spirit of music in psychoanalysis*. Columbia University Press.

Boston Change Process Study Group (BCPSG). (2010). *Change in psychotherapy: A unifying paradigm*. Norton.

Bracken, P. (2003). *Trauma. Culture, meaning and philosophy*. Whurr Publishers.

Brauer, J. (2016). How can music be torturous?: Music in Nazi concentration and extermination camps. *Music & Politics, 10*(1). https://doi.org/10.3998/mp.9460447.0010.103

Bruce, C. (2022). Performing normal: Restless reflections on music's dis/abling potential. *Music Therapy Perspectives, 40*(2), 125–131.

Bruscia, K. E. (1987). *Improvisational models of Music therapy*. Charles C Thomas.

Bruscia, K. E. (2012). Introduction. In K. E. Bruscia (Comp.), *Case examples of music therapy for event trauma* (pp. 1–8). Barcelona.

Castaneda, A. E., Mäki-Opas, J., Jokela, S., Kivi, N., Lähteenmäki, M., Miettinen, T., Nieminen, S., Santalahti, P., & PALOMA Expert Group. (2018). *Pakolaisten mielenterveyden tukeminen Suomessa*. PALOMA käsikirja. [Supporting refugees' mental health in Finland. PALOMA handbook.] Guidance, May 2018. Publications of the National Institute for Health and Welfare.

Chornik, K. (2013). Music and torture in Chilean detention centers: Conversations with an ex-agent of Pinochet's secret police. *The World of Music, New Series, 2*(1), 51–65.

Christensen, E. (2019). Music in body and brain. In S. Lindahl Jacobsen, I. Nygaard Pedersen, & L. O. Bonde (Eds.), *A comprehensive guide to music therapy: Theory, clinical practice, research and training* (2nd ed., pp. 51–64). Jessica Kingsley.

Cloonan, M., & Johnson, B. (2002). Killing me softly with his song: An initial investigation into the use of popular music as a tool of oppression. *Popular Music, 21*, 27–39.

Cloonan, M., & Johnson, B. (2008). *Dark side of the tune. Popular music and violence*. Ashgate.

Crenshaw, D. (2006). Neuroscience and trauma treatment. Implications for creative arts therapists. In L. Carey (Ed.), *Expressive and creative arts methods for trauma survivors* (pp. 21–37). Jessica Kingsley.

Cusick, S. G. (2006). Music as torture/music as weapon. *Transcultural Music Review, 10*. http://www.sibetrans.com/trans/article/152/music-as-torture-music-as-weapon

Cusick, S. G. (2008). Musicology, torture, repair. *Radical Musicology*, 3. http://www.radical--musicology.org.uk/2008/Cusick.htm.

Cusick, S. G. (2013). Towards an acoustemology of detention in the 'global war on terror'. In G. Born (Ed.), *Music, sound and space: Transformations of public and private experience*. Cambridge University Press.

De Backer, J., & Sutton, J. (2014a). Introduction. The music in music therapy: Writing without a pen. In J. De Backer & J. Sutton (Eds.), *The Music in Music therapy. Psychodynamic music therapy in Europe: Clinical, theoretical and research approaches* (pp. 14–22). Jessica Kingsley.

De Backer, J., & Sutton, J. (2014b). Therapeutic interventions in psychodynamic music therapy: The music in music therapy. In J. De Backer & J. Sutton (Eds.), *The music in music therapy. Psychodynamic music therapy in Europe: Clinical, theoretical and research approaches* (pp. 338–349). Jessica Kingsley.

De Backer, J., & Van Camp, J. (2014). Music and psychosis: The answer from the patient to music therapy: Für Elise! In J. De Backer & J. Sutton (Eds.), *The music in music therapy. Psychodynamic music therapy in Europe: Clinical, theoretical and research approaches* (pp. 72–90). Jessica Kingsley.

Dimitrijević, A., & Buchholz, M. B. (2024). Introduction: Silencing the traumatised and hearing silencing. In M. B. Buchholz & A. Dimitrijević (Eds.), *Encountering silencing. Forms of oppression in individuals, families and communities* (pp. xv–xxxvii). Karnac.

Duey, C. J. (1991/1996). Group music therapy for women with multiple personalities. In K.E. Bruscia (Ed.), *Case studies in music therapy* (pp. 513–526). Barcelona.

Elliot, D. J., & Silverman, M. (2013). Why music matters: Philosophical and cultural foundations. In R. Macdonald, G. Kreutz, & L. Mitchell (Eds.), *Music, health, and wellbeing* (pp. 25–39). Oxford University Press.

Else, B. A., & González, M. (2023). Global trends in music therapy for disaster preparedness, response, and recovery. In L. E. Beer & J. C. Birnbaum (Eds.), *Trauma-informed music therapy. Theory and practice* (pp. 19–27). Routledge.

Erel-Brodsky, H. (2016). I'm all ears—Thoughts on psychoanalysis: The musical reverie. *Contemporary Psychoanalysis, 52*(4), 578–601.

Fisher, A., & Gilboa, A. (2016). The roles of music amongst Holocaust survivors before, during, and after the Holocaust. *Psychology of Music, 44*(6), 1221–1239.

Fonagy, P. (2004). *Attachment theory and psychoanalysis*. Karnac.

Fonagy, P., Gergely, G., Jurist, L. E., & Target, M. (2004). *Affect regulation, mentalization, and the development of the self.* Karnac.

Freud, S. (1900/1981). The interpretations of dreams. In *Standard Ed.* (IV–V). The Hogarth Press.

Freud, S. (1905a). Fragment of an analysis of a case of hysteria. In *Standard Ed.* (VII, pp. 7–122). The Hogarth Press.

Freud, S. (1905b). Three essays on the theory of sexuality. In *Standard Ed.* (VII, pp. 135–245). The Hogarth Press.

Freud, S. (1914a/1981). Remembering, repeating and working through (further recommendations on the technique of psychoanalysis II). In *Standard Ed.* (XII, pp. 147–156). The Hogarth Press.

Freud, S. (1914b/1981). The Moses of Michelangelo. In *Standard Ed.* (XIII, pp. 211–236). The Hogarth Press.

Freud, S. (1915/1981). The unconsciousness. In *Standard Ed.* (XIV, pp. 166–215). The Hogarth Press.

Freud, S. (1920/1981). Beyond the pleasure principle. In *Standard Ed.* (XVIII, pp. 7–64). The Hogarth Press.

Freud, S. (1923/1981). The ego and the id. In *Standard Ed.* (XIX, pp. 12–66). The Hogarth Press.

Freud, S. (1930/1981). Civilizations and its discontents. In *Standard Ed.* (XXI, pp. 64–145). The Hogarth Press.

Gallese, V. (2011). Intersubjektiivisuus neurotieteen näkökulmasta. Ruumiillinen jäljittely ja sen merkitys intersubjektiivisuudessa. [Intersubjectivity in the point of view of neuroscience. Bodily imitation and its meaning.] Trans. T. Välkki. *Psykoterapia*, 30(1), 4–17. (Original article: Embodied simulation and its role in intersubjectivity.)

Glaser, D. (2000). Child abuse and neglect and the brain—A review. *Journal of Child Psychology and Psychiatry, 41*(1), 97–116.

Gombert, D. J. (2022). Who is being silenced?: Sociocultural and privilege dynamics within music therapy education. *Music Therapy Perspectives, 40*(2), 164–173.

Grant, M. J. (2013). The illogical logic of music torture. *Torture, 23*(2), 4–13.

Grassi, L. (2021). *The sound of the unconscious. Psychoanalysis as music.* Routledge.

Gratier, M., & Trevarthen, C. (2007). Voice, vitality, and meaning: On the shaping of the infant's utterances in willing engagement with culture. Comment on Bertau's "On the notion of voice." *International Journal for Dialogical Science,* 2(1), 169–181.

Gravestock, J. (2021). *Music therapy in adoption and trauma. Therapy that makes a difference after placement*. Jessica Kingsley.

Grummitt, L., Baldwin, J. R., Lafoa, J., Keyes, K. M., & Barrett, E. L. (2024). Burden of mental disorders and suicide attributable to childhood maltreatment. *JAMA Psychiatry*. Published online May 8, 2024. https://doi.org/10.1001/jamapsychiatry.2024.0804.

Handler Spitz, E. (1987). Separation-individuation in a cycle of songs. George crumb's ancient voices of children. *The Psychoanalytic Study of the Child, 42*, 531–543.

Hannibal, N. (2014). Implicit and explicit mentalisation in music therapy in the psychiatric treatment of people with borderline personality disorder. In J. De Backer & J. Sutton (Eds.), *The music in music therapy. Psychodynamic music therapy in Europe: Clinical, theoretical and research approaches* (pp. 211–223). Jessica Kingsley.

Herman, J.L. (1992/2022). *Trauma and Recovery*. The Aftermath of Violence – From Domestic Abuse to Political Terror. Basic Books.

Hoi Yan Fu, J. (2023). Finding one's voice: Working through developmental trauma with vocal psychotherapy. In L. E. Beer & J. C. Birnbaum (Eds.), *Trauma-informed music therapy. Theory and practice* (pp. 113–121). Routledge.

Hole, J., Hirsch, M., Ball, E., & Meads, C. (2015). Music as an aid for postoperative recovery in adults: A systematic review and meta-analysis. *Lancet, 386*, 1659–1671.

John, E. (1991/2001). Music and concentration camps: An approximation (E. F. Livingstone, Trans.). *Journal of Musicological Research, 20*(4), 269–323.

Keinänen, M. (2017). Mentalisaatiohoitomenetelmien teoreettiset perusteet ja toteutus. [Theoretical grounds and practice of mentalisation methods.] In I. Laitinen & S. Ollikainen (Eds.), *Mentalisaatio*. Teoriasta käytäntöön (pp. 82–104). [*Mentalisation*. From theory to practice.] Therapeia Foundation.

Kennedy, R. (2020). *The power of music. Psychoanalytic explorations*. Phoenix.

Klein, M. (1946). Notes on some schizoid mechanisms. *International Journal of Psycho-Analysis, 27*, 99–110.

Klein, M. (1952). The origins of transference. *International Journal of Psycho-Analysis, 33*, 433–438.

Knoblauch, S. H. (2000). *The musical edge of therapeutic dialogue*. The Analytic Press.

Kohut, H. (1977/1980). *The restoration of the self*. International Universities Press.

Kohut, H., & Levarie, S. (1950/1978). On the enjoyment of listening to music. In P.H. Ornstein (Ed.), *The search for the self. Selected writings of Heinz Kohut: 1950–1978. Vol. 1* (pp. 135–158). International Universities Press.

Kreutz, G., Quiroga Murcia, C., & Bongard, S. (2013). Psychoneuroendocrine research on music and health: An overview. In R. Macdonald, G. Kreutz, & L. Mitchell (Eds.), *Music, health, and wellbeing* (pp. 457–476). Oxford University Press.

Laitinen, I. (2017). Mentalisaatioon perustuvan terapian peruskäsitteet ja hoitotekniikat. [The basic concepts and treatment techniques of therapy based on mentalisation.] In I. Laitinen & S. Ollikainen (Eds.), *Mentalisaatio*. Teoriasta käytäntöön. [Mentalisation. From theory to practice.] (pp. 55–81). Therapeia Foundation.

Lee, J. H. (2016). The effects of music on pain: A meta-analysis. *Journal of Music Therapy, 53*(4), 430–477.

Lehtonen, K. (1996). *Musiikki, kieli ja kommunikaatio*. Mietteitä musiikista ja musiikkiterapiasta. [Music, language, and communication. Considerations of music and music therapy.] Jyväskylän yliopiston musiikkitieteen laitoksen julkaisusarja A: tutkielmia ja raportteja 17.

Lehtonen, K. (2007). Musiikkia, rakas Sigmund! Sigmund Freudin musiikkisuhteen arvoitus. [Music, dear Sigmund! The enigma of Sigmund Freud's relationship to music.]. *Psykoterapia, 26*(3), 176–191.

Lemma, A. (2006). *Introduction to the practice of psychoanalytic psychotherapy*. Wiley.

Levinge, A. (2015). *The music of being: Music therapy, Winnicott, and the school of object relations*. Jessica Kingsley.

Lombardi, R. (2008). Time, music and reverie. *Journal of the American Psychoanalytic Association, 56*(4), 1191–1211.

Mahler, M., Pine, F., & Bergman, A. (1975/1991). *The psychological birth of the human infant: Symbiosis and individuation*. Karnac.

McFerran, K. S., Lai, H. I. C., Chang, W.-H., Acquaro, D., Chin, T. C., Stokes, H., & Crooke, A. (2020). Music, rhythm, and trauma: A critical interpretive synthesis of research literature. *Frontiers in Psychology, 11*, 324. https://doi.org/10.3389/fpsyg.2020.00324

McWilliams, N. (2021). *Psychoanalytic supervision*. Guilford.

Miller, A. (1979/1984). *Lahjakkaan lapsen tragedia ja todellisen itseyden etsintä*. [The drama of the gifted child.] (T. Lahti, Trans.). WSOY, Finnish edition.

Miller, A. (1980/1985). *Alussa oli kasvatus*. Kätketty julmuus ja väkivallan juuret. [For your own good. Hidden cruelty in child-rearing and the roots of violence.] (M. Rutanen, Trans.). WSOY, Finnish edition.

Monaci, M. G., Gratier, M., Trevarthen, C., Grandjean, D., Kuhn, P., & Filippa, M. (2021). Parental perception of vocal contact with preterm infants: Communicative musicality in the neonatal intensive care unit. *Children, 8*(6), 513. https://doi.org/10.3390/children8060513

Moreno, J. (1999). Orpheus in hell: Music and therapy in the holocaust. *The Arts in Psychotherapy, 26*(1), 3–14.

Mukamel, R., Ekstrom, A. D., Kaplan, J., Iacoboni, M., & Fried, I. (2010). Single-neuron responses in humans during execution and observations of actions. *Current Biology, 20*(8), 750–756.

Music, G. (2022). The body as the new royal road to the unconscious. In J. Stubley & L. Young (Eds.), *Complex trauma. The Tavistock model* (pp. 74–92). Routledge.

Myerscough, F., & Wong, D. (2022). (Un)learning from experience: An exposition of minoritized voices on music therapy training. *Music Therapy Perspectives, 40*, 132–142.

Naliwajek-Mazurek, K. (2013). Music and torture in Nazi sites of persecution and genocide in occupied Poland, 1939–1945. *The World of Music, New Series, 2*(1), 31–50.

Nathanson, A. (2022). Relational trauma and oppression: Clinical work with young men groomed and sexually abused as children. In J. Stubley & L. Young (Eds.), *Complex trauma. The Tavistock model* (pp. 130–142). Routledge.

Neustadt, R. (2004). Music as memory and torture: Sounds of repression and protest in Chile and Argentina. *Chasqui, 33*(1), 128–137.

Orth, J., Doorschodt, L., Verburgt, J., & Drožđek, B. (2004). Sounds of trauma: An introduction to methodology in music therapy with traumatised refugees in clinical and outpatient settings. In J. P. Wilson & B. Drožđek (Eds.), *Broken spirits. The treatment of traumatised asylum seekers, refugees and torture victims* (pp. 443–480). Brunner–Routledge.

Papaeti, A. (2013a). Music and 're-education' in Greek prison camps: From Makronisos (1947–1955) to Giaros (1967–1968). *Torture, 23*(2), 34–43.

Papaeti, A. (2013b). Music, torture, testimony: Reopening the case of the Greek Junta (1967–1974). *The World of Music, New Series, 2*(1), 67–89.

Papaeti, A. (2020). On music, torture and detention: Reflections on issues of research and discipline. *Transposition* [Online], Hors-série 2 | 2020, http://journals.openedition.org/transposition/5289; https://doi.org/10.4000/transposition.5289.

Pickard, B. (2022). Anti-oppressive pedagogy as an opportunity for consciousness raising in the music therapy profession: A critical disability studies perspective. *British Journal of Music Therapy, 36*(1), 5–15.

Pitkäniemi, A., Sihvonen, A. J., Särkämö, T., & Soinila, S. (2020). Musiikki-interventiot kivun hoidon osana. [Music-based interventions in pain management.] *Lääkärilehti* [Finnish Medical Journal], 75(37), 1843–1848.

Priestley, M. (1975). *Music therapy in action*. Constable.

Rechardt, E. (1987). *Experiencing music. The psychoanalytic study of the child, 42, 511–530.* Yale University Press.

Reik, T. (1948/1998). *Listening with the third ear. The inner experience of psychoanalyst*. Farrar, Straus and Giroux.

Reik, T. (1953/1960). *The haunting melody. Psychoanalytic experiences in life and music*. Grove Press.

Robarts, J. Z. (2003). The healing function of improvised songs in music therapy with a child survivor of early trauma and sexual abuse. In S. Hadley (Ed.), *Psychodynamic music therapy: Case studies* (pp. 141–182). Barcelona.

Rose, G. J. (2004). *Between couch and piano. Psychoanalysis, music, art and neuroscience*. Brunner–Routledge.

Salberg, J. (2024). Historical overview of theories of trauma and transgenerational transmissions. In J. Salberg & S. Grand (Eds.), *Transgenerational trauma. A contemporary introduction* (pp. 5–22). Routledge.

Saraneva, K. (2002). Trauma ja pakolaisuus. Psykoanalyyttinen käsitys traumasta ja sen hoidosta pakolais- ja siirtolaiskohtaloissa. [Trauma and refugees. Psychoanalytic conception of trauma and its treatment in the destinies of refugees and immigrants.] In S. Haaramo & K. Palonen (Eds.), *Trauman monet kasvot*. Psyykkinen trauma sisäisenä kokemuksena (pp. 49–96). [Many faces of trauma. Psychic trauma as an inner experience.] Therapeia Foundation.

Saraneva, K. (2018). Vieraasta kulttuurista tulevan pakolaisen kohtaaminen ja hoitaminen—Haasteet terapeutille. [The encountering and treatment of refugee coming from foreign culture—Challenges for the therapist.] In A. Zonzi & N. Söderblom (Eds.), *Pakolaisuus*. Merkitykset ihmiselle ja yhteisölle (pp. 90–108). [Refugeeism. The meaning for individual and community.] Therapeia Foundation.

Schulman, G. (2002). Sietämisen kestämisestä eheytymiseen. Objektin sisällyttämiskyky ja trauman integrointi. [From bearing resilience to cohesiveness. The internalising of object and the integration of trauma] In S. Haaramo & K. Palonen (Eds.), *Trauman monet kasvot*. Psyykkinen trauma sisäisenä kokemuksena (pp. 162–187). [Many faces of trauma. Psychic trauma as an inner experience.] Therapeia Foundation.

Scrine, E., & Koike, A. (2023). Questioning the promise of safety in trauma-informed music therapy practice. In L. E. Beer & J. C. Birnbaum (Eds.), *Trauma-informed music therapy. Theory and practice* (pp. 37–44). Routledge.

Siirala, M. (1966/1969). *Medicine in metamorphosis. Speech, presence, and integration*. Tavistock.

Siirala, M. (1983). *From transfer to transference. Seven essays on the human predicament*. Therapeia Foundation.

Siltala, P. (2014). Ydintietoisuuden muotoutuminen varhaisen vuorovaikutuksen tilassa. [The shaping of core-consciousness in the state of early interaction.]. *Psykoterapia, 33*(2), 83–92.

Sinkkonen, J. (1997). Musiikin merkitys lapsen kehityksessä. [The meaning of music in the development of child.] In M. Kaikkonen & S. Mattila (Eds.), *Musiikki ja mielen mahdollisuudet* [Music and the possibilities of the mind.] (pp. 41–54). Publication Series of Sibelius Academy Continuing Education 1.

Sokira, J., Allen, J., & Wagner, H. (2023). The resilience framework for trauma-informed music therapy. In L. E. Beer & J. C. Birnbaum (Eds.), *Trauma-informed music therapy. Theory and practice* (pp. 9–18). Routledge.

Solms, M. (2017/2019). Mikä "tiedostamaton" on ja missä se sijaitsee aivoissa? Neuropsykoanalyyttinen näkökulma. [What is "the unconscious," and where is it located in the brain? A neuropsychoanalytic perspective.] (A. von Schulman, Trans.). *Psykoterapia*, 38(1), 62–70.

Solms, M. (2018). Psykoanalyysin tieteellinen perusta. [The scientific ground of psychoanalysis.] (A. von Schulman, Trans.). Psykoterapia, 37(2), 136–140.

Solms, M. (2021). *The hidden spring: A journey to the source of consciousness*. Profile Books.

Solms, M., & Turnbull, O. (2002/2018). *The brain and the inner world. An introduction to the neuroscience of subjective experience*. Routledge.

Solomon, Z., Laor, N., & McFarlane, A.C. (1996/2007). Acute posttraumatic reactions in soldiers and civilians. In B.A. van der Kolk, A.C. McFarlane & L. Weisaeth (Eds.), *Traumatic stress. The effects of overwhelming experience on mind, body, and society* (pp. 102–114). Guilford.

Standley, J. (1996). Music as a therapeutic intervention in medical and dental treatment: Research and clinical applications. In T. Wigram, B. Saperston, & R. West (Eds.), *The art and science of music therapy: A handbook* (pp. 3–22). Harwood Academic Publishers.

Stern, D. N. (1985/2004). *The interpersonal world of the infant. A view from psychoanalysis and developmental psychology*. Karnac.

Stern, D. N. (2004). *The present moment in psychotherapy and everyday life*. Norton.

Stern, D. N. (2010). *Forms of vitality. Exploring dynamic experience in psychology, arts, psychotherapy, and development*. Oxford University Press.

Strachey, J. (1934/1969). The nature of the therapeutic action in psychoanalysis. *International Journal of Psychoanalysis, 50*, 275–295.

Strehlow, G. (2009). The use of music therapy in treating sexually abused children. *Nordic Journal of Music Therapy, 18*(2), 167–183.

Strehlow, G., & Hannibal, N. (2019). Mentalizing in improvisational music therapy. *Nordic Journal of Music Therapy, 28*(4), 333–346.

Strehlow, G., & Lindner, R. (2016). Music therapy interaction patterns in relation to borderline personality disorder (BPD) patients. *Nordic Journal of Music Therapy, 25*(2), 134–158.

Stubley, J. (2022a). Complex trauma: The initial consultation. In J. Stubley & L. Young (Eds.), *Complex trauma. The Tavistock model* (pp. 11–33). Routledge.

Stubley, J. (2022b). The Tavistock trauma service. In J. Stubley & L. Young (Eds.), *Complex trauma. The Tavistock model* (pp. 34–55). Routledge.

Sullivan, J. M. (2007). Music for the injured soldier: A contribution of American women's military bands during world war II. *Journal of Music Therapy, 44*, 282–305.

Sutton, J. (2002). Trauma. Trauma in context. In J. P. Sutton (Ed.), *Music, music therapy and trauma. International perspectives* (pp. 21–39). Jessica Kingsley.

Svedberg Yinger, O. (2023). I am safe and I am strong: Understanding adverse childhood experiences and building resilience through trauma-informed music therapy. In L. E. Beer & J. C. Birnbaum (Eds.), *Trauma-informed music therapy. Theory and practice* (pp. 47–55). Routledge.

Swallow, M. (2002). The brain—Its music and its emotion: The neurology of trauma. In J. P. Sutton (Ed.), *Music, music therapy and trauma. International perspectives* (pp. 41–53). Jessica Kingsley.

Tähkä, V. (1993/1997). *Mielen rakentuminen ja psykoanalyyttinen hoitaminen*. [Mind and its treatment: A psychoanalytic approach.] WSOY, Finnish edition.

Temple, N., & Waddell, M. (1998/2002). Series editors' preface (pp. viiii–x). In C. Garland (Ed.), *Understanding trauma. A psychoanalytic approach*. Second enlarged edition. The Tavistock Clinic Series. Karnac.

Trevarthen, C. (2011). What is it like to be a person who knows nothing? Defining the active intersubjective mind of a newborn human being. *Infant and Child Development, 20*, 119–135.

Trevarthen, C., & Malloch, S. (2000). The dance of wellbeing: Defining the musical therapeutic effect. *Nordic Journal of Music Therapy, 9*(2), 3–17.

Uurtimo, Y. (2000). *On puhuttava siitä mistä vaikenemme*. Martti Siiralan ajatuksia elämästä. [We must talk from what we are silent. Thoughts of Martti Siirala from life.] Tammi.

van der Kolk, B. (1996/2007a). The complexity of adaptation to trauma. Self-regulation, stimulus discrimination, and characterological development. In B.A. van der Kolk, A.C. McFarlane & L. Weisaeth (Eds.), *Traumatic stress. The effects of overwhelming experience on mind, body, and society* (pp. 182–213). Guilford.

van der Kolk, B. (1996/2007b). Trauma and memory. In B.A. van der Kolk, A.C. McFarlane & L. Weisaeth (Eds.), *Traumatic stress. The effects of overwhelming experience on mind, body, and society* (pp. 279–302). Guilford.

van der Kolk, B. (2014). *The body keeps score. Mind, brain and body in the transformation of trauma*. Allen Lane.

van der Kolk, B.A., & McFarlane, A.C. (1996/2007). The black hole of trauma. In B.A. van der Kolk, A.C. McFarlane & L. Weisaeth (Eds.), *Traumatic stress. The effects of overwhelming experience on mind, body, and society* (pp. 3–23). Guilford.

van der Kolk, B.A., Weisaeth, L., & van der Hart, O. (1996/2007). History of trauma in psychiatry. In B.A. van der Kolk, A.C. McFarlane & L. Weisaeth (Eds.), *Traumatic stress. The effects of overwhelming experience on mind, body, and society* (pp. 47–74). Guilford.

van der Kolk, B. A., Burbridge, J. A., & Suzuki, J. (1997). The psychobiology of traumatic memory. Clinical implications of neuroimaging studies. *Annals of the New York Academy of Sciences, 821*, 99–111.

Volkan, V. D. (2004). From hope for a better life to broken spirits: An introduction. In J. P. Wilson & B. Drožđek (Eds.), *Broken spirits. The treatment of traumatised asylum seekers, refugees and torture victims* (pp. 7–12). Brunner–Routledge.

Volkan, V. D. (2018a). *Immigrants and refugees. Trauma, perennial mourning, prejudice, and border psychology*. Routledge.

Volkan, V.D. (2018b). Pakolaiskriisit, uhat ryhmäidentiteetille ja jaettu ennakkoluuloisuus. [Refugee crises, threats to the group identity, and the shared prejudice.] In A. Zonzi & N. Söderblom (Eds.), *Pakolaisuus*. Merkitykset ihmiselle ja yhteisölle (pp. 33–57). [Refugeeism. The meaning for individual and community.] Therapeia Foundation.

Winnicott, D. W. (1971/1997). *Playing and reality*. Routledge.

Wolf, H.-G. (2007). Grundlagen der Psychotraumatologie und der Traumatherapie. In H.-G. Wolf (Ed.), *Musiktherapie und Trauma* (pp. 11–20). Reichert Verlag.

World Health Organization (WHO) (2025). *International Classification of Diseases, Eleventh Revision (ICD-11)*. Geneva: World Health Organization; 2025. License: CC BY-ND 3.0 IGO.

Yeomans, F. E., Clarking, J. F., & Kernberg, O. F. (2015). *Transference-focused psychotherapy for borderline personality disorder. A clinical guide*. American Psychiatric Publishing.

Chapter 3
Music, Violence, and Trauma

This chapter will describe how music has been used as a part of the torture, interrogations, and war in history until recently (Alanne, 2010; Cloonan & Johnson, 2002, 2008; Cusick, 2006, 2008, 2013; Grant, 2013; Moreno, 1999, Papaeti, 2020). The long history of using music in torture and wars will be introduced and discussed. Also, the roots of music therapy, using music as an alleviation of pain and keeping up the spirit of forces in wars, and how modern music therapy evolved during WWII will be discussed (Alanne, 2010, 2023; Lee, 2016; O'Connell, 1990; Sullivan, 2007). This development will be discussed in the context how music is still used in modern warfare and interrogations as well as in prisons and camps to humiliate prisoners. This may also be a part of the propaganda and manipulation with music of oppressive governments and dictators (Alanne, 2010, 2014b, 2023; Grant, 2013; Papaeti, 2013a, 2020). The psychology of sounds and music as violence will be analysed in the light of psychodynamic theories such as object relations theory, music as a good and a persecuting bad object. Also, the ego psychology point of view will be discussed about how music has been illustrated as an "ego down" method in the earlier interrogation manual of Central Intelligence Agency (CIA).

Torture has a long history in punishments and interrogations of prisoners and accused. It was used by the Romans as they crucified people, which was depicted in the Holy Bible of Christians and the final moments of Jesus Christ. As a result of the Christian religion and tradition, the crucifixes of Jesus are in the numerous churches, schools, homes, and jewelleries people wear. In the front of us, we are seeing evident torture pictures even though we may not understand them consciously as such. I think, this is related to the contradictive relationship of torture and violence in punishment of how it is conceived today as something secret and hidden parts of war and legal practices that are not shown to the public. Earlier, things were much different as in in the story of Christ or how the religion after Christ was used in cruel torturing methods as part of the interrogations and penalties of accused criminals by the Church and courts. The torturing and violence were often made public to increase the humiliation and suffering of the law-brokers (Foucault, 1975/2001).

S. Alanne, *Music, Music Therapy and Refugees*,
https://doi.org/10.1007/978-3-031-94766-7_3

Violence and public death penalties, dead bodies, were processed in public places as warnings for the people; they served also as amusement that people gathered for and wanted to see.

Torture is still occurring in many parts of world in wars, conflicts, and prisons. In the beginning of the twenty-first century, torture and ill-treatment were reported occurring systemically in 80 countries according to different sources (Modvig & Jaranson, 2004, p. 42). Currently, it is assumed that torture occurs in more than half of the world's countries regularly even though it is systematically forbidden according to the international human rights and humanitarian laws in all situations (Castaneda et al., 2018; Modvig & Jaranson, 2004). It is estimated roughly that a quarter of refugees have torture experiences (Castaneda et al., 2018, p. 356). Frequently, torture is happening in secrecy, and only its results can be found in the stories of refugees, soldiers, and political prisoners, and as traces in their bodies including physical pains and dysfunctionalities (Modvig & Jaranson, 2004, p. 39). Frequently, torture is silenced because of the shame and burden of the victims as they are unable to speak about their humiliating experiences. As a result, in treatment and therapy victims may need a lot of time and long-term confidential environment to build trust towards their helpers before they can talk about traumatic experiences. Also, the society and those who were politically or administratively responsible for torturing and ill-treatment often want to hide and silence what happened partly due to the same reason of shame but also because of the fear of possible legal consequences. This is often making the research of the prevalence and the treatment of torture and its sequelae a complex situation (ibid.).

Torture is often targeted at the body even though the primary goal of the torture is the breaking of the mind and personality of victims. This occurs by causing them as much as possible physical and psychic pain and suffering that is leaving them to feel extremely helpless and anxious (Castaneda et al., 2018, p. 356). Torture may use physiological methods like unsystematic/systematic beating to different parts body like under the soles of feet and ears. Also, stinging, cutting, amputation, and shooting the body may be used as well as shaking. The tortured may be exposed to positional torture where the movements are restricted and/fixated with ropes and chains. A tortured may be forced to small boxes, rooms, or cages, and they may be suspended with their arms tied back as some examples of commonly used physiological torture methods (Modvig & Jaranson, 2004, pp. 40–41).

Physical torture methods may also include suffocating by near-drowning or near-suffocating as well as using heat, cold, or fire to cause a damage to the tissues and skin of the victim. In addition, chemical, pharmacological, and microbiological torture methods are used where electricity, acid, chilli powder, kerosene, toxic dose of neuroleptics, bacteria, and viruses like HIV are given to the victims forcibly. They may not also be provided with their necessary medicine like insulin as a means of torturing them. Other physical methods are sexual and animal torture where the victims are raped or forced to rape each other, or to see the close one being raped, and their genitals may be injured with electricity, for example. Animals like dogs, rats, and insects have been used to assault or attack a fixated victim (ibid.).

In addition to the physical methods, psychological torture methods are used that are often combined with the physical methods described (Modvig & Jaranson, 2004, pp. 40–41). Psychological methods include humiliation that may be verbal like sexual humiliation and mocking gender, race, family, culture, or personality of the victims. This can be done with forcing victims to humiliating actions where taboos are broken and ideological, political, and religious thoughts and values of person are renounced or mocked. In this regard, music has been used as a part of mocking and humiliating prisoners (Alanne, 2010, 2014b; Cusick, 2006, 2008, 2013; Moreno, 1999; Papaeti, 2013a, 2020). Other psychological methods of torture are depersonalisation or dehumanising of the victim by being called with a number instead of name, for example (Modvig & Jaranson, 2004, p. 40).

Victims may also be interrogated nude, and they may be kept blindfolded for weeks or months. Different kinds of threats may be given against the victims including death, rape, and torture that may also be targeted at the family of the victim. Mock executions may be a part of using threat and breaking down of the victim. Deprivation is one psychological method of torture where the sense and physiological need are manipulated by using light, sound, food, and drink that may be denied as well as denying access to toilet facilities. Victims may also be deprived with different methods like restricting their sleep, company, and access to medicine and medical assistance. Experiencing the torture of others by seeing, hearing, and while waiting one's turn as a threat is a means of psychological torture method (ibid.).

Using music and loud sounds as well as heavy lighting have been part of deprivation as non-touch methods of torture and interrogations (Alanne, 2010, 2014b, 2023; Cloonan & Johnson, 2008; Cusick, 2006, 2008, 2013; Grant, 2013; Papaeti, 2020). Music and sounds have also been used to manipulate, threat, humiliate prisoners and victims as psychological methods of torture that leave no traces in the body. Then, music and sounds are used as a weapon and violence to break the personality and identity of victims. Music and sounds may be combined with physical violence and torture, or they have been used to masquerade them. This may change the meaning of music and art for a refugee or a torture survivor that it is important for therapists, healthcare or social care workers, and educators working with music and arts to know. Music and sounds may be associated with violence, torture, and oppressive regimes and dictators, which is why music may be experienced as negative, or even traumatic, causing a threat and harm to their psychic integrity. In the next paragraphs, it will be described how music has been used unethically as a part of ill-treatment and violence and how it may psychologically affect the experiences in victims and their families.

3.1 Music in Torture Experiences

Music has been used in torture with refugees and political prisoners even though there seems not to be so much research about its direct use in torture or as torture. However, music is currently recognised and documented to be used in torture and as torture in warfare, interrogations, and prisons since WWII (Alanne, 2010; Cloonan & Johnson, 2002, 2008; Cusick, 2006, 2013; Grant, 2013; Moreno, 1999; Papaeti, 2020). It is also a question of what is considered as torture even though the use of music in such violent circumstances cannot be denied anymore. Not every disturbing behaviour like neighbours playing music loud the whole day or during the night is simply torture even though it may feel like it (Alanne, 2010, p. 58). It would be different if the music was played loudly to disturb, and even vandalise, other people as violence or a part of violence like some authors have suggested (Cloonan & Johnson, 2002, 2008; Frith, 2004). Then, music could have connotations that could feel or even be like torture. However, as I have argued earlier, it would be problematic to define every irritable noise or music as violence and torture juristically, philosophically, or medically (Alanne, 2010, p. 58). Basically, it is against the current general conceptualising of torture that is referring to the situations, methods, and goals where something is used deliberately to harm physiologically, psychologically, socially, or to increase the pain, suffering, and humiliating until breaking the psyche of victim (Castaneda et al., 2018; Modvig & Jaranson, 2004).[1]

The United Nations` (UN) Convention against Torture and Other Cruel, Inhuman or Degrading Treatment or Punishment (1984) Article 1 is defining the term "torture" as

> *—any act by which severe pain or suffering, whether physical or mental, is intentionally inflicted on a person for such purposes as obtaining from him or a third person information or a confession, punishing him for an act he or a third person has committed or is suspected of having committed, or intimidating or coercing him or a third person, or for any reason based on discrimination of any kind, when such pain or suffering is inflicted by or at the instigation of or with the consent or acquiescence of a public official or other person acting in an official capacity. It does not include pain or suffering arising only from, inherent in or incidental to lawful sanctions.*

This kind of juristic definition seems to separate the torture as a method and experience where the former is referring to the "official capacity" using the power and torture for its goals. However, as violence the torture is also referring to the painful, intimidating, discriminating, and coercing experiences of victim that are not as such referring to the official status of the tormentor. In this sense, the UN's definition of torture seems to lack the conceptualising of other similar violence as torture even though the applying and respecting of Universal Declaration of Human Rights (UDHR) by the UN are referred in their Convention against Torture and Other Cruel, Inhuman or Degrading Treatment or Punishment. In the UN's UDHR, Article 5, it is said: "No one shall be subjected to torture or to cruel, inhuman or degrading treatment or punishment". UDHR is not restricted to states and their official capacity; they are respected in all human relationships and activities. In this sense, also torture universally and experiences relating to it are forbidden and against the humanity. Thus, according to the UN's UDHR, using music in torture or as torture is against the human rights and forbidden, respectively.

---

[1] See Chap. 3 "Music, Violence, and Trauma" for the methods and consequences of physiological and psychological torture.

According to these medical, psychological, and juridical definitions of torture, it is also relevant to define "musical torture" as suggested by Cloonan and Johnson (2008, p. 150). They describe musical torture as "deliberate infliction of physical and/or psychological pain for a sustained period (ibid.)". In their opinion, musical torture is used in disorientation, humiliation, and causing pain for the victims. Cloonan and Johnson (ibid.) describe and report many circumstances where music has been used to disorient the victim or the target as a sonic weapon by the US troops. For example, in December 1989, they played loud AC/DC hard rock music outside the Vatican embassy in Panama City trying to force out the Panamanian President, General Manuel Noriega, from the embassy where he had retreated. Even though this tactic was successful, it is unclear what was the purpose of playing music loud.

Authors suggest that it may have been because music was used to mask the ongoing negotiations of the situation, cause fear, or offend the opera loving Noriega's musical taste and his cultural identity (ibid.). Considering the possible reasons of using music as a weapon by acoustically bombarding Noriega, it may have worked in disorientating, humiliating, and even causing pain to some degree. Frequently, all this seem to be the objects of using music in torture, warfare, or prisons in many reported cases (Alanne, 2010; Cloonan & Johnson, 2008; Cusick, 2006, 2008, 2013; John, 1991/2001; Moreno, 1999; Papaeti, 2013a, 2020). Using music as violence, torture, and a weapon has been systematic and continuing in the modern times. In the following chapters, it will be described more thoroughly, how it has been used in wars, as the non-touch method of interrogations, and for deceitful purposes in prisons and camps.

3.2 Music as a Weapon in War

Music has been used as a weapon and as the part of military tradition from the ancient wars (Alanne, 2010, p. 46). It has been a part of the parades and composed for specific military orchestras and purposes like tattooing, marching, building morale, and religious observances until this day (Cloonan & Johnson, 2008, p. 32). In 218 BC, Hannibal's army confronted the Gallic warriors who howled and sang in Italy (pp. 28–29). Hannibal won this battle but 16 years later he lost against the Romans who sung and cried in unison that was more effective than the mix of different tunes and mother tongues of Gallic warriors' war cries he was confronted earlier. Around 400 BC Greek galley oarsmen had chants and one of them was for battle (Cloonan & Johnson, 2008, p. 32). In the Old Testament of Bible, the Book of Joshua, Chap. 6, it is described how Joshua used trumpets and loud shouts to win the Jericho as its walls came tumbling down. Trumpets and war cries are reported to be used by the Cato the Elder with his men, so that the enemy fled. Also, King Richard I caused fear and dread for the citizens with resounding trumpets and loud horns in his crusade to Sicily (ibid.).

As we know, making loud sounds with singing and drumming when the soldiers are marching has been used to cause a fear and threat in enemy that can hear them approaching from the far. At the same time, singing has strengthened the spirit of the troops to overcome fear and give them vital physical energy of keeping their hunger in long marches. In the US War Department document during WWII, music is described as "one of the most effective vehicles for bringing a group together, for releasing the emotions, and for creating a spirit of fellowship and spirit de corps—if he simply listens to music, his interest are broadened and his sense of well-being is generally increased" (Sullivan, 2007, p. 288).

In this statement, the therapeutic effect of music to release emotions and increase wellbeing is recognised but also its usefulness for war likc bringing group together and broaden the interests of soldiers from losses, fears, and traumatic experiences of war. Music, songs, and their sounds may protect the soldiers from psychic traumas by strengthening their resilience and recovery from the fights. Music may also help psychotherapeutically to keep psychic distance from the battlefield and its threatening soundscapes and scenes that are stressful. Thus, music and sounds appear to have potential for the good and bad, trauma and recovery, in wars. Psychologically, they are representing themselves as the good and bad objects in the psychic structures of human minds from the psychodynamic point of view (Alanne, 2023, pp. 11–12).

In the history of humankind, it is evident that there has been knowledge of how to use music as a weapon or therapy long before their modern conceptualisations in trauma work and psychoanalysis (Alanne, 2023, pp. 11–12). Plato (2007, 427–347 BC) thought about the effects of music: How it may have good and bad influences for the people living in the state and what it could do for their morales. From time to time, societies including politicians, researchers, educators, and health professionals are considering music like rock ´n` roll, heavy metal, rap, and their relationship to the wellbeing of people. For oppressing governments and dictators, the possible effects of music may be the reason to forbid it for controlling their citizens like in the former Eastern Bloc (Alanne, 2023, p. 11).[2] In some Islamic countries the playing of rock and metal music as well as dancing has been forbidden as sinful (LeVine, 2009).

In the twenty-first century, music has been used in the war against terrorism (Alanne, 2010, pp. 46–47, 51). In the war of Iraq, it has been reported that music and sounds were used as a weapon by the US Army's PsyOps company (Cusick, 2006, p. 2). There was also sonic bombardment used in the Iraq War and use of special acoustic weapons developed for this kind of strategies since 1997 by the US Department of Defence (p. 1). For example, the "Acoustic Blaster" device was developed by the US forces, which was used in the Iraq War. This weapon could produce impulse waveforms up to 165 dB, and it could be targeted at over 15 metres (50 feet). In addition, such infrasound weaponry was developed that could be

[2] See the following paragraphs, particularly Sect. 3.5 "Transformed Experiences of Music, Violence, and Trauma", for the discussion of how music may have been used in propaganda and as a tool of power.

adjusted for disabling or killing the human as their targets when fired from helicopters in the Iraq War. These weapons were included with inputs for the MP3 and CD players, so that the soldiers could use music with them.

Soldiers could use their creativity and favourite music like *Hell's Bells* and *Shoot to Thrill* from AC/DC when they bombed Fallujah in November 2004 (Alanne, 2010; Cusick, 2006). It seems that there were no official orders or guidelines what kind of music should be used. At the command level sounds seemed to be considered as a similar strategy to smoke bombs to upset the enemy. Similar sonic weaponry was reported to be used in Israel, Gaza, and the Lebanon, where the effects of it have been described as "being hit by a wall of air that is painful on the ears, sometimes causing nosebleed and leaving you shaking inside" (Cusick, 2006, p. 2). This is more than using music and drums to frighten up the enemy psychologically as it is also injuring the enemy physically with the power of sound with the modern warfare high technology.

Music has been also used as a weapon in Europe during the Balkan War when Serbian soldiers forced Muslim prisoners to sing before they were killed in the 1990s. Also, in Zimbabwe, Africa, 300 members of the Movement for Democratic Change were frog-marched to a tree where they were tied and beaten with machetes, batons, and axe handles for five hours. During these manoeuvres they were forced to sing ZANUF-PF party's liberation song and slogans, which were used for humiliation purposes and music as a weapon in torturing them apparently (Alanne, 2010; Cloonan & Johnson, 2002, 2008).

Recently, music like hip hop and especially gangsta rap has been reported to be a part of the conflicts and violence with different mobs in the US and Europe. Gangsta rap, like Eminem, or earlier Body Count and Ice T's *Cop Killer* in the 1990s, has increased its success since 2000s with the lyrics and moods that may commonly include incitement to violence and misogyny (Cloonan & Johnson, 2008, p. 99). In these raps, music is used to emphasise the power of own group, and it is used as a threat for violence including gloomy moods of death and threatening gun-like sounds and gestures. Often, the violent lyrics are combined with the open substance abuse and explicit sexual content to underline their message in music videos of the artists like Migo, 6IX9INE, and Lil Pump's *Drug Addicts* (Alanne, 2018). However, sometimes it may be difficult to tell that the threats are really targeted to people and opposite groups. Or are they maybe reflecting the moods of poverty and threat of violence related to the drug culture and society as the current blues of modern times. Then, music, like metal, punk, and rap, may have therapeutic meaning for the people and substance abusers when music is reflecting and expressing their inner experiences and not only inciting to aggression in boosting one's ego, hyper hedonistic sexual behaviour, and substance abuse for the antisocial objectives (Alanne, 2019a, 2021; Miranda et al., 2013; Penn & Kojo Clarke, 2008).

In wars, soldiers as well as other people have used music and songs to keep up the fighting spirit for themselves and aggression towards the enemy. US soldiers in Iraq played music, for example, the Bloodhound Gang's *Fire Water Burn* song, when they were in a battle (Cloonan & Johnson, 2008, p. 157). In Finland, during WWII, there was a polka *Silmien välliin* (Between the Eyes) that was a particularly brutal and dehumanising song towards the Russians, which Finnish people considered as unacceptable (Alanne, 2010; Kirves, 2008). In Rwanda genocide, Simon Bikindi's music and his song *Nanga Abahutu* (I Hate Hutus) was reported to be played in radio constantly as people were beaten to death at the same time in its rhythms (Ervamaa, 2002, p. B4). Later, Bikindi was accused of genocide and crimes against humanity with his songs (Cloonan & Johnson, 2008, p. 97). On 2 December 2008, he was sentenced to 15 years in prison from incitement to commit genocide, however, not because of his songs that were made earlier than 1994 homicide according to the United Nations International Criminal Tribunal for Rwanda court decision.[3]

On the other hand, music may provide hope for surviving the war, imprisonment, and even execution like in the concentration camps of Nazis during WWII when music and concerts, singing Yiddish songs, provided the players and audience some "freedom of will" and reaffirming experiences for a worthwhile (Moreno, 1999, p. 12). Some of the prisoners sung *Hatikva* (The Hope)[4] while marching into the gas chambers to keep their faith and group identities as Jewish people (Alanne, 2010; Moreno, 1999). In the violent use of music in wars, interrogations, and deceiving, this conflictual meaning of music in keeping the spirit of aggression and survival has been taken further as the means of psychological torture in causing and increasing suffering.

3.3 Music as a Non-touch Method of Interrogation

Using music as a weapon has been especially developed for the methods of interrogations (Alanne, 2010; Cusick, 2006, 2013; Papaeti, 2020). There has been systematic research of using music as a non-touch method of interrogation since 1950s. It has been conducted by the intelligence organisations such as CIA (USA), MI6 (UK), and CSIS (Canada). US universities like Yale, Cornell, and McGill were a part of the organised research and development of such methods that was funded by the intelligent agencies in the Cold War. Research at the McGill University was funded by Canada for the sensory deprivation and sensory manipulation including hooding, noises, and soundproofing (Cusick, 2006, p. 7). CIA funded the research at the Yale and Cornell Universities, where the effects of self-inflicted pain, stress positions, and possibilities of provoked personal, sexual, or cultural humiliation were studied. In addition, at Yale, CIA funded the studies on common people and their capability to cause lethal pain on other people (ibid.). The interest of intelligence agencies towards these dark methods arose from the needs to compete with Soviet Union's brainwashing in debriefing the returning US soldiers from the Korean War in the 1950s (Papaeti, 2020, p. 5).

[3] See the ICTR Case Profile. *The Prosecutor v. Simon Bikindi*, ICTR-01-72.

[4] A current national anthem of Israel.

During this era there were also psychological experiments with lysergic acid diethylamide (LSD) that was given to the soldiers (Alanne, 2023, pp. 21–22). At the same time, LSD was studied as therapy and medicine that included using of music as a comparison. Helen Bonny, a pioneer of music psychotherapy, was involved in these experiments that were allowed with a special permission of government at the universities where music was found to have similar effect to LSD (Bonny and Pahnke, 1972). As the harmful effects of drugs and LSD became more evident in the 1970s, this kind of studies was abandoned. This led Bonny to develop her method of Guided Imagery and Music (GIM), which was sadly used to help the withdrawals of those clients that had LSD psychotherapy alone. In this regard music therapy and psychological interest towards music in war have a connection relating to their basic research. However, it must be stressed that there is not such evidence that Bonny and her methods were involved directly with military purposes like music as a weapon or as an interrogation method.

The specific funded non-touch interrogation methods by the intelligent agencies and investigated by the mentioned universities appear to have included effects of sensory deprivation; different kinds of manipulation; as well as personal, sexual, and cultural humiliation (Alanne, 2010, p. 47; Cusick, 2006; Papaeti, 2020). As discussed earlier, these methods of physical and psychological torturing that included self-inflicted pain, for example, using of stress positions, hooding, and continuous noise, loud or not, including music as well as soundproofing sensory deprivation (Alanne, 2010, p. 47; Leave no marks, 2007; Modvig & Jaranson, 2004; Papaeti, 2020; Report of the Senate Select Committee on Intelligence Committee Study of the Central Intelligence Agency's Detention and Interrogation Programme, 2014[5]).[6] The McGill University research with sounds in the sensory deprivation is mentioned in the 2014 declassified CIA's (1963, p. 88) *KUBARK*[7] *Counterintelligence Interrogation* manual among other experiments relating to them, including experiments at the US National Mental Health Institute. At the experiments of National Mental Health Institute two subjects were immersed with their whole bodies and hooded in the black-out masks in the 34.5 C water not more than three hours hearing only "faint sounds" from their breaths through the piping in the water. The subjects imposed such an experiment had personal reveries and fantasies and, in the end, visual imagery that resembled hallucinations, feeling like "afresh" from the bed and "out of step with the clock for the rest of the day" according to the report (pp. 88–89).

In the US army training for the interrogators, there was described a famous child's song *I Love You* sung by the character Barney the Purple Dinosaur. It was used to interrogate the Iraqi detainees as well as heavy metal song *Enter Sandman* of the Metallica. They were played in high volumes repeatedly for the prisoners in the shipping containers used at the time of Iraq War and the war against terrorism. An unidentified FBI agent has described how at least in three incidents, Guantanamo

[5] Report of the Senate Select Committee on Intelligence Committee Study of the Central Intelligence Agency's Detention and Interrogation Program together with Foreword by Chairman Feinstein and Additional and Minority Views (9 December 2014).

[6] See Chap. 3 "Music, Violence, and Trauma" for more detailed description of torture methods.

[7] KUBARK was a code name for CIA.

detainees were chained to the extreme heat, cold, or very loud rap music. Also, Christina Aguilera's pop music and water poured in the head were used in similar purposes of sensory deprivation and torture to wake up the prisoner during the nights in November 2002 to January 2003. One Ethiopian prisoner had to listen *The Real Slim Shady* of Eminem as well as Dr. Dre's music for days as the examples of psychological tormenting and pressuring. After that the music was changed to the ghost laughter and Halloween sounds for the similar purposes of frightening up the prisoner (Alanne, 2010, p. 47; Cusick, 2006).

It seems that the music used in violence, wars, and torture is reflecting the current trend or fashion of popular music of how they seemed to be creatively chosen or even improvised (Alanne, 2010, pp. 47–48). As mentioned earlier, there seemed not to be specific music lists for battle use in Iraq War, so it seems to be the case also within the non-touch methods of interrogations. During the Iraq War "high value detainees" were put into the "Black Room", a garage-sized place without windows, at the Baghdad International Airport (Cusick, 2006, p. 3). They were played loud rock `n` roll and rap music as they were tied up to the stress position, hands behind their legs and attached to an I-bolt. This kind of non-touch torture and deafening music was imposed on the imprisoned citizens of Afghanistan, Bosnia, Egypt, Ethiopia, Gambia, Indonesia, Iraq, Mauritania, Pakistan, Thailand, and United Arab Emirates. Also, British and Canadian citizens were among them during that war (pp. 2–3, 7).

Even though there seemed not to be any music lists for interrogations, the psychological effects and purposes were considered in the CIA field manuals (Alanne, 2010, p. 48). This kind of non-touch methods of interrogation and using music was under the tittles of "fear up" and "ego down" (Cusick, 2006, p. 3). This methodology of interrogations has its origins in the 2014 declassified CIA's (July 1963) *KUBARK Counterintelligence Interrogation* manual, where such interrogation techniques and using soundproofing and deprivation of sensory stimulus, for example, seemed to be first introduced (pp. 87–90). The interrogators' purpose was directly to break the prisoner's personality and induce them deliberately with symptoms like the later PTSD diagnosis included (Papaeti, 2020, pp. 4–6). This kind of state-of-the-art methods arouses from the Cold War era and interests in fighting with communism around the world. They were officially and literally forbidden as any inhuman treatment of subjects in the later revisited editions of CIA's (1983/1988) similar now-declassified *Human Resource Exploitation Training Manual*. However, as evident now, they were taken back to the repertoire during the War on Terror in the twenty-first century (Cusick, 2013, pp. 275–276).

Thus, the objective of music and sound was to scare and humiliate the prisoners and interrogated in a way described in the earlier examples of music as a weapon. It seems that music was not only used as physical sounds to deprive sleeping and cause pain, but use of it also had psychological elements in humiliating the prisoners like the mentioned *I love you* children's song. By playing children's song with a contradictory loving message, the tormentor is treating the prisoners and their adult egos like children. At the same time, interrogators are making a joke of the victim as a target of their cruelties and violence and psychological torture in increasing their pain and humiliation. As remembered, the objective of tormentor is the breaking of the victim's personality to a child-like depended and regressive state without own will (Castaneda et al., 2018, p. 356). This is also a target of fearing up, so that the victims would confess, give up resistance, and abandon their political and cultural views. Also, the goal of interrogator with the deprivation of sensory stimuli techniques may be to make "the regressed subject view the interrogator as a father-figure" and more compliant as is directly advised by the *KUBARK Counterintelligence Interrogation* manual (CIA, 1963, p. 90). There are a lot of examples of this kind of dark humour, psychological manipulation, and violent parody with asymmetric logic where the positions of victims are turned upside down in tormenting them (Alanne, 2010, p. 48). The asymmetric logic also relates to the deceitful use of music in prisons and camps where the music considered as safe has been used to calm prisoners in front of evident danger.

On 22 January 2009, President Barack Obama's executive order prohibited interrogation techniques and interrogation-related treatment that were against the UN Convention Against Torture.[8] This included the non-touch interrogation techniques mentioned that used music as well as the described CIA detention facilities where music was used as a non-touch method of interrogation to be closed "as expeditiously as possible" (Sec 4a) (Grant, 2013, p. 4). With the same kinds of conclusions, "—to help make sure that the system of detention and interrogation described in this report is never repeated" was made in the later *Report of the Senate Select Committee on Intelligence Committee Study of the Central Intelligence Agency's Detention and Interrogation Program* in the letter of the Committee chairman Dianne Feinstein (9 December 2014) to the President. Examples of using music in non-touch interrogations, sensory deprivation, and torture like described earlier are mentioned several times as a part of the unclassified documents included in this report. For example, according to the report of CIA records the Blues Brothers song *Rawhide* was used in conditioning fear in a detainee, so that he "knows when he hears the music where he is going and what is going to happen" (p. 429). This kind of fearing up of the prisoners including breaking, persuading, and cheating with music in the dark manoeuvres of "re-educating" and "rehabilitating" them has a long history in the twentieth-century conflicts and coups (Alanne, 2010; Papaeti, 2013a, 2020).

3.4 Deceitful Musical Experiences in Prisons and Camps

In addition to the music used as a technique and weapon in interrogations and torture, it has also been a part of torture and violence in hiding and masquerading them. During WWII, Nazis used music in their concentration camps systematically for

[8]Executive Order 13491—Ensuring Lawful Interrogations. https://obamawhitehouse.archives.gov/the-press-office/ensuring-lawful-interrogations

different purposes to humiliate, torture, and deceit prisoners (Alanne, 2010; John, 1991/2001; Moreno, 1999; Naliwajek-Mazurek, 2013). For example, in the concentration camp of Majdanek, loudspeakers were used in cars that blasted music incessantly so that the naked victims' screams down at the ground who were shot with the machine gun fire could not be heard (John, 1991/2001, p. 280). This kind of use of loudspeakers and music by the execution squads of Nazis has also been reported in other locations in the murdering of Eastern Jewish population (ibid.). In the concentration camps, there were orchestras and bands that accompanied prisoners in their deaths (John, 1991/2001, pp. 279–280). The orchestra members were other Jews and prisoners who were forced to play music during "show executions" that were even photographed (p. 279). In Buchenwald camp, the whole camp of prisoners was forced to sing on the roll-call square to hide the shots of the mass executions of Russian war prisoners. In Auschwitz and other locations, the prisoner orchestras had to play during the selections who will work and die at their arrivals of new prisoners. They had to play for the people who were going directly to the gas chambers waving their hands joyfully because "they thought that a place where there is music cannot be so bad" according to a survivor's description (p. 280).

For example, music like Richard Wagner's *Lohengrin* played by a full symphony orchestra was used at the arrival of new prisoners in concentration camps to psychologically create an illusion of safe space (Alanne, 2010, p. 50, Moreno, 1999, p. 6). Music is a psychologically good object that was used deceitfully so that the prisoners would not be afraid of their lives, go panic, and try to escape or fight against the guards. The majestic sound of classical music played by symphony orchestra provided a false representation of the camps where they were taken and what was happening to the prisoners there. In the concentration camps, as remembered by many survivors, music was also used to humiliate and keep up the spirit of the prisoners who were forced to sing happy songs like *Steht ein Dörflein mitten im Walde* (A Little Village Stands in the Midst of a Forest) and *Im Schatten grüner Bäume lasst uns singen und fröhlich sein* (In the Shade of the Green Trees Let Us Sing and Be Merry) while working and marching (John, 1991/2001, pp. 276–277).

Camp orchestras had to accompany these repeated manoeuvres with "merry marches" and "gay little songs" (John, 1991/2001, p. 277). In Sachsenburg, 15 to 20 men were entitled by the SS as the "singing horses" as they were harnessed like horses and forced to pull heavy-loaded wagon running and singing led by the SS man in a motorcycle (p. 278). There were also songs made by the prisoners behind the back of SS that made a parody of the living in the camps like the song *Lied vom heiligen Caracho* (Song of Saint Caracho) in the Sachsenhausen. Caracho meant singing and working in a double pace for the prisoners in the language of SS men. In the Buchenwald, there was "Caracho Road", a street from the SS headquarters to the main gate of prisoners' camp. It seems that besides tormenting, songs and singing meant also keeping self-respect, own identity, and some kind of hope for the prisoners as the word "Caracho" symbolised freedom in the song (pp. 277–278). In this regard, the meaning and the purpose of music for the prisoners and SS men seemed to be conflictual representing torment, relief, entertainment, and even therapy. Nazi guards and tormenters were enjoying music after or during their working days and the camp orchestras had to play for them as a part of their duties in the camps (Alanne, 2010; John, 1991/2001; Moreno, 1999; Naliwajek-Mazurek, 2013, pp. 39–40).[9]

One example of grown violent madness accompanied with the mixed moods of music aesthetics was in Buchenwald, where after one Sunday afternoon roll-call according to a survivor, a band remained and played a beautiful Viennese music at the gate (John, 1991/2001, p. 279). Viennese prisoners applauded and were glad about the music; however, their happy mood was soon destroyed as a column of 300 Jews were marched at the square led by the SS man. The Jews were surrounded by the Kapos with the sticks in their hands. The camp orchestra was ordered to play Viennese waltz as the prisoners had to turn around into to the beat of music until they were feeling dizzy and felt down. Then, they were pulled up to a half crouching position and made to jump like frogs exactly to the beat. In the end of this "Strauss evening", a large group of prisoners came sided by the low-rank SS officers with the big whips in their hands. They were beaten into the rhythm of music, and as they screamed in pain with the blows, on the other side of square other prisoners were still dancing and hopping like frogs to the music.

This vignette of so-called punitive sport in the camps, one example of the many cruelties with music described by the holocaust survivors, shows how music was used in deception, torture, and humiliation in the concentration camps (John, 1991/2001, p. 279). Detainees had to sing happy songs in doing exhausting work, that is already a torment, as well as in the punishing actions imposed on them arbitrarily by the SS men. For example, in the beginning of the vignette described, the prisoners must have thought they will have some sympathy and even respect in the form of leisure music from their home country as there was also this kind of concerts arranged for entertainment in the camps, but instead they were fooled and forced to witness brutal violence of the other prisoners (John, 1991/2001; Naliwajek-Mazurek, 2013). In the concentration camps, there were also leisure music and concerts arranged for the prisoners that were experienced as empowering, entertaining, relaxing, and providing positive thoughts for the detainees (John, 1991/2001, p. 284). However, at the same time, musical tormenting and fooling, violence accompanied with it, seemed to be in the similar use by the SS men and guards making fun of the victims and entertaining themselves with sadistic and pervert cruelties.

The biggest deception manoeuvre of Nazis in the use of culture, music, and other art forms, however, was how it was presented to the detainees and the public as the "leisure programming" (John, 1991/2001, pp. 285–286). The Theresienstadt was a "show camp" in "white-washing" the real purpose of the many concentration camps and hiding their cruelties (p. 286). In Theresienstadt, German and foreign visitors that included diplomats and delegates of Red Cross were shown a happy and easy ghetto life with a lot of cultural activities. Many talented artists and musicians took their chances to survive in the leisure programmes of the camps. There were many

[9] See Sect. 3.5 "Transformed Experiences of Music, Violence, and Trauma" for the more thorough discussion of altered and mixed meanings of music and violence.

kinds of orchestras, choirs, studios, jazz bands, even though jazz was banned elsewhere in the Nazi Germany as a degenerated art, among other arts, drama, dance, fine arts, literature, sports, music lessons and lectures, new compositions, and cafes in the camps (p. 286). However, it was an "as if" world like described in the same titled sarcastic jolly chanson "*Als Ob*" composed by the prisoner and cabaret poet Leo Strauss in the Theresienstadt:

I know a little town,
A town that's really fine;
I don't call it by its name,
I call the town As-if.

Not just anyone may
Enter in this town—
Only the chosen people
Of the as-if race may come.

There they live their lives
As if it were a life,
And enjoy the rumors
As if they were the truth.

The people in the street,
They gallop very fast—
Though there's nothing to do,
They act as though there were.

There is a nice café
Just like the Café d e l'Europe,
And with the music play
One feels happy as if. (Cited according to John, 1991/2001, p. 287)[10]

This song is describing the ambivalent feeling and meaning of the leisure programme and the deception going on in the concentration camps. Music and arts seemed to provide some comfort, leisure, resilience, and repression as a defence mechanism needed even in the form of sarcastic humour of song. For the prisoners, musical experience was not the same; they could not fully enjoy it as it brought memories of loved ones. The forced singing and playing in the orchestras meant guilt as they were conscious about the corruptness of their forced musical performances participating to the violence and killing process of perpetrators who had exterminated their families in front of their eyes. In addition, the musicians were always reminded about the temporality of their own lives in the camps (Naliwajek-Mazurek, 2013, p. 34).

Even though the musicians in the camps played for their lives and had some benefits of it, like less physical labour, most of them died and were killed like other

[10] An excerpt from the beginning of song in German translated by John. The song was originally cited from the book *Und die Musik spielt dazu: Chansons und Satiren aus dem KZ Theresienstadt* edited by Migdal (1986).

prisoners in the camps. In addition to the psychological deceiving of singing happy songs while the detainees marched outside the Sachsenhausen camp to work and back like everything was fine; forced singing seemed to be also a way of deceiving the detainees' bodies in exhausting them with more work or otherwise tormenting them physically and increasing their exhaustion and mental anxiety (Brauer, 2016, pp. 10–13).[11] In spite of the fact that there were music lovers among Nazis, it did not seem to help the prisoners' situation in saving their lives or providing them with any empathy or respect as their methods are suggesting (Alanne, 2010; John, 1991/2001; Moreno, 1999). In contrast, it seems that Nazis used music and other art forms performed by the detainees selfishly to comfort and reward themselves from the work and augment the pain of detainees in manipulating and controlling them with music (Naliwajek-Mazurek, 2013, pp. 39–40).

The period of Nazi concentration camps during WWII seems to be the most devastating with the systematic use of music as a part of genocide and torture. Even though the cruelties of Nazis and concentration camps became very well-known and documented after war, the part of music and arts in these crimes against humanity has not been so familiar to the broader public and even for the researchers. It took decades since the war and camps until it became a more recognised subject of studies in musicology (Brauer, 2016; John, 1991/2001; Moreno, 1999). A part of the reason was that first there was not left many documents about the use of music and survivors who played in the orchestras of the camps because the SS destroyed the evidence and their documents (Brauer, 2016, p. 6). However, later more memorials, important testimonies, texts, and archives of survivors and musicians were discovered, including photographs of their performances in the camps (Brauer, 2016; Fisher & Gilboa, 2016; John, 1991/2001; Lefleur, 2022; Naliwajek-Mazurek, 2013).

Currently, it seems evident according to these multiple witness testimonies and documents, far beyond the scope of this book to repeat in their number, that the music was a regular part of Nazis' deceiving, mass-murdering, and soundscape in the concentration camps (Brauer, 2016; Fisher & Gilboa, 2016; John, 1991/2001; Lefleur, 2022; Naliwajek-Mazurek, 2013). However, it also seems, as there has been witnessing survivors of the manipulative and violent use of music in the camps, that this was a partly silent area of study in musicology and music therapy for a long time (Alanne, 2010; Brauer, 2016; John, 1991/2001; Moreno, 1999; Naliwajek-Mazurek, 2013). This seems to be related to the language reasons as much of the documents and studies were in Polish, Yiddish, or German, and they were discovered, published, and researched much later they were originally written and produced until quite recently (Brauer, 2016; John, 1991/2001; Naliwajek-Mazurek, 2013). The Iraq War and the described non-touch methods of interrogation with musical violence seemed to arise the interest towards the research of these phenomena again because of the ethical reasons to help the victims therapeutically and support the human rights and their development in the use of music (Alanne, 2005,

[11] See Sect. 3.5 "Transformed Experiences of Music, Violence, and Trauma" for more through discussion of psychologically and physically deceiving and tormenting the detainees' bodies with music by the Nazis in the concentration camps.

2010; Cloonan & Johnson, 2002, 2008; Cusick, 2006, 2008; Dixon, 2002; Papaeti, 2013b). However, the systematic manipulative use of music as a part of the interrogations and propaganda in prison camps continued in Greek and Chile after WWII before the Iraq War and the war against terrorism. Recently, they have become more known after studies in musicology (Chornik, 2013; Papaeti, 2013a, 2013b, 2020).

In Greece, there were post-WWII British camps of Makronisos and Gyaros during the Civil War 1946–1949, where music was used to "re-educate" prisoners (Papaeti, 2013a, p. 34). This included forced sinning and music from the loudspeakers as well as camp orchestras and choirs like there were in Nazi concentration camps in Germany since 1933 (Naliwajek-Mazurek, 2013; Papaeti, 2013a). In Greek internment camps, left-wing resistance fighters were prisoned, abused, and tortured during the Civil War after WWII (Papaeti, 2013a, pp. 34–35). Imprisonment of left-wing individuals continued long after the Civil War in different prisons and places until the early 1960s. It started again during the period of Colonels' Military Junta in 1967–1974 when folk music and patriotic songs were used to "cure" from the "disease of Communism" (p. 35). For example, on Gyaros, the prisoners were "bombarded" with folk and patriotic songs throughout the day from the loudspeakers (p. 36). This music reflected the personal and national preferences of Junta like the Colonel Ioannis Ladas' opinion that Greek folk music is important to man and society as "a moral art form" that is praising the noble emotions of love, friendship, and heroism (ibid.). With music 7000 communists that were shipped in Gyaros were tried to change from "beasts" to "good Greeks" according to Deputy Brigadier Patakos (ibid.). Marches were the other main acoustic marker of Junta and its cultural politics in Greek.

Being exposed to music throughout the day like 12 hours felt terrible for the one detainee who also considered music as the worst torture in her memories from Gyaros at that time (Papaeti, 2013a, pp. 35–36). She was among 150 women locked in one room with no windows, privacy, or nothing. Blasting music, folk and national-liberation songs including the march *The Enemies' Troops Have Passed* and the folk song *Famous Macedonia, Country of Alexandria*. Songs like that were played from the wake-up and the songs that were played were the ones detainees loved. Along with these patriotic songs were interruptions with slogans like "this country will be saved because of the patriots who were send by God", and "Don't forget that you are under the protection of Greek officers who will transform you into real Greeks" according to her memories (p. 37). Then they became the announcements of names who have signed a statement that they had denounced their beliefs. All this made the detainees feel "physically sick" and cover their ears (ibid.).

Other detainees, including men, had similar experiences of non-stop patriotic loud music, announcements, and "re-education" programme from 1947 to 1949 in Makronisos, Greece (Papaeti, 2013a, pp. 38–39): It was a rehabilitation station where the re-education including musical brainwash and torture were institutionalised long before Junta. It was a place for the Greeks with the infection of communism virus. The Greek concentration camps differed from the earlier Nazi concentration and extermination camps because they tried to "take away your soul" compared to Buchenwald, where "they had you for your labour" according to one detainee (ibid.). This seems to be true because the SS men played happy music for the detainees and themselves, so that the workers would work more in double tempo that musical rhythms accompanied. However, Buchenwald camp was also an extermination camp where the religion and culture of Jews were mocked as there was a "Caracho Road" as described earlier and the detainees were forced to dance waltzes while being beaten (John, 1991/2001, pp. 277–278). As remembered, "Caracho" meant also working double space in SS jargon (p. 279).

In Nazi concentration camps, it seems that they tried to make the prisoners do work as much as possible and exploit literally every piece of them, teeth, hair, gold, and so on, within the controlled industrial process developed for that (Naliwajek-Mazurek, 2013, p. 32). The act of using detainees' musical and artistic performances can also be seen as a forced slave work and exploitation of their talents and skills. It was forced work without the freedom for creativity, expression, or a free will of any kind which is against the current understanding of human rights and arts included in them. It seems that music, arts, and people, like choirs, orchestras, theatre, and music during the meals in Treblinka, were used like in a macabre amusement park or like visiting in a zoo of normal life for the German and Ukrainian as described by one survivor (Naliwajek-Mazurek, 2013, pp. 39–40).

This is reflecting the "as if" normal life of the concentration camps that their personnel tried to keep up by exploiting the detainees' artistic skills for mandatory performances and entertainment. Further it seems that they used music to camouflage the killing process from the victims as well as from themselves, so that both could do their jobs effectively without hearing the screams and shots all around as in normal life. In the Gestapo premises of Auschwitz, there were constantly radio playing dance melodies hiding the sound of torture, beatings, and the moans of detainees (ibid., p. 43). Also, torturers in Greek during the Junta and Chile at the time of Pinochet listened to the music and their own radio that was playing the popular songs at the camps in 1970s to torment the prisoners and hide the sounds of violence (Chornik, 2013; Papaeti, 2013b).

I would call this tormenting of Jews in the depicted musical games, forced singing, and shows with brutal violence as "soul murdering" and torturing respectively. Similar cases have been testified also in Greek and Chile later when music was used to psychologically break the identities and torment the prisoners at the camps and interrogation prison centres in 1970s (Chornik, 2013; Papaeti, 2013a, 2013b). It seems possible that such clear madness, parody of Jews and other prisoners served as the entertainment of sadistic urges, fun, and creativity, even as art for the SS men. They may have felt themselves bored, tired, and vicious like a group of abusing children, however, with an ultimate power and guns in their hands to lift up their energies. In addition to the possible unconscious group regression, music and other artistic manoeuvres including sadism could have been a kind of ego control and defence for them, to amuse them as well as torment their bad self-objects projected into the detainees. In this regard, the detainees were cruelly exploited and objectified in games, fun, and work without humanity for narcissistic purposes in the concentration camps of Nazis.

It is possible that the SS men were also influenced by the stress of their killing work that they unconsciously tried to comfort, normalise, or even augment in their experiences with the artistic manoeuvrers and jokes like any working man (Alanne, 2010; John, 1991/2001; Moreno, 1999). For example, it has been told that Joseph Mengele, a physician at Auschwitz, was whistling his favourite music while choosing the life or death for the arrivals, who was going to be gassed and who was capable for work (Alanne, 2010, p. 50; Moreno, 1999, pp. 3–4). Besides the stress, it seems that there was also enthusiasm and pleasure in the work of SS at the camps that seemed to be expressed within music (Moreno, 1999, pp. 3–4). One SS officer at Birkenau always wanted the camp orchestra to play him Schumann's *Reverie* after an especially hard-working day of selecting detainees to the gas chambers. This could suggest that maybe music had some therapeutic meaning and purposes for the Nazi perpetrators in elevating their experiences (Alanne, 2010; Moreno, 1999, pp. 3–4, 7).

However, it cannot be said for sure that did the destinies of victims affect or burden them anyway, at least consciously. Nazis had also a mission to accomplish in exterminating Jews where they felt they were doing history for good purposes. This may have also been the reason for the using of music in their work that they wanted to elevate and make art of itself in a macabre way that reflected their sadistic pathological personality traits as suggested by Naliwajek-Mazurek (2013, p. 45). This kind of malign narcissistic personality or sociopathological characteristics achieve pleasure from humiliating, degrading, and causing pain, or watching them, for the victims that the cruel jokes and music as a part of it can produce. As such it is uplifting for the perpetrators' omnipotent ego where music may be pure expression of these urges and physical violence itself. In this kind of malignant use of music, for other person it may not be easy to identify with it because the motives of music are different, often non-verbal, and not music as usual. This would explain the comments of some victims of musical torture and violence that the perpetrators' music did not feel like music or had no soul because it was used like an object or a game for their own purposes:

> *They treated music as—they were happy that they can shoot to the sound of music. This was accompaniment to their murders, to their shootings—and music in the background. From them shootings sounded nice—with music in the background. They did not treat music as we did—with a capital M—for them it was a game—a hideous game.* (A survivor and musician from Kurowice Nazi concentration camp Leopold Kozlowski, pianist, composer, conductor cited in Naliwajek-Mazurek, 2013, p. 44)

In the Greek concentration camps after WWII and during the Junta in 1970s, it seems that the target of perpetuators was more to break the identity of detainees and re-educate them with music and propaganda (Papaeti 2013a). It was clearly a national project to re-educate the supposed communists and left-wing to the patriotic values with music. In his speech of February 1970 Colonel Ladas, General Secretary of the Ministry of Interior, said that the patriotic folksongs are expressing "authenthic emotions" (pp. 37–38). He mentioned the Greek philosophers as "forefathers", especially Aristotle, who postulated that "music ennobles the soul", and how music was considered as a "medium of psychotherapy" at their time (p. 38).

Ladas goes even further to argue in his public speech that those theories were "confirmed in the medically advanced countries, using the so-called music-therapy in their hospitals" (ibid.). His statements concerning the history of music therapy and music psychotherapy in expressing emotions are in accordance with the current knowledge of their development and origins (Alanne, 2014a, 2023; Alvin, 1966/1975; Bonde, 2019). However, his other opinions in the speech concerning the patriotic folk music, its pureness, and continuing from antiquity that "was not composed by drug-addict hippies" cannot be agreed theoretically or ethically (Papaeti 2013a, pp. 37–38). These arguments and his reproach towards the "certain artistic circles whose works harm art and pollute society" in the same speech are like the earlier mentioned conceptions of the degenerated art of Nazi Germany in 1930/40s. In both countries, the regime controlled and censored arts because it was thought to "corrupt" society and arts themselves as explicitly said by Ladas (p. 38).

Interestingly, on the opposite, in the communistic Eastern Bloc countries like Soviet Union, Czechoslovakia, German Democratic Republic, Estonia, Lithuania, and Latvia, Western music and arts were also rebuked and banned because of similar reasons that it would pollute the minds of people with wrong values and ideas of capitalism. There were also purges of the "enemies of the working class" and "political prisoners" in the Soviet Union since 1920s and concentration camps, Gulags, where music was used to "re-educate" detainees in "cultural education work" in addition to physical work (Klause, 2013, pp. 25, 29). Cultural education of detainees included literature, sports, chess, and music. There were musical theatres, orchestras, and choirs in the numerous camps from the 1920s to 1950s. However, only about 2% of the detainees participated in the music and theatre (p. 25). According to some cases, music was used also in torture, but it seems not as widely as in Nazi concentration camps, even though it was used in oppression and humiliation too (p. 26). For example, in 1921, the detainees of the Arkhugub forced labour camp were forced to sing the *Internationale*, the Soviet national anthem at that time, in the long roll calls in the cold weather until every note was right to some extent. As a result of humiliating singing many detainees became sick. In one case from the end of 1920s from Solovetsky Islands, musicians were forced to participate in the profaning treatment of other detainees and accompany with inappropriate music for their sawing down of the crosses at the graveyard. This kind of forced work was torture for the prisoners and musicians as well because they saw the suffering of fellow prisoners from the gruelling dangerous work, even though it helped them to survive with easier work at Gulags (pp. 25–28).

In the memories of the poet and author Sergey Alïmov from barracks of Kem, familiar waltz was played during the night on 15 August 1930 from the English radio. He could not sleep as "the waltz melody was painfully screwed into my heart as though with a dentist's drill" (ibid., p. 27). He considered it to be "probably the most horrible torture" that he could not escape (ibid.). The waltz that he had danced frequently as free was broadcasted from English radio, including lyrics "I want [to] say good morning, I don't want [to] say good-by[e]" (ibid.). In spite of the clear torture with music, in most testimonies of former Gulag detainees, especially those who made music themselves, music had positive effects for their psychical and mental health in their experiences. For Boris Shiryayev in his memories from the Solovetsky Island on the White Sea in 1920s, music restored prisoners' right to see them as human beings and feel free inside according to him (p. 26).

Hundreds of thousands of people were sent to Gulags after WWII from Estonia, Latvia, Lithuania, and Poland, for example. Many of the taken, usually suddenly at night without warning, were arrested, judged, and shot according to the fast protocol in the KGB facilities like the one in Vilnius, Lithuania. Others were sentenced and taken to Siberia concentration camps, Gulags, for many years of forced labour under very hard and cruel conditions where their names were changed to numbers like in the Nazi concentration camps. These people included whole families and children who had to leave their homes, belongings, and homelands immediately. Many of them died and could never return to their home countries and see their families. Currently, it seems that not much is known about the role of music during the interrogations and camps: Was there similar systematic deceiving or tormenting with music and sounds in the Eastern Block and Soviet Union as they were used systematically by Nazis and other oppressive governments after WWII? (Klause, 2013, p. 26).[12] Even though it seems that in the Gulags of Soviet Union, the tormenting with music was not that widespread; however, there were a system of numerous "agitation brigades" (p. 29). They included ensembles like two guitars, two accordions, and one mandolin that played music in the roll calls of the camps and during the nights, so that the detainees could continue their working even though they may have worked 42 hours already. This seems to be similar punitive use of music with Nazis, where music was systematically used to increase physical energy in keeping up the slowed work and exhausting, respectively.

The purges, tormenting, and exterminating the people and their own cultures in the countries behind the "Iron Curtain" by the Soviet Union and communists continued from WWII until the collapse of Soviet Union and its allies in the 1990s. These atrocities that also included the rebuking and censoring of the arts, music, and the free expression of thinking were also manipulating, silencing, controlling, and re-educating of the people to think and behave in a new Soviet way. Re-education in Gulags including music was a part of this purpose of Soviet state to format a new human being (Klause, 2013, p. 26). The hideous purpose of it seemed to be that people would deceitfully forget their own past, history, nationality, religion, culture, and identity, to become Soviet citizens. Behind the communistic artistic propaganda for workers, state, and their shared values for common good, they had similar interrogation and police centres that were operated by German Gestapo before they were taken over by KGB. In Vilnius, detainees were deceived that they were taken to investigations or a court peacefully without worrying. Instead, they were shot in the back of head without trial and warning, in cold blood. The last thing they ever saw was the sudden stone wall in the dark KGB cellar premises.

[12] This would require further research of possible survivors, interviewing witnesses, and documentation in the light of the current literature and knowledge. This would be important as it is out of the scope of this book.

In South America, people disappeared and died in similar fashion during the military coups of Chile and Argentina in 1970s. In Chile, it is known that music was used systematically in the concentration camps and the prisons as was revealed from the questionary for the former prisoners and the interviewed former agent (Chornik, 2013, p. 52). Prisoners in Chile were forced to sing the national anthem, *Orden y Patria Es Nuestro Lema*, *La Novia Va Prendida en el Avión*, and sing or listen songs of Julio Iglesia, Edith Piaf's *La Vie en Rose*, George Harrison's *My Sweet Lord*, Félix Luna's *Alfonsina y el Mar*, and Nino Bravo's *Libre*. Also, the soundtrack for Stanley Kubrick's *A Clockwork Orange* cinema by Wendy Carlos was used (ibid.). According to the testimony of former agent "Gonzáles", a changed name, the prisoners were obliged to sing and march in the batch with the national anthem as they arrived in the Chacabuco camp. They also had to sing the national anthem every morning since then as well as the *Juramenta a la Bandera* every evening. The purpose was to "push them to breaking point", he knew now after visiting himself in the Nazi concentration camps (p. 54). Also, soldiers in the camp were obliged to sing most often the anthem and marches *Los Viejos Estandartes* (The Old Banners), *Adiós al Séptimo de Linea* (Farewell to the Seventh Row), *Las Glorias del Ejército* (The Glories of the Army), *El Himno de Yungay* (The Anthem of Yungay), and *Lili Marlene*, Gonzáles remembers. These are military marches and songs; *The Old Banners* was an official anthem of Chilean army (p. 55). It is easy to understand the nationalistic pressure combined with fear and anxiety that the continuing military music and patriotic soundscape of the camp must have created for the detainees.

González remembers that also detainees sung Violeta Parra's songs *La Jardina* (The Woman Gardener), *El Casamiento de Negros* (Wedding of Blacks), *Run Run Se Fue Pal Norte* (Run Run Left for the North), and *La Paloma Ausente* (The Absent Dove) at the Chacabuco camp (Chornik, 2013, p. 55). In Villa Grimaldi, where González worked later, there was own radio for the agents and guards where they were listening all the time songs like *La Váca Planca* and *La Loca Maria*, also during the torture sessions (p. 57). Officers did not like the mentioned kind of popular songs, but they liked classical music, González remembers. The music played during the session was decided by the agent in charge. In Villa Grimaldi, there were imprisoned and tortured an estimate of 5000 people (p. 56). The most common torture method used there among many others was "parrilla" (barbeque) where naked victims were tied to a metallic bed and given electric shocks. Other torture methods used there included hanging, cutting, beating, sometimes electric shocks added, and keeping the detainee's head under dirty water or other liquid. Detainees' heads were placed in plastic bags until they were suffocating. There was also raping of women, even who were pregnant. The premises at the Villa Grimaldi included very small lockers for the breaking of the victims and keeping them totally isolated in the water tank called "Tower" (ibid.) In spite of such horrible cruelties, detainees were sometimes allowed for some fun by the agents, like swimming and singing Mexican revolutions songs in the summer nights of 1974 when the commanders and officers were away from the Villa Grimaldi, González remembers (p. 59).

It seems that music was used systemically in Chile prison camps and centres to camouflage the sounds of violence and torture (Chornik, 2013, pp. 52, 60). González remembers that the DINA (National Intelligence Directorate) agents like him used to take LPs from the houses of people they had breaking in including the stereo equipment and loudspeakers they were using at the DINA centres. Loud music was used during the interrogations, so that the sounds and screams of violence and torture would not be heard and recognised on the street outside the centres like the Irán street and José Domingo Cañas 1305 in Santiago, where he was contacted in his work. González himself worked at the Villa Grimaldi and Londres 38 centres in Santiago. The Irán street centre was even nicknamed as "La Discothéque" among the agents because they used very loud music and popular songs like mentioned *La Loca Maria* (Grazy Maria), *Rosa, Rosa* by Sandro, and *La Gallina de los Huevos de Oro* (The Hen of the Golden Eggs), among others all the time (ibid.). The centre on Irán street was also called as "La Venda Sexy" because the blindfolded detainees were systematically sexually abused there (p. 60). In the José Domingo Cañas 1305 centre, called as "Ollahue" in the DINA, they used music too and played "cueca", a traditional dance where the man is imitating a cock and following a woman as a hen insistently to hide the torture like punches, electric shocks, rapes, mock executions, suffocating, and burning (pp. 60, 64).

According to the testimony of former DINA agent "González", in the Irán street centre ("La Discothéque"), they did not call or think music as a sonic torture there in his opinion (Chornik, 2013, p. 60). He also reflected his memories that he did not know whether their detainees felt or thought about the use of music in the centre like La Discothéque. It is difficult to review this testimony because it seems as contractionary to his other knowledge of music used and things like torture done at the centres and camps during his work in Chile. The torturers and criminals, like war criminals, or agents, may not want to be charged themselves or testify against their colleagues. Also, they may want to belittle and deny their crimes and their own participation in them for the same reasons as well as their actions in prison may seem as unhuman and criminal that should be hidden even from themselves or from more publicity. As discussed by Chornik (ibid.), it stayed unclear whether "González" was a witness, a participant, or both, of the severe human rights violations during the Pinochet's regime (1973–1981) in the torture and concentration centres of Chile (p. 61). So, it is wise to keep in mind that not everything is always told correctly in this kind of testimonies; and not everything is wanted to be remembered afterwards as these memories and especially possible own participation in them may be embarrassing or even traumatic for the interviewed. Such testimonies and discussions may also have therapeutic meaning as a possibility of having some relief and correction for the victims in this case as he collaborated with the Amnesty International campaign of raising awareness what happened in Chile after being a DINA agent (pp. 60–61).

In the era of Greek Junta (1967–1974), there were also similar systematic use of music and sounds in prisons and camps (Papaeti, 2013a, 2013b). Interestingly, it was not considered as the "scientific torture" by some involved, even though there were also sleep, food, and drink deprivation, especially salty food, accompanied by the repeated loud music from March to November 1973 (Papaeti, 2013b, pp. 79–80). Some working at the Greek Special Interrogation Branch (EAT/ESA) at the time denied their participation of using such cruel methods like wires, sockets, and wood planks with nails, and argued that they only did beating with truncheon to the hands and legs (p. 80). However, this may also need critical reviewing of testimony, including possible belittling of participating in torture and other violations of humanity. As described earlier, frequently it is difficult to find evidence of torture because the evidence of it is not easy to achieve because of the possibly sanctions. Because of the possible juristic consequences, there may be also a culture of silence and not wanting to remember old things around the torture and genocides discussed. Like correctly pointed by Papaeti (2013b, p. 80), the use of physical and psychological deprivation was "on the cutting edge of interrogation techniques at the time"; they were similar to that used during the Greek Junta. Papaeti (ibid.) refers also to the earlier described CIA's (1963) KUBARK manual and how CIA disseminated these methods to the allied countries worldwide.

There is evidence of such collaboration with Greek as there were a CIA and NATO military barracks outside Athens from 1957, where people from communistic countries were interrogated and tortured by Greek officers (Papaeti, 2013b, p. 81). Later, many of the Greek officers were trained in the US; among them was Theodoros Thefylogianakos, the former director of Greek Military Police (ESA) in 1970–1972. Many survivors testified that the tormentors had bragged they were "scientist interrogators" who had studied psychological interrogation in the US (p. 82). Virginia Tsouderou, the member of Greek Parliament, testified the use of sounds in torture and that the "science was put in the hands of torturers" in Greek as the torture methods were taken from a NATO manual and school in Germany of "how to resist torture" according to her (ibid.). It is documented and uncontroversial that US supported the Junta that President Clinton apologised in 1999 during his visit of Greece (p. 81).

It seems possible that in some degree, music used in torture camps and centres in Chile could have been spontaneous use of music of the torturers. Maybe they used it to entertain themselves like music was used in the Nazi concentration camps. All the soldiers and agents may not have understood the full psychological depths of using music in tormenting other than masquerading the violence and torture. However, the use of music seemed to be systematic and humiliating for the detainees, so they just could not have ignored it. They even had fun of it like the name La Discothéque for the torture centre suggests. In fact, their practices seemed to be so unmoral that it could not be denied; so maybe they need some humour as defence to cope with their actions? Or as it seems, they just did not care a bit for the sufferings of their victims after all.

In Greece, the use of repeated music and a song like *Tarzan* for the purposes of sleep and physiological deprivation in addition to keeping detainees standing seemed to be very similar to Chilean camps and centres (Papaeti, 2013b, pp. 75–76). Also, another humiliating song like the *White, Red, Yellow, Blue* by Vicky Moscholiou, a song about the boats in the Aegean where the narrator wants to take her loved one, was used for the Navy Movement and high-ranking officer detainees at ESA (p. 76). This kind of repeated systematic use of songs in the prisons seems to come from some kind of understanding and learning of psychological deprivation and tormenting. In addition to the mentioned US and NATO trainings, and the CIA's (1963) KUBARK manual for interrogations, there were US, Canadian, and British scholars studying these methods for the CIA; and these methods were spread for the US allies including Greek and South American countries like Chile (Papaeti, 2013b, pp. 80–81).

Also, there were some Germans like the Nazi colonel and convicted paedophile Paul Schäfer involved in the operations of camps like Tejas Verdes in Chile, where the detainees had to sing national anthem every morning and afternoon according to the testimony of former agent "González" (Chornik, 2013, pp. 55–56, 60). Similar forced singing and torture occurred also in the Greek barracks of the Training Center of Military Police (KESA) according to the several testimonies (Papaeti, 2013b, pp. 76–78). Later, González recognised a similar use of music in the Nazi concentration camps as in the Chile camps when he visited them after leaving his job as an agent and escaping to Germany (pp. 54–55, 60–61). According to the testimonies of survivors, who did not disappear and die during the Pinochet regime, Schäfer was murdering political dissidents with neck shots and torturing them to death with raising up the volume of Wagner's music and electric shocks in the underground dungeons (Davison, 2010, p. 3).

In the light of the many documents, testimonies, and research of using music in interrogation, torture, exploiting, and for hiding the violence and humiliation of detainees, it has a long history in modern times (Brauer, 2016; Chornik, 2013; Papaeti, 2013a, 2013b, 2020). Evidently, it has continued, developed, and spread around the world before WWII and Nazi concentration camps. Especially, this relates to the post-WWII political climate and cold and hot wars against the communism in different countries like the examples of Greek and Chile in the history show. This led the US and its allies to develop, teach, and use non-touch interrogation methods including sounds and music for the detainees. According to the Ireland against UK court case of 1978 in the UK, these coercive physiological psychological deprivation methods were used in the War on Terror when 14 IRA prisoners were hooded, afforced to stand, exposed to noise, and their diets and sleep were reduced (Papaeti, 2020, p. 7). Even though in the European Commission of Human Rights report it was defined as torture, in the trial it was considered only as "inhuman and degrading treatment" (ibid.). The victims of these "enhanced interrogation techniques", which were authorised by ministerial order, suffered from many mild, medium, or severe psychiatric and psychosomatic issues in medical reports (ibid.).

These methods originating from the 1960s' studies and mentioned in CIA's (1963) KUBARK manual were continued to be taught to some military personnel to resist them in the Survive-Evade-Resist-Escape (SERE) programme (Cusick, 2013, pp. 275–276). Later, after 11 September 2001, terrorist attacks in New York, these methods were used again in the War against the Terrorism and the prison like Guantanamo and Camp Cropper in Baghdad (Cusick, 2013). It also seems that at least in Chile, the dark psychological knowledge and notorious skills of Nazi German and SS in manipulating, interrogating, tormenting, and killing detainees, including music, were continued to be taught and practised along with the newer state-of-the-art deprivation techniques (Chornik, 2013). Finally, in 2009, President

Obama ordered the ending of such enchanted deprivation interrogation techniques in the US as discussed earlier.

However, music has been used in propaganda and manipulative purposes in other countries and cultures as well. In the former Eastern Bloc countries and Soviet Union there was no freedom of thinking and expression of oneself including music and other art forms. For example, in Russia, the recent development has gone towards a similar non-democratic system again where there is no freedom of press or expression of opinion. The current conflict against Ukraine is only allowed to call as the "special operation" in Russia officially; calling it a war, which it really is in the eyes of Ukrainians and their losses, Europeans, and the US among the most of countries, will cause sanctions in Russia. There is information how Russian military forces have tortured their Ukrainian prisoners of war using music as a part of their maltreatment, propaganda, and re-education (Julkunen, 2024): One Ukrainian prisoner of war, military musician Volodmyr, has described recently how Ukrainian detainees were beaten continuously without reason by the guards. They were also forced to stand 10–12 hours a day, practically whole day excluding the time for sleep between 2 and 6 am their breakfast (p. 10). A part of the day programme in prison was learning of the Russian folk poetry and military achievements while the Russian national anthem was played loudly every day (p. 13). During his 20-month imprisonment, Volodmyr lost 40 kg from his weight that changed his appearance so drastically that her spouse Inna could hardly recognise him. Volodmyr's family, Inna and children, as well as Inna's mother escaped from Mariupol to Finland as refugees during the imprisonment of Volodmyr (p. 14).

In Vietnam, refugees were exposed to nationalistic propaganda that affected their musical experiences (Reyes, 1999). In the Islamic countries, music and dance have been considered as sinful, and therefore they are not allowed to practise publicly until recently (LeVine, 2009). Currently, in China, it has been reported by Australian Strategic Politic Institute to existing prison camps where detainees have been tortured and re-educated from their religion, language, and culture (Ortamo, 2024, pp. 1–4). According to an interviewed woman "Aigul" escaped from China who had been in of one such camps as a Kazak minority, they had to memorise Chinese law, history, and songs where China and communistic party were appraised. In the evenings, detainees needed to sit on a stool watching TV propaganda of the president Xi Jinping. If the detainee failed in a lesson or broke the rules, there were penalties like a dark restriction cell or torturing in a "Tiger Chair" where the victims were chained from legs and hands 75 hours while their brains were "burnt" with some equipment above their heads. Interviewed herself had a penalty of forced standing in the glass room (pp. 9–10). Similar testimonies of the unhuman treating of people in camps, where 18 detainees lived in a 20-square cell, have been described by other survivors and in the revealed documents (ibid.).

In spite of the fact that the torturing and using of enchanted interrogation methods, including music, are not allowed anymore, there seems to be continuing of such dark operations and manipulating people with music. There seems to be development of new technologies and approaches producing sounds, lights, and pain in war, non-touch methods of interrogation, violence, and torture. Next, it will be discussed with the examples of survivors` experiences how it affected their musical experiences then and afterwards. Traumatised refugees with experiences of manipulative use of music as propaganda and violence may come to seek help where they need understanding of their traumas that relate to sounds, music, and their identities. In this, the research and documentation of such experiences is helping their rehabilitation and therapy after years or even decades of their traumatic events. In addition, building a psychological theory of what happened, their experiences relating to music and sounds, consciously and unconsciously, may help them to regain their lives and music in a more positive way. The possibilities to testify and speak about such experiences with anyone are important but also in-depth therapy and treatment are needed. Also, the possibilities of new positive transforming experiences of music with peers and music therapy may be important in working through and recovering from their traumas.

3.5 Transformed Experiences of Music, Violence, and Trauma

Possible consequences of violence, torture, and propaganda are altered music experiences for the detainees and refugees during the violence, imprisonment, and afterwards (Alanne, 2010, 2014b, 2023; Brauer, 2016; Cloonan & Johnson, 2008; Cusick, 2013; Grant, 2013; John, 1991/2001; Naliwajek-Mazurek, 2013; Papaeti, 2013a, 2013b, 2020). In traumatic experiences of refugees and asylum seekers, music may represent sad memories of their imprisonment, violence, and suffering that are related to the cruelty and political persecution of oppressive government in the home country. As a result, they may not want to listen to the music of their home country as it brings negative feelings and even dissociated experiences of violence and torture in their minds (Alanne, 2010, 2014b). Then, psychologically music may be experienced as a persecuting bad object where the former negative experiences and feelings of imprisonment, interrogation, and torture are projected. In such a traumatised music experience, positive associations relating to music as a good object that is bringing pleasure and positive thoughts are transformed into the negative ones (Alanne, 2023). Earlier positive associations, memories, and imagery of nationality, home country, and its culture may be even avoided because of the traumatic experiences and losses.

Refugees, especially young people, may like to identify more with the Western culture and its music as something that associated with hope and freedom instead of gloomy experiences relating to their former national culture and old values connected with it (Alanne, 2010, LeVine, 2009). National music and culture may have been the symbols of oppressing government and dictators that have been used to re-educate the detainees and citizens systematically like described earlier (Alanne, 2010; Brauer, 2016; Chornik, 2013; Klause, 2013; Papaeti, 2013a, 2013b). It may have been even considered as a sort of music therapy and psychotherapy for the communists and political opponents in camps by the oppressors like publicly expressed in the speech of colonel Ladas in 1970 during the Greek Junta (Papaeti, 2013a, pp. 37–38).[13] National music and culture may have also been emphasised in the politics, education, and used as a part of propaganda to manipulate in prisons and camps of the victims (Chornik, 2013; Ortamo, 2024; Papaeti, 2013a). Similar, ethnic, and folk music or art music inspired by them may also be favourite music of such regimes that they are also representing as a symbol of their force and politics (Chornik, 2013; Ortamo, 2024; Papaeti, 2013a). This kind of music like patriotic military music and forced singing and listening of them has been used in humiliating and tormenting the detainees (Chornik, 2013; Klause, 2013; Papaeti, 2013a).

In such circumstances of forced singing or listening of nationalistic folk songs, for example, the earlier good representations of music may have transformed into negative representations of music as a bad object in the refugees' experiences (Alanne, 2014b, 2019b, 2023; Chornik, 2013; Klause, 2013; Papaeti, 2013a). These transformed negative experiences towards music may relate to the music in general as the bodily experiences of pain and exhaustion while being forced to sing and work simultaneously in the Nazi concentration camp with popular songs, for example (Brauer, 2016, pp. 10–12). This kind of singing and marching is a long military tradition that seemed to be used to deceit the prisoners with positive feeling and impression as well as for the villages and people the prisoners passed (p. 11). However, this singing of popular songs at the time was not only positive therapy for all the detainees like in some experiences but also a part of the violence as the continuous forced singing was also physically exhausting and mentally anguishing for the detainees in Sachsenhausen, one of the re-education concentration camps for the people not fitting the National Socialistic ideology beginning in the 1930s (pp. 10, 12). Singing in hunger and standing in attention in prison yard in any weather for hours took the energies much needed for the survival in the camps.

As discussed earlier relating to the use of music as a deception by the Nazis, it seems that the music and singing in the concentration and termination camps appeared to have many purposes, to keep and speed up the work of the forced labour with entertaining them and their guardians as well as increase their humiliation and suffering with music. Also, the bodies of the detainees seemed to be deceived as the positive energy of music vitalising their work and marching was physically used to increase their exhaustion and stress until they collapsed according to the many memories of the survivors. One survivor of the Sobibor camp is describing that "The SS men were interested in keeping up our spirit, so that we should not be depressed and we would work better" (Moreno, 1999, p. 5). The purpose of this was, according to his testimony cited, "that we should not feel that were doomed for extermination and think about an uprising" (ibid.).

One German Jew survivor Hans Reichman considered collective singing as effective physical and mental torture. He remembers that if the detainees did not

[13] See Sect. 3.4 "Deceitful Musical Experiences in Prisons and Camps" for more discussion of the Colonel Ladas and the use of music in the prisons and camps during the Greek Junta.

sing the "Juvivalera" loudly enough, they had to sing it again even though they did not feel like it as jubilation to sing it loud melodically laughing like in jubilation in the freeze (Brauer, 2016, p. 13). Their faces were numb and like masks in the dark; they did not know how many songs they still had to sing. Reichman and other detainees experienced this singing manoeuvre as "drudgery" and there was no doubt about its "evil purposes" that it was intended to be so according to him (ibid.). So, it seems that there were intentions to keep some hope for the detainees with music to fully exploit their energies and labour as well as sadistically punish and torment them with forced singing to physically exhaust and break them for extermination purposes.

As there were always present the possibility of violence and death with noises, gunshots, machines, shouts, smells, in the concentration camps, for example, music and sounds may trigger bodily reactions, flashbacks, nightmares, and alertness as the post-traumatic stress reactions in refugees. In the experiences of survivors of torture and violence, loud noises are often associated with traumatic experiences, memories, and fears that music may trigger. This may be the reason why the traumatised refugee does not want to listen to music or cannot concentrate to it anymore (Alanne, 2010, 2023). However, in music psychotherapy this may be possible which may help to transform the traumatised experience of music and build communication and trust with music as the goals of rehabilitation (Alanne, 2010; Beck, 2019; Castaneda et al., 2018). Also, other kinds of musical activities in the context of music therapy and as the hobbies may help the refugee traumatised clients in general which is discussed in the end of chapter (Beck, 2019; Beck et al., 2021; McFerran et al., 2020; Orth et al., 2004; van der Kolk, 2014). One important goal of such therapeutic use of music in the treatment, rehabilitation, and education of different aged refugees would be returning and transforming the traumatised negative music and sound experiences into the positive experiences (Alanne, 2010, 2014b, 2018, 2019b, 2023).

As described earlier, the survivors of Nazi concentration camps remembered that there was always music in the soundscape of camps for many purposes to entertain or masquerade the shootings and screams. Music and singing were also used according to a military tradition in marching to keep up the positive spirit, rhythm, and the direction of work that were conducted by the Nazis with the force (Brauer, 2016, pp. 11, 14). For example, if the guards did not like the singing of the marching detainees or when they did not know the song, there were punishments like *Strafsingen* (punitive singing) where the detainees needed to be "practicing and practising again the songs that would be sung during the march out and back again", Adam König, a former political prisoner described (ibid., p. 14).[14]

One survivor, Aleksander Kulisiewicz, has called this kind of manoeuvres as "musical sadism" where the song was "painful contrast to reality" in increasing the humiliation, exhaustion, and suffering of detainees (Brauer, 2016, p. 15). Another

[14] Compare the earlier description of similar "punitive sports" by the Nazis where music was also used to torment the detainees as well as with the "singin horses" manoeuvre (Brauer, 2016; John, 1991/2001).

concentration survivor Leopold Kozlowski considered that the Nazis destroyed the experience of music abusing it like "a game" where they could happily shoot and murder accompanied with it (Naliwajek-Mazurek, 2013, p. 44). The shooting "sounded nice" for the Nazis "with music in the background" (ibid.). This made the musical experience different and emotionally ambivalent for the detainees as they could not fully enjoy it while listening, singing, and performing it. For musicians like Kozlowski, it did not feel like music "with a capital M", as he described, even though playing in the camp saved his life (ibid.). Similar ambivalent experiences relating to music as an entertainment in the as-if false life were others like some sick detainees in the infirmary who did not want to hear the orchestra playing music for them but instead shouted that they wanted to die in peace (Moreno, 1999, p. 8). For some survivors, music like Mozart's Sonata in A Major played by violinist Jacques Stroumsa was an experience that was enthusiastically remembered and thanked for him even 30 years later (Brauer, 2016, p. 23). For others like Szymon Laks, music like marches played regularly at the gate of Auschwitz was musical violence that "demoralized the poor wretches" instead of keeping their sprits (ibid.).

The writer Primo Levi, another survivor of Nazi concentration camps, experienced the marching tunes in the camp as blood freezing in his veins when he heard or remembered them years after. They made him conscious how lucky he was because he could escape and survive from Auschwitz (Moreno, 1999, p. 8). One detainee described the listening of happy songs in the camp as "heartbreaking" because "it reminded us so much of normal life … the life that other people still led" (ibid.). There were also experiences of envy for the orchestra members who had some privileges like more food and less work. However, in the end many orchestra members had the same fate of death like the other detainees even though many also survived because of their musical talents and skills (John, 1991/2001; Moreno, 1999; Naliwajek-Mazurek, 2013). Even though playing in a camp orchestra seemed to increase the possibility to survive and at least live a bit longer, it caused guiltiness in some musicians (John, 1991/2001; Moreno, 1999; Naliwajek-Mazurek, 2013). Also, the orchestra members or singers were aware that the detainees like Jewish children were going to die, and they felt helpless, shame, and despair as they could not warn them when they were selected for gas chambers (Brauer, 2016; Moreno, 1999). Sometimes detainees singing and marching as a part of the general deception saw even their own relatives and friends going to the gas (Moreno, 1999, pp. 5–6). Also, singing, dancing, or playing nice songs and pieces for the Nazis to cheer up or comfort them during or after their killing was a torturing experience for the detainees (Brauer, 2016; Moreno, 1999; Naliwajek-Mazurek, 2013).

It has been argued by the survivors and researchers that this forced playing and singing was demoralising for the detainees as they could not themselves choose the music and the time it was played (Brauer, 2016; John, 1991/2001; Moreno, 1999; Naliwajek-Mazurek, 2013). This was also the objective of the Nazis to increase the humiliation, suffering, and exhaustion by torturing the detainees with music. According to researcher Brauer (2016, p. 23), Nazis used music like marches as a symbol of their "absolute power". With music and sounds they could penetrate the "mindful body" of the detainees who were unable to avoid or resist them (ibid.). Psychologically, Nazis were able to affect the detainees with music that moved their feelings and bodies involuntarily. As Brauer (ibid.) argues, in such a way Nazis could pass the control of their bodies and minds. Currently, it is known how music affects the neuro and limbic systems of the brain making conscious the presence of music with its chilling effect and startle reflex (Alanne, 2010, 2023; Christensen, 2019; Levitin, 2007; Rose, 2004). They can be described as auto-affects how people are moved by their senses and experiences in their bodies. I have called this non-verbal level of musical experience in body as the presentational knowledge of music and arts, whereas the symbols, memories, and imagery related to music are verbal representational knowledge of music respectively (Alanne, 2014a, 2016a, 2016b, 2020, 2023, p. 65; Blum et al., 2023).

Nazis were attacking the physical bodies of detainees with violence, hunger, and exhausting work that arose fear, rage, and helplessness, and while simultaneously singing and marching, these experiences were mixed with the positive feelings and memories of music (Brauer, 2016, p. 23). In such a way prisoners were forced to listen or sing music in despair and exhausted state that was psychologically shattering for some detainees as they could not even control their feelings and bodies (p. 24). Music seemed to transform their experience of despair, pain, and suffering with the contrast of their happier life in the past that assaulted their identity, dignity, and even the hope for the future purposively (ibid.). According to Brauer, who is also referring the researcher Wolfgang Sofsky in this context, this assault to the social body of music creates pain and despair that are linked to the physical body that begins to fragment and loses its will to survive and finally give up.

As described in the earlier paragraph and vignettes, with violent or sadistic use of music, Nazis seem to prolong their absolute power to the mind, body, and social/situational aspects of detainees' being with music that they could not escape or control themselves. This left them even in more vulnerable situations as music and sounds passed their psychological defence mechanisms of ego through body. It created a holistic attack for their personalities and bodies where the purpose was to break and exhaust them to their deaths finally. For survivors of such torture with music, the embodied musical experience may change from the former pleasurable experiences of music to hurtful ones (Alanne, 2010, p. 86). This may affect their general attitude towards music in their life and therapy when traumatised or tortured may not want to listen to music because music is involuntarily bringing forth their fear reactions connected to their mindful bodies (ibid.).

I have earlier considered that logic of music in violence is asymmetrical because it is experienced and used differently from its original purposes (Alanne, 2010, pp. 48, 51). For example, in the many described vignettes of using music as torture in prisons, interrogations, or camps, the message of the song like with the romantic love songs of popular music, the purpose of the music has not often been to comfort or bring pleasure in detainees. Instead, such popular music has been used to provide directly the opposite meaning for the music to humiliate the detainees with cruel jokes and parody of music. Even a children song *I Love You* sung by the character Barney the Purple Dinosaur was used in the Iraq War according to the "non-touch" manipulative tactics of "ego down" and "fear up" in the interrogation manuals of CIA (Cusick, 2006, p. 3). Often also the religious identity of detainees is attacked by forced singing, listening, or playing of spiritual music or music that is otherwise insulting like sexually the religious values of detainees. Even the use of music per se may be insulting for some Muslims, especially Western music, because music may be forbidden as sinful or like argued by former ayatollah Khomeini because it blunts the mind with its pleasure like a drug (LeVine, 2009, pp. 217–219, 224–227).

In this context, using Western hard rock music like Metallica or AC/DC as a weapon or other pop/rock/rap music with explicit contents of sexuality, nudity, hedonism, and substance abuse may feel like a direct psychological threat for the identities and egos of the people who have grown up in such religious Islamic cultures. Like described, for such a detainee, even the pleasure, rhythms, and the embodied feelings brought forth with music may be experienced as dreadful as drugs and satanic powers coming in. This is the goal of tormentor with the ego-down technique to go to the mind of detainees through their bodies with music and weaken the ego's capability for the self-protection and sustainment of one's identity. Using music in such a forced way, as a bad object, against one's religious beliefs and identity is cruel violent use of music as a weapon and unethical. However, not every Muslim considers heavy metal or other Western music as sinful or bad, but as something that is providing hope and a way of expressing their hard feelings towards life in the totalitarian systems (LeVine, 2009). In spite of the circumstances, music is continued to be practised underground, privately, or in terms of the totalitarian systems in the Islamic cultures as it is possible even though it may even endanger the lives of musicians (ibid.).

There is a clear pattern of using absolute power for the breaking of the detainees' own will and ego with music. The techniques used by the US forces during the Iraq War and the War against Terrorism were asymmetrical use of music and tactics in war like the strategies of terrorists (Report of the Senate Select Committee on Intelligence Committee Study of the Central Intelligence Agency`s Detention and Interrogation Programme, 2014). Using methods of enhanced interrogation later prohibited by President Obama was a torturing and dehumanising practice of war and music, and against the human rights, international laws, and agreements of war (ibid.). In the War against the Terrorisms after 911 terrorist attacks similar, symmetrical methods were revisited like in the Cold War against communism. Music was not used for therapy of pain, mental issues, and traumas like in WWII, where music therapy has its roots in the rehabilitation and treatment of war veterans (Alanne, 2010, 2023; Lee, 2016; O'Connell, 1990; Sullivan, 2007).

Like in the earlier-mentioned US War Department document of the World War II, music was considered as "one of the most effective vehicles for bringing a group together, for releasing the emotions, and for creating a spirit of fellowship and spirit de corps" (Sullivan, 2007, p. 288). In addition, music listening was described to broaden the interests of soldiers and increase their sense of wellbeing (ibid.). This kind of use of music in transforming the experiences of troops is different than the described strategies of using music in prisons, interrogations, and wars after WWII, where the music's operational function seemed to be more asymmetrical use of music as a weapon. In this, it seemed to continue the strategies developed in the

Soviet Union Gulags and Nazi concentration camps of 1930s in Germany and during WWII (Brauer, 2016; John, 1991/2001; Klause, 2013; Moreno, 1999; Mensfelt, 2017; Naliwajek-Mazurek, 2013).

Music was systematically used for many purposes, elevating the group sprits as well as in empowering and keeping the hunger of troops by the Nazis. This psychological understanding of transforming and elevating powers of music was also used to systematically deceit the detainees in addition to keeping their spirits in slavery while exhausting them to their deaths. It seems that with the asymmetrical use of music as therapy and weapon, Nazis deceit even the bodies of detainees because music passed the psychic defences of the detainees increasing their suffering and exhaustion. Music also seemed to keep the pain and hunger way like a drug that fooled the minds and bodies of detainees to carry on their slavery work even though they would have needed crucial rest.[15] Currently, it is known that music increases the endorphin production, a form of endogenic opioids, in the brain that provides pleasure and reduces pain, for example (Alanne, 2010, 2014a, 2023; Christensen, 2019; Kreutz et al., 2013; Swallow, 2002).

Music can also be viewed as the acoustemological object that is providing meaning from the acoustic environment (Feld, 2015, p. 12). It is a way of knowing and being in the world with music and sounds as they are vibrating with the body and the senses of listening and sounding. As such a situational experience, musical and sounding experience is relational being with the sounds like knowing and learning from the nature sounds as described by Feld (ibid.). His concept "acoustemology" is coming from the words "acoustic" and "epistemology". Feld came up with the idea when he was doing ethnographic studies in the Bosavi rainforest region of Papua New Guinea beginning from the 1976 (p. 15). During his studies he noticed and learnt how Bosavi people's songs were not just adaptation to the acoustic rainforest environment but how they had mapped the forests with their focalisations. The songs were attuned with the sounds of nature and sung from the bird's point of view, for example. Even the children could easily and quickly differentiate the sounds of forest like which bird was singing and where the sounds were coming from (p. 18). Children also knew about the location of bird's food, nest, and partners which they had already learnt by coinhabiting with them in the rainforest ecosystem. Thus, as argued by Feld, co-living within the rainforest and its sounds became a transformative learning process through singing for the Bosavi people during their lives (pp. 18–19).

Suzanne G. Cusick (2013) has studied the acoustemology of detention of how described enchanted interrogation methods and torturing with sounds and music affected the interviewed former prisoners of the War on Terror. In contrast to the transformative knowing or learning as sounds or through sounds that happens in

[15] This is like the biochemical strategy of Blitzkrieg War, where soldiers were fighting and keeping up their energies with the powerful amphetamine derivative Pervitin developed in the Nazi Germany. Also, Finnish special military intelligence forces had these tablets from the ally German during WWII. It enabled them to ski and escape without the need of rest or sleep. Some of them became drug addicts after the war.

symmetry with the nature and in the co-relational attuning or opposing to its sounds and places, as argued by Feld (2015, p. 19), the acoustemology of detention is asymmetric and forcing the use of sounds. According to Cusick (2013, p. 276), it is "ultimate violence that batters prisoners' bodies, shatters (however temporarily) the capacity to control the acoustical relationality that is the foundation of subjectivity". Cusick is referring to the ego-down experience that is the goal of tormentor where the ego cannot control anymore the sounding objects and the environment which may produce a chaotic experience of losing one's boundaries. With the loud sounds, detainees are arrested from all their senses of privacy as they cannot even think because of the blasting sounds. At the same time, they are isolated from the others with sounds and music, however paradoxically feeling not private, Cusick is arguing (ibid.).

In this kind of acoustemological situation, I have argued that the former pleasure-providing good objects of music and sounds are transforming into persecuting bad objects in the senses of self (Alanne, 2010, 2023). It may mean even that the victim loses one's self-integrity and regress to the non-organised chaotic thinking of part-object experience of the early self-experience. This can bring annihilation anxiety and show as terror of not being able to control one's experience anymore like within the psychotic experience. In the clinical situation of psychotherapy, a traumatised client may not want to listen or produce music because there is resistance of ego that is trying to sustain the object constancy of self-experience. It has been detected that neonates are producing a Moro reflex where their hands and feet are grabbing in when they are hearing a sudden loud noise (Alanne, 2014a, 2020, 2023; Kohut & Levarie, 1950/1978; Lehtonen, 1996). Later this reflex vanishes in a normal development; however, the bodily effect and the feeling of fear remain as when we are hearing a sudden siren, a gunshot, a slamming door, or loud music that our brain cannot predict (Alanne, 2023, pp. 102–105; Levitin, 2007, p. 186). The loud sounds are activating the limbic system, amygdala, and increasing the adrenocorticotropic (ACTH) stress hormone in the autonomous nervous system (Alanne 2010, 2014a, 2020, 2023; Christensen 2019; Lehtonen 1996; Solms & Turnbull 2002/2018; Swallow 2002; van der Kolk 2014).

Thus, in the acoustemological situation of detainee, music and sounds are like constant thunders, predators, and other threats of the nature that one tries to predict and avoid (Levitin, 2007, p. 186). However, in the nature environment one knows through habituation that the thunderstorm and sounds of it will pass eventually, but in the acoustic situations of prison like in the War on Terror, a detainee could not know, learn, and avoid the loud sounds, or even hear one's own voice or the others (Cusick, 2013; Levitin, 2007). This is an unnatural situation because humans are communicating with each other using sounds. Even foetuses are in relationship with sounds and feeling their vibrations in their bodies as well as sensing the body of the mother and its rhythms (Grassi, 2021; Siltala, 2014). This kind of communication through sounds, vibrations, touches, and feelings of bodies with others continues in human relationships for the whole life. We are also sensing music with vibrations in our bodies and how it is reverberating with our minds and bodies even only by listening or feeling it. In a way, music is not an object, a thing, in this context, because we are sensing and feeling it within our bodies as a subjective experience when music is felt, heard, and sung through body like argued by Ruud Welten (2002) (Alanne, 2010, p. 15).

Thus, music and sounds are in the core of human self-experience and subjectivity that are disrupted in musical manipulations of detainees, in isolating and perturbing their bodies as objects. This is one reason why the detainees and victims of Nazi concentration camps felt that the music of Nazis had no soul and they could not relate to it as it was like a game. It is also possible that some of the detainees were fighting against that their bodies were treated as the objects of tormenting with music that they could not enjoy. This probably required exhausting psychic resistance and use of defences like repression, splitting, and restriction of feelings that made them vulnerable to traumatisation. According to Roger Kennedy (2020, p. 7), "music can create a sense of wholeness or can confuse or even fragment us by its power". It can have multiple meanings and provide mixed emotional states like giving force for battle, sexual arousal, lament for the dying, sense of social belonging, and imaginative world of privacy (ibid.). Understanding music requires holistic and empathic attuning into music of how it can affect the mind, body, and the situation of the person simultaneously (Alanne, 2010, p. 81).

Using music asymmetrically is violent use of music as it is objectifying of the subject with music that is not considering the possible emotional, physical, or contextual effects of music for the person. Doing so, it is breaking the norms of "music as usual". Therefore, it is feeling irritating for the people because their brains, bodies, and minds cannot synchronise it as the regular sounds that they have learnt through former experiences and find their changes pleasurable (Levitin, 2007, pp. 191–192). In fact, the detainees may find the forced music bringing aversion in their experiences. Cusick (2013) is describing how one detainee "Z" at Camp Cropper in Baghdad interviewed by her first felt continuous blasting of music by the US forces as annoying but later considered that it as a "war of wills" and "a personal attack" against him (p. 281). He was using music and sounds from the outside, guards talking, practising shooting, doors slamming, and people going and returning from interrogations for his benefit. He was trying to create his own imaginable world in the unknowable space where he was locked by talking with himself or with the guards, telling jokes and stories to himself. He was plucking his ears with fingers to hear himself through music. With this kind of activity, he was trying to keep his acoustic agency and create a mental image from outside the cell as well as figure out the time of day. This was fighting against of interrogators and their systematic goal to break the mind of detainee with isolating music when he could not hear outside or hear himself. He found it difficult to resist the unpredictable "jumping" of hard rock, country, and rap music, and especially when he knew some song from the outside and started singing along, he knew they "once again began destroying me" (pp. 280–281).

With irregularities of food, sounds, and music, jumps from the predictable usual hard rock in the morning, country music in the afternoon, and rap in the evening programme of Armed Forces Radio, the interrogators tried to confuse the temporality of detainees (Cusick, 2013, p. 281). Also, Z suffered from fatigue and hunger that distracted his vocalised resistance and then "boom, it hits you", the devastating feeling he was trying to fight against and which he could not describe more thoroughly (p. 282.). It seems that this was the goal of the interrogators to break the psychic defences of detainees with the enhanced methods of interrogating and sense deprivation, torture, described and studied already in the described KUBARK (CIA) manual of interrogation in the 1960s. This kind of use of music is asymmetrical to the bodily and daily rhythms of a person as well as to their feelings towards music. It is breaking the possibility to learn and enjoy the music, and "groove" with it like Cusick (ibid., 281) notices as the music styles changed unpredictably. This kind of ambient music may probably feel annoying because you cannot relax with it but maybe achieve a quite opposite experience to be unable to concentrate, for example. It may also produce stress to the minds and bodies of detainees if one cannot calm down in the evening or sleep in the night as the pulses and sounds of music are vibrating and affecting their bodies. This seems to be like the musical manipulation of Nazis in the concentration camps of how to confuse the bodies of detainees, exhaust them, and break their identities as discussed by Cusick (ibid.).

In Guantanamo, musical torture was used in interrogation as described by Cusick (2013, p. 283): One interviewed "X" was chained in a stress position with strobe lights and loud music. X was also isolated during the interrogations. X could not move when he was forced to be on the tips of his toes, hands beneath and behind his knees, and he could move backwards or on sides to get relief and weight from his toes. When X was put in his place during the interrogations, the lights went out and music was turned on. Music almost always heavy metal or hard rock. During these sessions of musical torture and sense deprivation, X was left alone except with sounds and sight sometimes for five minutes, sometimes for three days he estimated. According to the videotaped interview of X after his releasement, the purpose of the interrogators was to prevent him from concentrating to his mind and distracting himself from the physical pains of stress position that made the pains more vivid in his experiences. He remembered that the experience made him feel like "going mad" (ibid.). After the music-accompanied torture and induced pain, he was uncuffed, music and strobe were turned off, lights were back, and he was marched cuffed again to his isolation cell until another interrogation (pp. 283–284). After this he was feeling very exhausted, felt asleep until waking to the feeling being "like crap … like you're not yourself … depressed" (p. 284).

This kind of methods was also used to the detainee "Y" held in the "dark prison" of CIA near Kabul (Cusick, 2013, pp. 285–286). Y was forced to listen repeatedly to the tape of music in his imprisonment. Y described that looped tape was "not music music" as it consisted of "very aggressive, intrusive, annoying sounds" (p. 286). There were breaks of only a few seconds without sounds as the tape was turned over or otherwise set to start again. The same sounds repeated all over again so loud that he could not hear himself. During the few seconds of silences, he was trying to listen to the sounds of other detainees and communicate with them in the dark which was usually difficult, and he usually received only some calls back. In addition to the darkness, there came aggressive repeated sounds from the speakers that appear to be mounted to the walls of cell, there was cold, and the food and water were provided scarcely in the unpredictable timing. Later, at Guantanamo, Y experienced music as physiologically and psychologically even more violent and harmful than in the dark prison: "Like your body is being bombarded with something—in Guantanamo the music affects your mind, your body, your senses—It's like you're being hit with a hammer, din, din din" (p. 288). In Guantanamo, it seems that there were used even bigger loudspeakers directed at the detainees from the outside of cell that produced even ten times sound than in the dark prison according to the interview of Y. Y described that he was unable to read, focus, or concentrate in mental disorientation produced by the forced music soundscape (pp. 287–288).

In this kind of use of music and sounds, the physical vibration and acoustical force was used against the bodies and minds of detainees. Like Cusick (2013, p. 288) argues, music and sounds in the interrogations and imprisonments of detainees were used to disrupt the human reflexive being with sounds in the acoustical environment to "construct and sustain subjectivity". This I have called as asymmetrical use of music and sounds that in this context are used as a weapon and not as music as usual; the interviewed detainee Y in the dark prison called it as "not music music" (p. 286). Similarly, one earlier-mentioned holocaust survivor Kozlowski did not feel forced music of Nazis as music "with a capital M" but like a "game" (Naliwajek-Mazurek, 2013, p. 44).

It is a sadistic use of music like the name given by the Nazis for this kind of manoeuvres as punitive singing or sports is suggesting. Music was used as a power, even as an ultimate power argued by Brauer (2016), and acoustical monopoly that is no longer only a metaphor and use of symbol "but power itself" as argued by Cusick (2013, p. 288). It is not a play or musing like the word music suggests for the listener but rather its opponent—transformed sadistic violence—that is vibrating within the flesh and bones as well as messing the mind like a repeated cruel joke. With pervading and detaining sounds persons are reduced to the objects with no subjectivity as they no longer cannot control their privacy with fingers in their ears (p. 288).

In a way, with music, the tormentors are impenetrating into the soul of person, how Kennedy (2020, p. 13) has described the effects of music and its power to affect the tangible emotions and the inner experiences. Other kinds of sense deprivations may be easier to fight back to some degree, like mentioned lack of food, water, temperature, sleep, sanitation, genital privacy, or prayers used in interrogation centres besides music (Cusick, 2013. pp. 288–289). With music and sounds, and the "acoustical monopoly" of the interrogators, the psychological strength of detainees to sustain their identities and fight back was affected (ibid.).

The detainees were not only tormented and disturbed with harmful sounds, but they were also listened and reported in the acoustical surveillance for every sound they made for the interrogators. This reduced their "acoustical agency" as argued by Cusick (2013, p. 288), when the detainees could not use music and sounds, even speak, and communicate with others or even with themselves. They could not sustain their personal dialogue with themselves or express their musical needs by singing, dancing, or grooving with music and sounds within their bodies because music was jumping unpredictably according to the terms of interrogators and their sensory deprivation and manipulation.

The detainees of US interrogation centres could not enjoy or use music as therapy or for their personal psychological protection because the loud sounds and stressful physical experiences made it impossible. In a way, music with an "M" that has soul and vitality for the person was taken away from them like the rest of their humanity in the detainment. Instead, with music and sounds their embodied experience of self was violently attacked and manipulated as a part of the ego-down strategies of interrogators.

Similar approaches of forced music listening were used at the Greek prison camps of Junta in 1967–1974 (Papaeti, 2013a, 2013b). A difference to the strategy of US forces during the War against Terrorism was that the goal of the blasting music played non-stop during the days at the camps was a sort of therapy and re-education of communists (Papaeti, 2013a, pp. 36–37). As discussed earlier, this musical re-education really had the agenda from the Junta like directly expressed by earlier-mentioned Colonel Ladas, the General Secretary of the Ministry of Interior, who was referring even to music therapy and its continuum from the antiquity until the present day in the form of "patriotic folksongs" that "sprang from the pure authentic emotions" (pp. 37–38).[16]

Therefore, patriotic folksongs and national-liberation songs were played constantly to the women at the Gyaros Prison Camp. One interviewed former detainee remembers as "terrible",—the morning wake-up with loud, blasting music: folksongs and national-liberation songs—Essentially they played what we loved. I can still dance ´Famous Macedonia`. I came from Macedonia. We had learned the dance at school and I loved it. But when this was taken by them … they appropriated as if they were the Greeks and we the non-Greeks" (ibid., p. 37).

This describes the asymmetry of musical experience of detainee how music once felt as positive experience transformed into a forced terrible experience that one does not belong to the same nationality. At the same time, the detainee continues, there were slogans like "this country will be saved because of the patriots who were send by God" or "don't forget that you are under the protection of Greek officers who will transforms you into real Greeks" (Papaeti, 2013a, p. 37). In this kind of "treatment", one is under the acoustic monopoly and idealism of the authority who are considering themselves as the allies of the God in the war against communism. Also, their protection is promised, and if they turn to good citizens, they will become real Greeks, which sounds like a totalitarian brainwash instead of therapy. Currently, this kind of use of music as a re-education of supreme authority and totalitarian regime seems to continue by China and Russia according to the recent testimonies and reports in public (Julkunen, 2024; Ortamo, 2024).

It is a form of cultural owing and intersectional use of music for oppressive purposes where folksongs and similar patriotic folklores and symbols are linked only

[16] See Sect. 3.4 "Deceitful Musical Experiences in Prisons and Camps" for more discussion of the Colonel Ladas and music during the Greek Junta.

with one ethnicity and their politics—a dictatorship. In society, this increases the feelings and thoughts of not belonging here, otherness, and fear. This seemed to be the message of Junta with music and slogans in the camps, so that the detainees would give up their own identities and sign a statement for the Junta, that "they have denounced their beliefs" so that they could leave the camps (Papaeti, 2013a, p. 37). The interviewed former detainee described how "all this unravelling with a music began to make us physically sick" (ibid.). When they heard the loudspeakers, they started to cover their ears with hands, she continued.

In the earlier-described situations of detainees held in Guantanamo and similar centres, the detainees were not able to protect themselves from hearing the noises and loud music as they were chained in the stress positions (Cusick, 2013). However, in both cases, as well as in the Nazi concentration camps, the victims of forced music listening or singing had physical experiences of sickness. This seems to relate also to the psychological experiences of being cheated or mistreated by the ones you had learnt to trust that they are following and respecting the laws. The same feelings of sickness seemed to also relate to the need to do something unmoral that is against their own will, identity, ethnicity, culture, and nationality like writing a false statement after torture in the Greek Camps (Papaeti, 2013a, p. 37). In the Nazi concentration camps, the fellow Jewish detainee musicians were forced to do wrong and play deceitfully for the other detainees who were coming from the transportations and led to the gas chambers, for example (Brauer, 2016; Moreno, 1999).

As a combined psychological and physical experience of sickness in addition to the social and moral notions of the pervert use of music and power against them, it must have increased the feeling of music and sounds as the persecuting bad objects in their experiences. The detainees tried to protect themselves with covering their ears and talking to themselves, so that they would survive psychologically and physically. This is like being in a paranoid-schizoid (PS) position of development and trying to split the experience of ego so that it would maintain its control and not regress to an unorganised position of development and chaotic experiences. Under continuing extreme stress, sense deprivation, and exhaustion, this could lead to the collapse of ego, dissociation, and cause even psychotic states with hallucinations. However, in that condition, the detainee probably would not be useful for the interrogators anymore. In the interrogation torturing that are often monitored by medical personnel like in Guantanamo, it seems not to be the case but the breaking of the victim until the breaking point of "going mad" like described by one interviewed former detainee of Guantanamo (Cusick, 2013, p. 288).

One former detainee of Greek Junta "F" described in his trial testimony his experiences of violence and constant same songs: "You felt like going grazy … In the end I had hallucinations. I thought the wall was a fridge and went to get a Coke. They hit me and their faces would transform. I thought that they were my friends and family.—And with all this, to hear this music 'The guys, the guys, the good buddies' [*We Will All Live* song] and 'I will go to the jungle with Tarzan' [*Tarzan* song]. When the torture time was up, for it never occurred at fixed times, they would play the song, 'Stefanos is dead, the good man' [*O Stefanos* song]" (Papaeti, 2013b, pp. 77–78).

Like correctly argued by Papaeti (2013b, p. 78), in the context of torture these songs, their lyrics, and their order were insulting for the victim as belittling and making a parody of him. At the same time his mind was manipulated with the repeating of these songs that brought fear like the *Tarzan* song seemed to be played as a sign for a torture session approaching and meeting the beasts of jungle. *We Will All Live* song played during the actual torture and beating seemed to symbolise the tormentors as the "buddies" and the "family" of victim with positive connotations and feelings. In the mind of F, this song may have also worked as some kind of psychic defence towards the sadistic violence and the tormentors because their faces transformed into the faces of his friends and family in the hallucinations. Thus, music at the same time appeared to be a kind of therapy for the F in my opinion because it created a positive illusion of family and good people around him. This may be compared to a temporary psychosis that can be a psychic escape and defence from the harsh reality the ego cannot confront. However, this also seemed to have a manipulative and betraying purpose to make the victim F to believe that the torturers are his friends and had the undertone "confess, say everything and then you can go, everything will be ok between us" (ibid., p. 78).

In the end of the torture session, the song *O Stefaanos* (1972) by Antonis Kalogiannis was played, which is about the death of good man Stefanos and friends mourning him (Papaeti, 2013b, p. 78). The order of other songs was not coincidence according to the experiences of F. Placing this song in the end of session seemed to underline the experience of F after torture. In addition, it appears to be a threat of violence and suggestion of possible death by the interrogators. It is similar song communication and manipulation with music that were used in the Greek Junta camps (Papaeti, 2013a). This approach of song communication, mocking, demeaning, insulting, and betraying was also used in the Nazi concentration camps as discussed earlier. Also, US forces in the War on Terror used song communication like the mentioned *I Love You* song by the Barney the Purple Dinosaur as an example.

Communication with songs is one of the key techniques in music therapy and music psychotherapy, where the words and feelings of song and their psychological meaning are sung, played, or talked together (Bruscia, 1987, 1998; Alanne, 2010, 2014a, 2023). When working with traumatised refugees and especially with those who have been possibly tortured, it is important to be very sensitive with the use of music and songs. They may have been a part of the oppressors' methods and manipulative song communication for the refugees during the imprisonment, interrogation, torture, and propaganda (Alanne 2010, 2014b, 2018; Cusick, 2006; Papaeti, 2013a, 2013b). As a result of this, the former experiences of music have been possibly changed like for the former detainee "F" of Greek Junta, who later became melancholic when listening to the music he heard in prison (Papaeti, 2013b, p. 78). One interviewed former detainee "B" of Greek Junta remembered his friend was also forced to listen to repeated music during his imprisonment; after his releasement he bought 15 LPs of that song and broke them on his knees (p. 77). The breaking of the records of torture music can be seen as a counteraction of song communication and symbolic resistance of the oppressors.

F also was afraid of choking experiences from the dry saliva in his larynx because of the forced singing during the imprisonment that traumatised him (Papaeti, 2013b, p. 78). It was very painful for him to testify this in the trial. Later, when interviewed for the research, he did not talk about it possibly because he was suppressing the traumatic experiences relating to music and his humiliation (pp. 78–79). Therefore, it is important for the music therapist, psychotherapist, or any other person treating refugees and torture survivors with music to assess the possibility of supressed traumatic memories relating to music. In the long-enough music psychotherapy process it may be possible to work through also this kind of traumas where they can be contained safely. When there are no possibility of continuous appointments and trauma therapy, then it may be better to try and avoid such strong experiences with music if possible. Instead, the more adequate goal for the treatment and use of music in the very short interventions would be trying to maintain and stabilise the experience of traumatised refugee and not retraumatise the client with music.[17]

The memories of music used by the interrogators or oppressive government in their propaganda or "re-education" of the camps may bring forth confusion and insecurity. One former detainee "C" of Greek Junta described his abuse and torture relating to music and a particular instrument of clarinet for the interviewer: "I am so fed up with the clarinet … had they put a clarinet player inside the isolation cell […] I would have said everything. They would not have to torture me, I would surrender myself entirely, so much I can't take it" (Papaeti, 2013a, p. 41). This strong experience and inversion towards the clarinet are relating to the use of it in the Greek folk music and dance tsamiko favoured by Junta in the collective memory of era (ibid.). It is an example of how particular music and even one instrument may become a symbol of oppression and violence in the minds of detainees. Music therapists or educators should be aware of the possibility of how the experiences of folk music in education may be different for the traumatised refugees. It may not be music as usual when it brings forth unsecure feelings, sad memories, or even traumatic experiences of the former homeland they had to leave (Alanne, 2010, 2014b, 2018, 2023; Reyes, 1999). The same goes with the education or therapy if they have included manipulative propaganda or forced learning and changing of behaviour or identity like at the prison camps after WWII in Makronisos and during the Junta in Greek (Papaeti, 2013a, 2013b).

There may be people of different ages who have traumatic experiences of music during the wars in history and current conflicts from around the world who are refugees, immigrants, or their children that have affected their experiences towards music in the family. The culture of one's homeland and the history of family as immigrants or refugees may be considered as something old that is not talked about. This also relates to the traumas and torture as shameful experiences that are repressed and avoided. Therefore, the refugees may not want to listen to music that could bring such memories and sad feelings from their past. There is not much research on

[17] See Chaps. 4 and 5 for more information and discussion of the music therapy methods and their goals with different clients.

the musical transfer of traumas to the other generations about how the later generations are experiencing the Greek folk music as an example.

It may be also possible that younger generations will find the music that once was used in the propaganda of oppressive positive again if they have not experienced the dark history of that music themselves. In this musicological research and music therapeutic work, there is a possibility to make a difference so that there would not develop musical or cultural transfer of traumas that would transform to generational traumas. Then, important to study and understand is whose way of remembering is represented in music and culture: trauma victims or perpetuators? Whose memories are right as the memory is a social phenomenon as well as political sometimes when considering refugees and detainees that have been manipulated and oppressed with music? (Välimäki, 2015, pp. 133–134).

From my own clinical experiences of music psychotherapy, I remember one client from Chile who could not listen to music anymore after detainment and torture. In music psychotherapy, he was first a bit afraid what I was doing with music to him. This was probably because of the torture and detainment experiences of how he had been treated and manipulated. After attending music psychotherapy and listening to music in a secure relationship, he was able to go to listen his children's concerts that were important for him. This was one of his own motives for music psychotherapy and an example also how music therapy may lessen the consequences of torture and trauma. It is also showing that music in the treatment may prevent cultural or musical traumas passing over generations if the parent can enjoy and support the musical hobby or career of their children. There is a discussion of development of negative musical identity and its continuation over generations as a burden if one feels that s/he is incompetent to sing, play, or understand music after negative music experiences at school (Alanne, 2017; Lehtonen et al., 2016). This negative experience and the feeling of incompetency in music may also transfer to the music therapy process with similar resistance towards music and unreluctance to play or participate in musical activities (Alanne, 2023, pp. 48, 86).

In music psychotherapy of traumatised refugees or torture survivors, this kind of resistance and doubt in the beginning of treatment is natural because of their traumatic experiences (Alanne, 2010, 2013, 2019b, 2023). They have affected into their capability of enjoying music and being in relationships which is why it is important for them to trust their therapist first. Then, the goal of music therapy or music education may be to return to capability to enjoy and consume music in their lives. However, it is good to remember that for many detainees, music was also giving hope, relief, and empowerment in their experiences. For example, in South Africa during the apartheid, music and songs in prison became life-affirming practice (Buis, 2013, p. 58). Songs often improvised between the detainees in their own language and lyrics brought hope and defiance. Many former detainees of Robben Island have told how music and dance were in a therapeutic role and enabled keeping up their identities against the brutal inhuman treatment (p. 56).

The former President of South Africa Nelson Mandela, a Nobel Peace Prize winner, like the earlier-mentioned President Barack Obama later, was also a detainee on Robben Island for a long period in his life during the apartheid (Buis, 2013, p. 58).

During his imprisonment he was often listening praising songs of him sung by other detainees. Music and dance were important for Mandela, and he cited songs and described musical activities like singing religious hymns with a priest from the prison in his autobiography (p. 61). As the president, Mandela was also known for dancing in his public appearances (p. 59). Songs like the *Nkosi sikelel` iAfrika* [God Bless Africa] were often sung on the Robben Island. In the minds of detainees, South African, and other African people it became a resistance song towards colonialism and apartheid (p. 61). After apartheid and the inauguration of Mandela in 1994, it was chosen as the part of national anthem in South Africa officially. Mandela has said that "music and dance make me feel alive" (p. 56). It reflects the importance of music and dance in the South African and African cultures in general, but also the elevating, empowering, and therapeutic effects of music and dance in his own experiences during his long imprisonment and apartheid (Buis, 2013).

In his memoirs, Mandela is describing how parodic songs were sung by the political prisoners like him in rivalry towards the criminals and the brutal system on Robben Island prison (Buis, 2013). This helped the political prison to "invert the power structure" in prison argued by Buis (2013, p. 62). In my opinion, political prisoners could protect themselves psychologically with songs that seemed to be psychotherapeutic objects for the prisoners (Alanne, 2016a, 2023). In this regard, music as humour and parody seemed to be also a personal structured defence and non-violent resistance of prisoners that helped them to keep their identities against the oppression (Alanne, 2016a). For example, the political prisoners were singing overt political songs like *Amajoni* that was ironically referring to the guerrilla soldiers (Buis, 2013, p. 62).

Other parodical political song mentioned by Mandela that the political detainees sung on Robben Island prison was the *Tshotsholoza* [Shoshloza]. According to Mandela, it talks about the struggle against the motion of train coming onwards. The name of song is onomatopoetic expression for the sound of train (ibid.). Symbolically, I think it was the expression of self with sounds that could be interpreted also as the resistance towards the steel wheels and cold mechanisms of oppressive system and apartheid that was driving on the people. On the other hand, sounds and songs as the expression of identity and will for freedom could have meant opponent force for the political prisoners symbolically that inverted the asymmetry of power structure in prison as argued by Buis (ibid.).

The songs, their expression with sounds, improvising, and communicating with them, seemed to also affect the acoustemology of prison as the rivalry sounds and symbolical signifiers in the space (Cusick, 2013). Mandela told in his memoirs that they were singing about the freedom, and one of such songs was the *Transkei* (Buis, 2013, p. 62). Its lyrics said: "There are two roads, one road is the Matanzima road and one road is Mandela road, which will you take?" (Mandela in Buis, 2013, p. 62).[18] The song was referring to the Chief Matanzima, who was the representative

[18] The memoirs of Mandela about the prison and music cited and studied by Buis (2013) referred in this book were originally published in Mandela's book: Mandela, N. (1994). *Long Walk to Freedom*. New York: Little Brown & Co.

and the “puppet” of oppressive government in South Africa (Buis, 2013, p. 62). Later, the rivalry gang member became silent as they could compete in singing with the political prisoners like Mandela. Then, also one guard could understand fluently Xhosa language and the parodies in songs and soon they were banned. At the same time, even whistling was forbidden according to Mandela (p. 63).

This was creating acoustical monopoly in prison argued by Cusick (2013, pp. 288–289) in restricting the prisoners to express themselves freely with singing. It was also a form of absolute power argued by Brauer (2016, pp. 23–24) of how the oppressive regime wanted to control the free expression of music and thoughts. By this, they also seemed to want to affect the spirit and identity of political prisoners as their rivalries, who were already jailed, and resisted the system. Using language that the guards could not fully understood made possible such an underground activity and resistance with music and arts that also occurred in the Nazi concentration camps. There were sarcastic songs like the earlier mentioned *Als Ob* (As if),[19] which criticised the asymmetry in the picture given to the public and harsh reality of the concentration camps like the Theresienstadt (John, 1991/2001, p. 287).

This seemed to be a similar “counter-world” in the Nazi concentration camp life like on Robben Island prison, where the Jews and other prisoners could construct their own sociological meaning and identity with music and arts (Fisher & Gilboa, 2016, p. 1228; John, 1991/2001, p. 291). Such activities enabled a chance to escape the reality in fantasies and free one’s mind and soul even temporarily from the nightmares of the camps. For example, there were underground chamber music ensembles, string quartets, choirs, and jazz bands rehearsing in the secrecy of the nights. Sometimes they were performing Beethoven, Mozart, Haydn, among the preserved human skulls, bullet-pierced hearts, and tightly stretched tattooed human skins in the pathology barrack (ibid., p. 285).

According to John (ibid. p. 291), this helped the prisoners to achieve psychological strength and balance, at least to some degree, their spirit in the fight of their survival. Similar songs that expressed the hope and freedom like on Robben Island were also done in the concentration camps like the Sachsenhausen. From there is known a song called *Wir shreiten fest* that says:

> *We march with firmness and keep step,*
> *we brave all trouble and sorrows;*
> *for within us marches hope*
> *for freedom and the future.* (John, 1991/2001, p. 296)

This kind of songs and musical activities on Nazi concentration camps were resistance towards the Nazi regime (ibid., pp. 296–297). Even though they could not prevent from physical exhaustion, torture, and death, where music and other activities were used as a weapon in punitive sports like the mentioned forced singing, they “helped to preserve life” as the “counteract” of “total demoralization” by the Nazis (p. 297). On Robben Island, political prisoners felt that singing gave strength to

[19] See Sect. 3.4 “Deceitful Musical Experiences in Prisons and Camps” for the more description of song.

work remembered by Mandela in addition to its social meaning in keeping and constructing their identities as counteracts against the oppressive regime (Buis, 2013, pp. 63–64).

There were also educational and cultural aspects as discussed in the singing of political prisoners that lightened their workload and reinforced cultural and socio-economic inter-ethnic identity in their experiences (Buis, 2013, pp. 63–64). Music as a social capital and a building block of togetherness seemed to create a social, political, and cultural community in prison on Robben Island. As such, in improvised songs and within song communications seemed to be a sort of cultural dialoguing in musicking and music that had therapeutic importance for the victims of oppression on Robben Islands as well as on Nazi concentration camps (Alanne, 2010, 2019b; Fisher & Gilboa, 2016, pp. 1232–1234).

Mandela remembers how music, singing, and dancing transcended ethnic differences and produced a common internal ontology in sharing thoughts and experiences with people in prison (Buis, 2013, p. 64). Music and dance as universal non-verbal and non-formal way of communicating transcended the cultural and lingual differences in the prison. Buis (ibid.) refers to Mandela's experiences and writes:

> *Accomplished ballroom dancers, sluggards who knew neither traditional nor Western dancing, all joined in the indlamu, the traditional Zulu war dance. Some moved gracefully, others resembled frozen mountaineers trying to shake off the cold, but all danced with enthusiasm and emotion. Suddenly there were no Xhosas or Zulus, no Indians or Africans, no rightists or leftists, no religious or political leaders; we were all Nationalists, patriots bound together by love a love of our common history, our culture, our country, and our people.* (Buis, 2013, p. 64)

This extract from the memories of Mandela described by Buis is clearly showing the power of music, how it can affect people emotionally and socially in uniting them. For this reason, oppressive governments and dictators often forbid and restrict the freedom of arts. Like in this example from the history and experiences of late President Mandela (1918–2013) in South Africa, the sounds, expression, and the freedom of people and music were tried to silence (Buis, 2013). In the experiences of political prisons of South Africa, music and dance seemed to pave a road to the enlightenment of people from their history, roots, ethnicity, will to freedom, and shared thoughts and emotions towards them (Alanne, 2014a, 2017, 2018, 2021, 2023).

In a historical view, it appears that music and dance were the forces of resistance and change that led a way to the collapse of apartheid atrocities and oppressive system in South Africa (Buis, 2013). In the experiences of prisoners in South Africa as well as victims of Nazi concentration camps, music became a counteraction and resistance towards the oppression and violence. Also, in Chile during the dictatorship of Pinochet in 1970s and 1980s, there were protest songs and prodemocratic punk music even though popular cultural music was first banned and silenced because of its symbolic, emotional, and psychological power (Neustadt, 2004, pp. 129, 134). In the beginning of coup, military changed the programme of TV and radio playing Nazi military marches temporally. However, there continued underground protest music movement that supported the political identity of people under oppression and gave them hope. These are examples of peaceful resistance and activity with the means of culture and creativity that can be compared to the singing revolution in Estonia. Estonian people began to sing patriotic songs that raised the national spirit and awareness in Tallinn. This led a way to the freedom and independence of Estonia peacefully from the former occupier Soviet Union in 1991.

The horrible witness-experiences of detainees, how music has been used as a weapon among other violence and torture from around the world, depict the dark use of music usually not publicly addressed. However, it is important to discuss and study them publicly because otherwise they would mean a burden for the victims, their children, families, and other persons who witnessed or even were a part of such cruelties. Without discussing and encountering traumatic experiences including music and other cultural representations, the traumas could transfer to the next generations and their families (Välimäki, 2015, p. 133). In addition, if music included in violence is not openly discussed and confronted, the dark culture of using music in the wars, prisons, interrogations, and torture would continue.

There seems to be a tradition of such strategies and methods that has developed before WWII and the Gulags of Soviet Union in 1920s and Nazi concentration camps in Germany in 1930s. As discussed in this book relating to the earlier research, the use of music in violence, torturing, and brainwashing manoeuvres continued after WWII in the Cold War against communism when it was further developed from the methods earlier used by the CIA in 1960s. This line of development of using music and sounds as a part of deprivation and sensory manipulation of detainees and their interrogation continued until the twenty-first century. A part of continuation of such strategies and music had former German Nazis who used and trained these methods in Chile, for example.

In the 2000s decade, these so-called enhanced methods of interrogations were taken back in the War on Terror by the President George W. Bush's administration. This time these methods that were grounded on the former interrogation methods were further refined in interrogation centres and prisons like in Guantanamo. Using of these enhanced methods including music in interrogations was publicly criticised and studied, which led to the official forbidding of applying them by the President Barack Obama in 2009. In 2014, The *Report of the Senate Select Committee on Intelligence Committee Study of the Central Intelligence Agency's Detention and Interrogation Program* was published, which included reports of using music non-touch interrogations, sensory deprivation, and torture. In the attached letter of the Committee chairman Feinstein to the President Obama was a conclusion that this kind of detention and interrogation system should be never repeated.

Unfortunately, according to the most recent reports and knowledge this kind of tactics of using music for the detainees has been used in China and the War of Ukraine by Russia. Therefore, it is important that the phenomena relating to music, violence, torture, and detainees are studied, reported, and documented in the present and history as suggested by Papaeti (2020, pp. 9–11). This is also a part of helping the victims and their traumas that their stories and suffering are told even though they are horrible and hard to bear. It is especially important also to notice the meaning of music for the traumatised detainees discussed in this book because for many of them music and sounds were psychotherapeutic. It helped the survivors to resist the "rehabilitation", terror, and isolation with the music's capability to build companionship, community, solidarity, and communication as argued by Papaeti (ibid., p. 10) in the context of Greek camps. In the light of this book, there were similar experiences with other survivors, especially with those who survived from Nazi concentration camps. There were also sadly survivors and murdered from Nazi camps who did not experience music as therapeutic, instead they remembered or witnessed it increasing their pain, exhaustion, and humiliation as a form of absolute power (Brauer, 2016).

During the War on Terror, it seems like the use of music and sounds were refined, so that the detainees would not have any possibility to feel music as therapeutic (Cusick, 2013). It seemed to increase the pain and isolation of victims until they were in their breaking points and feeling going insane. Music seemed not to give any hope, empowerment, or possibility to keep one's identity or build companionship. The acoustemology of prison was totally taken with absolute power by the guards and interrogators, so that the detainees could not hear even their own voices for keeping their identity and sanity. This seems to be different to the use of music in the Nazi concentration camps where there were detainee orchestras, leisure activities, and even underground possibilities for playing music that were highly important for keeping up the hope and spirit (John, 1991/2001; Moreno, 1999). In the War on Terror detainees were not used as a forced labour, so it seems that there was not such a need to keep the spirit of detainees, so that they could work more.

As discussed by Papaeti (2020, pp. 10–11), it is important to recognise different voices and experiences for the traumatised detainees when working with refugees, for example. For some detainees, sounds and music may have meant escape and resistance from the harsh reality of prison and society like in South Africa and for President Mandela (Buis, 2013). For others, it could have been the breaking point of their oppression that relates to their traumatic experiences and torture. In clinical, social, and educational contexts, it is important to be able to discern such individual experiences and multiple voices, tones, and dynamics relating to the musical experiences. As discussed by Brauer (2016, p. 26), when music has been used as violence and torture like in the Nazi or the War on Terror camps later, the positive emotional attitude, a sense of humanity, is "under attack". It can destroy and degrade the "contact zone" with oneself and music that are important for self-assurance and vitality for survival in contrast to despair and helplessness (ibid.). These are ego functions that the interrogators and torturers are consciously attacking with music and other methods.

When treating with music therapy or psychotherapy survivors of torture and traumatised refugees, it is essential to understand this dark psychology and manipulation of them with music and sounds. It may begin to relive in the musical relationships with them as a part of their transference to the therapist negatively. Music, sounds, and the therapist may transform in their experiences as bad objects symbolising momentarily the oppressor. It can make them suspicious and resistant towards music and treatment because of their traumatic backgrounds. Then, music and sounds may touch and reverberate with their traumatised mindful body described by Brauer (2016, p. 26) that is sensitive to them. For example, they may trigger unsafety experiences as trauma-responses that the therapist should monitor in their appointments with music to provide them with security and holding of their experiences with music (Alanne, 2010, 2023; Sokira et al., 2023).

In music therapy with traumatised detainees and refugees, there are the same elements and object relationships affecting the therapy that the detainees and victims described have experienced or witnessed. In the dynamics of music and transference, the past is relived in the musical experiences. Music may bring forth the traumatic experiences of clients that are related to music or not depending individually on clients and their stories. The most important is to be there sensitively with music, to attune and dialogue with their experiences, sounds, noises, and feelings to hear what they have to say or have experienced. In this music and sounds can be similar sound and song communication that brings hope, safety, and empowerment to rebuild their identity and capability of being in relationships, including music, and a part of community like it was for those who came before and survived, and for those who did not survive. In the memory of them.

References

Alanne, S. (2005). Music psychotherapy for torture survivors. *Music Therapy Today*, 6(4), 682–697. Special Issue: Proceedings of the 6th EMTC 2004 Conference, University of Jyväskylä. D. Aldridge & J. Fachner (Eds.), MusicTherapyWorld.net Witten: University Witten/Herdecke.

Alanne, S. (2010). *Music psychotherapy with refugee survivors of torture. Interpretations of three clinical case studies*. Sibelius Academy. Studia Musica.

Alanne, S. (2013). Psykodynaaminen musiikkipsykoterapia kidutuksesta traumatisoituneiden pakolaisten kanssa: Kliininen näkökulma. [Psychodynamic music psychotherapy with the refugees traumatised from the torture: A clinical point of view.]. *Psykoterapia, 32*(4), 264–276.

Alanne, S. (2014a). *Musiikkipsykoterapia*. Teoria ja käytäntö. [Music psychotherapy. Theory and practice.] Acta Universitatis Ouluensis D Medica 1248.

Alanne, S. (2014b). The ethnocultural and psychodynamic meaning of music for traumatised refugees. *Music Therapy Today*, 10(1), 48–49. Special issue: Proceedings of the 14th World Congress of Music Therapy Vienna/Krems, Austria, July 7–12, 2014.

Alanne, S. (2016a). Music as psychotherapy and the structure of personal identity. In M. Degli Stefani & F. Facchin (Eds.), *PerSona. Voce e identità. Opportunità musicali per la salute e il benessere* (pp. 131–137). CLEUP—Cooperativa Libraria Editrice Università di Padova.

Alanne, S. (2016b). Musiikki ja äänet tienä varhaislapsuuden kokemusmaailmaan—Kokemuksia mutismin psykoterapiasta. [Music and sounds as the road into the experience world of early childhood—Experiences of mutism's psychotherapy.]. *Psykoterapia, 35*(3), 186–195.

Alanne, S. (2017). Musiikillisen kokemuksen rajapinnat minuuden heijastajina. Milan Kunderan Naurun ja unohduksen kirjan avaamia näkökulmia. [The edges of musical experience as the reflections of self. The points of view unfolded from The book of laughter and forgetting by Milan Kundera.]. *Psykoterapia, 36*(2), 116–126.

Alanne, S. (2018). *Transformations of fear in music, sounds, and therapy*. A paper presented 19th October 2018 at the XX International Forum of Psychoanalysis, Firenze, Italy. International Federation of Psychoanalytic Societies (IFPS).

Alanne, S. (2019a). Musiikki, vuorovaikutus ja sisäinen kokemus psykoterapiassa. [Music, interaction, and the inner experience in psychotherapy.]. *Psykoterapia, 38*(1), 39–49.

Alanne, S. (2019b). Musiikkipsykoterapia traumatisoituneiden pakolaisten ja maahanmuuttajien kuntoutuksessa. [Music psychotherapy in the rehabilitation of refugees and immigrants.]. *Psykoterapia, 38*(4), 306–318.

Alanne, S. (2020). Musiikin ja kielen suhteesta—sekä psykoterapeuttisesta arvosta. [About the relationship of music and language—And their psychotherapeutic value.]. *Psykoanalyyttinen Psykoterapia, 16*, 6–15.

Alanne, S. (2021). *Väärän tiedon puu.* Mallintava tieto ja kulttuurin elämästä vieraantuneisuus. [The three of ignorance. Modeling knowledge and the estrangement of culture from life.] BoD.

Alanne, S. (2023). *The theory and practice of psychodynamic music psychotherapy.* Barcelona Publishers.

Alvin, J. (1966/1975). *Music therapy.* Basic Books.

Beck, B. D. (2019). Music therapy for refugees. In S. Lindahl Jacobsen, I. Nygaard Pedersen, & L. O. Bonde (Eds.), *A comprehensive guide to music therapy. Theory, clinical practice, research and training* (2nd ed., pp. 342–352). Jessica Kingsley.

Beck, B. D., Meyer, S. L., Simonsen, E., Søgaard, U., Petersen, I., Arnfred, S. M. H., Tellier, T., & Moe, T. (2021). Music therapy was noninferior to verbal standard treatment of traumatised refugees in mental healthcare: Results from a randomized clinical trial. *European Journal of Psychotraumatology, 12*(1), 1930960. https://doi.org/10.1080/20008198.2021.1930960

Blum, A., Goldberg, P., & Levin, M. (2023). *Here I'm alive. The spirit of music in psychoanalysis.* Columbia University Press.

Bonde, L. O. (2019). Music therapy—A historical perspective. In S. Lindahl Jacobsen, I. Nygaard Pedersen & L.O. Bonde (Eds.), *A comprehensive guide to music therapy. Theory, clinical practice, research and training* (2nd ed., pp. 17–28). Jessica Kingsley.

Bonny, H., & Pahnke, W. (1972). The use of music in psychedelic (LSD) psychotherapy. *Journal of Music Therapy, 9*(2), 64–83.

Brauer, J. (2016). How can music be torturous?: Music in Nazi concentration and extermination camps. *Music & Politics, 10*(1). https://doi.org/10.3998/mp.9460447.0010.103

Bruscia, K. E. (1987). *Improvisational models of Music therapy.* Charles C Thomas.

Bruscia, K. E. (1998). An introduction to music psychotherapy. In K. E. Bruscia (Ed.), *The dynamics of music psychotherapy* (pp. 1–15). Barcelona.

Buis, J. S. (2013). Music and dance make me feel alive: From Mandela's prison songs and dances to public policy. *Torture, 23*(2), 55–67.

Castaneda, A. E., Mäki-Opas, J., Jokela, S., Kivi, N., Lähteenmäki, M., Miettinen, T., Nieminen, S., Santalahti, P., & PALOMA Expert Group. (2018). *Pakolaisten mielenterveyden tukeminen Suomessa.* PALOMA käsikirja. [Supporting refugees' mental health in Finland. PALOMA handbook.] Guidance, May 2018. Publications of the National Institute for Health and Welfare.

Central Intelligence Agency (CIA). (1963). *KUBARK counterintelligence interrogation.*

Central Intelligence Agency (CIA). (1983/1988). *Human resource exploitation training manual.*

Chornik, K. (2013). Music and torture in Chilean detention centers: Conversations with an ex-agent of Pinochet's secret police. *The World of Music, New Series, 2*(1), 51–65.

Christensen, E. (2019). Music in body and brain. In S. Lindahl Jacobsen, I. Nygaard Pedersen, & L. O. Bonde (Eds.), *A comprehensive guide to music therapy: Theory, clinical practice, research and training* (2nd ed., pp. 51–64). Jessica Kingsley.

Cloonan, M., & Johnson, B. (2002). Killing me softly with his song: An initial investigation into the use of popular music as a tool of oppression. *Popular Music, 21*, 27–39.

Cloonan, M., & Johnson, B. (2008). *Dark side of the tune. Popular music and violence.* Ashgate.

Cusick, S. G. (2006). Music as torture/music as weapon. *Transcultural Music Review, 10.* http://www.sibetrans.com/trans/article/152/music-as-torture-music-as-weapon

Cusick, S. G. (2008). Musicology, torture, repair. *Radical Musicology*, 3. http://www.radical--musicology.org.uk/2008/Cusick.htm.

Cusick, S. G. (2013). Towards an acoustemology of detention in the 'global war on terror'. In G. Born (Ed.), *Music, sound and space: Transformations of public and private experience.* Cambridge University Press.

Davison, P. (2010, May 24). Paul Schäfer: Nazi colonel who established an anti-Semitic colony in Chile after the war. *The Independent.* https://www.independent.co.uk/news/obituaries/paul-schafer-nazi-colonel-who-established-an-antisemitic-colony-in-chile-after-the-war-1981014.html

Dixon, M. (2002). Music and human rights. In J. P. Sutton (Ed.), *Music, music therapy and trauma. International perspectives* (pp. 119–132). Jessica Kingsley.

Ervamaa, T. (2002, April 6). Rapin tahdissa kansanmurhaan. [With the beat of rap to the genocide.] *Helsingin Sanomat*, p. B4.

Feld, S. (2015). Acoustemology. In D. Novak & M. Sakakeeny (Eds.), *Keywords in sound* (pp. 12–21). Duke University Press.

Fisher, A., & Gilboa, A. (2016). The roles of music amongst Holocaust survivors before, during, and after the Holocaust. *Psychology of Music, 44*(6), 1221–1239.

Foucault, M. (1975/2001). *Tarkkailla ja rangaista*. [Surveiller et punir.] (E. Nivanka, Trans.). Otava.

Frith, S. (2004). Why does music make people so cross? *Nordic Journal of Music Therapy, 13*(1), 64–69.

Grant, M. J. (2013). The illogical logic of music torture. *Torture, 23*(2), 4–13.

Grassi, L. (2021). *The sound of the unconscious. Psychoanalysis as music*. Routledge.

John, E. (1991/2001). Music and concentration camps: An approximation (E. F. Livingstone, Trans.). *Journal of Musicological Research, 20*(4), 269–323.

Julkunen, E. (2024, February 24). Sodan erottama pari: Volodmyr jäi sotavangiksi, Inna pakeni Suomeen. [A couple separated by the war: Volodmyr was captured in war, Inna escaped to Finland.] *Ilta-Sanomat*. https://www.is.fi/ulkomaat/art-2000010246418.html

Kennedy, R. (2020). *The power of music. Psychoanalytic explorations*. Phoenix.

Kirves, J. (2008). "Päivittäinen myrkkyannoksemme"—sensuuria ja propagandaa jatkosodassa. ["Our daily portion of poison"—Censorship and propaganda in the continuing war.] In S. Näre & J. Kirves (Eds.), *Ruma sota*. Talvi- ja jatkosodan vaiettu historia (pp. 13–62). [*Ugly war. Silenced history of winter and continuing wars*.] Johnny Kniga.

Klause, I. (2013). Music and 're-education' in the Soviet Gulag. *Torture, 23*(2), 24–33.

Kohut, H., & Levarie, S. (1950/1978). On the enjoyment of listening to music. In P.H. Ornstein (Ed.), *The search for the self. Selected writings of Heinz Kohut: 1950–1978. Vol. 1* (pp. 135–158). International Universities Press.

Kreutz, G., Quiroga Murcia, C., & Bongard, S. (2013). Psychoneuroendocrine research on music and health: An overview. In R. Macdonald, G. Kreutz, & L. Mitchell (Eds.), *Music, health, and wellbeing* (pp. 457–476). Oxford University Press.

Leave No Marks. (2007, August). *Enhanced interrogation techniques and the risk of criminality*. Physicians for Human Rights and Human Rights First.

Lee, J. H. (2016). The effects of music on pain: A meta-analysis. *Journal of Music Therapy, 53*(4), 430–477.

Lefleur, J. (2022). *Music in the Holocaust: The roles of music in Nazi concentration camps*. MA Thesis. Hunter College, The City University of New York.

Lehtonen, K. (1996). *Musiikki, kieli ja kommunikaatio*. Mietteitä musiikista ja musiikkiterapiasta. [Music, language, and communication. Considerations of music and music therapy.] Jyväskylän yliopiston musiikkitieteen laitoksen julkaisusarja A: tutkielmia ja raportteja 17.

Lehtonen, K., Juvonen, A., & Ruismäki, H. (2016). Musiikkirajoitteisuus sukupolvien välisenä siirtotaakkana. [Music restrictiveness as a transfer between generations.] *The Finnish Journal of Music Education*, 19(1), 29–42.

LeVine, M. (2009). *Heavy metal Islam*—Vainoa, vastarintaa ja taistelua muslimisieluista. [Heavy metal Islam—Rock, resistance, and the struggle for the soul of Islam.] Johnny Kniga.

Levitin, D. (2007). *This is your brain on music: Understanding a human obsession*. Atlantic Books.

McFerran, K. S., Lai, H. I. C., Chang, W.-H., Acquaro, D., Chin, T. C., Stokes, H., & Crooke, A. (2020). Music, rhythm, and trauma: A critical interpretive synthesis of research literature. *Frontiers in Psychology, 11*, 324. https://doi.org/10.3389/fpsyg.2020.00324

Mensfelt, J. (2017). *Auschwitz-Birkenaun muistopaikka*. Opas. [Auschwitz-Birkenau Memorial. Guide.] Auschwitz-Birkenau State Museum.

Miranda, D., Gaudreau, P., Debrosse, R., Morizot, J., & Kirmayer, L. J. (2013). Music listening and mental health: Variations on internalizing psychopathology. In R. Macdonald, G. Kreutz, & L. Mitchell (Eds.), *Music, health, & wellbeing* (pp. 513–529). Oxford University Press.

Modvig, J., & Jaranson, J. M. (2004). A global perspective of torture, political violence and health. In J. P. Wilson & B. Droždek (Eds.), *Broken spirits. The treatment of traumatised asylum seekers, refugees and torture victims* (pp. 33–52). Brunner–Routledge.

Moreno, J. (1999). Orpheus in hell: Music and therapy in the holocaust. *The Arts in Psychotherapy, 26*(1), 3–14.

Naliwajek-Mazurek, K. (2013). Music and torture in Nazi sites of persecution and genocide in occupied Poland, 1939–1945. *The World of Music, New Series, 2*(1), 31–50.

Neustadt, R. (2004). Music as memory and torture: Sounds of repression and protest in Chile and Argentina. *Chasqui, 33*(1), 128–137.

O'Connell, A. (1990). Fifty years of music therapy at the University of the Pacific. *Music Therapy Perspectives, 8*, 90–92.

Ortamo, S. (2024, January 6). Aigul pakeni Kiinan vankileiriltä—hän kertoo minkälainen kidutusväline on "tiikerituoli". [Aigul escaped from the prison camp of China—She tells what kind of torture equipment is a "Tiger Chair".] *YLE*. https://yle.fi/a/74-20065432?utm_source=social-media-share&utm_medium=social&utm_campaign=ylefiapp

Orth, J., Doorschodt, L., Verburgt, J., & Drožđek, B. (2004). Sounds of trauma: An introduction to methodology in music therapy with traumatised refugees in clinical and outpatient settings. In J. P. Wilson & B. Drožđek (Eds.), *Broken spirits. The treatment of traumatised asylum seekers, refugees and torture victims* (pp. 443–480). Brunner–Routledge.

Papaeti, A. (2013a). Music and 're-education' in Greek prison camps: From Makronisos (1947–1955) to Giaros (1967–1968). *Torture, 23*(2), 34–43.

Papaeti, A. (2013b). Music, torture, testimony: Reopening the case of the Greek Junta (1967–1974). *The World of Music, New Series, 2*(1), 67–89.

Papaeti, A. (2020). On music, torture and detention: Reflections on issues of research and discipline. *Transposition* [Online], Hors-série 2 | 2020, http://journals.openedition.org/transposition/5289; https://doi.org/10.4000/transposition.5289.

Penn, M. L., & Kojo Clarke, P. (2008). Art, culture, and pediatric mental and behavioral health: An interdisciplinary, public health approach. In B. J. Koen (Ed.), *The Oxford handbook of medical ethnomusicology* (pp. 72–92). Oxford University Press.

Plato. (2007). *Valtio*. [The state] (M. Itkonen-Kaila, Trans.). Otava.

Report of the Senate Select Committee on Intelligence Committee Study of the Central Intelligence Agency's Detention and Interrogation Program together with Foreword by Chairman Feinstein and Additional and Minority Views. (2014, December 9). 113th Congress 2d Session. S. Report 113–288.

Reyes, A. (1999). *Songs of the caged, songs of the free: Music and the Vietnamese refugee experience*. University Press.

Rose, G. J. (2004). *Between couch and piano. Psychoanalysis, music, art and neuroscience*. Brunner–Routledge.

Siltala, P. (2014). Ydintietoisuuden muotoutuminen varhaisen vuorovaikutuksen tilassa. [The shaping of core-consciousness in the state of early interaction.]. *Psykoterapia, 33*(2), 83–92.

Sokira, J., Allen, J., & Wagner, H. (2023). The resilience framework for trauma-informed music therapy. In L. E. Beer & J. C. Birnbaum (Eds.), *Trauma-informed music therapy. Theory and practice* (pp. 9–18). Routledge.

Solms, M., & Turnbull, O. (2002/2018). *The brain and the inner world. An introduction to the neuroscience of subjective experience*. Routledge.

Sullivan, J. M. (2007). Music for the injured soldier: A contribution of American women's military bands during world war II. *Journal of Music Therapy, 44*, 282–305.

Swallow, M. (2002). The brain—Its music and its emotion: The neurology of trauma. In J. P. Sutton (Ed.), *Music, music therapy and trauma. International perspectives* (pp. 41–53). Jessica Kingsley.

Välimäki, S. (2015). Musical representation of war, genocide, and torture: Treating cultural trauma with music. *Acta Translatogica* 3: Pax R. Hartama-Heinonen & P. Kukkonen (Eds.), (pp. 122–136). University of Helsinki, Nordica/Department of Finnish, Finno-Ugrian and Scandinavian Studies, Swedish Translation Studies.

van der Kolk, B. (2014). *The body keeps score. Mind, brain and body in the transformation of trauma*. Allen Lane.

Welten, R. (2002). I sing the body. On the corporeality of music. *Tijdschrift voor muziektheorie, 7*(3), 196–199.

Chapter 4
Music Therapy in the Treatment of Refugees

This chapter will describe how music therapy may benefit different refugee client groups, adults, children and adolescents, and families in their treatments. Documented published clinical work and research of music therapy with traumatised refugees will be discussed (Beck, 2019; Beck et al., 2021; McFerran et al., 2020; Orth, 2005; Orth & Verburgt, 1998; Orth et al., 2004). Also, my own clinical experiences from music psychotherapy as well as other work related to the topic such as supervision of families whose child was in music therapy will be reflected (Alanne, 2005, 2010, 2014a, 2019, 2023). In this chapter, the forms of music therapy, individual and group therapies, will be introduced and how their settings can be arranged: Examples and guidelines will be given on how to proceed with the beginning of an individual music therapy for an adult, child, or an adolescent client with a refugee and trauma background. This will be discussed concerning the clients in the private practice as well as in the public sectors, clinics, centres, and hospitals. Group music therapy and music in the groups with refugees and asylum seekers will also be described regarding what kind of experiences there are from the groups within the different clinical settings and clients (Ahonen & Mongillo Desideri, 2014; The BZFO reports 2000–2002; Zharinova-Sanderson, 2004a, 2004b).

The diagnostic aspects of traumatised clients and what kind of goals would be relevant in their treatments concerning their refugee and asylum seeker status will be discussed. The possible time limits for their music therapies and how it affects the goals of treatment will be reflected in comparison to those refugee clients who already have a refugee status and thus may have a possibility for a long-term music therapy/psychotherapy (Alanne, 2010, 2019, 2023). Finally, special aspects of treating traumas from different cultures and nationalities in individual and group therapies will be paid attention concerning the cross-cultural meaning of music and cultural sensitiveness in therapy (Castaneda et al. 2018; Saraneva, 2018). Also, the possible traumatisation related to music and sounds of refugees and how to approach such clients in music therapy adequately will be discussed (Alanne, 2010, 2019, 2023).

S. Alanne, *Music, Music Therapy and Refugees*,
https://doi.org/10.1007/978-3-031-94766-7_4

4.1 Adults

Music therapy with adult refugees have a long history beginning from the 1982 Netherlands where a music therapist Jaap Orth started working with severely traumatised refugees (Orth et al., 2004, p. 449). He was using methods that had been already used by other music therapists treating traumas like the vocal holding techniques of Dianne Austin (1999, 2002) and the improvisational music therapy approaches and techniques collected and integrated by Kenneth E. Bruscia (1987). Also, the Guided Imagery and Music (GIM) method of Helen L. Bonny (2002) was used in treating traumas. In addition, he was adapting and developing new methods in his work when he noticed from his clinical experiences that some standard approaches and methods of music therapy like the GIM did not necessarily suit as such very well for the traumatised refugees (Orth, 2005; Orth et al., 2004). GIM has been studied and developed since to adapt more to the often-difficult clinical situations of severely traumatised refugees like torture survivors (Alanne, 2005, 2010, 2013, 2019; Beck, 2019; Beck et al., 2021).

A Danish music therapist Bolette Beck has studied with his colleagues the effects of music therapy and adapted GIM in the treatment of traumatised refugees (Beck, 2019; Beck et al., 2021). In their studies of adult Danish refugees, they have compared music therapy to other therapies like cognitive behavioural therapy (CBT) and the current standard treatment, the treatment as usual (TAU) including cognitive, psychodynamic, and narrative techniques (Beck et al., 2021, pp. 5–6). Short-term phase-orientated music therapy of 16 to 20 one-hour sessions was found not inferior to other therapies after the treatment and during the six-month follow-ups (pp. 5, 12). According to their research, music therapy lessened trauma symptoms like the standard treatment as there were improvements in wellbeing and fewer symptoms of dissociation after music therapy.

All compared therapies including music therapy consisted of stabilisation, working-through/trauma-exposure, and integration/reorientation phases adapted from Herman's (1992/2022) model for trauma recovery (Beck et al., 2021, pp. 5–6).[1] In the beginning, there was a supportive approach to therapies where the goal was to establish a relationship with a client. Also, clients had psychoeducation about their trauma symptoms as well as breathing exercises. Their purpose was to develop affect regulation and increase the affect tolerance. This kind of relaxation and breathing exercises can be used in music therapy with adult traumatised refugees in the beginning of session before music listening, for example. Music in the form of free improvisation can also be a method for grounding and holding of emotions (Alanne, 2023; Bruscia, 1987; De Backer & Sutton, 2014a; Levinge, 2015; Priestley, 1975).

GIM and other guided imagery methods of music psychotherapy can be used with traumatised refugees, where the client is often sitting with eyes opened instead of lying on the bed or couch like in the classic Bonny method of GIM (BMGIM) or

[1] See also the discussion of Herman's (1992/2022, p. 224) three-stage recovery process in Chap. 2.

in psychoanalysis (Alanne, 2005, 2010, 2023; Beck et al., 2018, 2021; Orth et al., 2004). The sessions are often shorter from 45 to 60 minutes instead of 90 minute sessions of BMGIM with other clients. Also, music other than classical music may be used by the therapist for guided imagery, projective music listening, and free association to music. A therapist is not necessarily using BMGIM music programmes and predefined themes, but the therapist can also improvise in the session what kind of music and theme would be suitable today according to the client's mood, situation, and issues in therapy (Alanne, 2010, 2013, 2023).

Also, clients themselves may participate in choosing music from the therapist's CDs or music files what music would fit their feelings and thoughts best in the current situation (Alanne, 2010, 2013, 2023). This is usually the safest way to start working with music with severely traumatised refugees and torture survivors who may dissociate easily to provide them with a feeling of safe space in music therapy (Scrine & Koike, 2023, pp. 42–43). It is also good to ask first if the client wants to listen to music and is s/he capable to listen to music, sing, improvise, and play a particular instrument depending on the current trauma symptoms of client. A client may feel too stressed, exhausted, anxious, or s/he may have different pains that are making the situation too uncomfortable for the client. Then, music and sounds as the bad objects may trigger traumatic experiences and feelings of unsafety and be threatening for the psychic integrity of client. In the trauma-informed GIM study discussed, clients were able to stop the music anytime or decrease the volume of music if they were having flashbacks (Beck et al., 2018, p. 71).

In the next phase of working-through of the discussed GIM study with traumatised refugees, traumatic memories of clients were processed, the goal of which was to enable the clients to change their avoidant behaviour and integrate their traumatic experiences and memories into the narrative of their current lives (Beck et al., 2021, p. 6). In music therapy with traumatised refugees, the traumatic events can be first discussed after a short relaxation and breathing exercise if that seems to be suitable for the client's situation, who maybe needs calming down from anxiety, panic attack, or if the client is otherwise feeling unsecure. Then, a therapist may propose a theme or a feeling from the discussion that a client may improvise with an instrument (Alanne, 2023; Priestley, 1975). In the applied GIM study with refugees, music was chosen as safe and supportive for the clients (Beck et al., 2018, p. 71). Listened music pieces were also shorter and included possibility to listen to the music of their own culture. The possibility to choose music from own culture increases the safety in therapy, so that the music and the therapist would not present the power structures of cultural oppression in music therapy with refugees (Scrine & Koike, 2023, pp. 42–43).

To avoid this, a therapist may also propose a theme for the improvised music that comes up from the psychotherapeutic discussion in the beginning of the session. It can be a feeling of a client like anger, suffering, love, sadness, and so on. A theme may also be a situation from the client's life, a conflict, or a traumatic experience that a client and a therapist are free improvising in music therapy (Alanne, 2023; Priestley, 1975). This should be done in collaboration and discussing with a client first, so that a client has a right to choose or reject the theme of the improvisation.

Music like a song, instrumental, classic, or pop music that is reflecting the feelings of a client can be listened and discussed during the music listening and afterwards. The music listening, discussion, and the whole session is good to happen in a holding environment with a client. Music can be holding and containing music where the clients are feeling themselves safe to reflect and share their thoughts and memories during the sessions (Alanne, 2010, 2023; De Backer & Sutton, 2014b; Priestley, 1975).

In the described trauma-informed GIM with refugees, the reorientation phase encourages the patients to retain and develop their social connections as well as to place goals for work or education (Beck et al., 2018; Beck et al., 2021). In this study that compared the GIM and TAU with traumatised refugees, the recovery phases were considered to proceed similarly with every therapy and client but there were natural therapeutic processes followed individually like proposed by Herman (1992/2022). As discussed earlier in this book, the treatment of severely traumatised clients with PTSD of C-PTSD, which many torture survivors have as their diagnoses, may proceed in many ways, and there may be a lot of individual variation in clients. Frequently, 16 to 20 sessions of therapy are not enough for these clients that may require years of rehabilitation and different therapies including psychiatric treatment, psychotherapy, physiotherapy, occupational therapy, music/arts therapies, and their different combinations.

It seems that the developing of short therapies, often manualised, are reflecting the current social, political, and economical needs that are tangled with the current psychiatric treatments and their research, including traumas, refugees, psychotherapy, and music therapy. These studies may not therefore address the whole picture of clients' needs that should be remembered in the clinical work and research. For instance, in the 16 sessions it may be quite impossible to set goals and new directions for the education and work of clients and at the same time work through their traumatic experiences even with music as the method. Especially, severely traumatised clients like refugee survivors of torture who are dissociating may need longer periods of containing and stabilising their traumas in therapy.

The clients with C-PTSD and personality disorders may need years of psychotherapy in stabilising, working through, and integrating their experiences before real new directions in life are possible. In music psychotherapy with refugees, this could mean more modest goals in the short therapy; however, it is very important for the recovery of trauma, like giving hope, empowerment, and reorientation to future in the beginning of treatment (Alanne, 2010, 2013, 2019; Beck et al., 2018). In addition to music psychotherapy, music therapy with adults may include musical workshops, bands, choirs, and other musical activities like music education as a part of their treatment and rehabilitation (The BZFO reports 2000–2002; Zharinova-Sanderson, 2004a, b). This can happen in the community level of refugees, in their natural social environments, as well as at the rehabilitation centres, refugee camps, or at the reception centres for asylum seekers, and cultural centres where musical practices and artistic projects may provide structures of safety and belonging together.

In Berlin, Germany, at the Centre for the Treatment of Torture Survivors, there has been Community Music Therapy (CoMT) in addition to the individual music therapy provided for the refugees (Zharinova-Sanderson, 2004b). The clients in music therapy varied in their age, culture, nationality, and education. Their traumatisation also varied, but many of the clients had symptoms of PTSD like acute insomnia, nightmares, extreme psychosomatic pain, phobias, and problems with communication (ibid. p. 236). In Helsinki, Finland, there has also been music psychotherapy at the Rehabilitation Centre for Torture Survivors. There it was mainly individual music therapy of clients with similar PTSD symptoms as in Berlin (Alanne, 2005, 2010, 2013). Also, short music therapy group for women was arranged that used clinical improvisation with instruments. Individual music psychotherapies were psychodynamically oriented and used music listening methods such as guided imagery, projective music listening, and free association to music.

In Berlin, 70–80 refugees from all over the world were gathered singing together at the clients' party in a church that was arranged by the centre where they were in treatment (Zharinova-Sanderson, 2004b, p. 233). Music therapist was conducting their singing in a circle that is an example of music therapy for the whole community of client from different nationalities and ethnicities including men, women, and families. Clients did not speak common language, and their German was limited. However, with chanting a simple melody, clapping, and stamping, they were communicating with music to each other sending and answering questions musically with the rhythms they were producing. The clients were energised and their eyes and faces lid up from their experiences of music and being united in a community.

The goal for such music therapy practice in communities, or with individuals and groups, was the re-establishment of trust in humanity with music (Zharinova-Sanderson, 2004b, p. 241). Severely traumatised people including refugees and torture survivors may experience strong disbelief and disappointment in humanity, other people, and their home countries who have betrayed their trust. Traumatised persons in general may have lost their trust towards other people and may feel alienated from them. However, with refugees and especially with torture survivors like the survivors from the Holocaust and concentration camps, their lack of trust may be even greater because of the massive traumatisation and the systematic violence and murdering of people they have experienced or witnessed by the legal authorities in their societies. This includes police, army, officials, leaders, even doctors and psychologists; they have learnt to trust in their communities (Alanne, 2010).

Music and music therapy, musical interaction, can be an antidote for such poisonous traumatising experiences and inhuman experiences of torture according to Dixon (2002) and Zharinova-Sanderson (2004b, p. 241). With musical interaction in music therapy or in other music therapeutic practices like music workshops, choirs, or bands in communities, music helps the traumatised to connect with themselves and the others with its vitalising energy noticed also by van der Kolk (2014) when he was observing the dancing and singing of the traumatised women in Africa described earlier. I have also used similar methods of improvisation, bodily instruments, clapping, and stomping of feet in the group of women torture survivors where joint musical interaction brought laughter and happy experiences, humour among women similarly (Alanne, 2010). These kinds of positive experiences in music build trust and reconnect also the belief in humanity with traumatised refugees as the goals for music therapy (Alanne, 2010, 2013, 2019; Zharinova-Sanderson, 2004b).

In addition, this kind of music projects and therapy may decrease the isolation of refugees and help in their homing and integrating to the new homeland (Zharinova-Sanderson, 2004b, pp. 241–242). This also creates trust and builds resilience for the refugees. Together such good object experiences of music, interaction, nurture, and community are reconnecting the belief in humanity. If traumatised clients like refugees or the victims of torture have lost their capabilities of enjoying music because of the disturbed experiences relating to music and sounds because they trigger dissociation and other trauma symptoms, one goal for music therapy would be the returning of music in the clients' lives (Alanne, 2010, 2013, 2019).

This is also reconnecting of the traumatised client's belief in humanity because music and culture are integral parts of the humanity where they have been alienated. Especially, the re-establishing of the client's capability to listen, play, and enjoy music is important for those traumatised who have been tortured with music and they cannot therefore bear music and sounds anymore. Then, returning the music in their lives is also working through and recovering from their trauma in music therapy. Overall, music, music education, and music therapy may support the mental health and general health, social, and wellbeing of refugees that may prevent from their further traumatisation and the transmission of their traumas to the next generations (Castaneda et al., 2018; Fancourt & Saoirse, 2019).

Thus, one step of avoiding further traumatisation and intergenerational transmission of trauma through music by avoiding it is the returning of music in the lives of refugees with music. In individual music therapy, playing songs with clients can be one method of music therapy with traumatised refugees (Zharinova-Sanderson, 2004b, pp. 237–238). Zharinova-Sanderson played Kurdish songs together with a Kurdish male client from Turkey who was imprisoned many times as well as beaten and tortured. The client was very depressed, unhappy, and could not see anything positive in his life before attending music therapy. For this man, music was a rescue of his bad thoughts he had noticed himself while playing the Kurdish instrument saz.

In this music therapy, there was also an interpreter in the session, which is a common practice with refugees. The interpreter was even drumming together with the therapist, and the client directed his musical questions and communication to the interpreter as well. First, the client had difficulties to look at the eyes of the female therapist. However, after few sessions there was more trust and acceptance in the client and they were able to play together a Kurdish song in developing their relationship, and positive transference, the therapist being a fellow musician, a person, instead of just being a woman for the client (Zharinova-Sanderson, 2004b, p. 238). The client had felt too embarrassed being alone with a young woman as the music therapist where the male interpreter and music helped him to be in relationship with the therapist first (pp. 237–238).

Eventually, the client playing Kurdish songs with a guitar together with the music therapist playing piano, and the interpreter the drum, developed to a repertoire of songs (ibid., 2004b, pp. 238–241). Later in the process, these songs were also performed in a concert for the politicians and other VIP supporters of the centre. The performance with the music therapist at the concert included also dancing and a song where the audience was activated to join in singing. When music therapy progressed, the client sometimes came still depressed but was energised and focused during the sessions and rehearsals for the concert. The responsibility of performing in the control seemed to strengthen his ego as he looked straighter, stronger, and more alert in the sessions according to the therapist.

After the successful concert he received many thanks and congratulations for sharing his soul and culture from the audience (Zharinova-Sanderson, 2004b, pp. 240–241). There was pride in his eyes in this moving experience where he was more than a traumatised refugee, a real person, also in the eyes of the audience that they could empathise with. According to Zharinova-Sanderson, this musical performance of "Herr A" as a part of his therapeutic process built bridges between refugees and their host society (p. 241). Music seemed to strengthen the relationship between the therapist and the client, building bridges also between them in my view. It became like a transitional object representing the thirdness in therapy when the interpreter was ill, and Herr A could come to meet the therapist without him. Then, Herr A said that they were not alone anymore, because "the music is there with us" (p. 239). In this way, musical dialogue, which seemed to also become cultural dialogue, helped to overcome the cultural attitudes and bringing trust between the therapist and the client of different genders in the beginning of therapy.

I think that this case of music therapy with a refugee adult client represents well the possibilities of music therapy, even though it is not necessarily a typical process in music psychotherapy. In general, music therapy may also include performances of clients for other patients and staff in a hospital, a centre, or a school that are not common methods in individual or group music psychotherapy because of the privacy and confidentiality of the treatments. In music psychotherapy, the psychotherapeutic working-through in the sessions is more emphasised. It includes discussions of personal issues and their musical or other artistic expressions through free improvisation, which are not always in the form of song or a performance. Even though songs and song performances are psychodynamic music psychotherapy methods as well as many others including GIM, they are not often made as public performances (Alanne, 2023; Bruscia, 1998, 2002).[2]

Also, not all the clients want to or are able to perform publicly because they do not have enough musical skills. They may also feel it to be too stressful. With C-PTSD clients, it may be too overwhelming because of their avoiding patterns of behaviour and anxiety, if their dissociative symptoms are not stabilised enough, so that they could feel safe and function normally in their performance. However, sometimes recording of songs and music can be done as a method of music psychotherapy that clients can play to their friends and families if they want to. Even

[2] See Chap. 5 "Music and Music Therapy Methods with Traumatised Refugees" for the introduction of different techniques and methods of music psychotherapy.

though not every music therapy client may not want or be able to perform publicly, for someone like Herr A it can be very empowering and build trust towards oneself and the others.

Sometimes like in the case of Herr A, music and creativity of the therapist, client, and the interpreter may build bridges, so that the unique individual music therapy and recovering processes become possible. It may not be a manualised psychotherapy of limited sessions, methods, and diagnoses currently emphasised in public health services but may need a living need-adapted process, between people, and in encountering severely traumatised refugees that seemed to make a difference in music therapy. However, this kind of working is not possible with every traumatised client and refugee why also other kinds of approaches and methods of music therapy and psychotherapy are needed depending on the clients' situations and their phases of the treatment.

It is important to understand that music can be a part of the client's normal functioning and ego strengths that can help the client in recovering trauma like it seemed to be in the case of Herr A (Alanne, 2023, p. 49). Similarly, music may build bridges in developing and broadening the ego's capabilities to bear and contain the stress of the traumatic experiences in daily life. This music ego of clients is representing health and functionality that can be contacted and supported also in the treatments of traumatised refugee children and adolescents.

4.2 Children and Adolescents

With children and adolescents, music and music therapy may provide good possibilities in treating their traumas of forced immigration and refugeeism. During their often dangerous and long journeys away from their home country and family, they may have experienced threats of violence, or they may have seen torture, rape, physical abuse, even deaths, including their relatives, other people, and other children (Beck, 2019, pp. 342–343). Frequently, refugee families and children have been living under the fear of violence or near the war in their home countries that has affected their mental health as ACEs (Bensimon, 2020).[3]

Sometimes the whole family cannot necessarily travel and escape together but a part of the family, parents or siblings, are still in the home country. Also, during the journey away from the home country may include human trafficking under life-threatening conditions at the sea or in the dark container of a boat or a truck. Also, a family member may have disappeared completely, or the family members have divided to go in different routes when children cannot see the other parent, for example. In addition to other possible ACE-producing situations, refugee children

[3] See the discussion of adverse childhood experiences (ACEs) in Sect. 2.3 "Impacts of Trauma in People's Lives".

and adolescents may have to stay long periods of time at the refugee camps and centres waiting their asylum in the new country.

In such circumstances of refugees, music and music therapy may provide children and adolescents safety structures in their lives. Music, music education, and music therapy that may be sometimes mingled and near each other's goals can be seen as a part of the normality in the children's lives in the refugee camps or reception centres. Music projects and music therapy may be provided there for the children and adolescents as groups where children can learn to play instruments, improvise, and jam together. Currently, hip hop music in music therapy is popular among adolescent refugees as well as with other adolescents that they can perform and record as a part of their therapeutic processes (Baker & Jones, 2005; Einarsen et al., 2024; Gulbay, 2021; Jones & Baker, 2004).

Using music workshops with refugees and traumatised war children has already a long history in music therapy since the 1990s and the Balkan War. For example, during the Balkan War in 1991–1995 a lot of musical instruments and other artistic equipment like audio tapes, music for guided imagery, and music and Orff instruments were given for the war-traumatised children in Croatia (Alanne, 2010; Barath, 1996). During that period creative workshops including music were provided for 100,000 children to support their mental health. According to the report, 75–100% of the war-traumatised children benefitted from the recovery programmes regardless of their age, gender, or residential status. The methods used in music workshops with children included active music playing and improvisation that were screened with many inventories including standardised screening scales for PTSD which improved their wellbeing significantly (Alanne, 2010, p. 33).

In Brisbane, Australia, music therapy has been used in working with traumatised Sudanese refugee children of the reception centre at the school (Jones & Baker, 2004; Baker & Jones, 2005). Studied music therapy methods included mirroring improvisation with instruments, hip hop, and rap music in a group music therapy of adolescents. Music therapy affected their generalised behaviour positively decreasing the maladaptive behaviour, hyperactivity, aggression, anxiety, depression, and attention problems of refugee adolescents significantly (Alanne, 2010, p. 27). Even though this was quite a small study of 31 new arrival refugees, it is still showing a clear example, how music therapeutic approach can help in trauma-related symptoms as well as in their homing and integrating into the new culture, society, and home country.

Music therapy with child refugees has included methods such as improvisation, singing of songs, music and movement, and song writing of hip hop and rap (Alanne, 2010, p. 27; Akombo, 2001; Gulbay, 2021. Hunt, 2005). One common approach in music therapy with refugees with children and adolescents has been Community Music Therapy (CoMT) that is emphasising the ecological and social perspectives on music and health in everyday life (Enge & Stige, 2021, p. 2). A goal of such music therapy with children has been to empower clients and foster their sense of belonging to a community (Alanne, 2010, p. 27). This is important because of the possible racism and rejection encountered in the new society. For example, in Kenya, traumatised children have sung Kenyan folk songs in storytelling with music

(Akombo, 2001). Singing, drumming, and moving culture of music are strong in African cultures where the storytelling of children was depicting the emotions of children with drums and voices. They were also singing stories of survival and hope as proposed in music therapy.

In Africa, there is not a separate word for music, dance, and movement as they go together naturally which is different from Western culture (Alanne, 2010, p. 11; Jones & Baker, 2004). In Western cultures, it is common to sit still and listen to music quietly sometimes also in music therapy and music education, which may feel awkward for children and people from Africa. This is good to consider and discuss in planning music therapy with refugees that can be a part of the cultural dialoguing approach with them (Alanne, 2010, 2019). There are also still natural and spiritual healing traditions in Africa, where music, dance, and ritual are used like in Sudan, where music is used to talk with gods. There is a long history and tradition of how music and sounds have been thought to be in contact with spirits and higher forces that may need to be sometimes considered and clarified if necessary for the children and parents of refugees how music is used in music therapy.

However, as a part of the growing number of refugees in Europe, for example, the Western music styles, genres, and music therapy seemed to have become well-received. Children and adolescents adapt and identify more easily to the Western cultures of new societies than their parents. In Norway, there was a music therapy project from 2009 to 2014 for asylum seeking and refugee children, the purpose of which was to support the refugee children's daily life (Enge & Stige, 2021, p. 3). There were open events like music cafés and concerts arranged at school. Music therapy was also implemented in the Introductory Programme for Foreign Students.

These kinds of methods are typical for CoMT as they are not necessarily music psychotherapy orientated even though they are trauma-informed and are considering that music is providing continuity and stability in difficult situations of refugee children (Enge & Stige, 2021, p. 2). In such situations, music therapy in the community may support their safety, nurturing relationships, and sense of mastery, as well as help in the emotion regulation of primary school children (Krüger et al., 2018). These goals of music therapy refugee children are in accordance with the goals and theories of psychodynamic music therapy in this book. They can also be applied in the individual, group, and community work with them respectively.

With children and adolescents, different kinds of music therapy approaches with refugees are possible, depending on how long it is possible to work with them. The therapist must plan and assess the therapeutic process individually, concerning is the client an asylum seeker who does not have an asylum decision and a refugee status yet. If the children or family do not know whether they are able to stay in the country, the longer music psychotherapy process may not be possible in the time limits. Then, it is better to plan shorter music therapy projects if it is unsure how long children and adolescents can participate. Also, a short music therapy from 16 to 20 weekly sessions may be possible that will take time approximately 6 months, or 3 months if the sessions are twice a week.

Even shorter music therapy consultations and treatments may be useful to support the children's mental health when they are living at the reception centre waiting for the asylum decisions. In such circumstances, short, closed music therapy groups with changing participants after one participant leaves are possible. Also, open music therapy groups or workshops with children and adolescents where music is improvised or listened, performed, or sung can be arranged where there may be varying participants in each session.

This kind of music therapy activities may be close to music education practices where music may be taught and supervised by the music therapists or music educators, or as a part of their collaboration in schools, like in Australia and Norway, where music therapy was implemented at the primary school programmes for refugees. This kind of music workshops may be a part of the cultural dialoguing with children and adolescents from different cultures in the community that can support their safety and mastering of their experience and crisis of being a refugee in a foreign country (Bensimon, 2020; Enge & Stige, 2021; Krüger et al., 2018).

Longer music psychotherapy/music therapy processes are possible when it is known that the children and adolescents can participate in it for a year or more, or even 6 months. Then, there are possibilities for more deep working-through of traumatic experiences and their integration safely. In the short-term individual and group music therapy from eight to ten sessions, there is not enough time for such analytic processes of music psychotherapy. Instead, music therapy must be focused on some issues in the clients and the stabilisation of their traumatic reactions and stress. Also, building trust and giving hope are essential goals in the short-term therapies. The clients have possibilities to feel secure in therapy and have some good nurturing experiences from the therapist and music as the good objects. The playfulness and creativity in music therapy are important ways to find ego control for the threatening traumatised experiences with children and adolescents when they are reexperienced as safe and less threatening in music and songs, for example (Bensimon, 2020, pp. 308–309).

In a short-term group music therapy with children and young people, as well as adults and families, clients can receive important peer support and empowerment for their lives in the new country. These can also be goals for the other music and music education projects with refugees. In this kind of educational and therapeutic approaches including short-term music therapy, a music supervisor or a therapist must keep the focus and limits of the therapy or group, so that it will not go too deep in their processes of trauma work. When there are only a few sessions or the possibilities for therapy process will be short and limited, the stabilisation of trauma is the goal of the treatment often in collaboration with other health and social care professionals. Also, if the music therapist does not have clinical experience and training for treating traumas, then the trauma-informed music therapy and the stabilisation of trauma are the recommended goals for music therapy (Alanne, 2019).

4.3 Families

In the treatment of traumatised refugees, it is important to notice the situation of the whole family. For example, many times the children and adolescents of the family may suffer because their parents are traumatised and cannot focus on their family and children because of their own trauma symptoms and dissociation. Also, the treatment system of the host country may be adult oriented, so that they are also focusing to treat the parent who has been tortured or has been otherwise traumatised because of the violence and being raped. The parents who are anxious, depressed, or otherwise worried and stressed because of the crisis being a refugee cannot necessarily be there with their children and contain their daily worries. This increases the risk of intergenerational trauma that the burden of situation will transfer to the children who will be anxious or depressed next. Also, if the parents do not treat their traumas they may project and transmit their traumatic experiences and symptoms of war and refugeeism to their children. As a result, their children may suffer from odd fears, dreams, thoughts, and experiences of being in danger.

It is important to assess the background of family when working with immigrant or refugee children. In my opinion, it is recommendable that a music therapist could meet the family or parents of the child or adolescent in music therapy to describe them about the possibilities of music therapy. During the music therapy process, a music therapist can be a parental consult/supervisor for the parents, so that the parents and family could better support and understand their child who is maybe traumatised too. This will increase the security of treatment and will give the parents guidance on how to see the symptoms like fears, apathy, tantrums, nightmares, clinging to parents of their child differently from the point of view traumatisation. However, this will need time for the parents and regular appointments with a therapist, so that the parents could find new ways of encountering their children. This kind of family work and supervising the parents is collaboration that enables the therapeutic process with children. Without the right kind of support of parents and the same direction with a therapy, music therapy or psychotherapy cannot necessarily help the child, and the therapy may also interrupt.

Refugee parents, and those waiting for asylum, may want something good for their children like music, music education, and music therapy, when they understand their difficult situation and that they are missing some parts of their normal life and activities as a child. They may also be motivated for music therapy or psychotherapy themselves, so that they could be better parents in their families. This is one motivation for psychotherapy of many adults generally: By helping themselves they can help their family and children. In a case of adult refugee being in music therapy or treatment, it is also important to keep in mind the situation of their children, do they need some kind of care or help, that parents cannot see or does not know where to receive it because of their own serious psychic symptoms, social withdrawal, and often many physical symptoms and illnesses.

Music and music therapy may provide the children with activity and good empowering experiences when there is a refugee crisis and stress in the family.

Positive musical experiences, games, and learning in a group, for example, provide children and their families with security, hope, and trust of being treated as fellow humans and persons in their host country. Also, other family members, siblings, and parents can be a part of musicking if all feel it comfortable, so that the parents could be a part of the positive energy and vitalising effects of music.

In music groups, there is also a possibility of sharing experiences with music without a need of common language. Instead, in musical improvisations, games, band, choirs, and workshops, music is the method of communicating with others that may lessen the feelings of loneliness and isolation in refugees as social interventions. Music and music therapy including siblings, family, and parents may also develop and strengthen their relationships in a positive way that will increase the resilience of the family and children in their crisis (Bensimon, 2020). In this kind of music therapy, performances, workshops, and concerts of children, adolescents, or adults, where their families can participate, could be empowering experiences for the recovery of the whole family and community of refugees.

Such musical experiences where music, music education, or music therapy is implemented in the community, refugees and their families including children have a possibility to be and be seen as normal persons, instead of being just a refugee, an asylum seeker, a traumatised person, or a patient (Zharinova-Sanderson, 2004b, pp. 240–241). For the severely traumatised person, these kinds of experiences are important for their self-dignity, humanness, and trust because they are feeling easily alienated from other people, activities, and life in general (van der Kolk, 2014). Making music together and sharing it is being in the music together that is rebuilding the trust towards others, oneself, and the humanity (Zharinova-Sanderson, 2004b, p. 241).

4.4 Individual Therapies and Groups

It is important that there could be possibilities for the individual and group music therapies for the refugees because they both are having their advantages. In the individual music (psycho)therapy, clients can go deeper into their traumatic experiences with a therapist alone. This setting may feel more secure for the traumatised clients who are maybe afraid to discuss their personal issues like being tortured or raped. In a group, some clients may feel themselves unsecure and anxious because of their traumatisation. Not all the clients, who have social phobias, or they are shy otherwise, are able to discuss and participate in the groups necessarily. Then, the personal therapeutic process in an individual therapy may be more beneficial.

However, as discussed already in the context of music therapy for refugee children, adolescents, and their families, musical groups may be very uplifting and empowering for the refugees. Some clients, who may not be ready yet for more deep working-through of their trauma and discussing them, may benefit from group activities and group music therapy. There they can express themselves with others and be together in music that can help in reducing their restriction of feelings, the feelings of being numb, splitting their experiences, and dissociation (Bensimon, 2023, p. 155).

In group music therapy, refugees can communicate with music when there is no need for an interpreter. Instead of verbalisations, clients can discharge their feelings that are encountered and shared by other members of the group and the therapist. In musical groups, traumatised refugees have a possibility to mirror and see the faces of other people and their expression that may help in noticing and expressing own feelings. In this regard, the peer group and music therapy with different methods, especially free improvising, may support and contain the emotional processing and outlet of trauma (Bensimon, 2023; Carr et al., 2012). Similarly, music therapy groups and workshops may also help the refugees to encounter themselves and the others in the same situation. This may help in the integration of traumatic experience of being a refugee and support their identity building process of third individuation in the host country.

There has been research of group music therapy with PTSD clients that compared the 10-week short-term music therapy once a week and the standard treatment after CBT provided at National Health Services (NHS) in the UK (Carr et al., 2012). The clients in music therapy (MT) included adult in working age of different nationalities and ethnic groups such as British, African and non-African blacks, and any other (p. 6). The clients in MT suffered from traumatic symptoms after torture, civilian casualties of war, terrorism, rape, childhood sexual abuse, and bullying.

In their results, group music therapy appeared feasible and effective for the treatment of PTSD clients who have not benefitted sufficiently from CBT. Clients participating in music therapy experienced it as helpful. In this small RCT research (n=17), that used mixed methods including quantitative measurements (BDI II, IES-R) and qualitative interviews, videotaped sessions, and process notes that followed the effects of music therapy after CBT treatment. In spite of the small sample size, this research showed that music therapy may help in the PTSD symptoms like reexperiencing, dissociation, avoidance, and hyperarousal relating to trauma.

Group music therapy was based on psychodynamic music therapy methods common in the UK training and practice of music therapists that consisted of one-hour meetings once a week (Carr et al., 2012, pp. 6–7). This is typically a good length for the group session with clients suffering from severe mental disorders like C-PTSD or psychoses. Depending on the group size and the method of music therapy, the session can be also of 90 minutes, so that there would be enough time for the participants to discuss their memories, thoughts, and imagery relating to music. This is important to notice if the interpreter is used. Also, the time of the music used in the session must be considered if music listening methods like GIM are used (Beck, 2019).

However, too many participants and too long sessions may be too demanding for severely traumatised clients like refugees and torture survivors in the group. The size and length of the groups should be considered and planned to depend on the clients in the group: Are they all torture survivors in the beginning of their rehabilitation where the stabilisation and smaller and shorter groups could be better? Or are there different kinds of traumatised clients whose situations are already more stable when the larger group and the longer session might be possible?

In the described music therapy study of persistent PTSD clients, common music therapy methods of psychodynamic-oriented music therapy in adult psychiatry in the UK were used (Carr et al., 2012, p. 7). These methods included receptive and active techniques where an emphasis was on free improvisation (Alanne, 2023; Bruscia, 1987; Wigram, 2004). In free improvisation, also called as clinical improvisation, clients were introduced to the instruments that included xylophones, maracas, Indian bells, gato drums, djembe, tone bars, and cabassas available for the group. Also, more complex musical instruments like a guitar and two pianos were used. In the group, clients were encouraged to improvise, and therapists were providing support for the instruments. Like in a psychotherapy group, sometimes two therapists may also be used in music therapy like in this study when there is a need for more psychological, physiological, or musical support for the clients. In this study, there were two music therapy groups where the other received MT after being a control group for another (Carr et al., 2012, pp. 5–6).

In the free improvisations with the PTSD clients, the therapists were listening carefully to the clients' music and provided them their close accompaniment (Carr et al., 2012, p. 7). Music therapists were responding to the group with their own improvisation by imitating some aspects in the music of the group member like the pitch, resonance, and timbre. Therapists were also providing a broader musical structure where the whole group was included (Wigram, 2004). Even though this study of MT was manualised for the research purposes, music therapists used various instruments, a flute and a piano, as their primary instruments and percussions. When the therapies progressed, they were extending and varying their musical interactions with the groups. This is a naturalistic use of methods and instruments in MT, where free improvisations are developing in accordance with the psychological and musical processes with clients that a therapist can approach psychotherapeutically within improvisations using different techniques (Ahonen-Eerikäinen, 2007; Alanne, 2010, 2014a, 2023, Bruscia, 1987; De Backer & Sutton, 2014a; Wigram, 2004).

The goals for the group music therapy with PTSD clients were fostering the safety and encouraging to use the MT setting and instruments in communication by regular and complete attendance in the group (Carr et al., 2012, p. 7). Other goals for the groups of this study, which can also be goals for the traumatised refugee groups, were increasing the self-agency and questioning the assumptions of leadership by increasing the independence, autonomy, and the initiatives of musical ideas in the groups. Also, alleviation of PTSD symptoms, like reexperiencing and avoiding the trauma as well as hyperarousal and depression associated with the traumatic experiences, was the monitored goal of the study.

Other general music therapy goals of psychiatry in the UK for these groups included offering opportunities for socialisation and support, providing experiences of making music for psychological, physical, and emotional benefits (Carr et al., 2012, p. 7). Also, utilising music to lessen anxiety and increase self-esteem, providing a space for thinking freely and promoting relaxation, was set as the general goal.

Goals for music therapy groups included also providing opportunities to speak in a group and enabling the participants an opportunity to play creatively without dependency of verbal instructions. These goals are also suitable for group music therapy with refugees in general.

In these music therapy groups, PTSD clients described that music sometimes gave them a "bad head" and memories, or they felt sounds unpleasant even though flashbacks did not occur (Carr et al., 2012, p. 11). It seems like music was then a bad object for these clients; however, they considered that music therapy was grounding their dissociative states. One female client in a study described the decreasing of dissociation with the help of music: "To be yourself again. You feel like you're you and not just somebody else walking around as if you're up there watching down on you" (ibid.). "When I'm in this room and I'm playing, I feel me again … like I was before … before everything that happened. When I go out that door—out there—I feel as if I'm up there again in a cloud watching me" (ibid.).

These experiences with music are examples of music being a good object and container for traumatised. It is also showing the effects of music therapy techniques like the *grounding* from Analytic Music Therapy (AMT) used for the dissociative/split experiences in the study (Alanne, 2023; Carr et al., 2012; Priestley, 1975; Volkman, 1993). In music therapy with traumatised, group or individual, music can be used to create safe space and trust with musical grounding that may lessen the avoidance of traumatic experiences and help in encountering of them with music. Music as a direct stimulus and sounding object can be difficult to avoid. This potential of music has been used by the interrogators for the detainees like described earlier. However, in music therapy, clients have told that music provided them a point of focus and link to the present (Carr et al., 2012, p. 18).

In this regard, musical stimulus upon and making music seemed to help the clients to distract from the PTSD symptoms and increased their focus and attention in the present (ibid.). This enabled the clients to associate and incorporate safer memories alongside their traumatic memories in music therapy. This capability of music in music therapy is crucial for the treatment of traumatic experiences and refugees in individual or group music therapy. In therapy, music is used professionally to enable good object experiences and working-through of the bad object experiences relating to trauma. With musical grounding, the integrating of the past, present, and the future is possible as music is distracting the dissociation, avoiding, and reexperiencing of trauma as it also provokes good memories, experiences, imagery, and hope (Volkman, 1993). In this regard, music therapy is working in different directions from those of the torture where the goals have been to break and disturb with music and sounds.

Trauma clients may also use music for the defensive purposes in avoiding and tolerating bad memories. The PTSD clients in the UK study of group music therapy told that they used music in blocking out or getting rid of their evocative emotions, especially anger and sadness (Carr et al., 2012, p. 12). This kind of use of music may be therapeutic self-care or escapism, and acting out if it does not include conscious working-through and containing of traumatic experiences that a therapist should monitor in individual or group music therapy: Is music a part of the client's resistance or acting out in therapy where the experiences, feelings, and their discussion are avoided? Or is it helping the client to stabilise, work through, and integrate traumatic experiences and memories?

In working-through of the avoidance symptoms, the feelings that music, sounds, and instruments bring can be reflected verbally in music therapy. This helps the clients to integrate their experiences musically and verbally, instead of avoiding or numbing them. For example, one male client in the UK music therapy group study noticed that the instrument flute itself brought sad feelings and memories in him that he wished to avoid. However, these feelings were relieved as the others in the group joined in playing. He said: "The sadness is good shared. It gives you back memories that you don't wanna have and it makes you feel depressed. So when other people join in it kind of evens out that it's meeting the other so you don't feel like that" (Carr et al., 2012, p. 12).

This kind of psychotherapeutic reflection of music can be done in music therapy with traumatised and refugees: What kind of associations and feelings music is bringing. They can be discussed in a group where the participants can share their experiences relating to music and instruments. This can provide important peer support verbally and musically how to deal and cope with difficult feelings like in the cited experience from group music therapy. Also, the therapist may discuss, confront, clarify, interpret, and emphatically describe the emotions of the group or the client in individual therapy (Alanne, 2010, 2023). This can be done also musically by using music that is somehow depicting or matching the emotions of clients that they are unaware of. In this, a therapist may use recorded music or improvisation in portraying the different emotional and personality aspects of clients (Alanne, 2010, 2023; Alvin, 1966/1975; Priestley, 1975).

The therapist can propose a theme for the free improvisation according to the theme that is discussed with a client. After the free improvisation, the therapist and client may continue again with psychotherapeutic discussions and explore verbally the contents, and the experiences shared in music. In an individual music therapy with traumatised refugees this kind of psychotherapeutic process may continue and develop according to the personal issues and traumas of clients. In such an individual music therapy process, the therapy may clearly manifest the phases of trauma work, stabilisation, working through, and integration. As discussed earlier, these phases may vary during the therapeutic recovery process (Herman, 1992/2022).

However, in my clinical experiences as well as according to literature, usually in the beginning of therapy, there is usually more need for the stabilisation of traumatic experiences and dissociation. But as can be seen with music that is integrating the experience in the present, also the other phases of recovery can be involved simultaneously. The therapist must assess what kind of techniques and processes are possible for the client or a group individually depending on the clinical situation of a client and the length of the planned therapy respectively.

From the mastering of trauma point view, music and other creative media like drawing with children enable the reexperience of trauma safely when it can have symbolic form in arts instead of physical symptoms, dissociation, avoidance, and acting out (Bensimon, 2020; Castaneda et al., 2018). The defence mechanism acting out which can be even self-destructive for the clients of different age should be discerned from playing out of feelings and traumas in music or psychotherapy that is natural, healthy social activity especially for children and adolescents (Alanne, 2023; Bensimon, 2020; Erikson, 1950/1964). In child psychotherapy playing is considered as free associating of the child like the free improvisation techniques in music psychotherapy respectively (Alanne, 2014a, 2023; Brummer, 2005).

In the referred UK study of group music therapy, one effect of music therapy was the relaxation and enjoyment of the PTSD clients (Carr et al., 2012, p. 13). Drumming and playing of different instruments like guitar were experienced as fun and soothing. It is very important for the traumatised people and refugees to be able to enjoy things in life again where they may feel to be detached from. Also, the clients may feel so anxious and depressed or have different kinds of pains like torture survivors that they cannot necessarily think or feel anything else (Alanne, 2010). Music and music therapy may return positive feelings and imagery for them. In group music therapy of PTSD clients, participants enjoyed the most on meeting other people, which is also important for their recovery to see and trust other people as the basic needs of humans for the company and community (Carr et al., 2012, p. 13). For the brains, music can transmit the presence of the other people with its sounds and singing (Alanne, 2023; van der Kolk, 2014).

Another music therapy technique for relaxation and expressing emotions like anger is drumming, which the clients found helpful in another group music therapy study of soldiers suffering from PTSD (Bensimon et al., 2008). Drumming as a technique of music therapy increased the clients' sense of openness, togetherness, belonging, sharing, closeness, connectedness, and intimacy, which are important feelings for the recovery of PTSD because these clients are restricting and avoiding their emotions as well as other people. This may increase their isolation and alienation from the social life. Drumming also achieved a non-intimidating access to the clients' traumatic memories and helped in regaining a sense of self-control for their anger. Even though these studies are examples of group music therapy with PTSD clients, similar methods can very well be used in individual therapy, where the therapist can mirror the clients' music and facilitate their expression and control of experiences.

For the relaxation and promotion of emotional processing in traumatic experiences of traumatised refugees Orth (2005) used music-making and song writing. They were also a part of the autobiographical collection of trauma narrative in music therapy. Both Orth (ibid.) and Bensimon et al. (2008) are suggesting that music can provide pleasure and safety structures and limits for the experimentations and expression of experiences (Carr et al., 2012, pp. 3–4). According to Orth (ibid.), often familiar music, standard instrumentals, is predictable for the traumatised refugees where there are even rhythms and slow paces. Also, the using of hands in drumming and playing other instruments may help the ego and brain in controlling the traumatic experiences and the feelings relating to it like the outbursts of anger (Alanne, 2010; Slotoroff, 1994).

When the feelings expressed in music are also verbalised and reflected, they are activating the verbal coding system of brain and the declarative memory process that is integrating and symbolising the trauma. The symbolisation of traumatic experiences is important with all the PTSD clients and traumatised refugees where music and other art forms may help in the recovery process with children, adolescents, and adults (Bensimon, 2020, p. 308). The symbolisation of trauma from non-organised states of procedural memory and somatic experiences, beta elements, to alpha elements, thoughts, memories, feelings, imagery, and symbols is the goal of individual or group music psychotherapy for traumatised (Ahonen-Eerikäinen, 2007; Alanne, 2019, 2020, 2023; Robarts, 2003, Schulman, 2002).

In an individual or group music therapy, the music's capability to synchronise experiences between the clients and the therapist is also important (Alanne, 2014a, 2023; Bensimon, 2023; Rose, 2004). PTSD clients and traumatised refugees may feel themselves lonely and isolated from other people where music therapy can enhance their feelings of belonging and connectedness as discussed earlier (Bensimon, 2023, pp. 154–155). This synchronisation concerns also the body and brain of the clients, how clients may find group cohesion in the rhythms of music, body movements, how they move their heads and limbs. This is also social synchronisation and finding the "we-ness" in the group (p. 154). In addition to the psychological and social synchronisation in music, also the brains of clients are synchronised as there seems to be concordance between psychic structures and the brains (Alanne, 2014a, 2023; Rose, 2004). When a traumatised client is off the track music and interpersonal emotions involved in the mirroring of music and the therapeutic relationship may produce corrective experiences neurobiologically (Alanne, 2023, p. 130).

Such methods like music, arts, and imagery in psychotherapy that are helping the client to look inside and learn from their experiences are useful in the rehabilitation of traumas (Alanne, 2023, p. 130; van der Kolk, 2014, p. 206). For example, music can increase the levels of the ACTH that the amygdala is producing in the brains. This is reducing the stress and alertness and is linked to the medial prefrontal cortex of the brain and its functions where there is the capability of self-awareness and interception ("looking inside") (Alanne, 2023, p. 130). This is crucial for the reexperiencing of the traumatic experiences, their mentalisation, and linking the traumatic stress to the verbal coding in the brain. In such a way, music can be an "external auxiliary ego" and a "prosthetic device" for the traumatised (Rose, 2004, p. 119). Music and singing songs as an example can integrate and synchronise psychic and neurological structures and functions in the brain also for the dementia, Parkinson, autism, and aphasia clients and increase their understanding of the time and place, memories, feelings, and language (Alanne, 2023, pp. 140–141).

In individual music therapy with traumatised refugees, there is usually better possibility for the working-through of trauma when the therapy is a long-term process of one year or more, with regular weekly sessions or more for 40 to 60 minutes depending on the clients and methods used. For the GIM, and if there is a need for an interpreter, then the session should be a bit longer than usual, so that there would be enough time for music listening and psychotherapeutic discussions that are translated for the client. If there is a need for a lot of discussion and music, then it could be better to meet once a week if that is possible for the client's situation. Sometimes severely traumatised clients cannot meet a therapist too often when they are needing time for their psychic stabilisation (Stubley, 2022b, p. 44).

Then, also sessions every second week can be useful, so that the therapy will not come too exhausting for the client if the dissociative symptoms are increasing between the sessions. Especially, in the beginning of rehabilitation during the consultation, the clients that have a narrow window of tolerance for the stress, who have lost their trust in the good object, have strong persecutory anxieties, disorganised attachment, excess of projective identification, and a history of problematic encounters with services, often repeatedly, could benefit from meetings twice a month (Stubley, 2022b, p. 44). Later, when these clients can settle into the therapeutic setting and work with their traumas, they may benefit from more intensive music psychotherapy. Music and music therapy as a part of the first consultations may motivate and help the clients to engage with their rehabilitation and continue music therapy with the regular meetings of once a week, for example.

In the groups similar deeper individual processes may not be always possible or in the short-term therapies. However, also in this kind of therapies clients may gain insights for their personal traumas and stories as they are hearing the other clients' experiences and trauma stories in the group. As discussed in the earlier clinical examples and research of music therapy groups, clients may benefit groups in many other ways like overcoming social fears and learning to trust others. They may also learn to control, share, express, and verbalise their experiences and feelings in group music therapy as well as in the short-term music therapy. However, in the short-term therapies, the goals of the treatment cannot be very extensive when considering the changes in the client's personality. Then, more supportive and re-educative goals of discovering feelings and expressing them could be enough. Also, more mature defences and coping towards trauma may be learnt in the short-term individual and group therapies. In the long group music therapy process, more analytic working through and integrating of traumas is also possible, especially if the group is a closed group with the same regular participants and not too many of them. This setting builds trust and safety for the participants to express themselves and discuss about their traumatic experiences.

Depending on the clients' age, clinical situation, the level of traumatisation, and the goals for the therapy, the time of the session and their frequency should be adjusted according to the time needed for the music and the discussion. Usually, the time for both and every participant respectively is good to assess when planning an individual or a group therapy and their setting. When working mainly with music, like using free improvisation or band playing, then the time for the discussion in groups does not have necessarily clear limits. However, it is good to think that in some point of the therapy, the traumatised refugee clients may be able to discuss more about their issues and feelings that should have time in the sessions. This is already achievement in music therapy with traumatised refugees like torture survivors (Alanne, 2010).

Especially within the groups the therapist must concern different nationalities and ethnicities participating the group. What kind of music they want to sing or play? Are there cultural differences? Is some music considered as unsafe or humiliating for some participants because of their culture or religion? It is good that the therapists would think this kind of questions while planning and doing their work because there may come situations like different songs and music that are asked or used in groups. Then, it is also good to discuss with the group, or in individual therapy, whether they feel safe to listen or play music. This can be a part of the cultural dialogue and therapeutic process in the group or between the therapist and clients that will be introduced more in the next chapter.

Discussions about the lyrics and contents on what they are meaning for the group participants or the client in individual therapy are important even though the discussed music will not be listened or played. Then, the clients have a possibility to tell how they are feeling about the music or song, what kind of feelings and memories it brings. The discussion about the music and songs may already be music psychotherapy as there may come associations and memories relating to songs from the homeland, the prison, or the camp where it was played as a part of the violence and torturing. Even the discussion of such musical experience may help the client to memorise and work through their traumas. However, as some music may be very touching and sensitive for the clients because of the sad memories from their home countries or how some music may be associated to the oppressive governments, it is important to discuss first about the music.

In a group, it can be asked from the other group members whether anyone is opposing playing and singing a song that has been suggested in the group. This is a good point in any music therapy group to consider like I have done with my clients for years, so that the group together is discussing and deciding the song, not a therapist or any other group member alone. This kind of sensitive approach in music therapy is increasing the safety and trust in clients. Clients can also feel that they have equal status as the group members or with a therapist as a fellow human in music and in the group that is fostering their agency in life.

As the many refugees are traumatised and suffering from the PTSD symptoms relating to sounds, it is also important to check the level of volumes in musical instruments like electric guitars, drums, and the PA system that the therapist may be using in a group or in individual therapy. The therapist can ask, is anyone feeling that the sounds are too loud? Then, the sounds can be adjusted so that everyone can hear and bear the sounds of music and the instruments. This is also important to ask in individual therapy of any other clients as well because many other clients may be sensitive to sounds and other stimuli because of their psychic disorder and stress relating to it (Stubley, 2022a, p. 20),

If the client, like a torture survivor, cannot listen or play music in one session because of trauma symptoms like headache, tiredness, or feeling bad, it should be notified and respected (Alanne, 2010). In this, like with the other trauma symptoms, a therapist may assess what is the window of tolerance for the client to discuss about traumatic themes or use music in therapy (Stubley, 2022a, p. 18). Is the client in a hyper- or hypoarousal state of mind when thinking or talking is not possible? In a hyperarousal, the client's nervous system is in the flight/fight mode, and in the hypoarousal in the freeze mode. Music in therapy may help the client and therapist to be in the window of tolerance where the clients can function and contain their experiences to some degree (Grassi, 2021; Gravestock, 2021).

In individual or even in group therapy music does not have to be listened or played if the clients do not want it when they cannot tolerate it. Then, the therapist and clients can talk about the experiences and associations that are coming to mind, for example. When the client is feeling better, music can be listened again. It is important to understand that many of the severely traumatised cannot necessarily express verbally their feelings and conditions. Instead, they may experience their traumas and psychic symptoms physically and often complain about their different kinds of pains, for example (Alanne, 2010). This is called alexithymia when the clients do not have language for their feelings and cannot talk about them because of their traumatisation in therapy (van der Kolk et al., 1996/2007, p. 60).

A therapist may also function as the container of the client's experiences of songs, playing and singing by listening, describing, and commenting them (Alanne 2023; Gravestock 2021). This is supporting of the client's capability for thinking from disorganised bodily states and beta elements to alpha elements (Alanne, 2020, 2023; Bion 1962/2007; 1970/2018; Erel-Brodsky 2016; Grassi 2021; Gravestock 2021). This containing and holding of experiences is especially important when the clients are feeling physically sick and cannot tolerate listening or playing music in therapy. However, as discussed, using music may help the clients to be in their window tolerance of stress, pain, and anxiety where there is a possibility for working through their hard experiences with music that is enabling symbolic distance for the therapy. For example, a listened song may be telling about the client's own feelings and experiences unconsciously or consciously in an individual or group therapy that can be reflected and discussed (Alanne, 2010, 2014a, 2023; Gravestock, 2021; Lehtonen, 2007).

It is also building of trust and alliance with clients when they can control the music in therapy according to their own willingness to use it. This is supporting their own agency like with the torture survivors whose own will has been taken from them. With the controlling of the music and sounds they are also learning to control and express their experiences and feelings. Therefore, introducing and playing music with clients must be done safely, so that the clients are feeling that the music is good for them and not felt as a persecuting bad object sound experience. This may take time in individual or group therapy, but when the clients can listen to or play more music in therapy, it is already a sign of psychic recovery like the capability of being able to discuss more, especially about their traumatic experiences and feelings, respectively (Alanne, 2010, 2013, 2019).

In general, music may help in symbolising the experiences of traumatised and refugees that is important for the differentiation of traumatic experiences and the flooding of unconsciousness as uncontrollable. Then, in music psychotherapy, symbolisation as the goal for therapy, the traumatic experiences are externalised into music where they can be controlled and internalised as a part of "me" experience in the psychotherapeutic process. In an individual or group work, various methods of music therapy, free improvisation, music listening, songs, drawing, painting, moving, clay-work, relaxation, writing a poem, collecting a self-narrative, and so on, can be used to increase the clients' capability for symbolisation as the goal of treatment (Ahonen-Eerikäinen, 2007; Ahonen & Mongillo Desideri, 2014; Alanne, 2010, 2019, 2023).

From the psychoanalytical point of view, arts like music are enabling the process of mourning when the clients are encountering their feelings in music. Sorrowing is an important goal for the recovery of trauma as it is moving the client into the depressive (D) position from the paranoid-schizoid (PS) position of the fight/flight state and alertness (Klein, 1946, 1952; Stubley, 2022a, pp. 22–23). Segal (1957) has pointed out that words are the possibility for imaginary thinking and emotional development from the early symbolic equation of the PS position to the D position. When the traumatised clients like refugees are producing their own narratives with music and music therapy methods like guided imagery, they may contain their non-organised thinking and feelings into the symbolic expression of music, arts, and words. They are promoting their emotional development to a more coherent narrative of their life history that their traumatisation has impaired (Stubley, 2022a, p. 22).

This is important because trauma is destroying the separation between internal and external realities through nightmares, terrifying thoughts, fantasies that are often felt as real and concrete (Stubley, 2022a, pp. 22–23). The traumatised is in the psychic equivalence mode of mentalising where the mental contents are felt to correspond with the physical realities. This may result as the avoiding of "knife" word or other words in therapy like one trauma survivor woman who had been attacked with a knife (p. 22.). Thus, trauma is destroying the links between the words, feelings, and knowledge of things that are experienced as unthinkable and unbearable (Bion, 1959). Instead, they are acted out or upon the body as trauma symptoms of dissociation or splitting and they cannot be remembered or reflected. In such cases, music and other art forms may help in reconnecting the psychic experiences, state of minds, parts of personalities, and identities for the traumatised. By doing so, they can also help in creating new meaning and psychic structures for the clients who are identifying with the therapist's empathic reactions, feelings of music, and their shared verbalising (Alanne, 2010, 2023).

Bensimon (2023, p. 155) has recommended five mechanisms—relaxation, playfulness, sense of control, super-expressive emotions, and interpersonal synchronisations—as important for the healing process of trauma with music. These mechanisms may also be used in music therapy with traumatised refugees, or in their preventive mental health work with music. It is also good to remember that not all music therapy, psychotherapy, and rehabilitation can be fully curative in its goals with severely injured or ill clients. There can also be preventive and ameliorating goals for the therapy, like with severely traumatised clients, including refugees and torture survivors (Alanne, 2010). They are also important goals in maintaining the psychic, physical, social, and global functioning and wellbeing of clients, like with the clients who are suffering from chronical illnesses, psychoses, and personality disorders. These may be comorbid disorders of traumatised refugees and other clients in music therapy that a therapist should consider when assessing, making the treatment plan, and evaluating it during the therapy process.

In conclusion, I recommend following goals and aspects that I have described and studied to be considered in music therapy and when using music in the treatment of refugees. The goals for the treatment of traumatised refugees such as torture survivors may include

(a) learning to control and confront disturbing thoughts and difficult emotional experiences by supporting the control functions of ego and developing the self-regulation of clients
(b) developing concentration, strengthening the experiences of stability, reality testing of clients with music
(c) desensitising of traumatic memories with music
(d) transformation of bodily neural experiences, brain dynamics (e.g. endorphins, amygdala) in the dual coding system and the procedural memory with music
(e) restructuring of thoughts, perceptions, and emotions (here-and-now moments, interactions, embodied experiences, and synchronisations)
(f) producing positive healing/corrective experiences, images, narratives, etc., with music
(g) returning security in the social relationships and networks of refugees
(h) reducing of trauma-related defences and action, like avoidance behaviour, acting-out, and reexperiencing of trauma
(i) rebuilding of the basic safety and trust (returning of dialogue in music and words)
(j) integration and containing of dissociated states of mind, personalities, or identities for the cohesive self-experience and narrative
(k) collecting a life story as a part of the verbalising, description, and sharing of traumatic experiences
(l) enabling grieving
(m) bringing back the capability to enjoy music as a part of the cultural and social integration of refugee immigrants
(n) returning the hope and joy for the lives of traumatised refugees, their families, and their communities (humour, playfulness, and creativity in music)
(o) promoting liberation and recovering from trauma individually, as a group, or as a community, including intergenerational traumatisation (Alanne, 2010, 2013, p. 274; 2014b, 2019, p. 311; Beck, 2019)

Many of these goals and aspects of treating traumatised refugees are possible in the longer processes of music psychotherapy, especially those that are concerning the defences and the personality structures of clients. Even the memorising and mourning of traumatic experiences and losses as a part of the refugee crisis may need often longer time. In the very short therapies and musical interventions this kind of durable changes cannot be set because the changing of the defences and behaviour like avoidance behaviour, acting out, and reexperiencing/reexposuring of trauma that are automatised and unconscious in the clients' personalities and nervous system may take years of therapy and rehabilitation. However, also in the shorter interventions and therapies including music they may be relevant to consider, confront, clarify, and interpret for the clients as their long-term goals for the treatment, and rehabilitation may include many treatments and professionals working with the client over the years. Also, the change in the rehabilitation including music therapy can occur in smaller pieces at the time.

With good experiences of music, in individual or group therapy, vitality and resilience may emerge for the often-long recovery from the traumatic experiences. Even in shorter interventions and therapies, music education with other people may become important for the motivation, empowerment, and encouragement for such a process. There may also be peer groups of men and women suffering similar traumas and disorders where music can provide elevating experiences and hope in recovering from difficult problems. The long-term therapies and working-through of traumas require a professional training in music therapy and psychotherapy combined with a specialised training/knowledge in trauma-related work. Also, other kinds of trauma-informed therapies, interventions, and techniques with music in the treatment may benefit the traumatised refugees. All this work can be planned and implemented according to the overall phases of recovery from trauma, stabilisation, working-through, and integration of trauma with music. However, not necessarily always in that order but depending on the individual processes of clients and their specific needs concerning also music in their lives (Alanne, 2019; Beck et al., 2021; Herman, 1992/2022; Sokira et al., 2023; Stubley, 2022b; Wolf, 2007).

References

Ahonen, H., & Mongillo Desideri, A. (2014). Heroines' journey—Emerging story by refugee women during group analytic music therapy. *Voices: A World Forum for Music Therapy, 14*(1). https://doi.org/10.15845/voices.v14i1.686

Ahonen-Eerikäinen, H. (2007). *Group analytic music therapy*. Barcelona Publishers.

Akombo, D. O. (2001). Reporting on music therapy in Kenya. *Voices: A World Forum for Music Therapy, 1*(1). https://doi.org/10.15845/voices.v1i1.45

Alanne, S. (2005). Music psychotherapy for torture survivors. *Music Therapy Today*, 6(4), 682–697. Special Issue: Proceedings of the 6th EMTC 2004 Conference, University of Jyväskylä. D. Aldridge & J. Fachner (Eds.), MusicTherapyWorld.net Witten: University Witten/Herdecke.

Alanne, S. (2010). *Music psychotherapy with refugee survivors of torture. Interpretations of three clinical case studies*. Sibelius Academy. Studia Musica.

Alanne, S. (2013). Psykodynaaminen musiikkipsykoterapia kidutuksesta traumatisoituneiden pakolaisten kanssa: Kliininen näkökulma. [Psychodynamic music psychotherapy with the refugees traumatised from the torture: A clinical point of view.]. *Psykoterapia, 32*(4), 264–276.

Alanne, S. (2014a). *Musiikkipsykoterapia*. Teoria ja käytäntö. [Music psychotherapy. Theory and practice.] Acta Universitatis Ouluensis D Medica 1248.

Alanne, S. (2014b). The ethnocultural and psychodynamic meaning of music for traumatised refugees. *Music Therapy Today*, 10(1), 48–49. Special issue: Proceedings of the 14th World Congress of Music Therapy Vienna/Krems, Austria, July 7–12, 2014.

Alanne, S. (2019). Musiikkipsykoterapia traumatisoituneiden pakolaisten ja maahanmuuttajien kuntoutuksessa. [Music psychotherapy in the rehabilitation of refugees and immigrants.]. *Psykoterapia, 38*(4), 306–318.

Alanne, S. (2020). Musiikin ja kielen suhteesta—sekä psykoterapeuttisesta arvosta. [About the relationship of music and language—And their psychotherapeutic value.]. *Psykoanalyyttinen Psykoterapia, 16*, 6–15.

Alanne, S. (2023). *The theory and practice of psychodynamic music psychotherapy*. Barcelona Publishers.

Alvin, J. (1966/1975). *Music therapy*. Basic Books.

Austin, D. (1999). Vocal improvisation in analytically orientated music therapy with adults. In T. Wigram & J. De Backer (Eds.), *Clinical applications of music therapy in psychiatry* (pp. 141–157). Jessica Kingsley.

Austin, D. (2002). The wounded healer. The voice of trauma: A wounded healer's perspective. In J. P. Sutton (Ed.), *Music, music therapy, and trauma. International perspectives* (pp. 231–259). Jessica Kingsley.

Baker, F., & Jones, C. (2005). Holding a steady beat: The effects of a music therapy program on stabilizing behaviours of newly arrived refugee students. *British Journal of Music Therapy, 19*(2), 67–74.

Barath, A. (1996). Creative therapies for war-traumatised children: 1991–95 Croatian experience. *Croatian Medical Journal, 37*(3), 174–184.

Beck, B. D. (2019). Music therapy for refugees. In S. Lindahl Jacobsen, I. Nygaard Pedersen, & L. O. Bonde (Eds.), *A comprehensive guide to music therapy. Theory, clinical practice, research and training* (2nd ed., pp. 342–352). Jessica Kingsley.

Beck, B. D., Messel, C., Lund Meyer, S., Cordtz, T. O., Søgaard, U., Simonsen, E., & Moe, T. (2018). Feasibility of trauma-focused guided imagery and music with adult refugees diagnosed with PTSD: A pilot study. *Nordic Journal of Music Therapy, 27*(1), 67–86.

Beck, B. D., Meyer, S. L., Simonsen, E., Søgaard, U., Petersen, I., Arnfred, S. M. H., Tellier, T., & Moe, T. (2021). Music therapy was noninferior to verbal standard treatment of traumatised refugees in mental healthcare: Results from a randomized clinical trial. *European Journal of Psychotraumatology, 12*(1), 1930960. https://doi.org/10.1080/20008198.2021.1930960

Bensimon, M. (2020). Perceptions of music therapists regarding their work with children living under continuous war threat: Experiential reframing of trauma through songs. *Nordic Journal of Music Therapy, 29*(4), 300–316. https://doi.org/10.1080/08098131.2019.1703210

Bensimon, M. (2023). Mechanisms of change in music therapy when treating adults coping with trauma. In L. E. Beer & J. C. Birnbaum (Eds.), *Trauma-informed music therapy. Theory and practice* (pp. 150–157). Routledge.

Bensimon, M., Amir, D., & Wolf, Y. (2008). Drumming through trauma: Music therapy with post-traumatic soldiers. *The Arts in Psychotherapy, 35*(1), 34–48.

Bion, W. R. (1959). Attacks on linking. *International Journal of Psycho-Analysis, 40*, 308–315.

Bion, W. R. (1962). *Learning from experience*. Karnac.

Bion, W. R. (1970/2018). *Attention and interpretation*. Routledge.

Bonny, H. (2002). *Music and consciousness: The evolution of imagery and music*. Barcelona.

Brummer, M. (2005). Psykoterapeuttinen suhde ja prosessi. [Psychotherapeutic relationship and process.]. In M. Brummer & H. Enckell (Eds.), *Lasten ja nuorten psykoterapia* (Psychotherapy of children and adolescents) (pp. 109–142). WSOY.

Bruscia, K. E. (1987). *Improvisational models of Music therapy*. Charles C Thomas.

Bruscia, K. E. (1998). An introduction to music psychotherapy. In K. E. Bruscia (Ed.), *The dynamics of music psychotherapy* (pp. 1–15). Barcelona.

Bruscia, K. E. (2002). A psychodynamic orientation to the Bonny method. In K. E. Bruscia & D. E. Grocke (Eds.), *Guided imagery and music. The Bonny method and beyond* (pp. 225–243). Barcelona.

Carr, C., d'Ardenne, P., Sloboda, A., Scott, C., Wang, D., & Priebe, S. (2012). Group music therapy for patients with persistent post-traumatic stress disorder—An exploratory randomized controlled trial with mixed methods evaluation. *Psychology and Psychotherapy: Theory, Research and Practice, 85*(2), 179–202. https://doi.org/10.1111/j.2044-8341.2011.02026x

Castaneda, A. E., Mäki-Opas, J., Jokela, S., Kivi, N., Lähteenmäki, M., Miettinen, T., Nieminen, S., Santalahti, P., & PALOMA Expert Group. (2018). *Pakolaisten mielenterveyden tukeminen Suomessa*. PALOMA käsikirja. [Supporting refugees' mental health in Finland. PALOMA handbook.] Guidance, May 2018. Publications of the National Institute for Health and Welfare.

De Backer, J., & Sutton, J. (2014a). Theoretical perspectives of music therapy. The state of the art. In J. De Backer & J. Sutton (Eds.), *The music in music therapy. Psychodynamic music therapy in Europe: Clinical, theoretical and research approaches* (pp. 37–57). Jessica Kingsley.

De Backer, J., & Sutton, J. (2014b). Therapeutic interventions in psychodynamic music therapy: The music in music therapy. In J. De Backer & J. Sutton (Eds.), *The music in music therapy. Psychodynamic music therapy in Europe: Clinical, theoretical and research approaches* (pp. 338–349). Jessica Kingsley.

Dixon, M. (2002). Music and human rights. In J. P. Sutton (Ed.), *Music, music therapy and trauma. International perspectives* (pp. 119–132). Jessica Kingsley.

Einarsen, O. K., Krüger, V., Engebretsen, I. M. S., & Stige, B. (2024). Collaboration between social workers and music therapists in a child welfare context for unaccompanied refugee children: A focus group study. *Voices: A World Forum for Music Therapy, 24*(3). https://doi.org/10.15845/voices.v24i3.4071

Enge, K. E. A., & Stige, B. (2021). Musical pathways to the peer community: A collective case study of refugee children's use of music therapy. *Nordic Journal of Music Therapy*. https://doi.org/10.1080/08098131.2021.1891130

Erel-Brodsky, H. (2016). I'm all ears—Thoughts on psychoanalysis: The musical reverie. *Contemporary Psychoanalysis, 52*(4), 578–601.

Erikson, E. H. (1950/1964). Toys and reasons. In M. R. Haworth (Ed.), *Child Psychotherapy: Practice and Theory* (pp. 3–11). Basic Books.

Fancourt, D., & Saoirse, F. (2019). *What is the evidence on the role of the arts in improving health and well-being? A scoping review*. Health Evidence Network Synthesis Report 67. World Health Organization. Regional Office for Europe.

Grassi, L. (2021). *The sound of the unconscious. Psychoanalysis as music*. Routledge.

Gravestock, J. (2021). *Music therapy in adoption and trauma. Therapy that makes a difference after placement*. Jessica Kingsley.

Gulbay, S. (2021). Exploring the use of hip hop-based music therapy to address trauma in asylum seeker and unaccompanied minor migrant youth. *Voices: A World Forum for Music Therapy, 21*(3). https://doi.org/10.15845/voices.v21i3.3192

Herman, J. L. (1992/2022). *Trauma and Recovery*. The Aftermath of Violence – From Domestic Abuse to Political Terror. Basic Books.

Hunt, M. (2005). Action research and music therapy: Group music therapy with young refugees in a school community. *Voices: A World Forum for Music Therapy, 5*(2). https://doi.org/10.15845/voices.v5i2.22

Jones, C., & Baker, F. (2004). From healing rituals to music therapy: Bridging the cultural divide between therapist and young Sudanese refugees. *The Arts in Psychotherapy, 31*(2), 89–100.

Klein, M. (1946). Notes on some schizoid mechanisms. *International Journal of Psycho-Analysis, 27*, 99–110.

Klein, M. (1952). The origins of transference. *International Journal of Psycho-Analysis, 33*, 433–438.

Krüger, V., Nordanger, D. Ø., & Stige, B. (2018). Music therapy: Building bridges between a participatory approach and trauma-informed care in a child welfare setting. *Voices: A World Forum for Music Therapy, 18*(4). https://voices.no/index.php/voices/article/view/2593

Lehtonen, K. (2007). *Musiikin symboliset ulottuvuudet*. [Symbolic dimensions of music.] Finnish Society for Music Therapy.

Levinge, A. (2015). *The music of being: Music therapy, Winnicott, and the school of object relations*. Jessica Kingsley.

McFerran, K. S., Lai, H. I. C., Chang, W.-H., Acquaro, D., Chin, T. C., Stokes, H., & Crooke, A. (2020). Music, rhythm, and trauma: A critical interpretive synthesis of research literature. *Frontiers in Psychology, 11*, 324. https://doi.org/10.3389/fpsyg.2020.00324

Orth, J. (2005). Music therapy with traumatised refugees in a clinical setting. *Voices: A World Forum for Music Therapy*. http://www.voices.no/mainissues/mi40005000182.html

Orth, J., & Verburgt, J. (1998). One step beyond. Music therapy with traumatised refugees in a psychiatric clinic. In D. Dokter (Ed.), *Arts therapists, refugees and migrants. Reaching across borders* (pp. 80–93). Jessica Kingsley.

Orth, J., Doorschodt, L., Verburgt, J., & Drožđek, B. (2004). Sounds of trauma: An introduction to methodology in music therapy with traumatised refugees in clinical and outpatient settings. In J. P. Wilson & B. Drožđek (Eds.), *Broken spirits. The treatment of traumatised asylum seekers, refugees and torture victims* (pp. 443–480). Brunner–Routledge.

Priestley, M. (1975). *Music therapy in action.* Constable.

Robarts, J. Z. (2003). The healing function of improvised songs in music therapy with a child survivor of early trauma and sexual abuse. In S. Hadley (Ed.), *Psychodynamic music therapy: Case studies* (pp. 141–182). Barcelona.

Rose, G. J. (2004). *Between couch and piano. Psychoanalysis, music, art and neuroscience.* Brunner–Routledge.

Saraneva, K. (2018). Vieraasta kulttuurista tulevan pakolaisen kohtaaminen ja hoitaminen—Haasteet terapeutille. [The encountering and treatment of refugee coming from foreign culture—Challenges for the therapist.] In A. Zonzi & N. Söderblom (Eds.), *Pakolaisuus.* Merkitykset ihmiselle ja yhteisölle (pp. 90–108). [Refugeeism. The meaning for individual and community.] Therapeia Foundation.

Schulman, G. (2002). Sietämisen kestämisestä eheytymiseen. Objektin sisällyttämiskyky ja trauman integrointi. [From bearing resilience to cohesiveness. The internalising of object and the integration of trauma] In S. Haaramo & K. Palonen (Eds.), *Trauman monet kasvot.* Psyykkinen trauma sisäisenä kokemuksena (pp. 162–187). [Many faces of trauma. Psychic trauma as an inner experience.] Therapeia Foundation.

Scrine, E., & Koike, A. (2023). Questioning the promise of safety in trauma-informed music therapy practice. In L. E. Beer & J. C. Birnbaum (Eds.), *Trauma-informed music therapy. Theory and practice* (pp. 37–44). Routledge.

Segal, H. (1957). Notes on symbol formation. *International Journal of Psycho-Analysis, 38*, 391–397.

Slotoroff, C. (1994). Drumming technique for assertiveness and anger management in the short-term psychiatric setting for adult and adolescent survivors of trauma. *Music Therapy Perspectives, 12*(2), 111–116.

Sokira, J., Allen, J., & Wagner, H. (2023). The resilience framework for trauma-informed music therapy. In L. E. Beer & J. C. Birnbaum (Eds.), *Trauma-informed music therapy. Theory and practice* (pp. 9–18). Routledge.

Stubley, J. (2022a). Complex trauma: The initial consultation. In J. Stubley & L. Young (Eds.), *Complex trauma. The Tavistock model* (pp. 11–33). Routledge.

Stubley, J. (2022b). The Tavistock trauma service. In J. Stubley & L. Young (Eds.), *Complex trauma. The Tavistock model* (pp. 34–55). Routledge.

The BZFO reports. 2000–2002. *Meeting the music* (pp. 20–28). Centre for the Treatment of Torture Survivors.

van der Kolk, B. (2014). *The body keeps score. Mind, brain and body in the transformation of trauma.* Allen Lane.

van der Kolk, B.A., Weisaeth, L., & van der Hart, O. (1996/2007). History of trauma in psychiatry. In B.A. van der Kolk, A.C. McFarlane & L. Weisaeth (Eds.), *Traumatic stress. The effects of overwhelming experience on mind, body, and society* (pp. 47–74). Guilford.

Volkman, S. (1993). Music therapy and the treatment of trauma. Induced dissociative disorders. *The Arts in Psychotherapy, 20*, 243–251.

Wigram, T. (2004). *Improvisation. Methods and techniques for music therapy clinicians, educators and students.* Jessica Kingsley.

Wolf, H.-G. (2007). Grundlagen der Psychotraumatologie und der Traumatherapie. In H.-G. Wolf (Ed.), *Musiktherapie und Trauma* (pp. 11–20). Reichert Verlag.

Zharinova-Sanderson, O. (2004a). Can music help? Music therapy with traumatised refugees and torture survivors. In D. Aldridge & J. Fachner (Eds.), *Info CD ROM V.* Dialogue and Debate—Conference Proceedings of the 10th World Congress on Music Therapy (pp. 2049–2060). MusicTherapyWorld.net. University Witten Herdecke.

Zharinova-Sanderson, O. (2004b). Promoting integration and socio-cultural change: Community music therapy with traumatised refugees in Berlin. In M. Pavlicevic & G. Ansdell (Eds.), *Community music therapy* (pp. 233–248). Jessica Kingsley.

Chapter 5
Music and Music Therapy Methods with Traumatised Refugees

In this chapter, the basic methods of music and music therapy that may be used with traumatised refugees are introduced. First, the common instruments and techniques of music therapy with traumatised clients such as drumming, performance, song writing, instrument playing, listening, and singing are discussed for those who are not familiar with music therapy (Alanne, 2010; Austin, 2009; Braak, 2007; Bruscia, 2014; McFerran et al., 2020; Orth et al., 2004). However, this will be described in a level of research that is also benefitting music therapists, researchers, and other practitioners working in the field of traumas and refugees as well as those who are beginning to work in these fields. The method of free improvisation in psychodynamic music therapy will be introduced first. It is a general approach to music therapy on how music and instruments may be used in producing sounds and music without former experience or education (Alvin, 1966/1975; Bruscia, 1987; Pavlicevic, 1997; Priestley, 1975; Smetana & Storz, 2020; Wigram, 2004, 2019).

Music and free improvisation in music therapy and free association in psychoanalytic/psychodynamic psychotherapy and psychoanalysis are compared as the similar approaches to studying unconscious and traumatised experiences (Alanne, 2014a, 2023; De Backer & Sutton, 2014a, 2014b; Grassi, 2021; Kennedy, 2020; Knoblauch, 2000; Stern, 2010). Next, it will be described how music may be listened with a similar approach of free associating to music and using guided imagery in the therapeutic process with traumatised refugees (Alanne, 2005, 2010, 2014a, 2023; Beck, 2019, Bruscia, 2002; De Backer & Sutton, 2014a; Grocke & Wigram, 2007; Orth et al., 2004; Priestley, 1975; Sutton & De Backer, 2009). Also, techniques for verbalisations and psychotherapeutic discussions with traumatised refugees will be described in the psychodynamic context of using interpretations, confrontations, clarifications, and mentalisations for the clients representing different age and clinical situation (Alanne, 2014a, 2023; Allen et al., 2008; Hannibal, 2014; Lemma, 2006 Strehlow & Hannibal, 2019; Yeomans et al., 2015).

Using other artistic media and functional methods in improvisations and therapy such as play, clay, drawings, games, paintings, movements, and so on will be introduced as possible non-verbal techniques with refugee clients like children (Alanne, 2023 Bruscia, 1987, 2014). They are reducing the need for interpreter in therapy (Castaneda et al., 2018). With music and other artistic approaches in therapy with traumatised refugees, there is a possibility of expressing the traumatic experience and symbolising it (ibid.). It is possible to collect a story or a narrative of the refugee

S. Alanne, *Music, Music Therapy and Refugees*,
https://doi.org/10.1007/978-3-031-94766-7_5

with words and artistic methods in the assessment, in the beginning of treatment, and during the whole process as the result of long-term psychotherapy. Some clinical examples and vignettes of using music therapy with the traumatised clients with a refugee background will be given to illustrate topics.

5.1 Active, Receptive, and Recreational Methods

Common music therapy methods used with refugees that have been studied include active and receptive methods (Beck, 2019; Bernard & Dvorak, 2022; McFerran et al., 2020). Active music therapy methods may include active music-making with refugee clients like free improvisation with different instruments in individual and group therapies. Receptive music therapy methods include music listening techniques like the earlier described GIM and its different kind of applications and approaches like the psychodynamic and integrative orientations discussed in this book. In spite of the name "receptive" method, it is also a method where the clients can be active in their minds and doing psychological work of reflection, analysing, and describing of their experiences and emotions. Receptive music therapy methods with refugees have also included relaxation with music listening that may be combined with breathing and body scanning exercises (Beck et al., 2018; Vibe Jespersen & Vuust, 2012).

The musical relaxation can be done by listening to a specific music that is suitable for the relaxation in the beginning or in the end of music psychotherapy sessions like in GIM (Alanne, 2010; Beck et al., 2018). Then, a client has a possibility to calm from the stress, hyperalertness, and restlessness of the possible traumatic experiences and dissociations. Peaceful music with verbal instructions to relax and calm the mind and body can help the client to orient for the therapy session, listening to more music and discussing. This can help the client's nervous system and the brain adapt into the safety expectations instead avoiding and numbing the experiences or by overreacting on them with automatised fight/flight reactions (Beck, 2019, p. 348). The relaxation in the beginning of session can help the client to stay in the window of tolerance for the therapy session, not having hyper- or hypoarousal, but being active and reflecting for the psychotherapeutic working-through in the session. In the very stressed and anxious state of mind, the thinking and normal functioning is not possible.

Similarly to the beginning of the session, musical or verbal relaxation can help the client in returning from the sometimes-painful thoughts and experiences of trauma into their window of tolerance and normal feeling. It is important to remember and understand, especially when working with GIM, or generally in music psychotherapy, that when traumatised clients are encountering their issues and trauma histories, experiences, memories, and images relating to them, they can be powerful experiences that are bringing strong and mixed emotions in the clients. These experiences such as before described torture experiences, in addition to the effects of listened music, may affect, so that they may feel overwhelmed or overarousal in their minds and bodies. Therefore, it is important that the clients have a possibility to calm down and orient themselves and their bodies for a while in these situations during the sessions and before leaving therapy.

Often when listening to music for relaxation or imagery, different kinds of themes like a "sunny beach" may be given to bring positive experiences for traumatised clients so that they would feel safe (Alanne, 2019b, 2023, p. 289). These kinds of themes like "a cave" used by Priestley (1975) may be also given for the free improvisation with musical instruments that is an active music therapy method. Active music therapy methods may include drumming with a therapist or a group as well as free improvisation with different instruments like the therapist in a piano or a keyboard and the client playing keyboards, xylophones, percussions and so on (Alanne, 2019b; Bernard & Dvorak, 2022; Erkkilä et al., 2011; McFerran et al., 2020).

Therapists may also use their own set of instruments like band and school instruments, including electric, acoustic, and bass guitars, ukuleles, drums, keyboards, and pianos. Also, amplifiers, mixers, and a public audio (PA) system with microphones are used in individual and group music (psycho)therapies (Alanne, 2023, p. 259). Percussion instruments often used in music therapy are congas, bongos, djembes, tambourines, agogos, chime bars, maracas, xylophones, triangles, and claves that are good for spontaneous free improvisations and musical games with clients of different ages. For the music listening purposes, a good-enough stereo system and speakers for CDs, vinyls, and portable digital devices such as mp3 players and mobile phones would be good to arrange. However, even some instruments and the possibility of listening or producing music together with therapists and other clients is a good starting point when there is no big budget for music therapy equipment. Clients may also have their own instruments that they can use for active music therapy.

Active music therapy with refugees and their children may include song writing and recording (Beck, 2019; Bernard & Dvorak, 2022; McFerran et al., 2020). For the recording of music, improvisations, or the clients' own compositions, a computer or a laptop with a digital audio interface and recording software can be used. Also, clients themselves may have digital music applications in their tablets or mobile phones that they can use at home and in therapy to continue their process of making music and songs in music therapy. One traumatised adolescent client of mine shortly described in the beginning of book made music for the relaxation of himself that he played in music psychotherapy.

Other studied active music therapy methods in the work with refugees are singing songs, karaoke, dancing, song learning, and performances with their different variations. For example, song performance and singing in group can be in a form of band playing from the songbooks and discussing them psychotherapeutically. Discussion, in general, has been a method in addition to music in the work with refugees. The choices of music can be ethnic and cultural music according to the clients' preferences and backgrounds that can be discussed sensitively. However, also many other kinds of music have been used with refugees including children's songs, folk songs, Western classical and pop music, depending on the clients and their age (Alanne, 2010; Beck et al., 2021; Bernard & Dvorak, 2022; McFerran et al., 2020).

In addition to the musical methods and discussions, where specific psychotherapeutic techniques can be used, also other creative media and recreational methods can be used in music therapy with refugees. Such methods like using drawing, painting, clay, videos, photos, literature, writing, movement, and dancing may be combined in the music therapy improvisations with clients (Ahonen-Eerikäinen, 2007; Ahonen & Mongillo Desideri, 2014 Alanne, 2014a, 2023; Beck, 2019; Bruscia, 1987). It is common practice in music psychotherapy process that clients may first listen to music and then, after or during the listening, paint, draw, write, and so on what has come in their minds during the music listening. After the verbal and recreational reflection of the listened music, the clients may also continue the reflection of their experiences by free improvisation with instruments.

In this process, receptive, active, and recreational music therapy methods can be combined, so that the clients can express, describe, and reflect their feelings and traumatic experiences. In working with refugees whose native languages may be different to the host country, using various creative media and musical approaches in addition to discussions enables the activation of both dual coding systems in the brain, the verbal and non-verbal (Rose, 2004). Using various media may also be important for the symbolisation of trauma because traumatisation has impaired the connections between the language, the feeling, the time, and the place of the client (Stubley, 2022a, pp. 22–23). In this way, refugee clients have many possibilities of expressing and grounding their emotions that can be reflected and connected to the symbolic thinking and language in therapy. Use of non-verbal methods of music and arts in communication is especially important and should be supported with children, adolescents, and those refugees without the common language with the therapist and the other treatment staff (Castaneda et al., 2018).

From the psychodynamic point of view, the disorganised experiences and the feelings of insecurity may transform from the beta to alpha elements of conscious thoughts, feelings, and words with music and arts, so that the traumatic experiences can be contained with the help of music therapy (Alanne, 2020, 2023). In this regard, music and other forms of recreational media may connect the external and internal, conscious and unconscious experiences of refugee clients, and making them more conscious thinking and expression. At the same time, they are making bridges between the mind and body, the non-verbal and symbolic systems (Alanne, 2014b, 2019b, p. 308; 2023; Ahonen-Eerikäinen, 2007; Alvin, 1966/1975; Beck, 2019; Trondalen & Bonde, 2013).

This capability of music and arts to synchronise the body and mind is helping the traumatised clients like refugees who may have been severely depressed to experience pleasure, enjoyment, sadness, and other feelings again (Alanne, 2019b, p. 308). This can happen in the body and brain as the endorphin levels are increasing, and the production of stress hormones is decreasing when listening to music, for example. Also, the normal psychological functioning of severely traumatised clients, the "top-down" thinking and processing of information, especially the perception, is impaired and disturbed (Stubley, 2022a, pp. 16–17). For example, with receptive music listening methods and the empathetic attuning of the therapist, the impaired stress regulation with easily activating fight/flight responses of the clients can be modified. This is also concerning the symbolising and transforming of the traumatic memories with music in the procedural memory that are not accessible through verbal discussions (Beck, 2019, pp. 348–349).

The impaired psychological functioning is often experienced as dissociations and flashbacks where the unconsciousness and trauma are flooding with an excess of external stimuli in the mind and body (Stubley, 2022a, pp. 16–17). Then, traumatised are reacting and acting out according to their fears and terrors. This flight/fight response is like the PS position of early infancy according to Caroline Garland (1998a/2002, pp. 212–215; 1998b/2002) where the traumatised clients are overwhelmed, anxious, feeling persecuted, and disintegrated with their terror and fear. They have lost their trust and safety towards the people, the world, and their goodness. As a result, they are feeling, treating, and controlling or identifying with them like their enemies and the primary objects of their worst childhood fears realised. They have lost their differentiation of their internal signal anxiety, anxiety of perceived danger, and automatic anxiety relating to the actual danger situation that is happening according to Garland (1998b/2002, pp. 16–17).

The automatic anxiety of traumatised persons is often occurring in the new situations that are potentially stressful (Stubley, 2022a, p. 17). Perceptions of smells, sights, sounds, facial expressions, and the tones of voice may trigger the automatic anxiety and flooding of the "this is it" feeling of the danger (ibid., Garland, 1998b/2002, p. 17). After that the full stress response system is activated and followed with the flight/flight or freezing defences. This is a disorganised state where the client's mind is filled with the bad object experiences of dread, horror, and persecution. Then, the client cannot think, feel, and observe outer reality rationally using top-down processing. There is a loss of symbolic thinking and therefore there is no capacity in the ego left for believing "warnings" and "signals" of anxiety (Garland, 1998b/2002, pp. 16–17). According to Stubley (ibid.), this flooding of unconscious and automatic anxiety will inevitably occur in some point of the first therapeutic encounters with severely traumatised clients.

In music therapy, Priestley (1975, p. 130) has warned about the flooding of the unconscious with very introverted clients who are needing a firmer hold on reality when using music. Very traumatised clients like refugees and torture survivors may also be introverted and vulnerable because of their flashbacks, fears, dissociations, compulsory thoughts, and so on, where the ego cannot maintain the control of anxiety and the psychic balance (Garland, 1998b/2002, pp. 16–17; Stubley, 2022a, pp. 16–17). Therefore, when using music psychotherapy methods and techniques such as directed music imaging and guided imagery, a therapist must be sensitive with clients and methods used like Priestley has explained. The purpose of music therapy is not to directly approach the trauma with music or a theme in music listening and improvising. If the clients do not want or cannot bear the encountering of their trauma yet, they cannot be forced to do so against their own will even though it might look like or be resistance towards therapy (Alanne, 2010, 2014a, 2023, pp. 289–290).

It could cause an unnecessary potential traumatic event for the client where the unconscious could be violently flooding into the conscious as the automatic anxiety and stress reactions. Producing such an insecure and stressful situation purposefully for a client, potential reexposuring, enactment, or acting out of trauma, would be unethical. Even temporally it could be a reminder of the stress positions in torture and the use of music as a weapon with similar psychic consequences of flooding traumatic experiences. Instead, the use of music and other recreational methods with traumatised refugees should aim at producing repairing experiences for the clients, and not retraumatising them with reexposuring to their traumas. Therefore, it is especially important to approach the traumatised refugees with music and other art forms sensitively. It should be done with understanding their defences and the possible resistance towards their treatments and music as the consequences of their traumatisation. This is also meaning the respecting of their cultural differences and ethnic backgrounds in therapy (Alanne, 2010, 2014b, 2019b, 2023, p. 290; Beck, 2019).

5.2 A Culturally Sensitive Approach to Music and Arts with Clients from Different Nationalities

In music therapy with traumatised refugees, or when using otherwise music with refugees, there is good to have some knowledge about the different cultures, music, and arts of the refugees. However, like Saraneva (2002, p. 74) has emphasised, it would be good to get to know the client's culture. But there is no need to know everything about different cultures when doing therapy with traumatised refugees as this could lead to generalisations. In addition, this would be impossible as it is impossible to understand and know perfectly any other clients and their experiences and problems in psychotherapy beforehand. It could lead to big mistakes if the therapists would be thinking that they would know the truth of the client right away. This would be objectifying of the clients, their problems, and owing the truth like Siirala (1966/1969, pp. 94–95) has warned about calling it as the "transfer" or the "vicarious illness". Then, the subjective experiences and needs of clients, their own unique personalities, possible traumatisation, are not noticed and encountered. If they will be overlooked, rejected, or denied, it may lead to further traumatisation and continuing of trauma over generations.

Concerning music and arts, it is therefore important to be open for different approaches and customs of doing music with refugees, so that the experience of making or listening to music will not be colonised. It could be like owing the music and the knowledge of music what musical activity would be good for the clients. Therefore, it is important to listen to the clients' own needs and preferences of music, what kind of music they are enjoying listening or playing. This kind of information from the client's musical history, knowledge, skills, what music they are listening now, or they used to listen or play before traumatisation or other issues in their lives can be already collected in the initial music therapy assessment and meeting with clients. This will increase the cultural sensitivity of the treatment.

Also, it is important to be trauma-informed when using music or music therapy with refugees from different nations that may have fled from natural disasters and wars (Else & González, 2023). Because of the possible traumatisation, a therapist would be good to be present and have a compassionate attitude towards the refugees and the victims of disasters. The therapist's capability to just listen to clients if the listening to music is not possible is just as important as music. This requires patience and flexibility from the therapist to wait the right time for the music and letting go of the preconceived plans and ideas with clients sometimes if necessary (p. 25).[1]

This is especially important to remember when the clients are still in acute crises of disasters, or the trauma has happened recently. Then, the mitigating of risks, remain safe and healthy, should be considered for the clients and therapist, especially if the music therapy is done at the catastrophe area or in the community near it (Else & González, 2023, pp. 25–26). When working in the catastrophe area, it is recommended to assess and understand the cultural context of the clients as well as their social customs. This may include finding information about the geographic features of the area clients are from and about the sociopolitical issues and personalities of the people in the community. There can also be different kinds of cultural, spiritual, and religious traditions in the community and areas people are from. Depending on the crisis, catastrophe, culture, or nation, there may be different sense of losses and immediate needs that should be assessed by the caretakers and music therapists in planning their interventions (p. 25).

This kind of cultural knowledge can increase the sensitivity of the treatment including music and arts with refugees also after their acute phases of crisis in their rehabilitation. However, this kind of information can be collected and shared also in their treatment and therapy that can also be a part of the getting to know and cultural dialoguing with clients. Some of the refugees and asylum seekers may have been interrogated and tortured with music in the interrogation centres and prison camps as discussed earlier that needs to be considered when using music with them. In the trauma-informed care this would mean the understanding of the importance of safe space with the clients who are potentially traumatised like refugees (Scrine & Koike, 2023, pp. 42–43).

This means structuring safety for the clients in the appointments, so that the physical place, the therapy office, would feel safety and clear for the clients, not including things that would trigger too much stress, anxiety, or possible fears (Scrine & Koike, 2023; Stubley, 2022a). As Scrine and Koike (2023, p. 42) have proposed, this does not necessarily mean that the music therapist's office should be "normalised" where, in fact, it could just represent the Western and white ideologies of neurotypical, middle class, and cisgender identities of otherness for some clients from different cultures. Other examples are the medical approaches and possible

[1] This is a part of the negative capability of therapist discussed later in the context of supervision and training of the therapists.

psychiatric protocols and registers and so on, implemented in the therapy settings in my opinion. They do not necessarily see the clients or treat refugees and their identities as fellow human beings with compassion, but as medical patients and the objects of treatments like in surgery.

This may trigger insecurity in any client but especially among refugees and torture survivors who may experience uniforms, sights, sounds, and smells of hospital as triggering because they may have been tortured in the medical setting. Also, providing information in different kinds of forms, questionnaires, and registers may make some clients like refugees feel insecure and suspicious for a reason because they may have fled from the countries where giving too much personal information could be a security threat for them and their families. Also, usage of music like songs that have been prohibited by the oppressive governments may trigger similar feelings of insecurity.

For example, in Vietnam during the Socialistic regime until the late 1980s, love songs and nostalgic sad songs of time before 1975 were prohibited (Reyes, 1999, p. 35). Singing those songs were considered as the act of defiance and self-differentiation from those who accepted the prohibitions. For the Vietnamese refugees, it also meant defying of the communist regime. This was the government that they have escaped for their lives, and it was not tolerated in their freedom because of that. Therefore, one refugee that has been considered as a "good composer" at the time was believed to be a communist and marginalised among other refugees because of that (ibid.).

In music therapy group of different nationalities, or within the same nationality, can be various cultural, political, social, and religious views that should be considered and discussed with a group if necessary. The music of communists, right-wing, or the music they banned may trigger negative transference, suspicious, and projects towards the therapists and the other group participants because music is symbolising the oppressor, aggressor, or the enemy in conflict. Therefore, it is good to be culturally sensitive in music choices, especially if there are ethnicities and citizens from the war countries fighting with each other in a group. In the camp of Vietnamese refugees, the prohibition of sad music brought vivid memories of cultural conflict and disapproval in the community even after years as an example of traumatised music experience (Reyes, 1999, p. 35).

Therefore, in structuring safety for the sessions, it is important to negotiate with the clients in therapy or in a group what kind of music can be played or sung (Scrine & Koike, 2023, p. 42). This would mean asking consents, building structures, and agreements with clients in a group or an individual setting that would be "safe enough" (ibid.). In some degree, this may also need stepping away from the binary "safe" and "unsafe" thinking with traumatised and refugees like suggested by Scrine and Koike (ibid.). Traumatised clients like any clients may also need to go into their uncomfortable zone of stress, insecurity, some pain, and even fears in the transference of therapy and music. This is a part of the therapeutic work in stabilising, particularly working through, and integrating the traumatic experiences that also music, sounds, and memories relating to them may trigger. An example of this would be the aforementioned music of Chilean Nueva Canción movement folk songs that were prohibited and silenced in the 1970s as socialistic (Neustadt, 2004, pp. 128–129). Decades later, in 1990s, after the area of Pinochet, the socialistic march *Venceremos* still arose strong anger and fear in some people.

Similarly, music from the time of disasters, conflicts, and war may bring sad memories and fear of the times that may not wanted to be remembered or discussed. Then, therapists must be gentle in their practices of approaching clients with music that is reverberating with their traumatic experiences of oppression, silencing, and violence by their home countries and governments (Alanne, 2010, 2014b). Even years or decades after oppression, conflict, and violence, some music may trigger feelings like anger, fear, anxiety, and sadness in refugees.

As a result of their traumatisation, they may not even be capable of listening and enjoying music first (Alanne, 2010, 2013, 2014b, 2019b). Some music, or any music, sounds, or activity, may be considered as provoking too much arousal, anxiety, and pain in their experiences. Then, they may need more relaxing and neutral music that is soothing their nerves first. Music and familiar language, for example spiritual songs from the homeland, may feel safe for the refugee in the host country. However, at the same time, music, language, cultural signs, and other people of the homeland and own ethnicity may also trigger negative feelings like fear and suspicion of the possible threat, political enemy, and traitor among the community and the group. For discussed Vietnamese refugees, prohibited sad songs were representing the true feelings they expressed that reminded them of the continuous warfare with Chinese, the French, the Japanese, the Americans, and the Viet Cong. The separation and loss were parts of almost every family's story relating to these songs (Reyes, 1999, p. 35).

It is assumable that modern pop, rock, hip hop, rap, r & b, and so on may trigger traumatic memories or fears for those who have been victims of musical torturing in the past decades. Also, ethnic and national music have been still used in detainee camps in "re-educating" prisoners by the oppressive governments like they were used in Soviet Union, Nazi Germany, Greek, Chile, and Vietnam during their dictatorships and persecution of citizens. In the experiences of Vietnamese refugees interviewed in Orange County, US, they did not like their traditional music and sounds because they were used by the communist government in their propaganda (Reyes, 1999, pp. 146–147).

According to interviewed, communists had included subtle and not-so-subtle messages into their traditional music (Reyes, 1999, p. 147). These negative feelings towards traditional music seemed to arrest the learning process of it later for one interviewed man, even though there were conscious interests to learn it. Also, his children did want to play traditional instruments bought for their learning which was an example of general ambivalence towards their traditional music and how it did not correspond anymore to their feelings and needs. This is showing how musical trauma may transfer over the next generation tragically.

The national and folk song may trigger fear, anxiety, and sadness in refugees of different nations because they are reminders of their persecution, killing, and their losses including their home countries and relatives there (Alanne, 2010, 2013, 2014b, 2019b). For the vast majority of the interviewed Vietnamese refugees in

Orange County, traditional music had become to symbolise Marxist ideology, the Vietnam that made them suffer, caused their losses, and used it as a tool of manipulation for the government's purposes (Reyes, 1999, p. 148).

Opposing paradigms emerged from the experiences of Vietnamese refugees relating to music as communists/non-communists, the current government/people, and the traditional music as propaganda/cultural heritage (Reyes, 1999, p. 148). Those Vietnamese refugees who did not identify with the communist government had dissociated themselves from the government-sanctioned traditional music. In their experiences it was mixed with political ideology and manipulation. This ambivalence towards their traditional music seemed to split their experiences of music in good and/or bad objects. However, in spite of their losses, sad music and love songs seemed to provide a possibility for the mourning of losses, especially for their homeland that they were longing as the forced migrants (p. 167).

According to this knowledge, it is recommended to have at least some caution with traditional music as well as with loud music and sounds first when using music in the treatment of refugees. Therefore, knowing something about the home countries of refugees; their political, social, and cultural histories; and conflicts may be helpful in attuning sensitively to their possibly ambivalent experiences with music. Even though some musicians, music therapists, and educators could think that music is all positive, therapeutic, and empowering experience, it does not automatically guarantee safety (Scrine & Koike, 2023, p. 42).

This is why it is good to negotiate with clients how music is produced where the clients like traumatised refugees could have a control and possibility of choice in their music (ibid., pp. 42–43). In music therapy methods like song writing, improvisation, and playlisting, there are possibilities for the stories of sad music described and narratives of resistance that can benefit the clients in working through and integrating their traumas. If the therapists would use their expert power position regarding the choices of music and psychologising them for the clients, this possibility of neutral and objective dialoguing with clients and their music would be lost. As discussed by Scrine and Koike (ibid. p. 43), then, the language and practices of therapists could be a part of the systemic oppression within therapy, or continuing of the silencing of the clients, their experiences, and cultures.

For the culturally sensitive, or humble, practice, relevant questions for the therapists working with refugees are (Edwards, 2023, p. 31) as follows: How the cultural identity of the clients have affected their lived experience and relationship with music? How the clients' oppression, trauma, or possible privilege has impacted their music in therapy and how they are manifesting in the therapy office? Also, important is to consider the relationships of refugee clients with their therapists and possible group members, how traumatisation has influenced them, and what are the clients' capabilities and options for social actions including music in and outside the therapy? Important is also to reflect what are the clients' needs in contacting them with music, and how music could encourage their own activity, social relationships, in elevating and stabilising their experiences?

When working with refugees, therapists should reflect and assess whether music could trigger traumatic experiences or insecurity in clients and, if so, in what degree.

Are there enough possibilities to encounter, hold, and contain such experiences in the therapeutic setting and by the therapist? Do the therapists themselves have enough knowledge, training, and experience to help their clients in such situations where traumatic experiences and unconscious are flooding, or the client is having a panic attack? These kinds of questions for the therapists themselves are helping them to maintain the security and the openness for their clients and themselves to share and express their cultural identities in the limits of the therapeutic setting (Edwards, 2023, p. 31).

The therapeutic setting and boundaries are holding the security of clients and therapists, so that the free expression and openness to cultural differences, various nationalities, people, and their traumatic experiences could be possible. Cultural sensitivity means also to see and hear the possible racism, misogynism, explicit violent or sexual contents of music that could be offensive for some clients and trigger insecurity in a group, for example. Then, clients should have also a freedom of choice not to play or listen to such music (Cadesky, 2023, p. 102).

In addition, at least, for the cultural humility and the therapeutic progress, there should be a possibility for the discussion of such triggering unsafe experiences that may directly relate to the trauma history of clients. Psychotherapeutic discussion of such songs can benefit the clients in working with their traumas even though this music will not be listened or played. This is also helping the clients to control their traumas and experiences by themselves. Therefore, the therapist should not be a censor, a sort of judge, or a teacher, who is deciding what kind of musical expression is allowed and beneficial for the clients either.

For some clients, like adolescents and adults as well, violent and misogynistic hip hop, rap, or hard rock are part of their subcultures and life that they are commenting. Music can be an outlet for the expression of their moods, anger, poverty, and their race-based traumatic stress that cannot be denied from them. Their music like any other music, if not villainised and silenced because of the hidden cultural biases or projections, and since it has been used in torture or propaganda before, can be a start for the alliance, going through of trauma, and therapeutic progress and growing in therapy (Holly, 2023, pp. 60–61; Zarate, 2022, p. 23).

5.3 Building an Alliance and Trust with Refugees: Cultural Dialoguing

Music may be a way of communicating with refugees from different ethnicities and cultures without language and a need for an interpreter when working with them. The culture and music refugees are possibilities of getting to know them. When a therapist is showing an interest towards the culture of clients, it is increasing the trust in clients because they are feeling that they are interesting and important respectively. This in turn is building alliance between the client and the therapist where different kinds of things and experiences are possible to discuss and share.

The trust of the clients is important because the psychotherapeutic work with traumas requires trust from both of the therapeutic dyad, so that reaching and sharing of traumatic experiences would be possible. In psychodynamic psychotherapy and music therapy, this is called as the analytic trust, that is the client's realistic view of the therapist understanding their subjective world (Elman, 1998, p. 187). The therapist cannot necessarily help the clients if they do not trust music therapy and its capability to help them. Also, therapists may feel insecure with some clients like traumatised refugees and those from different cultures (Alanne, 2023, p. 170; Klafter, 2017).

For example, therapists may be overtly polite and nice when they are unsure about themselves and too cautious about confronting and asking the clients about their issues like they could be breaking them with words and questions. The lack of trust in therapists may also show as the reluctance to use music in the treatment if they are afraid that it could break the clients respectively. Then, also the clients may feel unsure or insecure and are inhibited to talk or listen and play music in therapy. This may appear like the resistance of clients towards the treatment, that is a part of it, but it is lack of trust in therapy by both the therapist and the client (Elman, 1998, p. 189). In fact, it means impasse in therapy where the therapy is not progressing that is caused by the mutual fear of the therapeutic dyad to reach, talk, and express with music the traumatic experiences and vulnerabilities of client (Alanne, 2023, pp. 170–171; Klafter, 2017, pp. 187, 189, 191).

5.4 Cultural Dialoguing and Music

Because the severely traumatised like refugees have lost their basic trust towards people and world, it is especially important to develop this trust by creating a good alliance with them. Music as a good object experience may help in creating contact and positive transference with refugees. Like Saraneva (2002, 2018) has described, therapists may use the cultural dialoguing as the method of approaching their clients from different cultures like refugees. In cultural dialoguing, the therapist has a continuous "active and explaining approach" towards the cultural differences according to Saraneva (2002, p. 74).

From the beginning, a therapist must try to understand what reactions and issues of client in the communication are relating to the cultural differences between the therapist and the client before making conclusions and interventions (ibid., p. 74). In the beginning of treatment, the therapist may need to explain concretely the differences in the cultures what is the therapeutic setting and the treatment system in general for the clients. However, the cultural dialoguing begins when the therapist is separating in his/her mind the possible cultural differences of the clients where it can continue as open discussions about them with clients: For example, how is this thing in your country, the therapist may ask? In our country, it is thought like this, how about in your country? Topics for the discussion may include what the clients think about the treatment, values, family, children, and their education, for example.

Also, cultural activities like music, hobbies, and other life interests can be topics in the cultural dialoguing with traumatised refugees like torture survivors (Alanne, 2010, 2019b; Saraneva, 2002, pp. 74–75).

When using cultural dialoguing, equal relationships with clients are built where their own cultural backgrounds and roots are considered as a part of the treatment (Saraneva, 2002, pp. 74–75). In this regard, possible colonialised views, power relationships, cultural projections, and burdens relating to treatment can be avoided and deconstructed. This kind of critical thinking and questioning is also relating to the use of music by the therapist with the clients in the group, for example (Alanne, 2019b, pp. 313–314). Questions such as these: What is music? Why music or arts? How everyone in a group is experiencing music? What kind of cultural differences and habits there are between different cultures and ethnicities? These kinds of questions and topics can be raised for the open discussion in a group. This is supporting the alliance between the therapist and the group when everyone has a right to speak out their own opinions and conceptions relating to music and arts.

This kind of possibility for open discussions may be even a new experience for the clients because in their home country they have been oppressed and silenced because of their political views and opinions. Their freedom of speech and expression of their own culture may have been denied for them. Therefore, it is important that in the treatment of refugees, there should be a possibility to express their own opinion, will, and culture without a need to suppress it anymore in the host country. A part of the cultural dialoguing in the group, for example, is the critical perspectives relating to these power relationships in the treatment, group, and community that can be made visible (Alanne, 2019b, p. 314).

The core idea of critical perspectives is allowing the clients from different nationalities and cultures to speak and express themselves feeling safe (Alanne, 2019b, p. 314). The therapist is creating a safe and allowing climate for the group to discuss and share their opinions and experiences relating to music, for example. It can be new for some clients that everyone has equal rights to speak and express their feelings and memories relating to music not depending on their age, gender, education, or class. The therapist can explain this to the clients and take responsibility that everyone could express themselves in words or music. In decolonisation and desensitisation of power relationships, music, and their possible cultural differences for the clients, such topics as what does solidarity, freedom, and rules mean for the clients and the group can be discussed (ibid.).

With bringing up such issues in cultural dialoguing, the possible tensions and conflicts among the clients can be made visible and shared (Alanne, 2019b, p. 314). In the group of refugees, there may be participants from the countries that have been or still are in war, for example. Also, different kinds of religious and political values and views may inhibit the musical expression. There may also be musical transfers discussed earlier relating to the memories of homeland, great losses of closed ones, relatives, and violence, which are difficult to express and share. The people from other country and culture, or even of the same country, can be seen as enemies. Memories relating to them and their music may bring fear, anger, hate, bitterness, and a need for revenge.

Because there may be opponent political views and nationalities, it is especially important to discuss what is meant by different concepts, such as freedom and equality, and who are deciding and defining them in the group or community (Alanne, 2019b, p. 314). How people from different nationalities are understanding them? When they are confronted together in a group, they are also desensitised and made easier to discuss and express in music. When these things are talked out in music therapy or education, there is not one person or a group of people using systemic power who is deciding what is talked or played in a group. Therefore, the sense of feeling that everyone is belonging to the group as equal is emphasised and supported.

Like there is not one topic to discuss, there is not one music, as everyone has their own voices that are allowed to be heard (Alanne, 2019b, p. 314). Desensitisation of traumatic experience may also be working through of trauma with music like in free improvisation where the feelings relating to trauma are allowed to be expressed. After improvising or music listening like in the GIM, the traumatic experiences of client can be discussed and the memories and experiences relating to trauma can be shared and collected.

In an individual music psychotherapy, cultural dialoguing can be done similarly like with "Ben", a man in his 30s with a military background who was a refugee torture survivor from Central Africa (Alanne, 2010, 2013, p. 271). In the beginning phase of his treatment, we were discussing about the differences in African and Finnish cultures, customs, and climates. Also, music of Africa and his home country were discussed how people experience it in general. These kinds of discussions enabled Ben to talk and unlock his experiences. They also helped him to adapt in his host country, Finland.

Ben had experienced some threatening situations and racism when he arrived and lived at the reception centre that were discussed as a part of his therapy. As his therapy progressed, a guided imagery theme "a village in a jungle" brought him images and associations of witches and dead bodies that felt peculiar from the perspective of urban Africa. Cultural dialoguing with him was continued with cultural differences between the host and home countries about how some parts of the home country, villages, can be scary places where he did not ever want to go in real life. Later, in the working-through phase of his therapy, in his free association to music, he saw the scene where he was mock executed as a part of his torturing (Alanne, 2010, 2013, p. 271).

In music therapy or music education, funny musical games with percussions and other instruments, including body as an instrument, singing, and rhymes, can be techniques of "breaking the ice" with refugee clients of different ages (Alanne, 2019a, p. 314). In the beginning of the session, they can function as the opening for the expression and sharing of the experiences together among people. After this kind of musical games and exercises, which can be quite short, it is also easier to freely improvise and freely associate to music what kind of feelings, thoughts, memories, and experiences music is bringing. When music is experienced together, like the humour it may bring naturally, it is safer to talk and approach the other cultures, the otherness, even in own experiences, that maybe even looked like a threat in the beginning. Later, clients like Ben are more ready to go deep into their traumatic events with music, when there has developed alliance and enough trust first.

5.4.1 Free Improvisation

In music therapy, free improvisation or clinical improvisation is like the free association in psychoanalysis or psychodynamic psychotherapy (Alanne, 2023, p. 8). Instead of talking freely about whatever comes in mind, in free improvisations, music and sounds are expressed without censorship and thinking about their contents beforehand. However, also free association to music and psychotherapeutic discussions are used in tandem with improvisation. The experiences of clients and their traumatic events can be reflected verbally or musically in the music psychotherapy processes (Ahonen-Eerikäinen, 2007; Alanne, 2014a, 2023).

Free improvisations with clients can be musical dialogues with clients where the therapist and client both are playing instruments. Such improvisation techniques as imitation, holding, reflecting, rhythmic grounding, doubling, and synchronising surveyed by Bruscia (1987) are widely used in music therapy. They have their grounds in the psychodynamic encountering of clients in addition to other similar techniques used in music therapy commonly also outside the psychodynamic orientation (Alanne, 2023, pp. 1–2; Skinner et al., 2021; Wigram, 2004).

Originally, free improvisation like the Freud's free association in psychoanalysis was introduced in music therapy by Juliette Alvin (1966/1975, p. 85), who considered that "music can provide a bridge between the real and the unreal, the conscious and the unconscious". This was an important insight and discovery from psychoanalysis how music may reveal and express different layers of mind, including preconscious thinking, that made music therapy possible according to Alvin (2001). Whereas in psychoanalysis, words and talking are the roads to the different layers of mind and unconscious, in music therapy, music and songs are affecting the same levels of experiences according to her (Alanne, 2023, p. 14).

According to Alvin, no musical requirements were needed for free improvisation and expression of music that has become a general conception of free improvisation in music therapy (Alanne, 2023, p. 15). This idea enables the playing of music without notes and knowledge of Western or other music theory and history. Music is not taught either in free improvisations, but the purpose of the free improvisation is to express personal feelings and characters of clients. The clients are allowed to express their own feelings even when they are not sounding beautiful or clear but ugly and brutal sometimes.

Alvin (2001) considered that like the development of Freud's psychoanalysis paved the way for free improvisation and music therapy, so did the emancipation of Western classical music from its aesthetic canon like in the modern ballet *The Rite of Spring* (1913) by Igor Stravinsky. In it, music was not always necessarily aesthetically beautiful but also dissonant. The music and sounds were describing and expressing directly the feelings of a story and its brutality where the young girl is dancing to her death (Alanne, 2023, p. 15). Arthur Schoenberg and Gustav Mahler have been considered as psychoanalytic composers because of their expression of feelings and psychic contents in their music similarly.

In music therapy, Alvin began to portrait emphatically the feeling of clients in their "way of being" and reflected with improvised music their personalities and behaviour (Wigram, 2004, p. 89). In this regard, Alvin and her contemporary music therapists Paul Nordoff and Clive Robbins could create a rapport and contact with clients suffering from different disorders and disabilities including autism, intellectual disability, and mental disorders. With free improvisations, clients were tried to meet at their own level and develop relationship with melodic and rhythmical communication (Alvin, 1965/1972, pp. 110–111). Later, music therapist Mary Priestley (1975) developed further free improvisation techniques in her Analytic Music Therapy (AMT), where she even more directly portrayed the aspects of clients' conflicts and the different sides of their personalities (Alanne, 2023, p. 256).

The Splitting Technique

In AMT, there are techniques like the Splitting Technique, Holding Technique, and the Grounding that can be used and adapted to work with traumatised refugees of different ages (Priestley, 1975). In the Splitting Technique, the therapist and client are first psychotherapeutically discussing and then the therapist is introducing a theme where the client could improvise some aspect of his or her personality, feelings, or other object relationship. At the same time, the therapist is also improvising freely the opposite or another side of the client's experiences, personality, or relationships that have been discussed. The therapist may also improvise otherwise along with the client and holding or grounding their experiences like with traumatised clients (Alanne, 2014a, 2023, p. 263).

The Splitting Technique, or just Splitting as it is called currently, is a very confrontational technique where the client's unconscious sides are made conscious with music. It may be useful with those traumatised clients like refugees who are capable for interpretative and analytic reflection of their self-experiences and relationships. However, for many clients like severely traumatised torture survivors, taking the roles of victim and perpetuator could be a too direct approach to improvise their bad objects, conflicts, traumatic experiences, and events first. Use of it should be carefully considered and assessed individually according to the specific needs and psychic equilibrium of clients. In addition, this kind of analysing and probing of the client's unconscious projections towards the objects like another character, especially relating to traumatisation, should be first discussed with clients and make clear that there is their permission for such a theme that they can interrupt anytime (Alanne, 2023, pp. 263–264; Priestley, 1975, 123).

As discussed earlier, in the beginning phase of trauma work, the stabilisation is the main goal in therapy where more supportive elements of music and improvisation like holding and grounding are more adequate for the treatment. Later, in therapy, the clients may go into their traumatic experiences in music or in discussions themselves which is an indicator that they are working through and integrating their traumas. In the working-through and integrative phases of therapy more analytic and interpretative approaches are possible when there has been already stabilisation in the client's condition. Usage of such music psychotherapy methods like the Splitting requires professional music therapy and psychotherapy training, so that the therapist could assess the possible benefits and harms of technique for the clients. For example, those music psychotherapy clients who do not have enough capability for symbolisation, that are using splitting as a defence, their thinking and feelings are concrete, black or white, and they cannot see other perspectives than their own, it may be too demanding technique to confront their defences first (Alanne, 2023, pp. 264–265).

The Holding Technique and Containing with Music

The Holding Technique, or just holding, with music is a sort of basic method of improvisation that Priestley (1975) introduced for the AMT. The holding with music is using different elements and techniques of music where the clients' experiences and feelings are shared and carried by the therapist. Like with many clients and traumatised especially, it is often better to proceed with music safely, building trust and alliance first before confronting their traumas, characterological traits, and defences (Alanne, 2023, pp. 264–265). This can happen by discussing them first and letting the client play the different aspects of their feelings alone. The therapist is just listening or improvising along with the client and enabling them to express their feelings and traumas. Then, the therapist is holding the traumatic experiences of clients and their personalities with music like parents are holding their infants emotionally (Alanne, 2010, 2014a, 2023; De Backer & Sutton, 2014c; Gravestock, 2021; Winnicott, 1971/1997).

A part of the holding is the holding environment that a therapist is creating, sometimes together with other personnel, for traumatised clients. The holding environment is an ambience or climate, not a technique in that sense, that is caring (loving), understanding, and creating safe experience for the clients. It can be created by one person, group, family, treatment staff, school, and so on, where the clients or students are remembered, bore, and preoccupied in the thoughts of the other persons emotionally. Thus, holding is a part of the containment of traumatic experiences like the earlier containment of infant by the mother where the first experiences of being held are originated psychologically (De Backer & Sutton, 2014c, pp. 344–345).

In the Holding Technique, a therapist is creating a safe space and holding clients emotionally with music (Alanne, 2014a, 2023, pp. 265–268). Then, the therapist is reflecting and mirroring the client's music and the feelings expressed in it, however not pushing the client with music, sounds, and their dynamics over the client's experience, expression, and the window of tolerance. Holding with music is enabling the client to express all kinds of feelings like sorrow, anger, joy, guilt, fear, and so on. The Holding Technique differs from the *holding music* that is like a sonorous holding environment with music that is soothing, relaxing, and creating a safe atmosphere for the clients. I have used holding peaceful classical music during the psychotherapeutic discussions with torture survivors, for example (Alanne, 2010). The therapist may also improvise freely with a guitar or piano holding music when discussing with the client, or when the client like a child is drawing or painting on the floor. Then, holding with music can be a part of the musical reverie and play with clients (Alanne, 2023).

Thus, musical holding of client does not have to be very dramatic expression of feelings, but it can also be peaceful being together in music with the client (Alanne, 2023, p. 266). For example, the therapist can hum and sing for the client peacefully like a lullaby or something soothing for an infant (Levinge, 2015, p. 63). Singing or humming something peaceful may also benefit traumatised adult clients like Levinge (ibid.) has described: First she was humming non-verbally to the silent, frozen, and tensed adult client who could relax during her humming. After that Levinge added some words to her humming that described the client's fear. In her free improvisation with her voice Levinge used her body and countertransference she had experienced in the atmosphere of the room with a client. This attuning with music to the client's fear helped the client to integrate his experiences in music therapy.

In this regard, therapists can monitor and use their own feelings and countertransference for the benefit of their clients (Alanne, 2023, p. 266). Thus, holding can be a part of the other free improvisation techniques and probing of emotions like the splitting where the traumatised clients' feelings and characters are interpreted, described, held, and contained with music (Priestley, 1975, pp. 124–126). With musical holding, feelings of clients are supported to be fully expressed but the therapists should not consciously provoke, dramatise, act, or otherwise intentionally manipulate feelings in the clients (Alanne, 2023, p. 268). Rather, in the holding with music, the therapist is trying to move along and share their emphatic responses with musical understanding (Bruscia, 1987, pp. 552–553).

In the musical holding, a therapist is enabling the expression of clients' emotions and experiences with musical structures, not by using force, but by staying more in the background during the free improvisations (Alanne, 2014a, 2023, pp. 267–268; Bruscia, 1987). Bruscia's (1987, p. 536) definition of holding in the general clinical improvisation techniques is saying that "the therapist provides a musical background that resonates the client's feelings while containing them." Wigram (2004, pp. 97–98) has conceptualised holding a slightly differently as "a musical anchor and container for the client's music-making, using rhythmic or tonal grounding techniques" (p. 98). However, he is not excluding the Bruscia's definition but seems to consider it to be more related to specific clinical improvisation techniques such as musical grounding. Originally Priestley (1975, p. 121) like Bruscia and Wigram considered that techniques of holding and containing with music were overlapping in their definitions.

In clinical work, therapists may need to do both, hold the clients' expressions of their traumatic experiences as well as contain them personally and with music (Alanne, 2023, pp. 266; De Backer and Sutton, 2014c, pp. 342–345). In this sense, it is also useful theoretically to separate these concepts like originally conceived by Winnicott (1971/1997) and Bion (1962b/2007). With traumatised clients like refugees in containment with music, a therapist can offer the clients possibilities to express and share their unbearable traumatic experiences, anxiety, terror, and chaos of their unintegrated and dissociative states of mind. Then, within the elements of music and the therapist containing the intolerable, there is a possibility of these nonorganised and chaotic experiences to reform in a constructive and understanding way.

With containing, the bad objects of music and sounds relating to trauma can transform into good objects and a form of controllable play and enjoyment for the client's ego in the free improvisations. Often it is requiring the holding of the client's experience and expression from the therapist first, and then being a container, before clients can contain their unbearable experiences. This may take time before severely traumatised clients can work through, integrate, and contain their traumatic events and states of mind. Before it is even possible, the goal of treatment may be to stabilise these experiences where music may help in grounding and anchoring the intolerable feelings and anxiety. In this regard, the clinical work of holding and containing of trauma may consist of other free improvisation techniques like especially the mentioned musical grounding.

Musical Grounding of Trauma

With rhythmical grounding where a therapist is playing similar rhythms with clients, the therapist can sustain and make easier the free improvisation for the client (Alanne, 2014a, 2023, pp. 269–270; Skinner et al., 2021; Smetana & Storz, 2020). In addition to helping the client to freely improvise, rhythmical grounding may help the clients to psychologically anchor their traumatic experiences, anxiety, fear, panic, and so on to music. Bruscia (1987, p. 535) has defined that rhythmical grounding is "keeping a basic beat or providing a rhythmic foundation for the client's own improvising". In music therapy, it is used to help the clients in organising their improvising, controlling their impulses, and bringing safety and stability into their experiences (p. 541).

Even though free improvisations in music therapy may include techniques and elements of musical imitation of client's playing, notes, harmonies, or moods, affects, and behaviours, a therapist is not only reacting to or enacting according to the clients' expectations and experiences in therapy (Alanne, 2023, p. 122). This is especially important with traumatised clients like refugees who are needing holding and containing of their experiences instead of enacting or reacting according to the client's possible projective identifications in therapy. For example, this could be over identifying into the client's experiences where the therapist cannot separate and contain the client's trauma and is feeling the same with the client.

Stern (1985/2004) has discerned conceptually affective attunement, mirroring, and empathic responses of the therapist. As the basic methods of improvisational music therapy, he is mentioning the techniques of mirroring, matching, emphatic improvisation, grounding, holding, containing, dialoguing, and accompanying with music (Stern, 2010, pp. 139–140). Stern is referring to the interaction and affective attunement between the mother and infant where the mother is mirroring and matching the infant's experiences as essential for early internalisations in development as well as for therapy. Similar relational approaches in psychotherapy as well as in music therapy may help the clients to repair their dysfunctional and arrested development according to him (Alanne, 2023, p. 122).

This is in accordance with trauma and dissociation where the clients do not have necessarily words, language, and contact with their experiences and emotions. Music and other artistic approaches like free improvisation and guided imagery may help the clients suffering from early, cumulative, major traumatisation, and alexithymia, to build bridges with such experiences without mental representatives and contents that are only enacted or felt physically as symptoms.

In musical or rhythmical grounding, a therapist is attuning and matching to the musical and non-musical qualities and characteristics in the client's sounds (Zarate, 2022, p. 27). Zarate (ibid.) is describing how she is using "musical-cultural presence" in her attention with clients in building alliance with them. In her improvisations with clients, she is reflecting the client's cultural meaning and preferences in music (p. 23). This can be a part of the therapist's cultural dialoguing with clients discussed earlier and keeping in mind what kind of unconscious cultural projections and identities are present in the encountering of different clients. According to Zarate (ibid.), music with clients "should sound like based on the client's cultural background".

This is a good point of view considering the musical grounding with any clients but especially with traumatised refugees who often are clearly representing another culture and otherness for the therapist. A part of fun in free improvisations and musicking for the clients is the little differences and inconsistencies of music and interaction that are making it somehow unpredictable. Thus, some cultural differences in the expression and understanding of music and other things in therapy can also be meaningful sharing and cultural dialoguing. However, this kind of musical play, humour, and discussion in general needs to feel safe for the clients first.

Zarate (2022, p. 28) is emphasising the feeling of safety for the anxious clients and she is sending them a message "I see you, I am with you, I hear you" with empathic mirroring and reflection of the sounds produced by the clients. With clients who are experiencing panic, she is using the grounding technique and giving the clients simple musical harmonic structures, textures, and accompanying their vocalising, singing, and instrumental developments. Creating a safe space with music is also highlighted in the trauma-informative music therapy how the therapist can structure safety for the clients that is "safe enough" (Scrine & Koike, 2023, p. 42). It needs attuning into the cultural humility and background of clients what is considered as normal or good for the clients.

As discussed earlier, some music and songs may be triggering traumatic memories and experiences of clients that a therapist should consider before applying a musical technique or a specific song for the client (Cadesky, 2023, p. 102). In individual or group therapy, there needs to be clients' permission to use music and if music feels unsafe or there are possible triggering issues relating to music, it should be discussed and agreed to be played or listened to first. This needs to be done with free improvisations too where the clients are allowed to stop the music and playing anytime if they are feeling too anxious and unsafe. With clients who are refugees, torture survivors, and severely traumatised, the therapist needs to be especially cautious with their musical and other interventions before establishing a good alliance and knowing them.

Cadesky (2023, p. 102) recommends musical anchoring such as a familiar, simple, short, relaxing riff as a "home base" to bring back the focus and the co-regulation of the group. This is done according to the goals of Herman's (1992/2022) first stage of recovery from the trauma of structuring safety (Cadesky, 2023, p. 97). Hoi Yan Fu (2023, p. 116) has used musical grounding in free associative singing with clients suffering from developmental trauma. This is included in the vocal holding techniques of Austin (2009) how the therapist is providing a sustaining tone, frequently the root of the chord, that is a base for the clients' vocal improvisations. The therapist's voice and singing are the home base where clients can return to "refuel" themselves in the improvisations that is enabling the imitation and working of the separation-individuation development and object constancy with clients (ibid.).

Svedberg Yinger (2023, p. 50) has used a particular *I am Safe* song with traumatised children when they are feeling scared, anxious, and overwhelmed. In this kind of song, there has been added deep breathing and repeating of the affirmation in the song "I am safe, I am strong" (ibid.). This kind of singing and breathing bodily exercises as a part of the clinical improvisation can help the traumatised clients to regulate their traumatic experiences. Calming down and relaxing can be a goal of such exercises where the client's body is remembering the trauma with anxiety and panic attack during the improvisations and discussions with the client. In this regard, traumatised clients like refugees can develop self-agency for their often-repeating traumatic experiences that are making them vulnerable. To help in such panic situations, a therapist may continue after the grounding song and breathing with questions like "do you want to talk about it" and "do you want to sing" to increase the client's experience of self-agency and control of trauma (ibid.).

This kind of musical grounding included in free improvisations, like free associative singing, improvised songs, or raps with breathing exercises can also be used with adolescent and adult clients (Alanne, 2010, 2014a, 2023; Stephens Langdon, 2023). As the rhythmical grounding during the free improvisations, I have used calm and steady rhythms like the heartbeats of the mother that have provided the core physical feelings and emotional closeness and safety of early infancy for the clients (Alanne, 2014a, pp. 100–101; 2023, p. 270). In clinical situations, this may be used in a way that a therapist is not ending the playing and producing of sounds whilst the client has stopped improvising for a moment. Sometimes this may happen because clients are feeling shy, anxious, or unsafe and restricted to improvise. They may not be able to invent or produce new ideas and themes for their improvisations that may cause silences and the feelings of embarrassment and unsafety. This may also relate to the feelings of unsafe attachment and repeating of the patterns of separation-individuation process in music psychotherapy (Hoi Yan Fu, 2023, p. 116).

Then, a musical or rhythmical grounding of the therapist may provide a client a sort of a home base as discussed and help the clients to continue improvisation and study their feelings (Alanne, 2023, p. 270). I have used this kind of rhythmical grounding successfully with many clients of different ages to support the continuance of their own expression with instruments. In musical grounding, many kinds of instruments can be applied like discussed singing, own voice and breathing exercises, body instruments in general, as well as any other kind of instruments like drum sets, percussion, guitars, keyboards, xylophones, and so on. For example, I have used an electric guitar in keeping the tempo and boundaries for the improvisations when the client has played a keyboard or a drum set. With psychotic clients, I have played a drum set myself while the client has been improvising with an electric guitar. For such clients that are psychotic or emotionally disturbed, the rhythmical grounding has provided psychical structures for their chaotic experiences. In the therapeutic process, it seemed to integrate and "ground" them to physical reality as well (Bruscia, 1987, p. 541).

This kind of musical or rhythmical grounding with traumatised clients like refugees may stabilise the feeling of security in clients (Alanne, 2023, p. 270; Stephens Langdon, 2023). As Stephens Langdon (ibid., pp. 125–126) emphasises, when working with traumatised, music therapists should be aware of the importance of grounding. The traumatic experiences refugees and torture survivors are suffering can be overwhelming for their vulnerable psychic balance, and they can flood when they are brought up in an individual therapy or discussed in a group. Momentarily, clients may even dissociate in such situations, when traumatic experiences are activated during the discussion, music listening, or improvisation. Then, a simple breathing intervention from the therapist may help the client or the group in returning to the present moment.

Other grounding techniques during improvisations and discussions with clients are the sensations of body and bringing the client back from the dissociative states, panic attacks, and flashbacks with a contact and awareness of one's physical body (Stephens Langdon, 2023, pp. 125–126). In addition to the discussed breathing exercises, clients can be guided to feel their feet on the floor or to rub one's hands together to calm down and have a control of their overwhelming and chaotic experiences. Music is also psychophysical experience that can be helpful in grounding and supporting the clients' overwhelming experiences. As discussed, steady rhythms of a song or improvisations are providing a basis for expressing feelings and controlling them physically.

Then, a simple bass line can establish a foundation in the chaotic improvisation where the client can feel held by the therapist (Stephens Langdon, 2023, p. 126). Also, clients themselves can produce musical and rhythmical grounding for their experiences respectively. The therapist may ask the client to produce a simple beat or a tune with bodily instruments, or with drums, where there is a possibility of controlling the traumatic experience and feelings relating to it. This can be helpful in developing the client's capability for emotional regulation of their experiences like uncontrollable rage or silence. In music, a client can learn to control and manage with overwhelming experiences where they can move along with their feelings and stop when necessary. For example, in developing such a capability, a therapist can guide the client by choosing or improvising music that is changing from soft to loud and soft again (ibid.).

In improvising with different approaches and techniques with clients, therapists must also monitor their own thoughts, feelings, and countertransference towards their clients and avoid controlling and restricting the client's improvisation and expression with rhythmic grounding (Alanne, 2014a, 2023, p. 270; Bruscia, 1987). Stephens Langdon (2023, p. 124) is also rightly questioning the possible views of some music therapists and music therapy that with traumatic clients the catharsis of emotionally outpouring the traumatic experience would be a successful outcome of a session or even therapy. It is natural that after going through traumatic experiences in therapy, clients may feel the same feelings they experienced when they were traumatised as a part of their transference and working through of traumatic experiences. So, trauma survivors should not be encouraged or otherwise "pushed" to freely release strong emotions and their traumatic experiences or events. This can feel overwhelming and unsafe for them in the beginning of therapeutic process and early appointments.

This kind of practices may be even harmful for the trauma survivors in the early stages of treatment and cause them unnecessary traumatic stress and resistance towards the treatment if they are not solved and processed in therapy properly. In the early stages of psychoanalysis, the abreaction of feelings and traumatic memories was the goal of the treatment (Freud, 1914/1981). However, this conception was reconsidered by Freud (ibid.) himself when he noticed that it was not enough for achieving and maintaining the treatment results. Instead, it seemed that the traumatic experiences and memories needed to be worked through repeatedly in therapy, so that the durable change in psychic structures could be possible. This is the current view in psychoanalysis. Also, in the light of Herman's (1992/2022) phases of trauma work, traumatised clients need to feel safe, trust, and empowerment first to work through their traumatic experiences (Stephens Langdon, 2023, p. 124). This often requires many sessions, even years of therapies, and going through of trauma many times before the integration of trauma is possible.

However, in grounding and integrating the dissociation of clients, music has many possibilities where clients can freely improvise their intense memories and emotions (Stephens Langdon, 2023, p. 126). This can occur in the form of freestyle rap, for example, where clients can free associate with music and through their "flow" experience have a contact with themselves (ibid.). Because the experiences with music can be strong, therapists must understand the need of holding, containing, and especially grounding of such experiences where the client is in the musical hyperarousal state of mind. Also, verbal discussions of trauma may produce hyper- or hypoarousal in clients, which the therapist should be aware of.

Music in such situations can help the clients to return in a normal state. A catchy musical element, phrase, singing, or holding music listened or played in the background of discussions provided by the therapist that I have used with refugee torture survivors may help the clients to ground and tolerate their experiences (Alanne, 2010, 2023; Stephens Langdon, 2023, p. 126). In the group situations activating the other group members in music-making in addition to the therapist, playing a guitar, for example, may work as the grounding for the clients. Also, important is the verbal reflection and grounding after the improvisation, especially, if the therapist sees that some client in an individual or a group therapy is overwhelmed by the experience. In this, activating the other group members in discussion in addition to the therapist may help in grounding the situation and integrating the traumatic experiences. In the light of the discussed trauma theory and the dual coding system of brain, having contact through music and words both in the mind and in the body of the clients is increasing the possibility of building new connections in their brain and their recovery from trauma respectively.

5.4.2 Music Listening

With traumatised refugees like torture survivors such music psychotherapy techniques as free association to music and projective music listening are possible (Alanne, 2010, 2019b, 2023). Music listening and discussions relating to memories, feelings, images, and thoughts that music is bringing can be an easy way to begin music therapeutic work with refugees. Especially, if there are no other possible music or audio equipment than stereo system with speakers, a portable speaker, or a CD/cassette player available. If music therapy is done at the clinic or centre where there is a music therapy room, then there are already many kinds of instruments and equipment to produce or listen to music. When working at the camps, centres, or in the homes of clients, the therapist may need to bring their equipment themselves if the clients do not have their own instruments at home, for example. In such situations where music instruments are not available or they are not possible to use for other reasons, music listening methods may be the only choice possible for some clients.

Free Association to Music

Free association to music is a technique where clients are listening to the sounds or music and speaking or writing whatever comes to mind (Alanne, 2014a, 2023, pp. 284–285; Bruscia, 2014, p. 108). It is like the discussed free improvisation, free associative singing, and free association in psychoanalysis where clients are asked and encouraged to verbalise themselves freely (Hoi Yan Fu, 2023, pp. 116–117). In the free association to music, like in the other mentioned free associative psychodynamic techniques, there is an assumption that unconscious and repressed images, memories, and associated feelings gradually emerge as the streams of thoughts and words while listening to music or discussing it afterwards. To enable such a goal of accessing unconscious and repressed thoughts and feelings, the verbal associations relating to music are allowed to come out spontaneously with no attention given to their cohesion or meaning (Bruscia, 2014, p.108).

Free association to music can include techniques like writing of the associated words, or drawing, and painting of the imagery, and stories on the paper even though they are also their own techniques that will be discussed more later (Alanne, 2023, pp. 284–285). This can be useful with refugees when they have difficulties in finding words for their experiences with spoken language. Therefore, while listening to music with refugees, especially with children, it would be good to have some equipment for writing and drawing at hand. Free association to music can also have elements of play and storytelling where traumatised children may associate freely with music, like classical music, and continue their narrative like a fairytale. The therapist is listening and sometimes commenting the storytelling and fantasying with verbal psychotherapy techniques like confrontation, clarification, and interpretation (Alanne, 2010; Lehtonen & Heinonen, 2007).[2]

Free association to music like a song is a receptive music therapy technique as there is no prepared theme or image provided by the therapist (Alanne, 2023, p. 285). As such, it is different from the projective music listening and guided imagery techniques. Free association to music is also different from the free improvisation as clients are not improvising with instruments. However, a therapist may freely improvise for the clients who are listening, writing, or speaking freely whatever comes to mind (Bruscia, 1987, pp. 551–552). In the clinical music psychotherapy process, there are many music therapy techniques like body movements, drawing, painting, recording of song and improvisation, and so on, that can be combined with free association to music in their reflection (Ahonen-Eerikäinen, 2007; Alanne, 2023).

As a part of the music psychotherapy and phase-oriented trauma work, the free association to music technique can lead to the working through of trauma like in the case of Ben introduced earlier. In Ben's music psychotherapy, after a half year of therapy, session number 29, Ben's free association to music took him to the origins of his trauma and his mock execution (Alanne, 2010, 2013). Music listened and chosen by the therapist during the session was (1) Erik Satie: Gymnopedia; (2) Jean Sibelius: 2nd symphony, parts 1 and 2; and (3) Claude Debussy: Reverie.

At first, Ben's associations and imagery went to his home country in Africa. He was thinking about people living there in the city and countryside (Alanne, 2010, p. 140). He associated his hometown which felt good for him. In his imagery he was alone and did not experience any threat. Ben told the therapist about fishermen that he approached and how he sat down on a bench by the riverside after sightseeing. In the end of music, Ben was looking tensed, which was noticed by the therapist. When the music ended, Ben's experiences during the music listening and free association to music were reflected with the therapist. Ben told the therapist that his head had begun to ache and that he had felt heavy at the very end of the musical piece. He described to me that when he was coming down from the scenery, the view suddenly

[2] See Sect. 5.4.4 "Psychotherapeutic Discussions and Techniques" for more on the verbal techniques.

started to look peculiar. During that moment, the day of his execution came to his mind. He did not want to tell me as the therapist much about it but he told me only shortly that it was a mock execution. His images during the free association to music looked similar where he was taken, young trees, a bank, near the riverside (ibid.).

The analysis of his associations to music led to the reflection of his defences, particularly avoiding traumatic experiences in his life (Alanne, 2010, 2013). In that session, Ben told me that he did not want these pictures to come in mind; however, they just came like in the everyday life too. Ben described how he is usually absenting himself during the bad thoughts, memories, and imagery. Now he said that during the music listening he was present even though these thoughts and memories came to mind. He further explained that sometimes when these thoughts arrive, they destroy and "eat" the whole day (Alanne, 2010, p. 140).

It is noticeable, in this clinical vignette, how during the music listening and discussion Ben was mainly calm and relaxed (Alanne, 2010, 2013). Music seemed to function like a dream work during his music listening and transforming his symbolic associations and imagery of music to his traumatic memories. In this regard, free association to music can open defences and integrate traumatic experiences in the present moment. Music in music psychotherapy seemed to bridge the dissociation between the mind and the body of Ben as he was able to be present in his imagery as well as discuss his avoidance and dissociation patterns with the therapist safely. This was the first time Ben could discuss with me about his probably most traumatising experience when he was scared about his death but was instead for some reason rescued and let go to the aeroplane. He ended up in a very disordered, partly psychotic, state to Finland as a refugee.

Projective Music listening

Another music listening technique of music therapy is projective music listening that can include the described free association to music technique (Bruscia, 2014, p. 108). In projective music listening, music or sounds are used to work with the experiences of clients. The therapist is asking the clients to identify, describe, interpret, or freely associate to them verbally or through non-verbal means or expressions that differentiate it from the free association to music. Projective music listening can include *projective music identification*, where the client is listening to and identifying with ambiguous sounds, for example, that do not necessarily have musical structures or forms. They may be natural and ambient sounds, noise, as well as art combined with sounds for relaxing purposes or guided imagery (Alanne, 2023, p. 286).

In projective music identification, ambient sounds and noises may also be produced with acoustic and electronic music instruments or effects by the client and the therapist themselves (Bruscia, 2014, p, 108). A therapist may ask the clients what kind of imagery, thoughts, or feelings are associated with the sounds they have produced, recorded, or improvised. In projective music listening and identification clients may spontaneously describe and interpret the sounds created by themselves or the others like in the group, or by the therapist. This kind of exploring the sounds of synthesiser or other instruments with a therapist enables the possibility for verbalisations of projections and feelings relating to sounds and music like with children (Alanne, 2023, p. 286).

In this regard, traumatised clients like refugees, especially children in general, may learn from their experiences that they may have avoided or restricted because of their traumatisation. With a therapist or a group, projective music identification enables the identifications with the experiences of others that may help in identifying, integrating, and working through of feelings and experiences. These kinds of musical projective identifications are possibilities for the separation-individuation development in clients, where also the feelings and experiences of the others may be separated or identified from own experiences and thoughts without guiltiness, shame, or fear.

In projective music listening, music may also integrate experiences and memories that are identified in the given sounds and possible themes for the music. In projective music listening like in guided imagery, sometimes different kinds of themes like feelings or imagery may be given to clients where to begin the association verbally or non-verbally with music. Especially, with severely traumatised clients like torture survivors, refugees, or other clients who have difficulties to freely associate or express them, providing themes like a "sunny beach" or a "forest" chosen by the therapist may help them to encounter and explore their experiences safely (Alanne, 2010, 2014a, 2019b, 2023, p. 289).

From there clients can develop and continue their own associations, imagery, and narratives with music that can be painted, drawn, written, or discussed during or after the music listening with the therapist like in the case of Ben. This kind of projective listening can be done within an individual or a group therapy with refugees of different ages. Other functional and creative arts therapy approaches including dance, movement, clay-work, drama, storytelling, puppetry, and other toys, where clients may project and identify with themselves, will be discussed more later. They can be combined with projective music listening in describing and working through of issues verbally or non-verbally. For example, they can help in communication and psychotherapeutic work with refugees and lessen the needs for using an interpreter when there is no common language or words for some experiences (Alanne, 2023, pp. 286–288; Bruscia, 2014; Castaneda et al., 2018).

5.4.3 *Guided Imagery*

Guided imagery techniques in music psychotherapy are using imaginal listening with clients (Alanne, 2023, p. 288, Bruscia, 2014, p. 109). It means that music is listened to evoke and support imaginal processes and inner experiences of the client. During the music listening of guided imagery clients are often in a relaxed and nonordinary state of consciousness that is induced and helped by the therapist with relaxational or thematic instructions (Bruscia, 2014; Grocke & Wigram, 2007).

With severely traumatised clients like refugees and torture survivors the altered state of mind is not a prerequisite for the guided imagery process (Alanne, 2023, pp. 288–289). It can also be done in a normal state, and a therapist must assess according to the clients' problems, defences, and personalities what kind of imagery process is possible (Alanne, 2014a; Bruscia, 1998). With traumatised refugees, a therapist must be careful in the beginning of treatment and not to go deep into the imagery process with clients who are still in the acute phases of their trauma and their conditions are not stabilised yet.

Then, it is better to begin with guided imagery techniques like *directed music imaging*, where clients are imaging during the music listening according to themes provided by the therapist (Alanne, 2023, p. 289; Bruscia, 2014, p. 109). Often clients are in the altered state of mind and focusing their minds on music and their inner experiences. This kind of music listening is near meditation where clients are concentrating to the mental or physical themes selected by the therapist or themselves for the listening of music. The themes selected for the music listening may be from the lives of clients and relating to a specific situation or a relationship. The selected themes, which may be personal or general, are discussed before music listening and they are accepted by the clients.

The themes or images in the directed music imaging are meant to help the clients to work through a specific issue or feeling (Alanne, 2023, p. 289; Bruscia, 2014, p. 109). They may relate to the traumatic experiences, phases, and situations; however, the technique of directed music imaging does not refer to a direct exposure of a traumatic experience or an event for the clients. This may cause a flooding of the unconscious in a client and make them unstable and vulnerable to the negative acting out in their lives. Instead, it is used to help the clients in relaxing, concentrating, and producing imagery and creative processes with music (Bruscia, 2014, p. 109).

During the guided imagery and music listening, refugees are allowed to be with eyes open or closed (Beck, 2019, p. 346). They are instructed to let the music evoke inner imagery, experiences, and emotions, including body sensations. A typical theme with refugees that is often used is finding a "safe place that gives you a good feeling" (ibid.). The client is guided to relax their body and be aware of their feeling of grounding with music and focusing into the body. A therapist may increase the grounding and the experiences of holding and containing if clients are having many flashbacks during the relaxation. Then, the therapist may guide the clients to be aware of their body strengths and lighten their muscular tensions (pp. 346–347).

In guided imagery with refugees, there is also discussion that is helping the clients to ground their possible flashbacks and dissociations during the music listening (Alanne, 2010; Beck, 2019, p. 346). This way, the therapist is following and guiding the inner experiences of clients. If the client is having a flashback of traumatic experiences and memories, the therapist may guide and encourage the client to find a way to change the events with their imagination during the music listening (Beck. 2019, p. 346). In such circumstances during the guided imagery, clients may also be guided to a safe place and moving away from the too painful experiences. This can be done by guiding the clients towards positive experiences.

Therefore, as discussed in the context of projective music listening technique previously, such positive guided imagery like a "sunny beach" or a "forest" may be given to the clients in grounding and establishing their feeling of safety during music listening (Alanne, 2023, p. 289). In the beginning of the session or before the music listening, a therapist may discuss and observe the clients how they are feeling today. If they are feeling themselves difficult or unstable, a therapist may suggest some kind of general positive theme for the music listening to help the client to begin with the creative process. In this, a therapist may use relaxation and breathing exercises first to ground the clients' experiences and guiding them to focus on themselves and music listening.

Even this kind of quite simple musical exercises in therapy with refugees and traumatised may help in stabilising and grounding the dissociation and the hyperarousal of clients for a while in my experiences (Alanne, 2010). Music when it is listened or played can be like the meditative process when the focus of perception moves from outer reality to the inner experience and music (Alanne, 2023; Bruscia, 2014). Clients like traumatised refugees may also go deep in their imagery processes with music that are leading to their traumatic memories like in the case of Ben described earlier during projective music listening.

Priestley (1975) wrote that "[s]ymbols are accumulators and transformers of psychic energy" and that "it is the therapist's task to create a bridge from the manifest symbol to its meaningful expression in outer reality" (p. 129). Therefore, it is important that a therapist also discusses with traumatised clients like refugees during the music listening in guiding the experience as well as after the music listening. This is helping the client to return and reflect their experiences, often symbolic, in here-and-now reality. In reflecting the guided imagery process, a therapist may also instruct refugees to draw a mandala and discuss about it with clients (Beck, 2019, p. 346).

Priestley (1975) used this kind of guided imagery techniques and themes like "the cave mouth", "ascending a mountain", and "the pool in the meadow" in her AMT (pp. 131–133). The instruction she gave for her cave mouth guided imagery was "The client imagines that she is standing hidden behind a tree in a forest clearing, watching the mouth of cave. As she watches, something emerges" (p. 131). According to her, a therapist is working with "transformation of force" when using symbolic techniques with clients (p. 129). They can be powerful tools in themselves with no need to use unnecessary strong music, metaphors with music, or direct exposure to trauma that can lead to a violent flooding of trauma to consciousness that Priestley (ibid., p. 130) warned with very introvert clients (Alanne, 2023, pp. 289–290).

Often traumatised clients are focused on themselves because they are concentrating to keep the bad thoughts away like Ben described about himself (Alanne, 2010, 2013). Other traumatised clients may be extroverted, talkative, and very active in their hyperarousal because they are keeping off their feelings and bad thoughts with distracting, acting out, and avoiding of their experiences. Priestley (1975, p. 130) recommended using guided imagery techniques gently with such very extraverted clients who cannot easily see inside of themselves to ease their defences. In trauma work like with refugees, it is important to assess the personal structures and dynamics of clients, what kind of defences they are using to protecting themselves from traumatic experiences.

Therefore, it is safer to begin with peaceful music, relaxation, and positive imagery with refugees. Often, it is enough for the beginning of trauma work and in stabilising their experiences. Later, also the traumatic experiences may emerge during the music listening as the natural process and transference like in Ben's music psychotherapy described. In session 19 of Ben's music psychotherapy, the theme selected for the guided imagery by the therapist was "the river" (Alanne, 2010, p. 132; 2013, p. 271). During the music listening Ben had very strong transformative experiences that he wondered after music listening, "you are some kind of medicine man, you have some kind of magic. How is it possible that I see Africa and I am here? I am right here, sitting here, how can I see that far?" "So, you didn't make any spells?", he checked once more (Alanne, 2010, p, 132).

During the guided imagery process, Ben was in an altered state of conscious like in a dream, 80% in Africa and 20% here, he explained in the reflection of music listening. He was listening peacefully to music that was from the *Ambient Planet* CD including pieces (1) Goa-Kosafrica, (2) Nirbandh-Eastern Voices, (3) Magic Planet-Space Groove, which I have chosen for our session (Alanne, 2010, p. 133). In a positive experience of music, Ben seemed to go deep into his memories of homeland in Africa that really surprised and elevated him what was happening and affecting him so vividly. Like in some kind of emergency he wondered: "My physics is here, I am here and then I am completely there, suddenly with a help of some music. What really happens there because I was there in real? What is it that makes the memory turn upside down or something?" (ibid.)

From the cultural point of view, it is good to be aware that people from other than Western countries may have powerful experiences and memories relating to music like Ben. As discussed earlier, they may also have different kinds of spiritual beliefs and traditions that are influencing their imagery and conceptions of music and therapy. They may make them consider them as some kind of magic that may be even frightening for some participants. Therefore, it is important to try and explain such experiences also rationally with them and explain in some degree that is adequate and possible in treatment what music therapy is about. This may become a part of cultural dialoguing in therapy like with Ben (Alanne, 2010, 2013).

Important for the clients' experiences is to ground them after the guided imagery and other music therapy process with discussion, for example. Clients should be back in the normal state of consciousness and in realities before they leave the session with a therapist. Usually, verbal discussion in the end of the session is helping the clients in orientating to here-and-now situation after guided imagery or improvisation. A therapist should leave some time for the calming from the possible traumatic issues experienced and discussed in the end of the sessions. A therapist should also be aware of the boundaries of therapy session and the schedule, so that the sessions end according to a clock. This increases safety in therapy and supports also the boundaries of the clients and their integration.

However, the boundaries of therapy and its setting do not and should not mean abandonment of the flexibility and creativity in the treatment. Otherwise, the treatment may not be possible with clients suffering from severe disorders and traumata. For example, themes and instructions for the guided imagery and projective music listening can be developed by the therapists themselves (Alanne, 2023, p. 289). Therapists may use also different kinds of music depending on their clients where they come from and how old they are. In this sense, also music listening and guided imagery can be improvisatory and creative processes where the themes and music selected are depending on the clinical process and particular moods and feelings during the sessions with refugees (Alanne, 2010).

Synchronisation and Moving Along with Feelings of Clients in Music

By selecting music together with clients in improvisations, projective music listening, or guided imagery, it is possible to move along with the feelings, experiences, and the unconsciousness of clients (Alanne, 2010, 2023; Trondalen & Bonde, 2013, p. 54). Therapists are attuning with their counter-emotions to the feelings and situations of clients, which is helping them to choose specific music to hold and contain their experiences. In this regard, it is possible to synchronise the clients' feelings and experiences including body by listening to music or improvising it together (Alanne, 2023, p. 139).

As a bodily experience, music is activating the non-verbal system of the brain and when verbalising music like in the free association to music, projective music listening, or guided imagery, the verbal system is activated (Alanne, 2023, p. 139). When the therapist and client are attuned into music and moving along within the emotions aroused in the client during the music listening and guided imagery, the dual system of the brain is integrated. Similarly, like in the free improvisations of client where the therapist is attuning into the sounds, music, and their dynamics of clients with instruments, the therapist is moving along within the music and matching the feelings of clients during the music listening and guided imagery.

Moving along with the client's experiences requires a containing capability from the therapist as it is not just reacting to the client's feelings and expressions (Alanne, 2023, p. 167). It is also thinking and giving the time and space, "structuring sound", for the client in the psychotherapeutic work (Grassi, 2021, pp. 15–16). As such, it includes the container-contained psychotherapeutic relationship like the early relationship between a mother and her baby. Music is transforming the emotional unconscious experience where the dynamic forms of presentational knowledge may transform and synchronise into symbolic forms of conscious and representational knowledge, thoughts, imagery, words, and reflection in the client (Alanne, 2023, pp. 167, 168; Grassi, 2021, pp. 52–53; Trondalen & Bonde, 2013).

Moving along in the client's feelings in music allows the continuation of experiences for the client (Alanne, 2023, p. 308). It is a similar experience as in the early relationships between the mother and her baby and in verbal psychotherapy where the therapist can be in there now with a client (BCPSG, 2010; Stern, 1985/2004; 2010). In such a way, the therapist can also interpret the experience of being in a relationship with another person for the clients. In guided imagery, the therapist is monitoring the clients' experiences and communicating with them regularly during the music listening and moving along with clients' feelings (Alanne, 2023, p. 292).

The client's experiences during the guided imagery may be images of own body, body sensations, visions, feelings, and memories (Alanne, 2023, pp. 292, 308; Bruscia, 1998, p. 12). They may also include fantasies, allegories, metaphors, symbols, as well as all kinds of observed inner experiences that may be spoken to the therapist freely during the music listening. While speaking to the guiding therapist, the client may have an experience of continuation and being there with the other, the therapist and music. They are synchronising and connecting the experiences and neural activity "as an external auxiliary ego" in the client's brain (Rose, 2004, p. 119).

In the music psychotherapeutic process, musical synchronising is applied to support, stabilise, and strengthen the clients' responses (Alanne, 2023, p. 271; Bruscia, 1987, p. 539). It can promote the awareness and increase intimacy of a therapeutic relationship. It may also convey empathy, acceptance, identification, and understanding for the clients that are especially important for the traumatised like refugees who may have lost connections to themselves and their feelings. This provides a possibility for traumatised clients to be in a relationship with a therapist through music that is helping to stabilise, share, and discuss their traumatic experiences. In this way, music can support alliance, activation, calming, and building trust between the therapist and a torture survivor like one of my clients improvising with a guitar during the session. For another dementia client, guitar playing enabled discussion of losses during childhood and sorrowing them as examples of musical synchronisations in therapy (Alanne, 2023, p. 308).

In this regard, music as a non-verbal method may help to communicate with refugees and with other clients in general when there is no common language, or clients do not have connections to their feelings and experiences (Castaneda et al. 2018, pp. 291, 294). This may lessen the need for an interpreter. However, when using music and songs from the client's country, the therapist would be good to ask the interpreter to translate the lyrics, so that the therapist could understand the contents of the songs, are they hurting or insulting for the client, as they may belong to a certain ethnic group or a situation like a funeral (Beck, 2019, p. 346). Otherwise, it could be also difficult for the therapist to understand and identify with the feelings and lyrics of the song as well as move along with the client in music.

Even though all kinds of music may be listened and used in the guided imagery processes with clients, it is good to check with the refugee clients how they are feeling about listening to or using music from their native country (Beck, 2019, p. 346). This is important in avoiding listening something that would feel unnecessary confusion or unsafe for the client. However, using unfamiliar music where refugees can associate more freely may support their acculturation process in the host country and connect the old memories with new ones in the safe place (ibid.).

Therefore, it is good to remind that not everything can or should be always safe in music or therapy because otherwise working through of traumatic issues and recovering from them would not be possible according to the phase-orientated trauma work (Herman, 1992/2022). Also, free association to music and guided imagery as well as artistic and musical experiences feels more fresh, strong, and enjoyable because they are providing new experiences. They may be unfamiliar, uncanny, or strange, representing traumatic events, but may also feel very positive like in the guided imagery case of Ben. In the guided imagery processing, too familiar music cannot necessarily bring own experiences, images, and associations for the people because they may be too "used" already in commercials, movies, and so on. As such, they are belonging to a certain situations, social contexts, and cultural codes that they are too easily and even automatically associated with.

Music from the client's home country may support the therapeutic relationship and alliance as a part of the cultural dialoguing. One safe way to do it is to instruct clients like refugees to bring their own music and songs for the sessions that can be listened and translated by the client or the interpreter during the sessions (Alanne, 2010, 2013). This method of *song communication* enables the increase of the discussions and verbalisations of experiences in therapy where clients like refugees may be instructed to think and bring music that is relating to their current feelings and thoughts that can be listened in the sessions (Alanne, 2023, p. 280, Bruscia, 1998).

Clients may also bring their music on CDs or in other formats like in their digital phone applications to therapy or the music can be chosen from the therapist's music lists or collections (Alanne, 2023, p. 280). In this regard, clients may show their feelings, thoughts, and issues through music in therapy that can be listened, shared, and discussed during the sessions. Music listening and imagery work can be done with refugees and asylum seekers individually or in groups including families (Beck, 2019, p. 346). For the refugees, music listening may bring feelings of safety and peace as well as provide an access to positive feelings and memories. It can reduce or divert their pain or anxiety combined with psychotherapeutic discussions and reflections about the emotions and experiences music evoked (pp. 346–347).

5.4.4 Psychotherapeutic Discussions and Techniques

In a modern psychoanalytic thinking, procedural and declarative memories in the unconscious are discerned (Lemma, 2006, pp. 78–79). It seems that the emotional experiences and memories, like fears, are conditioned in our brains and unconscious behaviours. They are affecting how we are relating to the environment and our relationships with others. This is important considering the traumatisation of clients like refugees who often cannot understand why they are anxious with people and having panic attacks, for example. Their traumatic reactions are stored in their procedural memories and the body as speechless experiences outside their consciousness (Schulman, 2002, p. 172, van der Kolk, 2014).

Because of the traumatisation that is inhibiting their neural connections, as discussed earlier, there cannot be stored trauma memories in the declarative memory (Schulman, 2002, p. 172, van der Kolk, 2014). The feelings and sensations related to trauma cannot be integrated to concepts, words, and symbols, but they are experienced as hyper- or hypoarousal, fragments of feelings and sensations like the beta elements described by Bion (1962a/1967) that cannot be controlled. Therefore, when working with traumatised like refugees, therapists should keep in their minds that the traumatised do not necessarily have access to their traumatic feelings and memories.

However, a therapist can help their clients in verbalising their experiences through music and words. In psychotherapy, or in other therapeutic approaches like music therapy, when different kinds of feelings and issues of clients are worked and discussed, they can transform into a procedural knowing and learning (Alanne, 2023, p. 156). The repetition of the symbolised and verbalised contents as declarative knowing in therapy enables a change in the automatised patterns of feeling and behaving. Because of the automatised traumatic experiences, their repressing, avoiding, and acting out as a part of the client's developed transference, it is usually a slow process.

When stabilising and working through of the client's traumatic experiences, a therapist may move along in the expression of words, gestures, and silences of the client (Alanne, 2023, p. 156). As Stern (2004, 2010) and the BCPSG (2010) have described, in this regard therapists may provide non-verbal interpretations of the current situations and feelings that are meaningful in the present moment for their clients (Stern, 2004, pp. 150–151). In this, therapists may use their counter-emotions and implicit knowledge like in music and playing an instrument that is a familiar skill relating to the procedural memory of the therapist.

The therapist may match the moment of meetings and non-verbal understanding in the "now" experiences of such relational interaction with a client (Stern, 2004, pp. 150–151). According to Stern and his colleagues, this is adding something more to the verbal interpretations of clients that cannot be reached with the verbal knowledge of interpretations and the declarative knowledge (Alanne, 2023, p. 156). The implicit knowledge is mediated by the amygdala and the brain stem, and it is including the procedural memory, emotions, affects, and the bodily reactions of the clients (Lemma, 2006; Solms, 2017/2019).

Therefore, with traumatised like refugees, it is important to understand that clients are learning from their experiences with the so-called *here and now or transference interpretations* of the therapist. Otherwise, they may not achieve connection to themselves and their traumatisation in therapy. One useful approach for the traumatised and borderline/personality disorders as well as other clients who do have words or contact for their feelings is the *empathic describing*. In the empathic describing, the feelings and situations in therapy are described, so that the client may identify with the experiences of the therapist, how the therapist is feeling, seeing, and thinking about the clients and their traumatisation (Alanne, 2010, 2023; Schulman, 2002; Tähkä, 1993/1997).

The empathic describing of psychoanalytic psychotherapy is close to the *reflection* technique in music therapy where a therapist is portraying a child's emotions and actions using music and songs (Alanne, 2010, 2014a, 2023, pp. 161–162; Bruscia, 1987). This kind of musical reflection in music psychotherapy was developed by Alvin (1965/1972), where the therapist is mirroring the personalities and current moods of clients with an instrument or by singing. Reflection may also include musical imitation of the clients' movements, gestures, and sounds in different ways. Using both words and music to portray clients' personalities, moods, situations, and doings, the therapist is enabling the development of new internalised self and object representations for the clients like in the early relationship with a mother (Alanne, 2010; Levinge, 2015).'

Empathic describing with a client can be used in the verbal reflections with traumatised clients like refugees after listening to or playing music, guided imagery, and free improvisations. It enables the integration of their traumatic experiences, memories, and feelings and their verbalisations with the help of music as an "auxiliary ego" and "prosthetic device" for their brains (Alanne, 2023, pp. 140–141; Rose, 2004, p. 119; Schulman, 2002). This is important for the dual coding system of the brain in making new connections between the feelings and words, memories, time, and place like seemed to happen during the guided imagery process of Ben earlier shortly described (Alanne, 2010, 2013). It is important for the music therapy of traumatised that the therapists are discussing with their clients in addition to musical exercises and communication, to develop verbal capabilities and their brain connections for symbolisation in clients.

In the verbal reflection of musical experiences, a therapist may use *mentalising* techniques for the clients in verbalising the mental contents what they are doing and talking about. The mentalising capacity relates to the insecure attachment and the experience of unintentional being in a child because of the lack of marked mirroring of emotions by the caregivers (Alanne, 2023, pp. 134–135; Strehlow, 2009, p. 173).[3] Music and other artistic approaches can help the clients to depict and learn from their experiences and feelings in the here and now, especially with BPD clients and those who have insecure attachment patterns (Alanne, 2023; Lemma, 2006; Strehlow, 2009; Strehlow & Hannibal, 2019; Strehlow & Lindner, 2016).

The lack of mentalisation capacity refers to the difficulties in social perceiving and understanding of the cues from the other people's emotions in their faces, looks, and gestures (Alanne, 2023, pp. 134–135; Allen et al., 2008; Fonagy et al., 2004). In such situations, the verbal discussions with clients including music and other creative methods may help in developing understanding of such social cues and feelings relating to them. From the therapist's narrative and lived experience with a client, the client may internalise new ways of relating to social situations and relationships. This can happen explicitly according to the verbalising of the therapist or

[3] See the earlier paragraph "Mentalisation and Trauma" in Sect. 2.5 "Psychodynamic Understanding of Trauma" about the concept of mentalisation for more.

implicitly identifying with the feelings and experiences of the therapist in here and now.

In the explicit mentalisation people are describing and telling oneself and others what they are doing, thinking, and feeling (Alanne, 2023, pp. 134–135; Allen et al., 2008, pp. 315–316). Shortly, mentalising is "keeping mind in mind" and awareness of one's own and others' experiences and feelings that a therapist can help the clients to learn within the therapeutic relationship (Allen et al., 2008, p. 312). The techniques of mentalisation, empathic describing, and reflection in music psychotherapy are closely related. Their difference in the verbalisations of therapist seems to be that in mentalisation, the therapist is providing a psychic mind and feeling for the clients' perceptions of oneself and the other, which they do not seem to have an idea themselves. The therapist is providing such psychic contents and thinking that are poorly developed in the clients and their capabilities to feel and see themselves and the others. Because of the developmental trauma and ACEs their thinking may be very concrete and undifferentiated, for example (Strehlow & Hannibal, 2019, pp. 335–336).

When using the empathic describing, clients may have capabilities to mentalise themselves and the others as they have learnt to control their bad objects in the relationships, for example (Alanne, 2023; Cullberg & Johannessen, 2004; Tähkä, 1993/1997). However, because of the split, projection, projective identification, and other defences they are using because of their traumatisation and possible personality disorders including BPD, they cannot relate and accommodate with the feelings, opinions, and experiences of the others. Instead, they are often acting out that is causing trouble and conflicts in their lives and relationships. They necessarily cannot maintain their internalisation and control of good objects very long. In such situations, the therapist may modify and teach the clients, with their already existing feelings, psychic contents, and mentalisations, how to be with the objects in less destructive ways. The change occurs with identifications to the therapist's experiences and their descriptions for the clients.

I think that the empathic describing can also contain mentalisations and their learning because the mentalisation capability can be developed and learned in life and therapy even though it is referring to the innate incapability and prerequisites in the early development (Alanne, 2023, pp. 135–136; Fonagy et al., 2004). The capabilities of mentalisations do not refer directly to any psychological or medical disorders, but there may be differences and difficulties in some degree with all people and all kinds of clients (Allen et al., 2008). In the traumatic stress, difficulties in mentalisation may be emphasised in the flight/fight mode thinking temporally. However, the incapabilities in mentalisations are suggesting some difficulties in symbolic and undifferentiated thinking where the clients may think that what is said or seen is true, or that the therapist is thinking or feeling the same as the client (Strehlow & Hannibal, 2019, pp. 335–336).

With traumatised clients like refugees, a therapist may help the client to feel and become separate with the objects like the experiences of therapist. In the verbal or musical portraying of the client's experiences this may happen smoothly and by not confronting the experiences of clients but moving along with them separately in a different way. Then, a client has a possibility to identify with the experiences of the therapist without a need to deny or fight against them. However, this may need developing some trust between the client and the therapist first, so that the clients can let the therapist in and identify and internalise such new psychic capabilities to think, feel, reflect, and be in a relationship like the therapist.

In the stabilisation phase of trauma, the therapist may need to become an object first for the client's chaotic experiences like with psychotic clients respectively (Alanne, 2023; Cullberg & Johannessen, 2004; Tähkä, 1993/1997). The severely traumatised clients may be very vulnerable in trying to maintain their psychic balance and the control of it. In such circumstances, using of empathic descriptions and asking gently clarifications about the experiences of clients may be useful instead of early interpretations and confrontations of client's situation (Schulman, 2002, pp. 179–180). This is respecting the need of safety for the traumatised clients in holding and containing their experiences first before they are ready for working through and sorrowing their traumas and reorientating in their lives.

In this sense, verbal or musical reflection of clients' experiences is part of the returning of dialogue like with psychotic clients who have lost their differentiated object experiences. With verbal reflection of the clients and their experiences, a therapist may develop this capability as a goal with all clients how to think, discuss, and feel about oneself or the others separately. The therapist may support the clients' capability for self-awareness with verbal reflections that may develop new capabilities, thoughts, and insights in clients. As a part of the process, the therapist's reflections may be identified with and internalised in the therapeutic relationship. Particularly, this may relate to the working through and integration phases of trauma therapy. In these phases, clients may develop a new sense of their selves and traumatic experiences that can be discussed and reflected in therapy.

When the clients are stabilised, they are more likely to reflect their experiences and themselves. This enables more analytic approaches of using such psychotherapeutic techniques like direct confrontations and interpretations of clients' situations. However, depending on the clients and their situation, there may be needs to confront their feelings, behaviours, and issues in therapy if the client is acting out or is self-destructive, for example. Otherwise, confrontations, clarifications, and interpretations in therapy may relate to the here-and-now transference of the current feelings in therapy. They are providing some insight, awareness, and understanding for the clients how they are feeling music or themselves in therapy. This kind of psychotherapeutic discussion occurs typically in the beginning of the sessions where it can be decided together whether listen to or play some music during that session. After the music part of the session, the experiences of clients can be similarly discussed by the therapist. However, the emphasis is usually in the reflection of music and the experience of clients where the therapist may also need to support the reflection with raising up some feelings and issues in a client or a group.

In such a verbal reflection, a therapist may use verbal interpretations of the clients' experiences of music or what they have told about themselves. This may be confronting and clarifying some memories, associations, or imagery brought by music in clients. The therapist may also provide here-and-now/transference interpretations of the client's or group's feelings that are not discussed or are unconscious in the dynamics of the sessions. Also, so-called genetic/historical interpretations may be given to the clients suffering from traumas. However, these may be more effective and preferable when the client has already described and discussed them first in some degree. Genetic interpretations may help the clients to work through and integrate their traumatic pasts and consequences in their behaviour or life that they are unaware of.

This can help the traumatised understand their symptoms and behaviours like dissociation, acting out, and reexposuring to trauma patterns in their lives. As discussed earlier, some severely traumatised clients who are acting out and self-destructive may be completely unaware of their traumatic experiences and ACEs that can be raised up as a genetic interpretation. In this sense, genetic interpretations of the therapist may be a part of providing trauma knowledge for the clients. As such they can be provided indirectly or directly in clarifying, confronting, and interpreting the manifest trauma behaviours of clients and their possible acting out during the working through and integration phases of treatment.

However, with such interpretations that may also sometimes relate to the therapeutic relationship with strong feelings, transference, and reexperiencing of the trauma, the therapist needs to be cautious and assess the capabilities of clients for containing and understanding the connections of their reactions. Also, therapists must be careful and not to enact according to the clients' traumatic experiences when they cannot contain the unbearable experiences that are projected into them as a part of the client's transference and reexperiencing of the trauma. These may also be a part of the provocation and manipulation of clients where therapists may need to calm themselves and hold on with their interpretations, direct confrontations, and unnecessary conflicts with clients.

Often, the best that therapists can do then is to try to keep calm and maintain their own reflection of the clients, their situation, and themselves, and to help their clients in reflecting themselves and returning to a dialogue in therapy. Within the continuing of treatment, this may be beneficial in containing and holding the experiences of clients before they are possible to be contained and reflected for the clients themselves. This would be the long-term goal for the treatment as well as the capability to leave the trauma background in some point of their lives without the needless perennial mourning or controlling of bad objects (Tähkä, 1993/1997; Volkan, 2018a). To achieve this goal with traumatised and other clients, especially with refugees of different ages, therapists may use music, arts, and other functional methods, together or instead of language to support their communication in containing and reflecting their experiences (Castaneda et al., 2018).

5.4.5 Artistic Media and Other Functional Methods

With traumatised refugees and especially with children, therapists may also use other artistic activities and functional methods in addition to music in therapy (Castaneda et al., 2018). To achieve the goals of stabilising, working through, and integration of traumatic experiences, a therapist may use such methods as drawing, painting, writing, dancing, clay-work, relaxation, and so on to support the reflecting of clients (Ahonen & Mongillo Desideri, 2014; Ahonen-Eerikäinen, 2007; Alanne, 2023; Bruscia, 1987).

Clients like refugees may draw their experiences during their journeys from home country and refugee camps, for example. Use of free drawing or painting may bring forth their feelings, losses, and traumatic experiences. Methods like drawing, painting, and writing can be combined with music listening where the clients have possibilities to express themselves immediately while listening to music. After that the drawings and paintings can be psychotherapeutically discussed with a client and a group where they can further reflect their experiences verbally. An interpreter may be only needed after the music listening and painting/drawing to music which can help the therapists and interpreters in their work (Castaneda et al., 2018). Also, when using other artistic media combined with music, the interpreter may not be even needed, if it is not possible to arrange for some reason. Then, the clients can represent and symbolise their thoughts, imagery, and feelings in the form of pictures, for example.

In a music psychotherapy process, using music, words, and other creative media is considered as continuous reflection and externalising-internalising interpretative work with clients (Ahonen-Eerikäinen, 2007, pp. 94–95; Alanne, 2023, pp. 54–55, 284). Music and other artistic approaches like music movement, music-painting, and fantasies are helping clients in symbolising and containing their psychic contents and experiences. As such, they can be considered like dreams and day-fantasies of clients in therapy that are communicating personal unconscious thoughts and experiences to the therapist.

This can develop the client's capability of thinking and reflecting, the alpha function according to Bion (1962b/2007), from chaotic and fragmented beta elements to alpha elements (Alanne, 2020, 2023, p. 62). As discussed earlier, using different media in therapy may help the traumatised to connect their sensory experiences, anxiety, fear, hyper/hypoarousal with words, and symbols. Instead of splitting or acting out, they can be played out and reflected to name and have a meaning for the traumatic feelings and experiences with a therapist.

This kind of work in therapy where the emotional and symbolic experiences of clients are integrated may also include physical exercises and usage of relaxation, breathing, or yoga with traumatised like refugees (Ahonen & Mongillo Desideri, 2014; O'Rourke, 2022). The therapist may teach the clients to ground and relax themselves with the breathing exercises, for example. This may help them during their panic attacks or when they are feeling and fearing that the panic is coming, and they cannot control themselves. In this regard, using and combining words, artistic, and functional methods, therapy with traumatised refugees may support and develop their capability for interception, safe awareness, and understanding of their bodily reactions, perceptions, and their mentalisation (O'Rourke, 2022, p. 236).

5.4.6 Use of Play

With children and adolescent refugees, therapists may use playing as a method of therapy as music can be considered as a form of play (Alanne, 2023, p. 260). Music is a part of human culture in plays, games, and social dances. Music is combined with the funny stories and rhymes in the children's songs as well as in Christmas carols. Also, music targeted for the adult audiences may have funny and ironic lyrics in opera, rock, pop, or folk music. Musical ideas, rhythms, melodies, sudden changes in dynamics, and sounds can be playful and contain elements of joy, humour, and surprise elements like in a play. As discussed earlier, in Africa, there may not be a different word for music, dance, and movement as they are thought to be the same (Alanne, 2010, p. 11; Jones & Baker, 2004).

Therefore, music with refugees and traumatised may bring natural positive energy and elevation when listened to or played together with a therapist or a group. Musical improvisations, even with adults, may include elements of play when clients in a group are imitating with drum beats each other. In the group improvisations, group members can "pass the rhythmic message" with drums to each other in a circle, teaching the next one their rhythmic patterns that the next one must repeat, for example. This can be a very funny experience for the group and does not necessarily require former skills and knowledge. One player can try to teach their rhythms to the next one and accept it before the next ones can continue and teach their rhythms similarly.

I have used this kind of musical games and free improvisations with refugee children and adults, women torture survivors, where music, sounds, and rhythms are the communication between participants, and no speaking and teaching with words is not allowed in a game. For the depressed and traumatised, this can be an elevating experience. These kinds of musical games and improvisations can also be a part of the preventive mental healthcare interventions with refugees.

In the child psychotherapy, free playing with children including music is like verbal free association where the children's unconscious feelings and thoughts are played out together with a therapist (Alanne, 2014a, 2023, Bensimon, 2020; Brummer, 2005; Erikson, 1950/1964; Klein, 1955/1964). Instead of aggressive and destructive behaviour and acting out of feelings, it can contain healthy and social structures for the clients to express themselves in the form of fantasies and playing games with a therapist. For example, children of different ages may enjoy peek a boo game with music and sounds in therapy that can be a part of their therapeutic regression and reworking of their traumatic developmental issues with a therapist.

During the music (psycho)therapy, children or adolescents may want to play different kinds of children's board and card games or hide `n´ seek (Alanne, 2023,

p. 262; Bruscia, 1987; Reuter et al., 2021). Musical and other artistic elements like singing, drawing, and making things together may be implemented in the sessions. There can be toys, characters, puppetry, animal figures, toy cars, and so on that can help the children to express their feelings and issues in therapy. This can help the children to communicate their traumas in a form of play. The therapist can psychotherapeutically discuss with the children and verbalise things that are happening and experienced during the play. As the play may manifest symbolically or sometimes directly the object relationships and transference of the client, the therapist may also provide personal transference or genetic interpretations for the children about their situation.

Sounds, music, songs, and body instruments can also be a part of the games with children in therapy or playing board games like draughts with older children. The therapist may sing, produce sounds, or improvise music with instruments like keyboards to imitate and express the elements of game or story, plot, in a play with children. This may be empathic musical reflection of the children's or character's emotions and personalities like reading a fairytale. As with fairytales, fables, and myths, children can learn from their experiences when they are enchanted and identified with the unconscious feelings and themes included in their plays, games, and stories (Alanne, 2023, p. 55; Bettelheim, 1975; Schwartz, 1956/1964).

With traumatised children like refugees, children's stories and plays may also include elements of their losses and fears that they have encountered during their escape from the home country and war. In the context of playing and fantasies, children may represent symbolically their traumas and experiences that they may have no words. Also, music and sounds in the free improvisations and as a part of the playing may present such unconscious fears and dynamics of trauma that a therapist should attune and listen to with a "third ear" (Alanne, 2023; Lemma, 2006; Reik, 1948/1998, pp. 144–145): What a child or an adult is expressing within a story, play, or in music with a therapist? How are they using their voices or sounds in their speech or music? This may provide a therapist a key in understanding and verbalising the unconscious drama, feelings, and dynamics for the client directly or as an indirect interpretation in a play or music.

Winnicott (1971/1997, p. 50) thought that playing as a creative experience is "itself a therapy" and providing children a possibility to play "is itself a psychotherapy that has immediate and universal application". Furthermore, Winnicott considered that all psychotherapy is a creative process and that a therapist should also have a capability to play to help their clients in removing their developmental blocks (pp. 38, 50, 54). According to him, when children cannot play, a therapist must help them to play (Alanne, 2023, pp. 260–261).

This is especially important with traumatised children like refugees as well as with adults in therapy who may have lost their creativity, hope, interest, and joy of life because of their traumatisation. Music as a form of play and creativity may invite clients to open, join, and share with others their experiences naturally. Therefore, therapists should maintain their creativity, sense of playing, and attune with sensitive interest to the different expressions in playing, games, music, choices of words, language, and topics of clients in their work (Alanne, 2023, p. 262; Bruscia, 1987; pp. 564–565; Levinge, 2015, pp. 125–127).

5.4.7 Collecting a Story

When working with traumatised refugees, it is important to collect their stories, who they are, where they come from, and what has happened to them. It is a part of the clinical assessment of refugees like torture survivors to probe their possible traumatisation. This should also be considered in their music therapy assessment, so that the methods of music therapist and music used would not feel unsafe for the clients.

In therapy, the client's story including their traumatisation can be collected more thoroughly including their childhood memories and family experiences. ACEs and childhood traumatic attachments are important to share and collect because they may include the parents' transgenerational traumas of war, slavery, and death that have affected the resilience of clients negatively (Salberg, 2024a, pp. 40–41). Without a possibility to share this kind of experiences that many refugees, including children, have encountered may increase their vulnerability for traumatisation and its transmission over next generations and their children.

As the traumatised have learnt to match and "dance" with their traumatised parents forming a role reversal, it is especially important to hear and witness their own voices and stories (Salberg, 2024a, pp. 40–41). Within this kind of role reversal and empathic attuning to their parents, trauma survivors may have even developed a *traumatic attachment* where the parents' trauma story has entered their bodily cellular system preverbally with *dissociative attunement* before the narrative. This enables the transmission of trauma to a child.

With this background, it is evident that the story of the clients that is told should be their own in therapy. It should not be considered simply as a narrative of trauma because it might not be the story of the clients themselves and their experiences. As discussed earlier, memories can be social and political, so they can represent the denied and silenced collective trauma and narrative, and not necessarily the actual self-experience and losses of the citizens and refugees relating to their traditional music, for example (Reyes, 1999; Välimäki, 2015). Also, the narrative of refugees, torture survivors, and other clients often repeated does not necessarily transform their experiences as they may have told many times how they have been beaten and tortured by several people during their asylum-seeking process. It seems that these traumatic experiences should be worked through within their minds and bodies as well as be shared in the empathic encountering of therapy (Salberg, 2024b, p. 75). It should include the holding and containing of the experiences, so that the clients themselves could bear and contain their often-horrible experiences. If not so, it may be avoided to become just a narrative of their traumatisation and journey, and not a real lived story of themselves.

Because of the avoidance of traumatic experiences, there may be holes in the memories and stories of trauma survivors that may not be reached and sorrowed

(Grand, 2024, p. 47). Then, the traumatic events are not integrated in the memories but are staying as timeless, repetitive, and inchoate. Sometimes these memory blocks may be years of their childhood, adolescent, or adult life that clients cannot memorise at the beginning of therapy. However, during the regular appointments and continuing therapy process, clients are beginning to remember what happened during those years and times.

In this sense, a part of the therapy including music is collecting and witnessing the story of clients that needs to be restored for their knowledge (Grand, 2024, p. 47). This requires empathic witnessing of the traumatic experiences of clients like Holocaust, so that a traumatisation that has exceeded verbal knowledge could become registered in their own minds. This makes the testimony of torture, rape, violence, and so on, which refugees and other traumatised have encountered, a possibility for traumatic events to become "knowable" for them (ibid.). However, this needs empathic Other to receive and hear their trauma and to become a witness for the trauma that can be considered as "an event without a witness" or "a subject without history" (ibid.).

This is closely related to Siirala's conceptions of transfer and vicarious illness discussed earlier where the client is carrying the burden of trauma and cannot share it with anyone (Siirala, 1966/1969, pp. 94–95; 1983, pp. 137–138). It seems that in the dissociative attunement of family, where the child becomes a carrier of the parents' intensive emotions, affects are restored into their child unconsciously (Salberg, 2024a, pp. 40–41). This is causing a traumatic or dissociative attachment where the traumatic experiences are split from awareness.

Like explained earlier by Siirala (1983), a person seems to be a placement of the unbearable transfer of feelings and thoughts resigned by the parents, family, and society. Volkan (2018a, pp. 47— 48) has described an unconscious "deposit" of relocated, immigrant, or refugee parents' self and other images into their children's internal world. In this kind of transgenerational transmission, the images of war, terror, fear, anxiety, enemy, otherness, and so on are pushed into the fantasies of child or baby without their contexts. They may remain in the narratives and experiences of refugees and dislocated people as split from their own experiences and memories as a child.

However, with empathic encountering of these split and deposited experiences, they may become meaningful for the clients of different ages. Clients have a possibility to collect their own memories, experiences, and a story when they are mutually understood and shared during the therapy. Together with a therapist their holes in memories and experiences can be studied and communicated using discussion, playing and drawing with children, as well as music therapy methods like the described free improvisation, guided imagery, projective music listening, or song communication (Ahonen & Mongillo Desideri, 2014; Alanne, 2010, 2023; Beck, 2019; Bruscia, 1998, 2014; Orth et al., 2004).

The empathic encountering and collecting a story of traumatised may include use of autobiographical music and songs from the memories and different life situations of clients when they were feeling depressed and considering suicide as examples (Alanne, 2023, p. 288). Clients can bring their CDs, songs, or music in therapy, so that they could connect themselves with their feelings and life histories. Song communication or autobiographical music may also contain music from the good and happy memories as well as stories, sometimes funny, to be memorised and restored in therapy for the knowledge of client (Bruscia, 2014, p. 109).

Sometimes clients may have forgotten and lost these good experiences in themselves because of the massive use of defences like splitting, acting out, denial, and projective identification. However, with music bridging their experiences in the empathic encountering, they may restore their life-experience as meaningful. Therefore, any music like the guitar playing and improvisation of torture survivor during the session that a therapist is empathically listening may be a containing and restoring of a sense of meaning in the life for the severely depressed or psychotic client. Song communication may also include the clients themselves playing or composing their meaningful songs and stories that can be verbalised and integrated into their experiences.

Music therapy was used to collect the experiences and stories in one study of the six traumatised refugee and immigrant women in Canada (Ahonen & Mongillo Desideri, 2014). The short-term analytic group music therapy process of eight sessions used music therapy techniques like music listening, including adapted guided imagery, improvisation, art, writing, clay-work, and relaxation techniques. The refugee group participants worked with their experiences how they felt to be refugee women, dealt with being refugees, and how they felt themselves in the community of host country.

In therapy they shared their stories and experiences, how they felt helplessness, pain, fear, and anxiety for being refugee women (Ahonen & Mongillo Desideri, 2014). Music therapy seemed to enable grieving and acceptance of their refugee experiences and losses relating to that even though it was felt hard and painful according to their verbalisations in music therapy. They also had to deal with their guilt of being refugees and leaving their children, parents, not supporting them financially, and not filling their parents' dream in their lives.

With music therapy and other creative functional methods, these traumatised refugee women could collect and share their stories as well as grieve their losses (Ahonen & Mongillo Desideri, 2014). Music seemed to provide symbolic distance in the improvisations needed in raising, sharing, and verbalising their feelings in spite of the shortness of their therapy. During their therapy women could validate their being in a host country and a part of the community. They could feel content and liberated from their pasts as there were new sense of hope and future in the group's experiences with music that were shared in discussion and writing. After the discussion in the sessions, such themes like hope, freedom, and here and now were chosen for improvisation and further study of their experiences through music. Music and other art forms were used in tandem to enable discussion and reflection of their experiences as refugees in addition to sharing their stories.

Music can be used to collect a story of clients in music psychotherapy where the therapists and the group members become witnesses for the traumatised refugees like in the described cases of Ben and women in group music psychotherapy (Alanne, 2010, 2013; Ahonen & Mongillo Desideri, 2014). Witnessing is important for the recovery of traumatised psychologically, ethically, and juristically like with torture survivors and those other who were victims of violence and crime (Herlihy et al., 2004; Herman, 1992/2022; Grand, 2024; Salberg, 2024b). According to Herman (1992/2022, p. 191), recovery occurs "only within the context of relationships; it cannot occur in isolation." When sharing stories in the relationship, clients' unprocessed experiences are contained and metabolised in a new way as they are encountered affecting their relationships, including the therapist. Thus, witnessing makes possible the correction of ruptures of traumatised attachment and restoring humanity in clients when they become seen and heard as themselves (Salberg, 2024b, pp. 62–63, 75).

In collecting a story, music and other art forms are useful because they can empower and connect traumatised that is important for the recovery according to Herman (1992/2022, p. 191). Like in the group therapy of refugee women who were given positive themes by the therapists such as hope, future, positive, feelings, joy, faith for improvisation, combined with music they seemed to enable feeling and sharing of elevating experiences in the group (Ahonen & Mongillo Desideri, 2014). In addition to the empowerment that music and group provided in a short time, the participants could connect themselves to their own feelings and stories as well as with the experiences of others and their stories shared in the group.

However, collecting a story does not always have to include empowering themes for the music listening, improvisations, or discussions by the therapist. In the long-enough therapy process like in the case of Ben, positive experiences, feelings, and imagery relating to music and therapy may come naturally during the process. In fact, there is possibility that the traumatic events and experiences are not worked through and encountered properly if there are only some appointments and therapists are using very positive themes for the music listening and discussion. In very short therapies it may not be even possible to collect a story of clients because like discussed traumatic experiences are avoided, not even remembered, or wanted to talk about. So, in this regard there are no short-cuts in the treatment of severe traumas even with music and arts. However, as a part of other treatment and rehabilitation, even shorter music therapy interventions with positive themes may be very useful and help the clients in integrating their experiences and reconnecting themselves with positive thoughts and dignity.

In the end of the described case of Ben, he used music at home to relax and bring pleasure. He told that while listening *The London Pop Orchestra Plays Bee Gees CD, How Deep Is Your Love*, and *More than a Woman* songs, he had brought in music psychotherapy; he felt like he was a decent person with no negative thoughts as his consciousness was free and he was feeling "alive" (Alanne, 2010, p. 142; 2013, p. 273). While listening to music, he could almost feel like being a Finnish as his feelings were so good like at home, Ben explained. He continued that with music he "bracketed" his gloomy state of mind and living conditions in the host country (Alanne, 2010, p. 143). In the session 47/50, he said that "without music life would be like living in the cemetery" (ibid., 2013). He explained that during the past six or seven months in music psychotherapy, music had felt good as in the beginning even gentle music like this was annoying and made him angry. However, he said that he had learnt to use it, so that it freed him from all those thoughts and occasionally he was falling asleep.

Ben's case is one example of collecting a story of refugee torture survivor in music psychotherapy where Ben's experiences with music changed to more positive thoughts and feelings (Alanne, 2010, p. 143; 2013). He could even use music at home to relax and in his words to put away all the miserable—distract himself like some Holocaust survivors did with music at the camps to survive (Fisher & Gilboa, 2016, pp. 1228–1229). This kind of change in controlling and suppressing his thoughts, feelings, and calming down is an important capability and development for traumatised to learn in music psychotherapy. In such a way, music can create a safe place for the traumatised refugees, provide empowerment, and create connections in their body and mind as well as between people. There is also a possibility of reconnections in the brain dynamics and functions of clients when their experiences are verbalised and shared with music in therapy. Like in the described case of Ben, the clients can elevate and relax, even sleep, with the help of music and collecting their story in music psychotherapy.

5.5 The Self-Care and Empathy Fatigue of Therapist

Witnessing and collecting the story of the client can be demanding for the therapist as the traumatic experiences of clients are often relived in therapy and projected into the therapist (Castaneda et al. 2018; Salberg, 2024b, pp. 61–63; Steel et al., 2004, pp. 669–670). To listen traumatised requires attuning to their affective experiences; that is contagious for the therapists as they are going through some disturbing version of the clients' trauma. The therapy process including music may also feel contagiously disturbing because as discussed earlier in the context of torture and violence, music and especially loud sounds are passing the ego defences affecting directly to the mind and nervous system of the therapist. Similarly, the intensity and colours in drawings of trauma story or their enactments in a play of traumatised children may transmit horror in a therapist (Steel et al., 2004, pp. 669–670). Also talking with clients can transmit the suffering and disturbing dynamics and feelings of suffering, violence, grieving, insulting, annoyance, and so on into the therapist.

This is part of the traumatised client's transference and reexperiencing of trauma in the intersubjective process of therapy (Salberg, 2024b, pp. 61–63). The goal in therapy is to create a holding environment including music that is carrying and containing the traumatic experience for the clients. This is allowing the clients to come out from their dissociation and heal from what they have survived and what is happening here and now like the trauma of refugee children in their drawings or music. In this intersubjective space of therapy, therapists and other workers are constantly vulnerable to the empathy fatigue and vicarious traumatisation because they need to keep up the live contact in attuning with the experiences of clients (Steel et al., 2004, pp. 670–671).

Working with severely traumatised and depressed persons like refugee torture survivors holding and witnessing their suffering and experiences of cruelties can affect the capabilities of therapist to feel empathy towards them (Barnard & Jones, 2022, pp. 169–170). The therapist may give up the hope for such clients and feel powerless to help them. Therapists may develop negative thoughts and feelings towards their clients; even a potential universal "internal racist" towards otherness may emerge under stress when working with refugees, and their cultural and language differences (p. 169). This may affect their work in encountering clients negatively when unwanted aspects of their selves are projected onto clients.

As a result, the signs of empathy/compassion fatigue like withdrawal from client's and one's own experiences may develop when therapists are feeling anxious, burn-out, and depressed themselves because they are frustrated with their work, clients, and themselves (Castaneda et al., 2018, pp. 142–143; Lansen & Haans, 2004, p. 320). They may feel cynic, unhappy, and that they cannot affect their work and clients, and lose faith in their capabilities to treat their clients. This may also be caused by excessive workload, hurry, and witnessing too many tragedies of clients. In addition to the empathy fatigue, encountering unconscious dramas of victim, perpetrator, rescuer, victim, and witness transference constellations played out in therapy, therapist may develop similar symptoms as in PTSD and changes in their personalities when they are overwhelmed in their emotional connections with traumatised clients (Barnard & Jones, 2022, p. 170).

This may lead to vicarious traumatisation/secondary PTSD that is often felt as sudden ruptures in hope and meaning in therapists as well as mentioned experienced depression, difficulties in adapting and coping with stressful situations in and/or outside the therapy, and crying spells (Barnard & Jones, 2022, p. 170; Pérez-Martinez, 2023, p. 71). In addition, vicarious traumatisation and compassion fatigue may include psychophysical or social symptoms like sleeping problems, irritation, physical pains in head or stomach, difficulties in concentration, and intrusive anxious imagery (Castaneda et al., 2018, pp. 142–143). Compassion fatigue and vicarious traumatisation are referring to the same work-related symptoms that are considered as normal reactions to abnormal and inhuman situations. They are not primarily considered as illnesses, diagnoses, or malpractices, even though they may develop as such if they are prolonged.

Therefore, therapists need to monitor this kind of cynicism and tiredness as well as other negative distractive thoughts and feelings like fear, anxiety, and uncertainty, in their work (Wilson, 2004, pp. 294–295). They are emerging signs of empathy fatigue and vicarious traumatisation as well as countertransference issues that may relate to the activating defences of the therapist and failure of empathic attuning. The therapist should also be aware of the possibility of their tiredness, and reactions could be transmissions and projective identifications with the situations of clients. In this kind of situations, therapists are needing help and working together with colleagues as a team in containing clients' dissociation and psychic crisis, including possible suicidal thoughts and acting out of self-destructive behaviour. Then, also the support of centre or a clinic and supervision is needed in the reflection and understanding of the client's situation as well as in preventing the workers from empathy fatigue, depression (burn-out), and vicarious traumatisation (Barnard & Jones, 2022, p. 170; Casteneda et al., 2018, pp. 142–146; Swinburne, 2022, pp. 163–164).

When working with traumatised like refugees as well as with any clients, therapists should take care of themselves, so that they could help their clients (Castaneda et al., 2018, pp. 142–146). Working with severely ill and traumatised people from catastrophic situations, disasters, and wars, suffering from violence is also affecting the minds of the helpers as intuitive and empathic persons. The "music" in their lives may vanish and their world may seem unnecessarily negative without a self-care of the therapist. Therefore, it is especially important for music therapists and other therapists to take care of their own basic needs including their families and children (Pérez-Martinez, 2023, p. 71).

Working with traumas may exhaust a good-hearted therapist, so the therapists should not take too many clients to prevent themselves from depression and traumatisation. Therapists should also have a life outside their interesting work including some hobbies and other activities, connections, and relationships that are not directly related to their work. This helps in reducing stress, recovering from work, and balancing the life that is also maintaining the resilience for the therapists.

Individual activities and emotional experiences outside the work like physical exercises, relaxing, sports, culture, creativity, music, arts, literature, cinema, social relationships, nature, and so on help in maintaining the resilience and boundaries of the therapists. They are keeping them emotionally alive and interested towards their work, the others, and themselves. However, like with clients, therapists also need to reflect their work by thinking, reading, studying, discussing, learning, writing, sharing, and understanding their work and experiences. It is helping the therapists in containing and symbolising the unbearable and thus avoiding traumatising themselves (Young & Stubley, 2022, pp. 253–254).

5.5.1 Working with the Transference and Countertransference Issues

Reflection of therapy and intersubjective experiences between the therapist, client, and the group is the most important task of the therapist treating traumas (Stubley, 2022b, pp. 37–38). As discussed earlier, trauma is a two-way phenomenon that can interact and transmit itself with empathic attuning between the subjects. Even the witnessing of the client's story may affect the therapist as the embodied experience when the therapist is working empathically. This may happen as relational holding implicitly between the right-brain connections and activity between the therapist and the client as the "embodied witnessing" (Salberg, 2024b, p. 71).

This makes working with traumas and their witnessing, including music that is also affecting the brain connections in implicit/procedural memory, hard work (Salberg, 2024b, pp. 71–72). Therefore, therapists must be able to discern their own experiences from those of the clients to help them as well as to protect themselves from empathy/compassion fatigue and secondary traumatisation. In psychodynamic context, this phenomenon of memorising trauma, the past, by repeating it in behaviour and feelings generally and towards the therapist or the group members is called as transference (Lemma, 2006, pp. 231–232). It is an expressive and informative act of the clients' unconsciousness that can inform the therapist from the clients' transference feelings and enactments (Alayarian, 2024, pp. 76–77; Stubley, 2022b, p. 37).

Psychoanalytic witnessing and encountering of trauma are including the body and the psyche, deep understanding sometimes without words, when the "wounds" similar enough touch between the therapist and the client strongly (Salberg, 2024b, pp. 71–72). This can make a relational connection, which is experienced on a procedural level as a presentational level of experience and knowledge as auto-affects of music, thoughts, and feelings, in the communication (Alanne, 2014a, 2019b, 2020, 2023, p. 65). These kinds of experiences of the therapist are a part of the counter-emotions or countertransference of therapists that they should observe as a part of their therapeutic work, reflection, and communication.

Originally Freud (1910/1981, pp. 144–145) considered countertransference as some negative feelings and attitudes of therapist towards the client that were caused by unconscious complexes. They could become an obstacle for the treatment if the therapists are not aware of these experiences and their meaning in the relationship. According to Freud (1905/1981, p. 116) "transferences" were "new editions or facsimiles of the impulses and fantasies which are aroused and made conscious during the progress of analysis; but they have this peculiarity, which is characteristic for their species, that they replace some earlier person by the person of physician." Currently, in psychoanalysis, psychodynamic psychotherapy, and music therapy, countertransference usually means all the meanings and empathic reactions of unconscious communication, positive or negative, conscious or unconscious, in a therapist (Alanne, 2023, pp. 67–68; Alayarian, 2024, pp. 111–112; Lemma, 2006).

When working with traumatic experiences like those of refugees, the therapist may feel negative feelings, attitudes, and thoughts that are projected towards the therapist or therapy (Alanne, 2023, p. 70; Lemma, 2006, pp. 249–250). The therapist may have to deal with the clients' negative experiences of how they are feeling about the therapist as non-nurturing, angry, and fearful, according to their projections (Alayarian, 2024, p. 139). In negative transference, clients may deny their need of help from the therapist even though they could be in very vulnerable conditions themselves. This may be caused by the defences of clients towards the therapist or the group when they are fearing the opposite, the rejection of the therapist. Clients may also fear the judgement of therapist or avoid the emotional rapport and connection to the therapist and the group as a part their negative transference (ibid.).

In positive transference, a client may see the therapist as a dependable good object like a nurturing mother unconsciously (Alayarian, 2024, p. 139). In dealing with the negative transference, therapists must be careful with their interventions because often the clients are needing time to feel safe, so that their feelings can be reflected, confronted, or interpreted verbally (Alanne, 2023 p. 71). Vulnerable clients are needing more holding and containing of their negative experiences before they can calm down and reflect their experiences during the session and the whole therapy process. When the clients like traumatised are calmed down and relaxed, they are more able to think, function, reflect, and symbolise their experiences. Music and music therapeutic interventions like discussed methods of music relaxation, free association to music, projective music listening, and applied guided imagery may help the traumatised refugees and other clients in the stabilisation and symbolisation of their experiences (Alanne, 2010, 2023, Ahonen & Mongillo Desideri, 2014, Beck, 2019; Beck et al., 2021).

Often, in music therapy, negative experiences and anger are projected or acted-out into music where imagined chaos or war inside can be worked from the symbolic distance of music (Ahonen-Eerikäinen, 2007; Ahonen & Mongillo Desideri, 2014; Alanne, 2023 p. 71). Then, a therapist may more easily provide indirect interpretations and empathic descriptions for the child in therapy as example. Instead of discussing directly about the negative feelings and thoughts that could cause guiltiness and possible interruptions in therapy, images and feelings can be discussed as the elements of music like "this music sounded like war or chaos", "unhappy", or "tired" (ibid.). When a traumatised client like an adolescent or an adult is ready, the therapist may also provide direct transference interpretations and descriptions of the clients' playing or singing in music and how it could match the client's current feelings. This is helping the clients to contain and reflect their experiences as well as to verbalise them with a therapist—this music or song sounded like me, my experiences, and my story.

Before the transference interpretations of the client and the therapeutic relationship are possible, it is often necessary to develop a good alliance and positive transference with clients first. This is also stabilisation, building trust, and becoming a therapeutic object for the traumatised clients. Music as a mutual positive experience bringing hope, positive feelings, joy, and faith can support the alliance and positive transference between the therapist and clients (Ahonen & Mongillo Desideri, 2014). Later, in the process, also more conflictual feelings like anger, shame, guiltiness, and suicidal thoughts may come to a discussion and shared with music like in the context of free improvisations and songs. This is integrating and working through of the clients' traumatic experiences with music that is helping in expressing, witnessing, and verbalising such issues.

Sometimes the negative transference and feelings towards the therapist, music, and treatment become first with traumatised clients like children and refugees who are projecting their disappointments towards their parents, adults, and situation into music or the therapist. For example, negative feelings, turmoil, envy, and anger are often expressed in the drum, keyboard, or guitar playing of children in music psychotherapy first (Alanne, 2023, p. 71). This is possible when clients are feeling safe and allowed to express such feelings, which is important for the therapists to understand. Music in therapy must not always be aesthetically beautiful, or music at all necessarily, because the negative feelings and thoughts are allowed and supported to be expressed in music.

Music relating to early attachment traumatisation ruptures in the care and contact, abuse, neglect, and deprivation as ACEs may be true expressions of traumatisation that may sound aggressive, violent, chaotic, and feel sadistic in the unconscious experiences of clients (Alanne, 2023, pp. 71–72). Therapists need to bear and contain such expression of feelings and not deny them because music may represent a psychotherapeutic and developmental object for a client, like a transitional object of a child who is externalising the feelings and anger towards the mother safely in the teddy bear (Ahonen-Eerikäinen, 2007; Alanne, 2014a; Lehtonen, 1997; Levinge, 2015; Winnicott, 1971/1997).

In this regard the negative transference that is expressed in the symbolic distance of music or play may be helpful in therapy as it is not projected directly towards the therapist and treatment (Alanne, 2023, pp. 71–72). Some clients may experience the positive feelings and experiences such as love and intimacy in a relationship as a threat because of their early traumatisation and ACEs that are split underneath their negative transference and attitude towards the therapist and therapy (Priestley, 1994, pp. 80–81). Later, during the therapy process, new positive feelings like those of attachment towards the therapist and therapy may develop when the therapist can bear and contain the negative transference of a child client, for example.

Also, negative transferences may sometimes be hiding underneath the seemingly positive feelings towards the therapist and treatment, positive transference in therapy (Alayarian, 2024, p. 139). In this kind of situation, clients may be obedient and amenable, like everything is going well in treatment. However, these feelings and behaviour are not authentic towards their treatment as the negative experiences are split underneath the positivity. Therefore, the therapy of refugees may not progress if the negative thoughts and feelings cannot be encountered and shared in therapy. Then, music and other arts may help in bringing and playing out the authentic true feelings and negative transference, possible internal and external conflicts towards the treatment. These may relate to the losses, feelings, and situation of being a refugee in a foreign country, for example (Ahonen & Mongillo Desideri, 2014).

Some traumatised clients like refugees may refuse to collaborate, and they are challenging the therapists and their interventions (Alayarian, 2024, p. 139). There may be conflicts with therapists and other clients in a group, for example, that are projections of negative transference. These clients are reenacting their traumatisation and there may be similar failures and ruptures in their lives; they are also denying the progress in therapy for themselves, respectively. As discussed, this kind of reexperiencing and/or repletion compulsion of trauma may also be hidden underneath the compliance towards the therapy, but it may also show itself as continuous depression and acting-out behaviours like self-harm, self-injury, and interruptions in therapy.

These kinds of negative transferences and projections may cause frustration and even anger as the countertransference feelings in therapists, as the clients are unconsciously expressing their anger at the therapists (Alayarian, 2024, p. 139). Therapists may also feel hurt, ineffective, and incompetent because of the projections of negative transference towards them. However, a therapist should not consider these countertransference feelings and possible attacks on their personality and treatment as such but as the unconscious communication and defences of clients. This kind of behaviour and acting-out is a part of the purpose of the clients to control therapists and refusing of any intervention and interpretation of them.

Such negative transference towards the treatment and the therapist including complaints about suffering and being worthless is unconsciously implying taking a victim's role and the needing of a rescuer "if you care" by the clients (Alayarian, 2024, p. 139). There may also be blaming of the therapist for the problems as an unconscious appeal for the therapist to try and save the client from suffering. This may cause the therapists to identify and enact with the unconscious communication and projective identification of clients who are appealing in their suffering (Stubley, 2022b, pp. 37–38).

In such circumstances, therapists may forget their professional roles and blur their personal boundaries in work. They may do everything to help their clients, which may include taking responsibility for the client's life outside the therapy and their primary job. However, this may be fulfilling the traumatised client's unconscious wish when instead the clients should be supported to restore their own confidence and psychic capability to take responsibility from themselves. Also, in therapy clients should be encouraged to think and reflect their past experiences as well as to learn to live here and now (Alayarian, 2024, p. 139). Musical interventions like music listening, guided imagery, and free improvisation may help the traumatised refugees in understanding their traumatisation and pulling them away from such experience and dissociation (Alanne, 2010; Beck, 2019).

If the therapists do not recognise their countertransference feelings and the appealing of the clients to become their rescuers, it may cause a burn-out and vicarious traumatisation of a therapist. Especially, there is a possibility that therapists who have their own traumatic experiences and vulnerabilities become so-called wounded healers in their work (Alanne, 2023; Austin, 2002; McWilliams, 2021). As a result of the clients' projections and transmissions of their traumatic experiences, the therapist may begin to react and enact according to their own feelings of threat and try to help and save their clients. This is over-identification with the traumatised clients and refugees' situation where therapists may forget to take care of and protect themselves.

Therefore, therapists including music educators and others working with traumatised refugees should be aware of their limitations to help people in their work. It is important to identify emotional responses relating to trauma work, even negative feelings of tiredness and anger, as they may inform from the feelings of clients as well as from the therapists' own needs for resting and balancing their work (Pérez-Martinez, 2023, p. 71). Working with catastrophes in a general sense and with severely traumatised clients like refugees and their horrifying experiences like torture may reverberate with our basic feelings of needing safety. So that the therapists could do their work properly, they need to feel safe in order to reflect their clients' experiences.

In this, the rotation of work and different kinds of clients, regular supervision, peer partners and peer/team consultation, as well as continuing education in trauma cases and trauma-informed therapy are helping. Therapists and other helpers should also consider going through of their own psychotherapies if it has not been a part of their training to protect themselves from vicarious traumatisation and burn-out. Personal psychotherapy or psychoanalysis may also help the therapists to become better aware of their countertransference in therapy (Alanne, 2023; Austin, 2002; Else & González, 2023; Pérez-Martinez, 2023; Swinburne, 2022).

5.5.2 Supervision and Training

Working with traumatised like refugees requires some special theoretical knowledge of traumas as a phenomenon and how they are affecting the lives of people. In addition, it requires clinical knowledge and skills how to approach traumas and refugees with therapeutic interventions and music. As discussed, otherwise therapists like music therapists could have a risk of retraumatising their clients or suffering themselves from the effects of vicarious trauma and professional burn-out (Sokira et al., 2023, p. 9). Trauma-informed practices like in music therapy have developed to bring such a basic knowledge for therapists to encounter their traumatised clients safely. At the same time, it is helping therapists to protect themselves from the discussed risks of secondary traumatisation and potentially decreasing their professional competence, capability, effectivity, and ability to continue their work (ibid.).

The trauma-informed music therapy is including a resilience framework that is based on Herman's (1992/2022) three stages of trauma recovery of how to navigate through the effects of trauma with music (Sokira et al., 2023, pp. 11–12). The suitable and recommended stages for music therapists are (1) establishing of safety, (2) remembrance and mourning, and (3) reconnection. These stages are similar and included in the goals and phases of stabilisation, working through, and integration of trauma psychotherapy and music discussed in this book. They are well suitable for those therapists who do not have a specific psychotherapist or other training related to traumas. Psychotherapists or music therapists may benefit for trauma-informed approaches that can be integrated into their own clinical practices and theories like the complex trauma and its treatment in psychoanalytic psychotherapy respectively (Stubley, 2022b, pp. 40–41).

This kind of basic trauma knowledge could be a part of the standard training and seminars of music therapists and psychotherapists. Currently, they are already integrated in the studies of psychodynamic psychotherapists and psychoanalysts like in Finland. However, there could be more specific trauma-related theory and clinical seminars in psychotherapist and music therapist training programmes because so many people are suffering from trauma symptoms. Also, it would be good to arrange specific seminars related to work with refugees and immigrants. In Finland, there has been the PALOMA national project that has continued as a network to develop mental health actions for refugees, asylum seekers, and immigrants (Castaneda et al., 2018).

This kind of networks can educate and spread information, experiences, research, and clinical methods nationally or globally to help in working with traumatised refugees. They may also arrange training relating to the topics concerning traumas and refugees for the professionals working with them. This kind of collaboration is important for continuing education as well as peer support for those working with traumatised refugees. They are usually including the latest information and experiences in the field about how different people and organisations have developed their work and services with refugees. In addition to the new information and skills, these kinds of seminars and networks are supporting the resilience of those who are working with refugees and are facing similar issues in their work.

A possibility for clinical supervision is important for all the therapists including music therapists as well as for other professionals working with traumatised refugees (Lansen & Haans, 2004, p. 320). Especially important is the understanding of the emotional issues relating to traumas and how they are affecting therapists and those who are working and contacting them with music like music therapists and music educators. Traumatic experiences of the clients may horrify the therapists and affect their capability to work and understand their clients. In regular clinical supervision with a senior therapist or an expert in the field, it is possible to reach negative emotions and thoughts rising from the traumatic experiences of the clients. Often these may occur as unconscious bodily experiences and feelings like headache, tiredness, anhedonia, and anxiety relating to work.

As discussed, in a therapeutic relationship including music, there is developing transference where the therapist is taking a part and drawn into by the clients (Stubley, 2022b, pp. 37–38). If the transference phenomena are not familiar or the therapists are denying the possibility of the transmission of clients' feelings into their own experiences, there is a chance that a therapist will be enacting according to the unconscious drama of clients. Therefore, therapists should understand when their clients are acting out and reexperiencing their trauma, so that they would not join into the repetition compulsion of their clients in therapy. For example, therapists may begin to feel the same feelings of emergency, anger, anxiety, and so on as their clients that are transferring into their work and treatment decisions respectively without the much-needed reflection of their client's situation first.

As traumatisation causes incapability to think, remember, mourn, verbalise, and symbolise the experiences and losses, the traumatised experiences are often enacted in the therapeutic encountering (Stubley, 2022b, pp. 37–38). Clients may enact according to their powerful and unbearable anxieties where their early defences are activated. Then, a traumatised may regress and more likely function in a PS position where the roles of a victim, a perpetrator, a witness, and a rescuer are beginning to emerge in a relationship between the therapist and the client. If therapists are not aware of such a role offered by the clients consciously or unconsciously, they may be drawn to such a relationship where they are continuously and unconsciously reenacting according to the various traumatic scenarios of their clients.

In clinical supervision, different kinds of feelings and roles projected by the clients can be shared and discussed with a supervisor. Therefore, the supervised should be able to think, verbalise, and express their feelings and experiences relating to their work freely and confidentially like in therapy. This is to ensure that the unconscious traumatic scenarios and roles possibly projected by the traumatised clients like refugees could be studied and understood in the supervision relationship respectively. Then, it is possible to notice the acting out of the clients and how they are reexperiencing and repeating their traumas in their current relationships and treatments.

Also, the dynamics and interactions with music and sounds in music therapy may consist of musical and relational aspects of repeating trauma (De Backer & Sutton, 2014b, pp. 42–44). The anxiety and pain of the clients may have a sonorous form in the sensorial playing of clients at the undifferentiated and affectional/procedural levels. This kind of free improvisation of a client may be chaotic and fragmented playing of an instrument without clear structures, melodies, and rhythms in sounds that may also feel similarly chaotic, unpleasant, and disturbing for the therapist.

In supervision this kind of musical transferences and repetitions of trauma can be studied where the music, sounds, and the therapist are the objects of transference like a perpetrator or a father/mother figure where the negative feelings of clients are projected. In the supervision process, such projections and needs of the clients to reexperience their traumatic feelings and conflicts may be identified, so that the therapist could bear and contain the powerful and often unorganised and non-verbal anxieties in music and sounds. As such, they can be understood as the clients' unconscious communication that the therapist should be containing, not enacting or trying to get rid of it (Stubley, 2022b, p. 38).

Sometimes it happens when working with severe traumas as well as with other problems that the clients are splitting and acting out their feelings outside of therapy. This kind of behaviour may be self-harmful repeating of trauma and unconscious attempts to control it. This may bring negative feelings in the therapist as well as in the team treating the client who may split persons and things in good/bad, black/white, and who are often expressing themselves through negativity and aggression like complaining and opposing. Clients may also be very needy and demanding about their treatments. Then, in addition to the therapist, the whole team may need a group supervision how to encounter and communicate with such clients who are acting out and reexposuring to traumatic experiences.

Treating severely traumatised clients like refugees can be very demanding as the traumatic experiences seem to affect the therapist as well as the whole team or the centre/institute treating them (Lansen & Haans, 2004, p. 320). The feelings and experiences of clients may cause countertransference and acting out in a staff that can appear as compassion fatigue, helplessness, disappointment, anger, emphatic enmeshment, microaggression, guiltiness, emphatic repression, and tiredness towards the clients and their treatment. Similar issues may also emerge among teams that could be signs of burn-out. However, they can also be parallel processes relating to the feelings and situations of their clients that have been transferred into the staff and the team (McWilliams, 2021, pp. 33–34). As such they are unconscious reenactments of trauma where the group, team, or individual supervision may help in recognising the similar feelings or behaviours in clients and how they are affecting the therapists, other treatment personnel, and the lay volunteers.

This kind of parallel processes and their understanding in supervision or through the regular introspection of the therapist can be useful for the treatment as it may help in identifying unconscious communications and projections of clients (McWilliams, 2021, pp. 33–34). Then, a therapist or a team may use the information of their own countertransference in understanding and benefitting their clients. It is familiar in psychoanalytic psychotherapy that the countertransference feelings of the therapists towards their clients may unconsciously evoke similar feelings in a supervisor towards the therapist (p. 33). Therefore, it is also important for the supervisors to monitor their countertransference feelings and possible signs of projective identifications towards the supervisees and their clients.

Sometimes the communication in supervision may reveal a parallel process to the treatment in how things are discussed and felt, how the relationship between the supervisee and supervisor feels (McWilliams, 2021, pp. 85, 100). Are there difficulties in discussing something—what topic or feeling is missing, how the supervisee or supervisor is saying or reacting in the supervision? These may show as the different kinds of offered roles for the supervisor or the supervisee, like a rescuer or a perpetrator that may also spread into the transference between the supervisor and the supervisee. In such cases, it is the responsibility of supervisor to interpret and educate the supervisee about the transference affecting the treatment and supervision respectively.

This is helping and educating the supervisee in supervision about the treatment and the role of the transference. As discussed, sometimes also the therapists may have traumatic experiences in their backgrounds in addition to that therapists are using themselves as the instruments emotionally that can deeply affect and make them vulnerable to reenactments (Austin, 2002, p. 241; McWilliams, 2021, p. 173). Therefore, also supervision should be sensitive, confidential, and built on good alliance between the supervisor and the supervisees like therapy (Sutton & De Backer, 2014, p. 315). Negative supervision, or educational, relationships may affect the treatments of supervisees/trainees negatively as there may occur acting out of negative relationships and the repetitions of reenactments included in the supervision or teaching respectively (McWilliams, 2021, pp. 33–34).

As discussed, enactments in a therapeutic work are not necessarily harmful to the treatment if they are not continuously acting out and reexposuring the clients to traumatic experiences. When enactments are understood by therapists as the unconscious communication and appealing, or even forcing sometimes, of the therapist to take a specific role in their transference, then a therapist may help their clients. The supervision relationship should be safe, confident, and strong enough to also discuss and solve such issues, even when they are also concerning the supervision itself (Sutton & De Backer, 2014, p. 315).

Supervision is helping the therapist in bearing the experiences of clients and themselves. However, it is not therapy even though it can have therapeutic goals in supporting the mental health and capability of therapists and other workers to work with their clients. This can increase and develop the empathy towards the clients as the one goal of supervision. Other goals of clinical supervision are the clarification of feelings, exploration of preconscious and unconscious experiences, differentiation of the therapist's feelings from the clients, and studying the therapeutic relationships of therapists (ibid., pp. 315–316).

When working with music, in achieving these goals, it is also important to see, hear, and feel the countertransference of the therapists relating to music in therapy. In addition to the discussion, it may be possible to listen to audio recording from improvisations or songs/music listened or produced in therapy. Also, the drawings/paintings to music of clients may be studied in supervision to understand the experiences, unconscious communication, and the therapeutic relationships with clients, and their transference dynamics. They may manifest from the products of clients in therapy. When it is possible, a therapist may also improvise their feelings in supervision like in therapy to explore their own transference, countertransference, their differentiation, and to understand the inner/outer conflicts, personality, and defences of clients (ibid., pp. 316–317).

Working directly with music in balance with verbal reflections is a recommended asset for the music therapists, however, depending on the individual needs of the supervisees and their clients (ibid., pp. 316–317). Music can also be used in the supervision of other workers/therapists very well because it may provide a live contact with the feelings of therapists and their clients. On an affective level, using music and sounds may increase the understanding of the clients' feelings and experiences in therapy that are difficult to verbalise for the supervisees and the clients respectively. In supervision, expression of music and sounds by the supervisees or together with the supervisor may develop the symbolisation and reflection of the client's experiences that supervisees may use verbally or musically in their work.

One important goal in the education, training, and supervision of therapists is the so-called negative capability (Sutton & De Backer, 2014, pp. 315–317). Negative capability means the capability to think, feel, reflect, doubt, bear uncertainty, mystery, and to be patient in the position of not knowing yet, instead of understanding and acting immediately in therapy (Bion, 1970/2018; Hägg, 2020; Salo, 2024). This capability of therapists relating to their working with traumas and refugee clients' experiences can be developed in the supervision where the supervisees are held and contained themselves. This experience of bearing uncertainty of therapy processes and themselves, and being patient with clients in supervision, they can bring back to their work in helping their clients.

In such a holding and containing supervision relationship, supervision is co-creation of musical and therapeutic experiences that are shared and reflected without the client (Sutton & De Backer, 2014, p. 317). This happens verbally or by using music where the supervisee and the supervisor are freely associating or/and improvising the experiences of clients and giving them meaning between rational and unconscious thoughts. This is an intersubjective imaginative process, a reverie, of the clients and their psychic material that is allowed to be dreamed and stayed open in personal thoughts, embodied feelings, imagery, and associations during the supervision (Alanne, 2023, Hägg, 2020, Kennedy, 2020; Ogden, 1999/2005). Like in therapy, it may help therapists to empathise with their clients, their situations, and provide new meaning for the experiences of clients and themselves respectively.

References

Ahonen, H., & Mongillo Desideri, A. (2014). Heroines' journey—Emerging story by refugee women during group analytic music therapy. *Voices: A World Forum for Music Therapy, 14*(1). https://doi.org/10.15845/voices.v14i1.686

Ahonen-Eerikäinen, H. (2007). *Group analytic music therapy*. Barcelona Publishers.

Alanne, S. (2005). Music psychotherapy for torture survivors. *Music Therapy Today*, 6(4), 682–697. Special Issue: Proceedings of the 6th EMTC 2004 Conference, University of Jyväskylä. D. Aldridge & J. Fachner (Eds.), MusicTherapyWorld.net Witten: University Witten/Herdecke.

Alanne, S. (2010). *Music psychotherapy with refugee survivors of torture. Interpretations of three clinical case studies*. Sibelius Academy. Studia Musica.

Alanne, S. (2013). Psykodynaaminen musiikkipsykoterapia kidutuksesta traumatisoituneiden pakolaisten kanssa: Kliininen näkökulma. [Psychodynamic music psychotherapy with the refugees traumatised from the torture: A clinical point of view.]. *Psykoterapia, 32*(4), 264–276.

Alanne, S. (2014a). *Musiikkipsykoterapia*. Teoria ja käytäntö. [Music psychotherapy. Theory and practice.] Acta Universitatis Ouluensis D Medica 1248.

Alanne, S. (2014b). The ethnocultural and psychodynamic meaning of music for traumatised refugees. *Music Therapy Today*, 10(1), 48–49. Special issue: Proceedings of the 14th World Congress of Music Therapy Vienna/Krems, Austria, July 7–12, 2014.

Alanne, S. (2019a). Musiikki, vuorovaikutus ja sisäinen kokemus psykoterapiassa. [Music, interaction, and the inner experience in psychotherapy.]. *Psykoterapia, 38*(1), 39–49.

Alanne, S. (2019b). Musiikkipsykoterapia traumatisoituneiden pakolaisten ja maahanmuuttajien kuntoutuksessa. [Music psychotherapy in the rehabilitation of refugees and immigrants.]. *Psykoterapia, 38*(4), 306–318.

Alanne, S. (2020). Musiikin ja kielen suhteesta—sekä psykoterapeuttisesta arvosta. [About the relationship of music and language—And their psychotherapeutic value.]. *Psykoanalyyttinen Psykoterapia, 16*, 6–15.

Alanne, S. (2023). *The theory and practice of psychodynamic music psychotherapy*. Barcelona Publishers.

Alayarian, A. (2024). *Group analysis for refugees experiencing trauma*. Routledge.

Allen, J. G., Fonagy, P., & Bateman, A. W. (2008). *Mentalizing in clinical practice*. American Psychiatric Publishing.

Alvin, J. (1965/1972). *Music for the handicapped child*. Oxford University Press.

Alvin, J. (1966/1975). *Music therapy*. Basic Books.

Alvin, J. (2001). Interview. VHS-Video. *Music Therapy in Europe in Occasion of the 5th European Music Therapy Congress*. Naples, April 2001. European Music Therapy Confederation (EMTC). Naples: ISFOM.

Austin, D. (2002). The wounded healer. The voice of trauma: A wounded healer's perspective. In J. P. Sutton (Ed.), *Music, music therapy, and trauma. International perspectives* (pp. 231–259). Jessica Kingsley.

Austin, D. (2009). *The theory and practice of vocal psychotherapy. Songs of the self*. Jessica Kingsley.

Barnard, L., & Jones, J. (2022). Bridging the gap: Developing a thinking space for refugees. In J. Stubley & L. Young (Eds.), *Complex trauma. The Tavistock model* (pp. 166–181). Routledge.

Beck, B. D. (2019). Music therapy for refugees. In S. Lindahl Jacobsen, I. Nygaard Pedersen, & L. O. Bonde (Eds.), *A comprehensive guide to music therapy. Theory, clinical practice, research and training* (2nd ed., pp. 342–352). Jessica Kingsley.

Beck, B. D., Messel, C., Lund Meyer, S., Cordtz, T. O., Søgaard, U., Simonsen, E., & Moe, T. (2018). Feasibility of trauma-focused guided imagery and music with adult refugees diagnosed with PTSD: A pilot study. *Nordic Journal of Music Therapy, 27*(1), 67–86.

Beck, B. D., Meyer, S. L., Simonsen, E., Søgaard, U., Petersen, I., Arnfred, S. M. H., Tellier, T., & Moe, T. (2021). Music therapy was noninferior to verbal standard treatment of traumatised refugees in mental healthcare: Results from a randomized clinical trial. *European Journal of Psychotraumatology, 12*(1), 1930960. https://doi.org/10.1080/20008198.2021.1930960

Bensimon, M. (2020). Perceptions of music therapists regarding their work with children living under continuous war threat: Experiential reframing of trauma through songs. *Nordic Journal of Music Therapy, 29*(4), 300–316. https://doi.org/10.1080/08098131.2019.1703210

Bernard, G., & Dvorak, A. L. (2022). Using music to address trauma with refugees: A systematic review and recommendations. *Music Therapy Perspectives, 41*(1), 30–43. https://doi.org/10.1093/mtp/miac013

Bettelheim, B. (1975/1994). *Satujen lumous*. Merkitys ja arvo. [The uses of enchantment. The meaning and importance of fairy tales.] (M. Rutanen, Trans.). WSOY.

Bion, W. R. (1962a). A theory of thinking. In W. R. Bion (Ed.), *Second thoughts* (pp. 110–119). William Heinemann.

Bion, W. R. (1962b). *Learning from experience*. Karnac.

Bion, W. R. (1970/2018). *Attention and interpretation*. Routledge.

Boston Change Process Study Group (BCPSG). (2010). *Change in psychotherapy: A unifying paradigm*. Norton.

Braak, P. (2007). Musiktherapie mit kriegstraumatisierten Menschen. In H.-G. Wolf (Ed.), *Musiktherapie und Trauma* (pp. 89–96). Reichert Verlag.

Brummer, M. (2005). Psykoterapeuttinen suhde ja prosessi. [Psychotherapeutic relationship and process.]. In M. Brummer & H. Enckell (Eds.), *Lasten ja nuorten psykoterapia* (Psychotherapy of children and adolescents) (pp. 109–142). WSOY.

Bruscia, K. E. (1987). *Improvisational models of Music therapy*. Charles C Thomas.

Bruscia, K. E. (1998). An introduction to music psychotherapy. In K. E. Bruscia (Ed.), *The dynamics of music psychotherapy* (pp. 1–15). Barcelona.

Bruscia, K. E. (2002). A psychodynamic orientation to the Bonny method. In K. E. Bruscia & D. E. Grocke (Eds.), *Guided imagery and music. The Bonny method and beyond* (pp. 225–243). Barcelona.

Bruscia, K. E. (2014). *Defining music therapy* (3rd ed.). Barcelona.

Cadesky, N. (2023). Group work with adults in short-term inpatient psychiatric treatment and recovery. In L. E. Beer & J. C. Birnbaum (Eds.), *Trauma-informed music therapy. Theory and practice* (pp. 96–103). Routledge.

Castaneda, A. E., Mäki-Opas, J., Jokela, S., Kivi, N., Lähteenmäki, M., Miettinen, T., Nieminen, S., Santalahti, P., & PALOMA Expert Group. (2018). *Pakolaisten mielenterveyden tukeminen Suomessa*. PALOMA käsikirja. [Supporting refugees' mental health in Finland. PALOMA handbook.] Guidance, May 2018. Publications of the National Institute for Health and Welfare.

Cullberg, J., & Johannessen, J.-O. (2004). The dynamics of acute psychosis and the role of dynamic psychotherapy. In J. F. M. Gleeson & P. McGorry (Eds.), *Psychological interventions in early psychosis: A treatment handbook* (pp. 80–98). John Wiley & Sons.

De Backer, J., & Sutton, J. (2014a). Introduction. The music in music therapy: Writing without a pen. In J. De Backer & J. Sutton (Eds.), *The Music in Music therapy. Psychodynamic music therapy in Europe: Clinical, theoretical and research approaches* (pp. 14–22). Jessica Kingsley.

De Backer, J., & Sutton, J. (2014b). Theoretical perspectives of music therapy. The state of the art. In J. De Backer & J. Sutton (Eds.), *The music in music therapy. Psychodynamic music therapy in Europe: Clinical, theoretical and research approaches* (pp. 37–57). Jessica Kingsley.

De Backer, J., & Sutton, J. (2014c). Therapeutic interventions in psychodynamic music therapy: The music in music therapy. In J. De Backer & J. Sutton (Eds.), *The music in music therapy. Psychodynamic music therapy in Europe: Clinical, theoretical and research approaches* (pp. 338–349). Jessica Kingsley.

Edwards, J. (2023). Cultural humility in music therapy practice. In L. E. Beer & J. C. Birnbaum (Eds.), *Trauma-informed music therapy. Theory and practice* (pp. 28–36). Routledge.

Elman, S. J. (1998). Enactment, transference and analytic trust. In S. J. Elman & M. Moskowitch (Eds.), *Enactment: Toward a new approach to the therapeutic relationship* (pp. 183–203). Aronson.

Else, B. A., & González, M. (2023). Global trends in music therapy for disaster preparedness, response, and recovery. In L. E. Beer & J. C. Birnbaum (Eds.), *Trauma-informed music therapy. Theory and practice* (pp. 19–27). Routledge.

Erikson, E. H. (1950/1964). Toys and reasons. In M. R. Haworth (Ed.), *Child psychotherapy: Practice and theory* (pp. 3–11). Basic Books.

Erkkilä, J., Punkanen, M., Fachner, J., Ala-Ruona, E., Pöntiö, I., Tervaniemi, M., et al. (2011). Individual music therapy for depression: Randomised controlled trial. *The British Journal of Psychiatry, 199*, 132–139.

Fisher, A., & Gilboa, A. (2016). The roles of music amongst Holocaust survivors before, during, and after the Holocaust. *Psychology of Music, 44*(6), 1221–1239.

Fonagy, P., Gergely, G., Jurist, L. E., & Target, M. (2004). *Affect regulation, mentalization, and the development of the self.* Karnac.

Freud, S. (1905). Fragment of an analysis of a case of hysteria. In *Standard Ed.* (VII, pp. 7–122). The Hogarth Press.

Freud, S. (1910/1981). The future prospects of psycho-analytic therapy. In *Standard Ed.* (XI, pp. 139–151). The Hogarth Press.

Freud, S. (1914/1981). Remembering, repeating and working through (further recommendations on the technique of psychoanalysis II). In *Standard Ed.* (XII, pp. 147–156). The Hogarth Press.

Garland, C. (1998a). Action, identification and thoughts in post-traumatic states. In C. Garland (Ed.), *Understanding trauma. A psychoanalytic approach* (pp. 199–215). Second enlarged edition. The Tavistock Clinic Series. Karnac.

Garland, C. (1998b). Thinking about trauma. In C. Garland (Ed.), *Understanding trauma. A psychoanalytic approach* (pp. 9–31). Second enlarged edition. The Tavistock Clinic Series. Karnac.

Grand, S. (2024). The wound and its social imperatives. In J. Salberg & S. Grand (Eds.), *Transgenerational trauma. A contemporary introduction* (pp. 45–59). Routledge.

Grassi, L. (2021). *The sound of the unconscious. Psychoanalysis as music*. Routledge.

Gravestock, J. (2021). *Music therapy in adoption and trauma. Therapy that makes a difference after placement*. Jessica Kingsley.

Grocke, D., & Wigram, T. (2007). *Receptive methods in music therapy. Techniques and clinical applications for music therapy clinicians, educators and students*. Jessica Kingsley.

Hägg, V. (2020). Reverie-käsite ja sen soveltaminen kliiniseen käytäntöön. [The concept of reverie and its application in the clinical practice.]. *Psykoterapia, 39*(2), 91–103.

Hannibal, N. (2014). Implicit and explicit mentalisation in music therapy in the psychiatric treatment of people with borderline personality disorder. In J. De Backer & J. Sutton (Eds.), *The music in music therapy. Psychodynamic music therapy in Europe: Clinical, theoretical and research approaches* (pp. 211–223). Jessica Kingsley.

Herlihy, J., Ferstman, C., & Turner, S. W. (2004). Legal issues in work with asylum seekers. In J. P. Wilson & B. Drožđek (Eds.), *Broken spirits. The treatment of traumatised asylum seekers, refugees and torture victims* (pp. 641–658). Brunner–Routledge.

Herman, J. L. (1992/2022). *Trauma and Recovery*. The Aftermath of Violence – From Domestic Abuse to Political Terror. Basic Books.

Hoi Yan Fu, J. (2023). Finding one's voice: Working through developmental trauma with vocal psychotherapy. In L. E. Beer & J. C. Birnbaum (Eds.), *Trauma-informed music therapy. Theory and practice* (pp. 113–121). Routledge.

Holly, S. (2023). Changing the narrative: Exploring how music therapy can assist adolescents dealing with race-based traumatic stress. In L. E. Beer & J. C. Birnbaum (Eds.), *Trauma-informed music therapy. Theory and practice* (pp. 56–63). Routledge.

Jones, C., & Baker, F. (2004). From healing rituals to music therapy: Bridging the cultural divide between therapist and young Sudanese refugees. *The Arts in Psychotherapy, 31*(2), 89–100.

Kennedy, R. (2020). *The power of music. Psychoanalytic explorations*. Phoenix.

Klafter, A. B. (2017). Mistrusting the analyst. In S. Akhtar (Ed.), *Mistrust. Developmental, cultural, and clinical realms* (pp. 165–177). Routledge.

Klein, M. (1955/1964). The psychoanalytic play technique. In M. R. Haworth (Ed.), *Child psychotherapy: Practice and theory* (pp. 277–286). Basic Books.

Knoblauch, S. H. (2000). *The musical edge of therapeutic dialogue*. The Analytic Press.

Lansen, J., & Haans, T. (2004). Clinical supervision for trauma therapists. In J. P. Wilson & B. Drožđek (Eds.), *Broken spirits. The treatment of traumatised asylum seekers, refugees and torture victims* (pp. 317–353). Brunner–Routledge.

Lehtonen, K. (1997). Is there correspondence between the structures of music and the psyche? *Nordic Journal of Music Therapy, 6*(1), 43–52.

Lehtonen, K., & Heinonen, Y. (2007). Musiikki psyykkisen työn edistäjänä. Tapausseloste 8-vuotiaan tytön musiikkiterapiaistunnon analyyttisesta tulkinnasta. [Music as a promoter of psychic work. A case study of an 8-year-old girl's music therapy session and its analytic interpretation.] In M. Laitinen & H. Westerlund (Eds.), *Musikaalisuuden ytimessä*. Juhlakirja Kai Karmalle (pp. 165–181). [In the heart of musicality. Essays in honour of Kai Karma.] Sibelius Academy.

Lemma, A. (2006). *Introduction to the practice of psychoanalytic psychotherapy*. Wiley.

Levinge, A. (2015). *The music of being: Music therapy, Winnicott, and the school of object relations*. Jessica Kingsley.

McFerran, K. S., Lai, H. I. C., Chang, W.-H., Acquaro, D., Chin, T. C., Stokes, H., & Crooke, A. (2020). Music, rhythm, and trauma: A critical interpretive synthesis of research literature. *Frontiers in Psychology, 11*, 324. https://doi.org/10.3389/fpsyg.2020.00324

McWilliams, N. (2021). *Psychoanalytic supervision*. Guilford.

Neustadt, R. (2004). Music as memory and torture: Sounds of repression and protest in Chile and Argentina. *Chasqui, 33*(1), 128–137.

O'Rourke, J. (2022). Therapeutic yoga and psychotherapy for facilitating posttraumatic growth. In J. Stubley & L. Young (Eds.), *Complex trauma. The Tavistock model* (pp. 226–239). Routledge.

Ogden, T. H. (1999/2005). *Reverie and interpretation. Sensing something human*. Karnac.

Orth, J., Doorschodt, L., Verburgt, J., & Drožđek, B. (2004). Sounds of trauma: An introduction to methodology in music therapy with traumatised refugees in clinical and outpatient settings. In J. P. Wilson & B. Drožđek (Eds.), *Broken spirits. The treatment of traumatised asylum seekers, refugees and torture victims* (pp. 443–480). Brunner–Routledge.

Pavlicevic, M. (1997). *Music therapy in context. Music, meaning, and relationship*. Jessica Kingsley.

Pérez-Martinez, C. (2023). Music therapy with children in the aftermath of a natural disaster. In L. E. Beer & J. C. Birnbaum (Eds.), *Trauma-informed music therapy. Theory and practice* (pp. 64–73). Routledge.

Priestley, M. (1975). *Music therapy in action*. Constable.

Priestley, M. (1994). *Essays on analytical music therapy*. Barcelona.

Reik, T. (1948/1998). *Listening with the third ear. The inner experience of psychoanalyst*. Farrar, Straus and Giroux.

Reuter, L., Grandke, V., Gumz, A., Tuinmann, G., & Bauer, S. (2021). Unbewusstes hörbar machen—psychodynamische Musiktherapie im klinischen Kontext. *Psychotherapeut, 66*, 545–558.

Reyes, A. (1999). *Songs of the caged, songs of the free: Music and the Vietnamese refugee experience*. University Press.

Rose, G. J. (2004). *Between couch and piano. Psychoanalysis, music, art and neuroscience*. Brunner–Routledge.

Salberg, J. (2024a). Between silence and words: Attachment, trauma and the mode of transgenerational transmissions. In J. Salberg & S. Grand (Eds.), *Transgenerational trauma. A contemporary introduction* (pp. 27–44). Routledge.

Salberg, J. (2024b). When wounds touch. Witnessing and enacting as embodied healing process. In J. Salberg & S. Grand (Eds.), *Transgenerational trauma. A contemporary introduction* (pp. 60–75). Routledge.

Salo, O. (2024). Negatiivinen kyvykkyys psykoanalyyttisen menetelmän läpäisevänä periaatteena. [Negative capability as the overall principle of psychoanalytic method.]. *Psykoterapia, 43*(4), 289–302.

Saraneva, K. (2002). Trauma ja pakolaisuus. Psykoanalyyttinen käsitys traumasta ja sen hoidosta pakolais- ja siirtolaiskohtaloissa. [Trauma and refugees. Psychoanalytic conception of trauma and its treatment in the destinies of refugees and immigrants.] In S. Haaramo & K. Palonen (Eds.), *Trauman monet kasvot*. Psyykkinen trauma sisäisenä kokemuksena (pp. 49–96). [Many faces of trauma. Psychic trauma as an inner experience.] Therapeia Foundation.

Saraneva, K. (2018). Vieraasta kulttuurista tulevan pakolaisen kohtaaminen ja hoitaminen—Haasteet terapeutille. [The encountering and treatment of refugee coming from foreign culture—Challenges for the therapist.] In A. Zonzi & N. Söderblom (Eds.), *Pakolaisuus*. Merkitykset ihmiselle ja yhteisölle (pp. 90–108). [Refugeeism. The meaning for individual and community.] Therapeia Foundation.

Schulman, G. (2002). Sietämisen kestämisestä eheytymiseen. Objektin sisällyttämiskyky ja trauman integrointi. [From bearing resilience to cohesiveness. The internalising of object and the integration of trauma] In S. Haaramo & K. Palonen (Eds.), *Trauman monet kasvot*. Psyykkinen trauma sisäisenä kokemuksena (pp. 162–187). [Many faces of trauma. Psychic trauma as an inner experience.] Therapeia Foundation.

Schwartz, E. K. (1956/1964). A psychoanalytical study of the fairy tale. In M. R. Haworth (Ed.), *Child psychotherapy: Practice and theory* (pp. 383–395). Basic Books.

Scrine, E., & Koike, A. (2023). Questioning the promise of safety in trauma-informed music therapy practice. In L. E. Beer & J. C. Birnbaum (Eds.), *Trauma-informed music therapy. Theory and practice* (pp. 37–44). Routledge.

Siirala, M. (1966/1969). *Medicine in metamorphosis. Speech, presence, and integration*. Tavistock.

Siirala, M. (1983). *From transfer to transference. Seven essays on the human predicament*. Therapeia Foundation.

Skinner, K., Kurkjian, A., & Ahonen, H. (2021). Bruscia's clinical techniques for improvisational music therapy in autism research: A scoping review. *Approaches: An Interdisciplinary Journal of Music Therapy, 13*(2), 162–177.

Smetana, M., & Storz, D. (2020). Psychotherapeutische Techniken in der Musiktherapie. In H. U. Schmidt, T. Stegemann, & C. Spitzer (Eds.), *Musiktherapie bei psychischen und psychosomatischen Störungen* (pp. 53–58). Elsevier.

Sokira, J., Allen, J., & Wagner, H. (2023). The resilience framework for trauma-informed music therapy. In L. E. Beer & J. C. Birnbaum (Eds.), *Trauma-informed music therapy. Theory and practice* (pp. 9–18). Routledge.

Solms, M. (2017/2019). Mikä "tiedostamaton" on ja missä se sijaitsee aivoissa? Neuropsykoanalyyttinen näkökulma. [What is "the unconscious," and where is it located in the brain? A neuropsychoanalytic perspective.] (A. von Schulman, Trans.). *Psykoterapia*, 38(1), 62–70.

Steel, Z., Mares, S., Newman, L., Bijou, B., & Dudley, M. (2004). The politics of asylum and immigration detention: Advocacy, ethics, and the professional role of the therapist. In J. P. Wilson & B. Drožđek (Eds.), *Broken spirits. The treatment of traumatised asylum seekers, refugees and torture victims* (pp. 659–687). Brunner–Routledge.

Stephens Langdon, G. (2023). Music therapy in the treatment of complex trauma in adult mental health. In L. E. Beer & J. C. Birnbaum (Eds.), *Trauma-informed music therapy. Theory and practice* (pp. 122–130). Routledge.

Stern, D. N. (1985/2004). *The interpersonal world of the infant. A view from psychoanalysis and developmental psychology*. Karnac.

Stern, D. N. (2004). *The present moment in psychotherapy and everyday life*. Norton.

Stern, D. N. (2010). *Forms of vitality. Exploring dynamic experience in psychology, arts, psychotherapy, and development*. Oxford University Press.

Strehlow, G. (2009). The use of music therapy in treating sexually abused children. *Nordic Journal of Music Therapy, 18*(2), 167–183.

Strehlow, G., & Hannibal, N. (2019). Mentalizing in improvisational music therapy. *Nordic Journal of Music Therapy, 28*(4), 333–346.

Strehlow, G., & Lindner, R. (2016). Music therapy interaction patterns in relation to borderline personality disorder (BPD) patients. *Nordic Journal of Music Therapy, 25*(2), 134–158.

Stubley, J. (2022a). Complex trauma: The initial consultation. In J. Stubley & L. Young (Eds.), *Complex trauma. The Tavistock model* (pp. 11–33). Routledge.

Stubley, J. (2022b). The Tavistock trauma service. In J. Stubley & L. Young (Eds.), *Complex trauma. The Tavistock model* (pp. 34–55). Routledge.

Sutton, J., & De Backer, J. (2009). Music, trauma and silence: The state of the art. *The Arts in Psychotherapy, 36*(2), 75–83.

Sutton, J., & De Backer, J. (2014). Supervision in music therapy: The jumping-off point. In J. De Backer & J. Sutton (Eds.), *The music in music therapy. Psychodynamic music therapy in Europe: Clinical, theoretical and research approaches* (pp. 300–319). Jessica Kingsley.

Svedberg Yinger, O. (2023). I am safe and I am strong: Understanding adverse childhood experiences and building resilience through trauma-informed music therapy. In L. E. Beer & J. C. Birnbaum (Eds.), *Trauma-informed music therapy. Theory and practice* (pp. 47–55). Routledge.

Swinburne, M. (2022). Helping the heroes: Psychoanalytic work with military veterans. In J. Stubley & L. Young (Eds.), *Complex trauma. The Tavistock model* (pp. 143–165). Routledge.

Tähkä, V. (1993/1997). *Mielen rakentuminen ja psykoanalyyttinen hoitaminen.* [Mind and its treatment: A psychoanalytic approach.] WSOY, Finnish edition.

Trondalen, G., & Bonde, L. O. (2013). Music therapy: Models and interventions. In R. Macdonald, G. Kreutz, & L. Mitchell (Eds.), *Music, health, and wellbeing* (pp. 40–62). Oxford University Press.

Välimäki, S. (2015). Musical representation of war, genocide, and torture: Treating cultural trauma with music. *Acta Translatogica* 3: Pax R. Hartama-Heinonen & P. Kukkonen (Eds.), (pp. 122–136). University of Helsinki, Nordica/Department of Finnish, Finno-Ugrian and Scandinavian Studies, Swedish Translation Studies.

van der Kolk, B. (2014). *The body keeps score. Mind, brain and body in the transformation of trauma.* Allen Lane.

Vibe Jespersen, K., & Vuust, P. (2012). The effects of relaxation music listening on sleep quality in traumatized refugees: A pilot study. *Journal of Music Therapy, 49*(2), 205–229.

Volkan, V. D. (2018a). *Immigrants and refugees. Trauma, perennial mourning, prejudice, and border psychology.* Routledge.

Wigram, T. (2004). *Improvisation. Methods and techniques for music therapy clinicians, educators and students.* Jessica Kingsley.

Wigram, T. (2019). Free improvisation therapy—The Alvin model. In S. Lindahl Jacobsen, I. Nygaard Pedersen, & L.O. Bonde (Eds.), *A comprehensive guide to music therapy. Theory, clinical practice, research and training* (2nd ed., pp. 189–192). Jessica Kingsley.

Wilson, J. P. (2004). Empathy, trauma transmission, and countertransference in posttraumatic psychotherapy. In J. P. Wilson & B. Droždek (Eds.), *Broken spirits. The treatment of traumatised asylum seekers, refugees and torture victims* (pp. 277–316). Brunner–Routledge.

Winnicott, D. W. (1971/1997). *Playing and reality.* Routledge.

Yeomans, F. E., Clarking, J. F., & Kernberg, O. F. (2015). *Transference-focused psychotherapy for borderline personality disorder. A clinical guide.* American Psychiatric Publishing.

Young, L., & Stubley, J. (2022). Writing trauma: Literary representations of traumatic experience. In J. Stubley & L. Young (Eds.), *Complex trauma. The Tavistock model* (pp. 253–265). Routledge.

Zarate, R. (2022). *Music psychotherapy and anxiety. Social, community, and clinical contexts.* Jessica Kingsley.

Chapter 6
Music and Arts Promoting the Health and Wellbeing of Refugees

This chapter is describing different kinds of music, music therapy projects, and programmes that have been developed for refugees during the years internationally. There have been different research groups and organisations participating in helping refugees and asylum seekers in the refugee camps, schools, as well as in the host countries. This kind of organisational support and collaboration including systemic intervention on micro and macro levels of society affecting refugees, their children, as well as their communities in the host countries has been developed in music therapy.

In the later paragraphs, some oppressive practices of music in education and therapy will be discussed and identified. This discussion relates to the cultural sensitiveness and power relations in music therapy and music education approaches that are grounded on Western conceptions of music, education, and therapy. This may include some potential cultural projections, microaggression, and prejudices towards refugees and other minorities concerning their "otherness", nationality, race, sexuality, gender, and mental and/or physical issues (Bruce, 2022; Gombert, 2022; Myerscough & Wong, 2022; Pickard, 2022).

The concepts of ableism and disablism will be introduced and discussed in how it is important to decolonise musical practices including power-orientated practices like potential violence, silencing, nepotism, and poisonous education in their cores (Bruce, 2022; Gombert, 2022; Ilmola-Sheppard et al., 2021; Pickard, 2022). Finally, some ethical considerations of music practices in therapy, education, psychology, mental health, health care, and society in general will be raised about how music and culture should be used safely for goodness, health, and wellbeing, not as weapon and oppression, considering the human rights and equality of the people (Alanne, 2010; Ilmola-Sheppard et al., 2021; Koivisto, 2022; Trondalen, 2023).

S. Alanne, *Music, Music Therapy and Refugees*,
https://doi.org/10.1007/978-3-031-94766-7_6

6.1 Music Projects and Music Therapy Programmes for Refugees: International Perspectives

There have been many music and music therapy projects that are related to refugees and other traumatised dislocated people because of wars and other catastrophes in European countries like in Netherlands, Norway, Germany, Spain, UK, as well as in Australia, North America, Canada and US, South America, Chile, Africa, and Kenya as examples (Akombo, 2001; Ahonen & Mongillo Desideri, 2014; Alanne, 2010; Baker & Jones, 2005; Barath, 1996; Bernard & Dvorak, 2022; Comte, 2016; Coombes, 2018; Einarsen et al., 2024; Else & González, 2023; Enge et al., 2024; Gulbay, 2021; Heynen et al., 2022; Hunt, 2005; Mallon & Hoog Antink, 2021; Muriithi, 2020; Orth, 2005; Storsve et al., 2010; Zharinova-Sanderson, 2004). This work has included individual and group therapies as well as music education and other music projects combined with music therapeutic goals targeted for the refugees and asylum seekers particularly. In the UK, there has been a specific charity organisation Music Action International for more than a decade, which has been actively supporting refugees' and asylum seekers' rights, wellbeing, and recovery from traumas. They are inviting refugees of different ages to participate in their music activities like bands, choirs, and projects in schools.

In the Health Evidence Network Synthesis Report of the WHO it is reported that the engagement with the arts including music after forced displacement is benefitting the creation of new support networks for the refugees and asylum seekers as well as developing their practical skills in finding work (Fancourt & Saoirse, 2019, p. 10). It is specified that songs, that are a method of music psychotherapy described earlier, are promoting social inclusion in reducing prejudice, discrimination, and aggression between groups. They are also promoting cultural understanding according to the WHO report, where the Norwegian music projects in schools are mentioned as an example. There, music around the world helped young people in changing their attitudes towards migrants (ibid.).

The community music therapy (CoMT) approach, developed and spread particularly from Norway, has been used in the music and music therapy projects with refugees and asylum seekers (Einarsen et al., 2024; Enge & Stige, 2021; Enge et al., 2024; Storsve et al., 2010; Zharinova-Sanderson, 2004). It has emphasised different kinds of collaborations in the community, like between refugees, asylum seekers, and other inhabitants of the host countries. Their projects have also included collaboration between music therapists, music educators, social workers, other therapists, and professionals in the health care.

In such projects like the music project among youth in a Palestinian refugee camp that began in 2002 and continued the whole decade (Storsve et al., 2010), music is actively used in contacting refugees to develop their skills and engagements in their lives. This project was related to the music education approach emphasising the role of music as the promoter of health in musical practices of learning and playing music (Alanne, 2010, p. 204). In this CoMT project, children and teenagers, boys and girls, were learning to play instruments, skills they also taught forward to other children. According to interviewed six participants aged 12–20, music learning provided them with hope, pride, motivation for school, as well as sense of belonging together (ibid.).

Aim of this project with music was to find collective balance to the difficulties that could have resulted from oppression and unbalanced power relationships (Alanne, 2010, p. 204; Storsve et al., 2010). This may be different from some other therapeutic approaches like individual and group therapies addressing individual explanations for their clients according to them. Rather, their CoMT approach combined with music educational goals was studying how their music project could strengthen the refugees' sense of self and cultural identity. According to the experiences of the interviewed young people, this music project seemed to go in that direction. There was also a concert arranged for Palestinian Land Day, where the students performed Norwegian Sunset. This kind of approach with music, cultural dialoguing, that is not necessarily always therapy, at least directly, but more like music education with therapeutic goals may benefit the children and young people in preventing them from traumatisation in the refugee camps.

It is common practice in CoMT approaches of music therapy that there may be concerts arranged where the participants can perform for the audiences in their community and social networks (Enge et al., 2024; Muriithi, 2020; Storsve et al., 2010; Zharinova-Sanderson, 2004). A part of the CoMT approach and treatment ideology identified is that natural social environments of the clients in music therapy are considered in their treatments. Even though there is individual CoMT, it often takes a place in schools and public projects with refugees (Einarsen et al., 2024; Enge et al., 2024).

In this regard, it is different from other therapy approaches and trauma therapy including psychodynamic music therapy or psychotherapy. In psychotherapeutic approaches, the subjective experience, confidentiality, and the boundaries of therapy do not usually allow deviations from the rules of therapy concerning treatment in public, for example. However, there can be similar therapeutic goals in treating traumas with CoMT like in the described identity formation, building resilience, sense of competency, and connectedness where music-orientated approaches are suitable parts of the traumatised refugees' rehabilitation (Einarsen et al., 2024, p. 4).

Music therapeutic and educational approaches relating to refugees and their traumatisation in their natural environments may be preventative mental health work when it lessens the feelings of alienation, shame, otherness, and resulting cultural stress in refugees. It is considered that the recovery from traumas should occur in connection with other people that can mean the psychotherapeutic relationship like discussed earlier but also important is the collective sharing and witnessing of the trauma and taking responsibility of it (Herman, 1992/2022, p. 191; Salberg, 2024b). This is preventing from the transmission of trauma and the vicarious illness because the responsibility, the burden of trauma, will be balanced in the community and the relationships with others. Then, it does not force the refugees into the otherness position of "blaming the victim" for their problems, or misunderstanding them through some diagnosis that is forced upon them (Alanne, 2010, pp. 204–205; Storsve et al., 2010).

By participating with music in schools or other public activities like performing live in concerts or in media may help traumatised refugees to decrease their isolation, loneliness, and integrating them into the community and society. For example, within the CoMT of African refugee musicians in the US, participants published their performances as videos in the YouTube (Muriithi, 2020). In their music therapy, they were able to express and communicate their losses of being refugees through the music that came from their own cultural preferences and backgrounds in Africa. According to the interviews of participants, refugees considered their musical activities as "healing" their pains. It also gave them hope and helped in the recovery of trauma and negative emotion. Some of the adult participants of the study did charity work at the refugee camp in Uganda to educate, inspire, encourage, and instil hope for the other refugees.

In Netherlands, there was a project in three schools with refugee children and adolescents that had often experienced negative or traumatic events (Heynen et al., 2022). This music therapy project developed and implemented for this group in the school setting strengthened the social connectedness and the sense of belonging of 6–17-year-old students. It also seemed to stimulate their inclusiveness and cultural sensitivity according to the study. After the music therapy intervention, negative affects relating to stress and mental health problems decreased. These results are important because refugee children have more concentration problems, aggressive incidents, anxiety, and worries related to their own safety compared to their peers. This is affecting negatively their class environments and relationships with other students and teachers (pp. 1–2).

Therefore, this kind of music and music therapy programmes with similar results like in Netherlands and Norway that were discussed earlier in the context of music therapy methods like music cafes and concerts of refugee children and adolescents is needed in the schools and communities (Einarsen et al., 2024; Enge & Stige, 2021; Enge et al., 2024; Heynen et al., 2022). As such trauma-informed music practices, they can help in the homing process of refugees and their children. Music therapeutic interventions and programmes in schools may also improve the psychosocial development and resilience of the children by reducing their stress that can help all the children and their teachers in the school environments (Heynen et al., 2022, p. 2). In schoolwork, music may also help in bridging the gap between different languages and cultures.

This can help the inclusivity of teaching and integrating the refugees into the so-called normal classes. As such, musical activities and music therapy implemented at schools and communities may decrease the cultural stress of otherness in refugee children and their families. The capabilities of music in reducing stress and physiological arousal as well as modulating and connecting the brain structures and their activity of emotional, motivational, and lingual processes may help in schoolwork and concentration like in therapy (Alanne, 2023; Heynen et al., 2022, p. 2; Rose, 2004).

In the described Dutch music therapy programme "Safe & Sound" implemented in three schools, music therapists, children, adolescents, and their caregivers were collaborating in stabilising the situation of their children (Heynen et al., 2022, p. 3).

Music therapy was a group intervention of 10 sessions that combined a verbal and a musical technique. The goals of music therapists in the programme were to work for a positive climate in the group. The aim was to optimise the prerequisites for the learning of the students with music therapy, so that the students would feel safe, relaxed, and open for new learning experiences. In addition to improve learning in classes, the goal was to strengthen the interpersonal skills and relationships in the groups like with listening, helping, and trusting each other. Every session had a specific theme like making new friends, sharing stories, and dealing with difficult situations and emotions. In the end, children and adolescents performed a song they have made during the sessions to their teachers, parents, or caregivers. Parents and caregivers were stimulated to discuss about the songs with their children.

In Germany, a COVER model of music therapy for a trauma-informative early intervention with refugees was developed (Mallon & Hoog Antink, 2021). It is providing guidelines for the music therapists working with refugees in the insecure circumstances of their natural living environments. This model was developed after experiences of music therapy provided by the German non-profit association of trained music therapists, the Musiktherapie-Initiative e.V., for the refugees and asylum seekers during 2013–2018 in Hamburg. Music therapy was provided in refugee reception centres and follow-on camps (pp. 1–2).

The COVER model that means "COntext-sensitive classification model for music therapeutic interVEntions with Refugees" is not based on any specific music therapy orientation like psychodynamic/psychoanalytic or behavioural (Mallon & Hoog Antink, 2021, p. 2). It relates to the CoMT approach discussed as the goals and methods of it are quite similar including nurturing of personal strengths, coping skills, and increasing social, cultural, and material resources of refugees. In addition, music therapy provided according to the COVER model is done in the natural environments of refugees in reception centres and follow-up camps, and not only in the external music therapy outpatient setting facilities (p. 3).

Music therapy methods used in the COVER model are open group, small group, and individual sessions for the refugees where the individual sessions are done in the outpatient setting including schools (Mallon & Hoog Antink, 2021, pp. 3–4). Participants of open groups may vary from 2- to 45-person large group. Small groups may include even 12 participants. Music therapy techniques used are instrument building workshops, drum sessions, singing group and small instruments, body instruments, and dancing for the open groups. Individual therapies are psychodynamic music therapy with a focus of trauma-based music therapy that may have all kinds of instruments used in a music therapy setting generally. In the small groups, small instruments, drums, and body percussion were used. For the open groups, participants were received with written announcements in different languages, and by verbal invitation of music therapists. Also, written and oral invitations by social workers and music therapists were used for small groups. For the individual therapies, consultations of schoolteacher, doctor, and psychiatrist were used.

Music used in the open groups was circle songs, familiar pop songs, simple rhythms, and songs taught by the participants for themselves (Mallon & Hoog

Antink, 2021, pp. 4–5). In the small groups, songs from the home countries of participants, producing of their own music, instrumental role plays, singing, as well as more complex rhythms were used. In individual work, music was chosen according to the emotions of clients as the goals of it were being "here and now" and supporting the clients' resettlement processes (p. 4). In the open groups, the goals were the empowerment, discovering resources, contacting other camp members, and creating a space for the individuality of participants. In the small groups, interventions used were supporting, grounding, mirroring of individual needs and wishes, and their exploration with music.

Participants of the COVER model/project in Germany included men, women, and children from different countries like Syria, Afghanistan, Iran, Iraq, Eritrea, and Somalia (Mallon & Hoog Antink, 2021, pp. 5–6). Songs learned together included music from different languages of the participants like Farsi and Arabic. Songs performed together included the Shakira's *Waka Waka*, which related to the soccer championships or *We Will Rock You* of Queen. Songs from the different nationalities, including German folk songs, were shared in the open group. Also, songs from the African music canon were learned as something new for all that were easy to learn for the open group as they only had few words. Teaching the song and the right pronunciation of the words, rhythms, and movements gave the participants joy and self-empowerment as well as developed their relationships towards the others and the therapists.

This work of COVER model is an example of cultural dialoguing with music in music therapy and its elevating powers for refugees, asylum seekers, and traumatised (Mallon & Hoog Antink, 2021). The model also shows the many possibilities of using music in different levels of groups and settings including standard procedures of outpatient psychodynamic music therapy made possible for refugees and asylum seekers of different ages. This is important because some traumatised refugees like children may require individual rehabilitation services and music (psycho) therapy that is recommendable for them as a part of the public mental health services in Finland (Castaneda et al., 2018, pp. 291–292).

Also, other kinds of musical approaches than individual music psychotherapy are benefitting refugees in their resettlement and adapting to the host country in the crisis of being a refugee. In this, the discussed collaboration with schools and communities, music educators, musicians, and other professionals is important. Especially collaboration with those who are providing health and social services like doctors, social workers, nurses, psychologists, psychotherapists, and other art therapists and professionals is important in creating the needed support and safety for the newcomers to foster their integration in the communities and schools.

In the COVER model of music therapy, it is shown that also different music therapeutical/psychotherapeutic approaches like those of mentioned CoMT, psychodynamic music therapy, and trauma-informed music therapy can be combined with their methods and goals in the work with refugees (Mallon & Hoog Antink, 2021). This is broadening the use of music and music (psycho)therapy and their possibilities for refugees as something natural in their environments where the clinical theories of psychodynamic psychotherapy and trauma can be integrated successfully.

6.2 Organisational Collaboration and Systemic Intervention in Encountering Refugeeism and Trauma

In the light of the positive experiences related to the use of music and music therapy on the refugee camps, centres, schools, and communities, it seems recommendable that such projects and collaborations would continue also between the organisations arranging services for the refugees and asylum seekers. For example, in Finland, there has been a PALOMA network supporting the mental health of refugees organised by the National Institute for Health and Welfare (Castaneda et al., 2018). From the beginning, it gathered experts from public services, administrations, universities, cities, schools, hospitals, clinics, associations including therapists, researchers, teachers, youth workers, psychologists, social workers, doctors, nurses, and so on, who are encountering refugees in their work of different organisations. These people that were representing expertise from different levels of organisations were planning together guidelines how to encounter refugees in the services.

As a part of this project that continued as an expert network for those professionals who are working with refugees and providing them therapy and healthcare services was published a PALOMA handbook (Castaneda et al., 2018). It was planned and written together with the described PALOMA expert group of professionals from different fields. As a result of hearing all the professionals including some refugees themselves, an open access handbook was published that provided basic information about the concepts, laws, cultural perspectives, mental health, positive empowering, and risk elements of being a refugee. This book also provided recommendations for professionals in encountering refugees and how to develop their services and skills including the wellbeing of professionals themselves and their supervision.

Recommendations were provided on the micro level for those who are working face to face with refugees and doing practical work like therapists, teachers, and nurses, and on the macro level for their superiors and stakeholders (Castaneda et al., 2018). Superiors were given recommendations on how to support the mental health and other professionals in their work, and how to develop their own work and services in meeting these goals respectively. In the specific recommendations of promoting, supporting, and treating the mental health of refugees were considered services from the early childhood and school to work life and adulthood including cultural and spiritual needs and services for refugees of different ages.

As a result of the PALOMAe collaboration of experts in different fields including myself as the author of this book, increasing of the music and art therapeutic work is mentioned in the recommendations, methods, and tools for professionals relating to psychotherapy and corresponding rehabilitation forms in the guidance of National

Institute for Health and Welfare in Finland for refugees: "*Increasing of possibilities to apply also creative or functional methods (e.g. music and art therapeutic), where the part of nonverbal expression in interaction and working is larger, and therefore the need of interpreter possibly lesser*" (Castaneda et al., 2018, p. 294). In the recommendations of progressing, supporting, and treating mental health of vulnerable groups, methods like music and arts are mentioned: "*Apply methods which enable opening from difficult situations. Relaxing, music, narration, fine arts, physical exercises and photographing help to build trustful relationships as functional methods and in achieving peer support from experts by experience and others in a same situation*" (p. 382).

Further, music, arts, and music psychotherapy are mentioned and recommended for refugees in the guidance: "*Clinical appointments include usually discussion, but they can also include different kind of creative or functional methods (e.g. art, music, body, dance, and movement or animal assisted therapy)*" (Castaneda et al., 2018, p. 289). In the context of current rehabilitation system of psychotherapy in Finland that is funding 200 hours of psychotherapy including music therapy for 16–67-year-old people, music and art psychotherapy are recommended for refugees: "*The rehabilitation psychotherapy subvention by Kela [The Social Insurance Institution of Finland] can be individual, group, family, or couple psychotherapy, and it can be also music or art psychotherapy*" (p. 289).

Also, music and art psychotherapy methods and applications used are discussed in the guidance that is mentioning clinical improvisation, playing in the form of free improvisation, projective music listening using imagery, memories, and associations relating to music with verbal psychotherapy. It is also described in the same context how in art psychotherapy as well as in music and other forms of creative therapy methods, a picture, or music like discussed earlier, functions as a method of expression and communication. It is described that a picture can construct and clarify the mind of refugees. It also has a direct connection to the psychic processes for refugees in forming a bridge between the past, present, and future (Castaneda et al., 2018, p. 291).

All this is also concerning the use of music with refugees of different ages in getting access and symbolising their traumatic experiences. The guidance continues: "*Clients with refugee background, children, adolescents as well as adults, can also benefit especially from such rehabilitative forms of psychotherapy, where in verbal therapy are integrated various creative and functional methods. With creative methods getting contact with different memories, fears and dreams and healthy loosening of traumatic memories are supported*" (Castaneda et al., 2018, p. 291). In the applicable methods for refugee children and adolescents in therapy, the guidance says: "*Methods can be playing, for instance with sand, toys and media. Also drawing, clay moulding, and music in addition to verbal communication are media to apply with children and adolescents*" (pp. 291–292).

In this regard, music, arts, and culture are recognised in the guidance of National Institute for Health and Welfare in Finland for refugees of different ages in supporting their mental health. This kind of collaboration of different professionals working with refugees is helping the accessibility of different therapeutic approaches for wider use. As such, it is an example of systemic intervention in all levels of encountering refugees and their families where music and arts as non-verbal methods can be implemented. This kind of collaboration of different professionals and fields may also be cultural dialoguing on a macro level if there are sharing, collecting, and discussion of experiences relating to refugees in supporting, promoting, and treating their mental health like there was in the PALOMA project described. This kind of working together enabled the hearing of different situations of refugees and their difficulties that all the participants could reflect how they could be helped. In this, other experts could bring their knowledge, skills, and experiences to help others in encountering refugees.

This development work occurred in a democratic way of discussing with people regardless of their title, status, or a profession in the field. The purpose was also to affect and develop the whole system of services and professionals working and encountering with refugees. In my experiences, like in the recommendations and guidance of the handbook, there was also a possibility for the professionals to be heard what support they would need for preventing them from the empathy fatigue and vicarious traumatisation as examples. In addition to providing and sharing such important experiences relating trauma work with refugees, also skills, readings, and guidance were provided for the workers and superiors respectively (Castaneda et al., 2018, pp. 142–146).

These kinds of large group of people working together that relate to many institutes and organisations may prevent from empathy fatigue, burn-out, and hopelessness as it is providing professional and peer support, as well as social contacts for those who are working with traumatised refugees. Similar collaborations and networks could be developed more between those who are practising, studying, and teaching music or music therapy with refugees internationally. As such, they could develop music and music therapy practices on a systemic level of interventions globally. For example, there could be consortiums of professionals in promoting music and music therapy research, practices, and their knowledge like the music and music therapy projects in this book with similar goals of helping refugees, their encountering, and homing in different countries. Also, it is important to build connections and collaborations with other networks helping refugees, so that the music, music therapy approaches, and their knowledge could be implemented within those networks, organisations, and their practices more widely like in the PALOMA project.

6.3 Challenging the Oppressive Practices of Music

In the light of this book as well as according to the former studies of music, violence, and torture, music as a method of oppression has a long history that has continued until the present (Alanne, 2010; Brauer, 2016; Cloonan & Johnson, 2002, 2008; Cusick, 2006, 2008, 2013; Dixon, 2002; John, 1991/2001; Moreno, 1999; Papaeti, 2013a, 2013b, 2020). As such, it has been used systematically as a weapon against humanity to break the personalities of detainees. This dark side of music and the poisonous education implemented in the practices of soldiers, interrogators, or tormentors in the prisons and camps against communism or other political views is the unethical use of music and manipulation. In addition to manipulative psychological purposes of using music, music and sounds have been used to produce physical pain and to socially isolate and humiliate people. In this sense, music and sounds have been representing total power and superiority of the perpetrators where the victims have been forced to feel weakness and otherness of not being even humans.

In the many cruel examples in this book, which some may find difficult or disgusting to read for a reason, music has been used sadistically to torment people, even for the sake of entertainment for the perpetrators. In such practices, music has not been music but a strange game and parody in the hands of perpetrators like remembered by one holocaust survivors of his experiences (Naliwajek-Mazurek, 2013, p. 44). Therefore, it should feel peculiar, embarrassing, bring anxious and sadness, not positive feelings, in the minds of the most people because it is pervert use of music without a soul. As such, it is lacking inherent feelings and social relatedness of music. Instead, it is asymmetrical and violent use of music in dehumanising, belittling, and exhausting detainees that is psychologically manifesting early narcissistic sadistical injures and psychopathological characters in the personalities of perpetrators (pp. 45–46).

These kinds of characters like having no empathy or feelings of guiltiness or shame towards people or music are relating to narcissistic, psychopathic, or antisocial personalities. Instead of empathy, sociopaths may enjoy inducing pain to people and animals like making fun of humiliating people with their cruelties. This is what happened with music in the Nazi concentration camps, and it has continued in other camps and interrogation centres after WWII until the present (Cusick, 2013; Naliwajek-Mazurek, 2013; Papaeti, 2013a, 2013b, 2020). It seems to relate with totalitarian systems and their absolute power where there is no personal superego and ego control of morality. The superego of the perpetuator seems to be cruel and punishing, the feelings of shame and guilt are restricted as bad objects, and their sadistic impulses are acted upon the humiliating and tormenting of the victim.

Identifying with absolute power, "Messianic sadism" proposed by Akhtar (2009, p. 171), is providing a perpetrator with an ideology where the subjective self-experience and the ego control of empathy and ethics are corrupted (Naliwajek-Mazurek, 2013, pp. 45–46). Without a sense of own subjective self-experience, judgement, reflection, and ethics relating to other people, their suffering, ethnicities, religions, nationalities, the evil is let in. Philosopher Michel Henry (1987/2012) has described how barbarism according to him is resulting from the situations where human self-experiences and self-reflections are denied and their meaning belittled and distanced in culture, technology, and science. This denying of self-experience, he calls fascism, is self-destructive cynicism towards life in general. The military jargon is an example of distancing of the lived experiences in killing and destroying with the technical terms of "removing of targets", "operations", "interventions", and "processes", similarly used in other fields like medicine, education, and therapy, and by the Nazis in modelling technologically the "exterminating" of Jews (Alanne, 2010, p. 105; 2021).

As a result of such technological modelling of exterminating "process", the aggression of id is rationalised with cruel superego identifications and prejudices of bad objects that are projected towards the otherness and which in turn are attacked and persecuted. This is making the violence and oppression guilt-free when it is encouraged by the authorities and distanced technically from the self-experiences and reflection of the perpetrators (Akhtar, 2009, p. 171; 2018, pp. 106–108; Alanne, 2010, 2021). Akhtar (2014, pp. 17–18) has also written about "unmentalized xenophobia" that is bland indifference and avoidance of others like Blacks, homosexuals, Muslims, or Jews for the Nazis, who are different. The psychic pain needed for the self-reflection of fear causes relentless need to externalise aggression, paranoia, and weakness to objects outside that are often representing minorities like refugees as easy targets. The result of unmentalised xenophobia may be homocultural simplemindedness that is making life easier because discordant cultures and people are not thought and their voices are not paid attention with (Akhtar, 2018, p. 106). It allows also a cold pragmatism of decision and policy making in communities and societies.

This seems to explain some of the systematic use of the music as violence and torture where also the using of music was a megalomaniac or pervert performance of externalising aggression with humiliating and inducing more pain in victims (Naliwajek-Mazurek, 2013, pp. 45–46). Then, music may resemble the paranoid superego identifications with often despotic authorities, even divinity, and gratifying pleasure achieved from obeying it. Emerging with such malicious superego identifications like national symbols and the power of despotism may explain some of the apparent ego regression to madness and loss of boundaries relating to the use of music in violence, torture, and killing of people (Akhtar, 2009; Akhtar, 2018, pp. 107–108; Naliwajek-Mazurek, 2013). Therefore, this kind of oppression with music may even increase the violence and cruelty acted upon the victims as it is boosting the weak ego and the feeling of the superiority in the perpetuator.

At the same time, the pervert use of music as a weapon to fear, humiliate, and induce more pain has been applied to demoralise and exhaust the victims to give up their politics, re-educate them, provide information, work, and consume them faster until their deaths (Brauer, 2016; Cusick, 2013; John, 1991/2001; Moreno, 1999; Naliwajek-Mazurek, 2013; Pieslak, 2009). However, as discussed earlier in this book, music may have also had a distancing function for the Nazis and the Holocaust victims and survivors as well, when it was used as an entertainment to keep up the spirits (Fisher & Gilboa, 2016, pp. 1228–1229). Also, the masquerading with sounds and music could have the same psychological function of distancing in addition to the hiding of the torturing and killing in the soundscapes of camps and centres. In this context, music and sounds were betraying victims and the public outside, even themselves, as when music is always played and sung what could be wrong? For interviewed holocaust survivor musicians, the moments of music represented "normality" and "sanity" as it was distracting them from the horrors of the camps (ibid.).

In this sense, music and songs may have normalised, distracted, and balanced the effect and stress of doing such cruelties in their work repeatedly for the SS men, soldiers, agents, and their egos like in any other work where the radio is on playing constantly their favourite popular songs and music. This can also be an example of "propaganda addiction" suggested by Akhtar (2018, p. 107), where music like bands is spreading prejudiced minority worldview, propaganda, and hate; they may feel even normal, rationalised, and consensual. However, at the same time, they were oppressive use of defeating sounds and music including national songs and military marches with no escape for the victims from their forced presence of representing symbolic power and superiority (Brauer, 2016; Chornik, 2013; Cusick, 2013; Hirch, 2007; Moreno, 1999; Pieslak, 2009).

Currently, Internet websites and social media applications may normalise the prejudices and hate towards the minorities like refugees (Akhtar, 2018, p. 107). When they are mirroring the worldview of a follower, they are fostering the hate and consensual distorted beliefs and propaganda addiction that is diminishing the inner loneliness and increasing the narcissism in the person. As argued by Akhtar (2014, p. 18), even the democratic countries are vulnerable to the regression of being mute or not expressing their opinions towards such prejudices, propaganda, oppression, and terrorism because of the culture of fear towards their citizens.

This may lead to the "extraordinary renditions" that made possible the torture including music and other enchanted interrogation methods like in the War on Terror (Akhtar, 2014, p. 18; Papaeti, 2020, p. 2). The culture of fear is also concerning organisations, their orthodoxy, and authority including psychoanalysis. For example, Freud and his followers supressed the dissidents in the beginning of psychoanalysis like Ferenczi, who was attacked and cast out with malign rumours of his mental issues because of his pioneering focus of real in trauma theories (Salberg, 2024a, pp. 10–11). Similar power hierarchies of authorities are relating to other fields as well, including music, and concerning citizens, governments, students, teachers, therapists, and other healthcare professionals. Especially refugees and asylum seekers have felt the fear and learnt to know the "click of the trigger" in their experiences of their home countries.

Often individuals or groups are blamed for the difficulties in the society as a part of the "villain hunger" (Akhtar, 2018, pp. 106–107). In the villain hunger, the feelings of aggression are externalised to other people instead of feelings of sadness and sorrowing of the hardships. This may relate to the global or domestic unrest, catastrophes, and wars like the falls of economy and states like Soviet Union, where the identity of large group is threatened. Then, paranoiac enemies like Jews, Muslims, Blacks, foreigners, or other imagined enemies including "refugees", "immigrants", "terrorists", or "Nazis" and "fascists" used by Russia in their attack to Ukraine, are needed. This can explain some of the use of music as a weapon and torturing of the enemy and detainees with music. The stress and losses of war, conditions of concentration camps, prisons, and their work may cause a need to externalise aggression to the detainees and minorities like refugees that is making the perpetrator feel strong because the feelings of being weak, mourning, and self-reflection are avoided.

Authoritarian sociocultural perspectives and cultural stress may relate to the use of music in music therapy and music education as well where different people and students like refugees may be silenced because of their cultures, ethnicities, genders, sexualities, or disabilities. This kind of oppression and unmentalised xenophobia is often hidden in the hierarchies and power structures of the organisations, governments, and nationalities in their symbolic traditions including weaponising of classical, folk, and popular or rock music (Brauer, 2016; Chornik, 2013; Cusick, 2013, Hirch, 2007; Papaeti, 2013a, 2013b, 2020; Pieslak, 2009).

Understanding even the subtle asymmetries of cultural and social relationships in music, and especially clear breaking of boundaries and using of music as oppression, is making easier the prevention of using music unethically and manipulatively as a weapon (Grant, 2013). It is also making the use of music feeling safe and not triggering fear for the refugees who are often traumatised as well as for the other people and minorities like students. Educating people in understanding their sometimes-unconscious dynamics of power in their relationships and music is also educating the people for the humanity and responsibility towards the world and each other.

6.3.1 Decolonising the Musical Experience

Understanding the asymmetries in power relationships and music is important when working with traumatised and refugees. This is because the refugees usually come from different cultures and ethnicities. They often have different kinds of customs and traditions that may relate to their spirituality and religious beliefs. Their cultural norms and values may differ to some degree from their host countries that are often representing Western way of life and culture as "normality". Therefore, encountering refugees from another countries and parts of the world needs to be culturally sensitive in music therapy and education treating them individually and without discrimination. This kind of understanding is a part of the cultural competency of the music therapist as well as the educator in creating services for the refugees that are equal with the citizens of the host country. Provided services should be respecting the rights of refugees regardless of their age, origins, nationality, religion, or conviction (Castaneda et al., 2018, p. 113; Comte, 2016; Ilmola-Sheppard et al., 2021).

For example, UN's Convention on the Rights of the Child (1989), article 31, is saying that children have a right "to participate fully in cultural and artistic life" that shall be promoted and encouraged, and have "equal opportunities for cultural, artistic, recreational and leisure activity" (p. 13). Therefore, also children of the refugees, asylum seekers, and immigrants should have free opportunities for music and arts in their host countries that may increase and maintain their health and wellbeing as well as prevent them from traumatisation and its consequences in the form of music therapy, for example.

Professional cultural competence is cultural awareness, knowledge, skills, encountering, and motivation to reflect own cultural rules, customs, values, and belief systems with those of the refugees respectively (Castaneda et al., 2018, pp. 113–114). It is a part of the cultural dialoguing of the therapist or the educator within oneself and with the other in therapy and in the encountering of refugees and students from the other cultural backgrounds (Alanne, 2010, 2019b; Saraneva, 2002, 2018). Cultural sensitivity means professionally respecting relationship skills and verbal or non-verbal encountering between the professionals and clients. It allows the differences in both parties and their "otherness" with respective rights on their own cultures, ways of expressing it, needs to be accepted and heard.

It is also important to note that refugees are not all similar and traumatised, but they are coming from different situations, countries, and representing various cultural identities (Comte, 2016). Thus, music therapists as well as other professionals need to be reflexive and challenge their possible neo-colonial assumptions about refugees being a homogeneous and traumatised group. It could unintentionally perpetuate oppression and strengthen negative connotations of the refugee identity being displaced and powerless as suggested by Comte (ibid.). Therefore, it is valuable to identify and strengthen the individual cultural identity in therapy or education that is making also possible the dealing with the grief and losses related to the forced migration. As an example, this kind of work was done in the earlier-discussed COVER model of music therapy in Germany, where refugees from different nations and cultures could bring and teach their own music for the other group participants (Mallon & Hoog Antink, 2021).

Working this way identifying and respecting the other cultural identities is decolonising of the musical experiences for the refugees. Shared music and safe musicking is allowing the witnessing and cultural dialoguing between different nationalities and ethnicities that may integrate traumas and ease possible prejudices, cultural projections, and conflicts transferred within the group dynamics (Gottesman, 2017, pp. 14–15). As discussed, otherness and minorities are easy targets for externalising anger where sharing of their own culture and subjective story may also inhibit forming of generalised narratives of being a refugee and belonging to a particular socio-ethnological group.

Therefore, it is important to hear and witness such unique refugee stories because as discussed becoming a refugee and a migrant in the host country can be a crisis (Akhtar, 1995). Opening, discussing, and musicking with peers in music therapy may also help in this respect to stabilise, work through, and integrate feelings and memories of being a refugee and an immigrant (Ahonen & Mongillo Desideri, 2014). In such a work, personalised stories with music from their home countries may elevate the immigrants and refugees enabling grieving and finding their true selves and identities. However, the goal of such therapeutic work is not to develop a prolonged refugee identity because it would be neo-colonising of the people with music (Comte, 2016).

The question of being a refugee, owing a refugee identity, or a narrative of oneself and the others is not simple as considered by Comte (2016). I think it is better to hear people and let them decide themselves how they are identifying and constructing their identities. Like with music, classical, popular, or rock music that may symbolise Western values and the host country that refugees, especially young people, may want to identify with (Hirch, 2007). Such Western music may confirm a new group identity and hope for the oppressed (Alanne, 2010; LeVine, 2009). For example, Western hip hop that has been very popular long time is used with refugees and other youth in music therapy commonly.

Therefore, listening, performing, or producing Western music or folk music from the home country of refugees in music therapy is not necessarily a colonising practice if the people in therapy have a real possibility to choose what kind of music they want to listen to. If it is gangsta rap or other music adolescents are listening and identifying with, it can be worth listening and discussing about in therapy openly. In prisons or camps, the detainees did not have this choice but music that represented the values and political agendas of perpetrators was violently and manipulatively forced upon them as "therapy", "re-education", or inducing fear like during the Greek Junta or War on Terror. Then, music like folk, hip hop, or metal was representing colonialised symbolic power and superiority of authorities and not people themselves like in real therapy. Instead, they were manipulated with music and sounds that should not be the objective of music therapy, music education, or any other practice with music.

When otherness is identified and respected mutually, it is not projected and imposed to another person. Then, it is not also colonised use of music and transferring of trauma to clients with cultural assumptions. However, as discussed, people may suffer from trauma symptoms they are not aware of that is requiring a trauma-informative approach from a therapist. Then, it may be good for the clients to develop a trauma survivor identity when it helps them to go therapy, work through, integrate their traumas, and continue with their lives.

Even though the trauma does not necessarily disappear and change in therapy, like a narrative may, a person may learn to accept and live with the history of trauma that is helpful. Finding a story of trauma that is heard, witnessed, and contained with a help of music can be also liberation and desensitisation from traumatic experiences. It is decolonising of musical experiences when a refugee torture survivor who may have been tortured with music can relax, listen, and enjoy music and sounds again in music therapy without disturbing feelings and thoughts (Alanne, 2010, 2019b).

6.3.2 Ableism and Disablism in Treatment, Education, and Music

Western health care and therapeutic as well as educational traditions with their practices may look refugees through trauma lenses that may be oppressive repetitive imposing of a trauma and a victim for the refugees (Comte, 2016). At the same time, there may also be difficulties in recognising mental issues and risk factors for health and wellbeing of refugees with the methods of Western health care (Castaneda et al., 2018, p. 133). The first point of view to the see all the refugees as potentially traumatised and having many risk factors for their health and wellbeing is an example of disablism relating to refugees. This kind of generalised assumption may lead to a self-silencing and disempowerment of refugees because of their internalised fear of persecution (Comte, 2016). Other cultural, ethnical, and sexual minorities may have similar risks of being silenced and fears of being discriminated or persecuted because of their identities and ideologies (Gombert, 2022).

With disablism, it is meant that something or someone is seen through the lenses of not being capable of doing something because of their health, dysfunction, social issues, gender, age, sexual issues, and so on. It relates to the ableism, where it is assumed that something or somebody is normal and capable to do something regardless of their cultural or social background and despite their illnesses and problems. It may lead to a situation where traumatised, or a person with autistic characters, learning, reading, and concentration issues, neurodiversity, or blindness, is performing normal and hiding the problems at school and their lives because of the minority stress (Bruce, 2022, pp. 126, 128; Davies, 2022, p. 23).

In this context, music and music therapy may be a part of the "normalising" and ableism of the students and clients like refugees that can be seen as a therapeutic possibility of providing accepted identity and empowerment as well as removing or reducing their symptoms. On the other hand, it could be a part of their avoidance and fostering of not accepting or seeing their differences and difficulties—the otherness of the individual students representing multiple oppressed identities like neurodiversity, for example—and their need for more recognition, support, and rehabilitation (Bruce, 2022, p. 126; Davies, 2022, pp. 22–23; Pickard, 2022, p. 9).

In this sense of ableism, music, music therapy, and music education, as well as other artistic approaches including music, may include possible oppression and excluding people who are not considered as "normal" (Ilmola-Sheppard et al., 2021, p. 36). This exclusion may cover the institutions of arts educating artists where idealised artists are considered as talented with an optimal body structure, coordination, and sensitive perception capabilities. Their audience is behaving according to the needs and schemes of the performance traditions idealised as normal respectively. Those who have disabilities or who cannot confirm with these rules of "normality" in their bodies or otherwise because they are handicapped and dysfunctional may be restricted outside of doing and consuming of arts in society (ibid.).

This kind of desired ableism relates to the ideology of being a valued/unvalued citizen that is ready and able to work in the contemporary society (Bruce, 2022, p. 128). Ableism is argued as species-typical, however, emphasising human individuality, in the neo-liberal culture of desiring the demonstration of normalcy and ability. In this thinking, disability is a bad object and linked to the racism in the structures of ableism like in the Nazi concentration camps, Gulags, or Greek and Chilean detainee camps during the dictatorships, where music was involved in marginalising and "educating" unvalued citizens. Therefore, especially refugees and immigrants are vulnerable targets for ableism because of their social status and otherness with different ideologies, ethnicities, possible poverty, illnesses, and unemployment; they are often suffering, and are seen as weak. However, as can be seen in the horrible away, ableism and disablism are connected and even essential for each other in the social and political systems of persecuting, dominating, and controlling of disability (ibid.).

Therefore, this hegemony of ableism may lead to a systemic oppression, poisonous education, and nepotism, even violence, of silencing the disabilities and otherness (Gombert, 2022, pp. 164–165). In addition to other music practices, such a systemic discrimination can be a part of the curriculums of music education and therapy studies emphasising certain music and theories related to privileged, often representing white male heteronormative people. However, systemic dynamics may also change; nowadays, it seems that therapists in the field like music therapists, music therapy educators, and researchers are more often women than men. So, the current discussions of normativity and otherness are not necessarily anymore about men and women or Blacks and Whites, but they are considering more broadly gender, sexuality, ethnicity, socioeconomic status, power, diversity, equity, and inclusion of different people to participate in music and other relationships (Ilmola-Sheppard et al., 2021).

Refugees and their treatment may involve multiple identities including clients and the therapists themselves that can be both from dominant and marginalised groups of the society (Bruce, 2022; Davies, 2022; Gombert, 2022, p. 165; Pickard, 2022). The experiences of black woman may differ from a black man's or white woman's experiences of marginalisation and internalised minority stress and fears relating to them (Gombert, 2022, p. 165). Therefore, it is important to remember often unconscious power dynamics in the treatment of refugees and other clients. In such a work, especially concerning the fact that we are living in more and more multicultural world where many cultures and cultural identities are co-existing, the cultural intersections of each person should be acknowledged.

This is also decolonising of the music experience where the dynamics of the therapeutic dyad or a group, including men and women, black or white, different age, and culture are in interaction. In a therapeutic work with refugees including music, the power dynamics relating to marginalised and minorities may be expressed through microaggression (Gombert, 2022, p. 165). Microaggressions may appear in the everyday subtle interactions and behaviours towards marginalised groups that can be intentional, unintentional, conscious, or unconscious. As continued, they can be as harmful as overt discrimination because they are harder to identify and not easily necessary admitted as biased, racial, sexistic, homophobic, or anti-immigrant attitudes by the white or other people belonging to a socially dominant group.

Microaggressions may have led to silencing, marginalising, or dismissing of the minoritised opinions according to some experiences of music therapy education because of their sexual (LGBTQIA+) or ethnic Latino/a, Black, or Chinese identity (Gombert, 2022, p. 167). In their experiences of microaggressions, a student or a supervisee had to carry special burden for the expectations of educating others about their minoritised identity. These kinds of microaggressions can quickly lead to a weathering and wearing down of therapists belonging to marginalised groups. In addition, music therapists and other music professionals are often belonging to a professional minority group in the health and social care that can cause them extra burden and stress because of the prejudices and continuous need to justify and show some evidence that their work is effective. This is a part of the systemic ableism and positivistic hegemony that is also influencing all health, social care, and education fields, including psychotherapy and other therapies as well. Also, working with minoritised group of refugees may invoke resistance and increase the pressure for the justifications of using music or music therapy in their treatments.

In therapy field, systemic ableism has led to a shortening of therapies and their research as many as possible people are tried to treat more effectively according to medical technological treatment procedures that are modelling the assembly line in factories (Alanne, 2019a, 2021). Usually, neither therapist's or their client's opinions and experiences are heard in planning or implementing such treatment procedures or research that are imposed upon them. Then, therapists and their clients are marginalised, and their voices are not heard. This is intersectional administration and biased use of power where the theoretical and political ideologies other than those constituting therapy like psychotherapy or music therapy are controlling the treatment from outside. As such, it is like poisonous education of the dominant group in excluding the feelings, experiences, and possible benefits of the clients and therapists that are de-centralised from their research, treatment, and narrative respectively.

It is also nepotism and exclusion in favour of particular people, stakeholders, professions, therapists, researchers, their careers, theories, studies, and treatments that should be acknowledged in the research and treatment policies. Especially, it is important to acknowledge the rights and the experiences of the vulnerable groups living in the institutions, mental health clients, elder people, children, or asylum seekers and refugees of different age so that they would not be excluded or distanced from the arts or therapy/rehabilitation services because their social status is marginalised as not "normal", "talent", or "equal" (Castaneda et al., 2018; Ilmola-Sheppard et al., 2021).

Otherwise, these beliefs of being inequal, disabled, and marginalised may become a part of the traumatisation of refugees and their internalised identity of otherness and being worthless. As such, they may transfer over generations if their mechanisms in the human relationships and society are not recognised, balanced, and corrected. This is also concerned with the clients like refugees and their relationship with music and arts where the experience of being worthless may transfer to music therapy and education as the marginalised core beliefs and transference of being poor in music. However, music and other arts may also be a part of correcting of such transgenerational traumatisation in music therapy, education, and society with positive experiences of their inclusion in the lives of different people (Alanne, 2017, 2023; Ilmola-Sheppard et al., 2021; Lehtonen et al., 2016).

6.3.3 Ethical Considerations for Music Practices in Therapy, Education, and Psychology

In the light of the recommendations of experts and researchers specialised in the study and treatment of refugees and arts, it seems relevant to foster the use of music for the special groups like refugees and asylum seekers (Castaneda et al., 2018; Ilmola-Sheppard et al., 2021). From the ethical point of view, music, arts, and cultural services are belonging to everyone and there should be equal possibilities to participate them in a society. Music has potential in treating, rehabilitating, and integrating the traumatic experiences of refugees in the different levels of services including therapy, education, and their encountering in the communities. Salutogenetic approaches that are promoting health and wellbeing with music towards good life should be encouraged in work with refugees as well as with other special groups. However, this should happen with shared musical situations and solidarity that are not objectifying identities of the refugees and not using or treating vulnerable people like hospitalised patients as commercial objects (Koivisto, 2022, pp. 82–83).

It would be good and recommendable that the use of music in health and social care as well as in education would have some psychological and especially therapeutic understanding how music can affect people. These musical approaches would also be good to develop towards the culture-sensitive and trauma-informed practices, so that the professionals could learn to use music in their work ethically (Koivisto, 2022; Sokira et al., 2023). Developing of safe practices with music would be important for encountering refugees from different cultures who are often traumatised.

Music therapists, pedagogists, and healthcare musicians working in hospitals and other institutions should be educated to understand the therapeutic and oppressive meaning of music concerning social justice and human rights in their work (Koivisto, 2022; Pickard, 2022). It would help in developing anti-oppressive practices including anti-oppressive pedagogy framework already in the core of the curriculums in these studies. Within this kind of education, the teachers of therapists and educators are in a crucial position as the role models for culture-sensitive and anti-oppressive pedagogy and practices that the students can identify with.

This is important to emphasise because otherwise there is a possibility of continuing of systemic ableism towards othering as unspeakable issues and conflicts, racism, in the community. The cultural dialoguing of differences and a safe dialogical space created for expressing different points of view freely and taking responsibility for others may help in dissolving conflicts and understanding differences (Gottesman, 2017). This way education for privileging and othering may be avoided if the students like therapists, pedagogists, and so on are educated not to feel superior and belonging to the elite from the beginning (Pickard, 2022, p. 10).

Instead, anti-oppressive pedagogy with cultural dialoguing is challenging the privileging, othering, and ableism with a critical discussion and theory approach (ibid.). As such, it can be transformative experience and learning, changing, growing as human being for the participants like students and refugees that can affect their ways of thinking and feeling life in future (Gottesman, 2017). At the bottom of anti-oppressive education and practices is equality of the people as a value that is a shared experience and not objectifying, excluding, or distancing experience with music. It is emphasising of the goodness of life in its standpoints with intersubjective lived experiences of music (Ilmola-Sheppard et al., 2021; Koivisto, 2022; Trondalen, 2023).

Using music as a weapon and oppression becomes from different origins of being privileged and superior to others. There is no responsibility with the use music and sounds for the victims or detainees at the wars, concentration camps, interrogation centres, and prisons. They are examples of institutionalised violence with music in its cruellest forms where the purpose is not only the breaking of the enemy but their personalities and dignities as well. Such musical practices are against the rules of war in international humanitarian law according to the International Committee of Red Cross (ICRC, 2014) and against the UN's Universal Declaration of Human Rights (UDHR, Article 5).

In this respect, there should be ethical education for military, soldiers, and their superiors about inhuman practices including using music and sounds in war, interrogation, and in imprisonment that would be symmetrical with the rules of war and human rights. Similarly to the discussed education of music in general, the teachers, superiors, stakeholders, and politicians in charge of soldiers and military personnel are holding great responsibility for being vital role models of controlling and not tolerating sadistic and manipulative use of music and sounds as a weapon or torture. The use of music and sounds in warfare should be discussed in the same context with other forbidden dehumanising conduct of soldiers, detainees, and civilians on war according to the rules of war (ICRC, 2014).

Also, medical personnel like doctors, psychologists, and therapists including music therapists are holding responsibility not to be a part of using music manipulatively as a weapon and torture during the conflicts and wars. It is ethically wrong to use psychological and medical knowledge and skills involving music in torture and otherwise in dehumanising of soldiers, detainees, civilians, and especially refugees, their children, and families, respectively. Especially violence, torture, and killing depicted in this book where music was used in increasing the pain of the often-civilian victims, their humiliation, and exhausting are committing and assisting a war crime or a genocide (ICRC, 2014).

Music and music therapy have long history of helping the pains of wounded soldiers in their rehabilitation, especially during and after WWII when music therapy academic training and practice began to develop in the US (AMTA, 2014). The use of music therapy in the military services has continued since then in helping the soldiers, veterans, their families, and children. Because of this history of modern music therapy in helping wounded, injured, and traumatised, it would be ethically suitable that music therapy would also continue to help refugees and others including civilians, their families, and children that have lost their homes and suffered the most from the wars and their consequences.

Especially, music therapists have a broad knowledge of music, sounds, and their psychological effects in helping wounded, minorities, and special groups that is different and should be discerned from music lessons, and other activities like hobbies arranged for the special groups like refugees. They are important too, but they are not the same as music therapy or psychotherapy that have, in addition to preventive goals, treating and rehabilitating goals for the use of music in their practices relating to health care (Alanne, 2010). Because of their education music therapists also have responsibility and Code of Ethics of not using their knowledge and skills of using music and sounds wrong (Trondalen, 2023, pp. 40–41). This includes teaching, understanding the power positions and culturally biased forms of using music in curriculums. As such, it also means teaching and using of music psychologically as a weapon, which would be disgraceful for the profession and its described honourable history in helping and providing psychosocial services for the minorities as well as for wounded and traumatised soldiers (AMTA, 2014; Bensimon et al., 2008).

References

Ahonen, H., & Mongillo Desideri, A. (2014). Heroines' journey—Emerging story by refugee women during group analytic music therapy. *Voices: A World Forum for Music Therapy, 14*(1). https://doi.org/10.15845/voices.v14i1.686

Akhtar, S. (1995). A third individuation: Immigration, identity, and the psychoanalytic process. *Journal of the American Psychoanalytic Association, 43*(4), 1051–1084.

Akhtar, S. (2009). *Comprehensive dictionary of psychoanalysis*. Karnac.

Akhtar, S. (2014). *Sources of suffering. Fear, greed, guilt, deception, betrayal, and revenge*. Karnac.

Akhtar, S. (2018). *Mind, culture, and global unrest. Psychoanalytic reflections*. Routledge.

Akombo, D. O. (2001). Reporting on music therapy in Kenya. *Voices: A World Forum for Music Therapy, 1*(1). https://doi.org/10.15845/voices.v1i1.45

Alanne, S. (2010). *Music psychotherapy with refugee survivors of torture. Interpretations of three clinical case studies*. Sibelius Academy. Studia Musica.

Alanne, S. (2017). Musiikillisen kokemuksen rajapinnat minuuden heijastajina. Milan Kunderan Naurun ja unohduksen kirjan avaamia näkökulmia. [The edges of musical experience as the reflections of self. The points of view unfolded from The book of laughter and forgetting by Milan Kundera.]. *Psykoterapia, 36*(2), 116–126.

Alanne, S. (2019a). Musiikki, vuorovaikutus ja sisäinen kokemus psykoterapiassa. [Music, interaction, and the inner experience in psychotherapy.]. *Psykoterapia, 38*(1), 39–49.

Alanne, S. (2019b). Musiikkipsykoterapia traumatisoituneiden pakolaisten ja maahanmuuttajien kuntoutuksessa. [Music psychotherapy in the rehabilitation of refugees and immigrants.]. *Psykoterapia, 38*(4), 306–318.

Alanne, S. (2021). *Väärän tiedon puu*. Mallintava tieto ja kulttuurin elämästä vieraantuneisuus. [The three of ignorance. Modeling knowledge and the estrangement of culture from life.] BoD.

Alanne, S. (2023). *The theory and practice of psychodynamic music psychotherapy*. Barcelona Publishers.

American Music Therapy Association (AMTA). (2014). *Music therapy and the military populations*. A Status Report and Recommendations on Music Therapy Treatment, Programs, Research, and Practice Policy. Silver Spring: American Music Therapy Association.

Baker, F., & Jones, C. (2005). Holding a steady beat: The effects of a music therapy program on stabilizing behaviours of newly arrived refugee students. *British Journal of Music Therapy, 19*(2), 67–74.

Barath, A. (1996). Creative therapies for war-traumatised children: 1991–95 Croatian experience. *Croatian Medical Journal, 37*(3), 174–184.

Bensimon, M., Amir, D., & Wolf, Y. (2008). Drumming through trauma: Music therapy with post-traumatic soldiers. *The Arts in Psychotherapy, 35*(1), 34–48.

Bernard, G., & Dvorak, A. L. (2022). Using music to address trauma with refugees: A systematic review and recommendations. *Music Therapy Perspectives, 41*(1), 30–43. https://doi.org/10.1093/mtp/miac013

Brauer, J. (2016). How can music be torturous?: Music in Nazi concentration and extermination camps. *Music & Politics, 10*(1). https://doi.org/10.3998/mp.9460447.0010.103

Bruce, C. (2022). Performing normal: Restless reflections on music's dis/abling potential. *Music Therapy Perspectives, 40*(2), 125–131.

Castaneda, A. E., Mäki-Opas, J., Jokela, S., Kivi, N., Lähteenmäki, M., Miettinen, T., Nieminen, S., Santalahti, P., & PALOMA Expert Group. (2018). *Pakolaisten mielenterveyden tukeminen Suomessa.* PALOMA käsikirja. [Supporting refugees' mental health in Finland. PALOMA handbook.] Guidance, May 2018. Publications of the National Institute for Health and Welfare.

Chornik, K. (2013). Music and torture in Chilean detention centers: Conversations with an ex-agent of Pinochet's secret police. *The World of Music, New Series, 2*(1), 51–65.

Cloonan, M., & Johnson, B. (2002). Killing me softly with his song: An initial investigation into the use of popular music as a tool of oppression. *Popular Music, 21*, 27–39.

Cloonan, M., & Johnson, B. (2008). *Dark side of the tune. Popular music and violence*. Ashgate.

Comte, R. (2016). Neo-colonialism in music therapy: A critical interpretive synthesis of the literature concerning music therapy practice with refugees. *Voices: A World Forum for Music Therapy, 16*(3). https://doi.org/10.15845/voices.v16i3.865

Convention on the Rights of the Child. (1989). United Nations. https://www.unicef.org/child-rights-convention/convention-text

Coombes, E. (2018). We all came from somewhere. *Voices: A World Forum for Music Therapy, 18*(1). https://doi.org/10.15845/voices.v18i1.915

Cusick, S. G. (2006). Music as torture/music as weapon. *Transcultural Music Review, 10.* http://www.sibetrans.com/trans/article/152/music-as-torture-music-as-weapon

Cusick, S. G. (2008). Musicology, torture, repair. *Radical Musicology*, 3. http://www.radical-musicology.org.uk/2008/Cusick.htm.

Cusick, S. G. (2013). Towards an acoustemology of detention in the 'global war on terror'. In G. Born (Ed.), *Music, sound and space: Transformations of public and private experience.* Cambridge University Press.

Davies, H. (2022). 'Autism is a way of being': An 'insider perspective' on neurodiversity, music therapy and social justice. *British Journal of Music Therapy, 36*(1), 16–26.

Dixon, M. (2002). Music and human rights. In J. P. Sutton (Ed.), *Music, music therapy and trauma. International perspectives* (pp. 119–132). Jessica Kingsley.

Einarsen, O. K., Krüger, V., Engebretsen, I. M. S., & Stige, B. (2024). Collaboration between social workers and music therapists in a child welfare context for unaccompanied refugee children: A focus group study. *Voices: A World Forum for Music Therapy, 24*(3). https://doi.org/10.15845/voices.v24i3.4071

Else, B. A., & González, M. (2023). Global trends in music therapy for disaster preparedness, response, and recovery. In L. E. Beer & J. C. Birnbaum (Eds.), *Trauma-informed music therapy. Theory and practice* (pp. 19–27). Routledge.

Enge, K. E. A., & Stige, B. (2021). Musical pathways to the peer community: A collective case study of refugee children's use of music therapy. *Nordic Journal of Music Therapy*. https://doi.org/10.1080/08098131.2021.1891130

Enge, K. E., Stige, B., & Øystein Nordanger, D. (2024). Refugee children's perspectives on participating in music therapy: A qualitative study. *Voices: A World Forum for Music Therapy, 24*(3). https://doi.org/10.15845/voices.v24i3.3998

Fancourt, D., & Saoirse, F. (2019). *What is the evidence on the role of the arts in improving health and well-being? A scoping review*. Health Evidence Network Synthesis Report 67. World Health Organization. Regional Office for Europe.

Fisher, A., & Gilboa, A. (2016). The roles of music amongst Holocaust survivors before, during, and after the Holocaust. *Psychology of Music, 44*(6), 1221–1239.

Gombert, D. J. (2022). Who is being silenced?: Sociocultural and privilege dynamics within music therapy education. *Music Therapy Perspectives, 40*(2), 164–173.

Gottesman, S. (2017). Hear and be heard: Learning with and through music as a dialogical space for co-creating youth led conflict transformation. *Voices: A World Forum for Music Therapy*, 17(1). https://doi.org/10.15845/voices.v17i1.857.

Grant, M. J. (2013). The illogical logic of music torture. *Torture, 23*(2), 4–13.

Gulbay, S. (2021). Exploring the use of hip hop-based music therapy to address trauma in asylum seeker and unaccompanied minor migrant youth. *Voices: A World Forum for Music Therapy, 21*(3). https://doi.org/10.15845/voices.v21i3.3192

Henry, M. (1987/2012). *Barbarism* (S. Davidson, Trans.). Continuum.

Heynen, E., Bruls, V., van Goor, S., Pat-El, R., Schoot, T., & van Hooren, S. A. (2022). Music therapy intervention for refugee children and adolescents in schools: A process evaluation using a mixed method design. *Children, 9*(1434). https://doi.org/10.3390/children9101434

Hirch, L. E. (2007). Weaponizing classical music: Crime prevention and symbolic power in the age of repetition. *Journal of Popular Music Studies, 19*(4), 342–358.

Hunt, M. (2005). Action research and music therapy: Group music therapy with young refugees in a school community. *Voices: A World Forum for Music Therapy, 5*(2). https://doi.org/10.15845/voices.v5i2.22

Ilmola-Sheppard, L., Rautiainen, P., Westerlund, H., Lehikoinen, K., Karttunen, S., Juntunen, M-L. & Anttila, E. (2021). *ArtsEqual*: Tasa-arvo taiteen ja taidekasvatuksen palveluiden suuntana. [ArtsEqual: Equality as the direction of the arts and the arts education services.]. University of the Arts Helsinki, CERADA.

International Committee of Red Cross (ICRC). (2014). *Rules of war (in a nutshell)*. Video, 22nd August 2014. https://www.icrc.org/en/document/rules-war-nutshell

John, E. (1991/2001). Music and concentration camps: An approximation (E. F. Livingstone, Trans.). *Journal of Musicological Research, 20*(4), 269–323.

Koivisto, T-A. (2022). *The (un)settled space of healthcare musicians*. Hybrid Music Professionalism in the Finnish Healthcare System. The Sibelius Academy of the University of the Arts Helsinki. Studia Musica 89.

Lehtonen, K., Juvonen, A., & Ruismäki, H. (2016). Musiikkirajoitteisuus sukupolvien välisenä siirtotaakkana. [Music restrictiveness as a transfer between generations.] *The Finnish Journal of Music Education*, 19(1), 29–42.

LeVine, M. (2009). *Heavy metal Islam*—Vainoa, vastarintaa ja taistelua muslimisieluista. [Heavy metal Islam—Rock, resistance, and the struggle for the soul of Islam.] Johnny Kniga.

Mallon, T., & Hoog Antink, M. (2021). The sound of lost homes—Introducing the COVER model—Theoretical framework and practical insight into music therapy with refugees and asylum seekers. *Voices: A World Forum for Music Therapy, 21*(2). https://doi.org/10.15845/voices.v21i2.3124

Moreno, J. (1999). Orpheus in hell: Music and therapy in the holocaust. *The Arts in Psychotherapy, 26*(1), 3–14.

Muriithi, B. A. K. (2020). Music as the medicine of trauma among refugees in Arizona. *Voices: A World Forum for Music Therapy, 20*(2). https://doi.org/10.15845/voices.v20i2.2891

Myerscough, F., & Wong, D. (2022). (Un)learning from experience: An exposition of minoritized voices on music therapy training. *Music Therapy Perspectives, 40*, 132–142.

Naliwajek-Mazurek, K. (2013). Music and torture in Nazi sites of persecution and genocide in occupied Poland, 1939–1945. *The World of Music, New Series, 2*(1), 31–50.

Orth, J. (2005). Music therapy with traumatised refugees in a clinical setting. *Voices: A World Forum for Music Therapy*. http://www.voices.no/mainissues/mi40005000182.html

Papaeti, A. (2013a). Music and 're-education' in Greek prison camps: From Makronisos (1947–1955) to Giaros (1967–1968). *Torture, 23*(2), 34–43.

Papaeti, A. (2013b). Music, torture, testimony: Reopening the case of the Greek Junta (1967–1974). *The World of Music, New Series, 2*(1), 67–89.

Papaeti, A. (2020). On music, torture and detention: Reflections on issues of research and discipline. *Transposition* [Online], Hors-série 2 | 2020, http://journals.openedition.org/transposition/5289; https://doi.org/10.4000/transposition.5289.

Pickard, B. (2022). Anti-oppressive pedagogy as an opportunity for consciousness raising in the music therapy profession: A critical disability studies perspective. *British Journal of Music Therapy, 36*(1), 5–15.

Pieslak, J. (2009). *Sound targets: American soldiers and Music in the Iraq war.* Indiana University Press.

Rose, G. J. (2004). *Between couch and piano. Psychoanalysis, music, art and neuroscience.* Brunner–Routledge.

Salberg, J. (2024a). Historical overview of theories of trauma and transgenerational transmissions. In J. Salberg & S. Grand (Eds.), *Transgenerational trauma. A contemporary introduction* (pp. 5–22). Routledge.

Salberg, J. (2024b). When wounds touch. Witnessing and enacting as embodied healing process. In J. Salberg & S. Grand (Eds.), *Transgenerational trauma. A contemporary introduction* (pp. 60–75). Routledge.

Saraneva, K. (2002). Trauma ja pakolaisuus. Psykoanalyyttinen käsitys traumasta ja sen hoidosta pakolais- ja siirtolaiskohtaloissa. [Trauma and refugees. Psychoanalytic conception of trauma and its treatment in the destinies of refugees and immigrants.] In S. Haaramo & K. Palonen (Eds.), *Trauman monet kasvot.* Psyykkinen trauma sisäisenä kokemuksena (pp. 49–96). [Many faces of trauma. Psychic trauma as an inner experience.] Therapeia Foundation.

Saraneva, K. (2018). Vieraasta kulttuurista tulevan pakolaisen kohtaaminen ja hoitaminen—Haasteet terapeutille. [The encountering and treatment of refugee coming from foreign culture—Challenges for the therapist.] In A. Zonzi & N. Söderblom (Eds.), *Pakolaisuus.* Merkitykset ihmiselle ja yhteisölle (pp. 90–108). [Refugeeism. The meaning for individual and community.] Therapeia Foundation.

Sokira, J., Allen, J., & Wagner, H. (2023). The resilience framework for trauma-informed music therapy. In L. E. Beer & J. C. Birnbaum (Eds.), *Trauma-informed music therapy. Theory and practice* (pp. 9–18). Routledge.

Storsve, V., Westbye, I. A., & Ruud, E. (2010). Hope and recognition: A music project among youth in a Palestinian refugee camp. *Voices: A World Forum for Music Therapy, 10*(1). https://doi.org/10.15845/voices.v10i1.158

Trondalen, G. (2023). *Ethical musicality*. Routledge.

Zharinova-Sanderson, O. (2004). Promoting integration and socio-cultural change: Community music therapy with traumatised refugees in Berlin. In M. Pavlicevic & G. Ansdell (Eds.), *Community music therapy* (pp. 233–248). Jessica Kingsley.

Chapter 7
Summary and Conclusion: Towards an Ethical Musicality

Music as a phenomenon is usually associated with positive things and comfortable feelings like in celebrating. Similarly, music studies including music therapy have emphasised the positive role of music for the humanity. As described by Papaeti (2020, p. 2), it took until the end of the twentieth century before the musicology and ethnomusicology began to be really interested in studying the use of music as a violence and oppression. For music therapy, it took even a bit more until the beginning of twenty-first century when the adverse effects of music were more discussed and studied, including the mechanisms and methods of using music as a violence and torture (Alanne, 2005, 2010; Moreno, 1999). This is in spite of the fact that modern music therapy developed as a treatment and science during WWII. Treating soldiers and their pain in wars had even longer roots. However, music therapists did not seem to study the other side of music used in wars but were focusing to study the benefits of it. First, anthropologists were studying more the mechanisms and methods of using music in violence (Papaeti, 2020, p. 2).

It remains open and would need more specific study of history why music therapists or other musicologists were not studying the adverse effects of music and violence relating to it before. It may relate to their positivist paradigms of science and former practice of musicology to study and analyse classical music, notations, and "pure music" from absolute music point of view and excluding the referential contexts like culture and symbolism. In music therapy, it has not been ethically right to study how to use music as a violence or torture or even think and discuss about it (Trondalen, 2023). On the other hand, in the therapeutic context, empathic people wanting to help others with music may not even have an idea about the possible negative effects of music like violence related to it. Therapists and students may have been more enthusiastic to study the good object side and the "magic" positive effects of music for moods without thinking the possibility that music would hurt someone as a bad object.

The positive effects connected with music may be like an addiction or mania where the addicted or a manic person is only seeing the good sides of the addictive

S. Alanne, *Music, Music Therapy and Refugees*,
https://doi.org/10.1007/978-3-031-94766-7_7

and all-good object and denying the other possibilities in their experiences. Like discussed, these kinds of all-good oceanic feelings without boundaries are related to the early infancy and the enjoyment of music as well as to religion. Freud (1930/1981, pp. 64–65) could not approach and enjoy the oceanic feelings because he could not explain what is moving him in music. This may have related to his rationalistic worldview of Enlightenment and psychoanalytic theory that made him reluctant to obey the forces of feelings, pleasure, and aggression, Eros and Thanatos, in music, in culture, and in himself respectively (Alanne, 2014, 2020, 2021, 2023; Kohut, 1977/1980; Lehtonen, 2007).

Similarly, it may be difficult to understand the bad object experiences related to music if the pleasant experience is so strong and holistic in soothing and comforting like milk or a breast for the infant. Then, the bad is away completely. This may explain why music is therapeutic and regulating moods and why the possible negative scaffolding of affects and feelings, even traumatising effects of music, like in torture and violence, in contrast to the positive scaffolding of music, have not much been focused, concerned, or studied before (Alanne, 2010; Fisher & Gilboa, 2016; Papaeti, 2020; Peltola & Vuoskoski, 2022; Taipale, 2023). However, negative experiences and dynamics of creating destroying acoustemology in symbolising the absolute power with sounds and music have been studied in the context of the musical torture in Nazi concentration camps and interrogation centres of US in the War on Terror (Alanne, 2010; Brauer, 2016; Cusick, 2013).

In addition to the possible psychological and paradigmatic difficulties to study adverse and traumatising effects of music related to the phenomena of violence and torture, war crimes have been hided and silenced. They may not have been wanted to study and discuss about these because of the shame and fear of punishment relating to those traumatising issues that are avoided and silenced over generations. This may have even negatively impacted the reputation of music as therapy and music therapy for the treatment of traumatised, torture survivors, and refugees because there may have been silent knowledge about adverse effects of music and how music and sounds have been used in manipulation, propaganda, interrogation, and torture.

As discussed earlier, often torture is silenced in a society, and they are difficult to study afterwards as people suffered from torture including music, or the tortures, do not want to memorise and talk about it. The same phenomenon has been noticed in the study of music that the use of music as a weapon or torture may be denied or it has not been even acknowledged as such even though it was documented in the court material, for example (Chornik, 2013; Papaeti, 2013, 2020). Also, soldiers may be afraid to discuss about the confidential matters relating to the use of music as a weapon in the battlefields or interrogations (Pieslak, 2009). This may result as the continuing of silencing, traumatisation, and exclusion of refugees and traumatised from musical activities and services if there is no research of music in their persecution or therapy stabilising their experiences respectively.

Musicologists including ethnomusicologists became more interested in music as violence and torture during the War on Terror and Iraq War when US forces used music in the battlefields and interrogations systemically (Cloonan & Johnson, 2002,

2008). Especially, the pioneering studies of Susanne Cusick (2006, 2008, 2013) raised objections towards using music as a weapon when the music societies reacted because of the use of music as torture by the US (Papaeti, 2020, p. 2). In 2007, the Society of Ethnomusicology (SEM) and the Society for American Music (SAM) condemned such use of music, and in 2008 American Musicological Society (AMS) followed with their resolution. In 2009, President Obama prohibited interrogation and interrogation-related treatment according to the UN Convention Against Torture. Finally, in 2014, The *Report of the Senate Select Committee on Intelligence Committee Study of the Central Intelligence Agency's Detention and Interrogation Program* admitted and similarly prohibited the use of such methods including music described in their report.[1]

Because the use of music as a weapon and torture in "re-educating" has continued elsewhere in the world, it would be relevant for musicologists, music therapists, and educators including their national and international societies to condemn such manipulative use of music and violence respectively (Grant, 2013; Dixon, 2002). This could increase the general knowledge and respect for the human rights that are violated in torture and violence including music. International studies, collaborations, and position papers that would condemn such treatment of fellow human beings could make a change in spreading knowledge and acknowledgement of such methods, including music, as not acceptable. This kind of study and education would be also relevant for the better understanding of the mechanisms of refugeeism, oppression, otherness, violence, and trauma including music. The developing of "ethical musicality" and Code of Ethics for music therapists, educators, musicians, and researchers studying music could contribute to this work internationally (Trondalen, 2023, pp. 50–51).

Ethical musicality means offering "a hope of good life" with music (Trondalen, 2023, p. 51). Such a musical goal suits well for the work with refugees, asylum seekers, torture survivors, and other traumatised. As discussed by Trondalen (ibid., p. 50), ethics in music and life require reflexivity how to use music, including laypersons as music consumers and performers as well as music therapy clients and therapists. Reflexivity means a capability to identify and "recognise oneself as an agent" in the social structures and norms with a capacity to think, question, and change one's position of thinking and doing if necessary (Zarate, 2022, p. 134). Thus, it can be a part of the reciprocal cultural and clinical listening as well as musical improvisation in music psychotherapy with clients and their encountering in music psychotherapy (pp. 134–135).

Similarly, music can also be a part of the cultural dialoguing and conflict resolving involving and developing reflexivity (Gottesman, 2017). With a capacity of reflexivity that means also self-reflection, the violent use of music as torture and humiliation maybe could have been avoided on War on Terror and Iraq War as it has been described by the soldiers that they had no specific tactics of using music in the

[1] See Sect. 3.3 "Music as a Non-touch Method of Interrogation" for more discussion on prohibitions in the US.

battlefield that came from their commanders. Instead, use of music seemed to be improvised and learnt from the fellow soldiers. Soldiers also used their own current favourite music like pop, rock, and metal for the purposes of frightening the enemy. Also, in the Chilean and Greek detention camps and centres as well as in the Nazi concentration camps, music seemed to be chosen randomly by the perpetrators according to their own preferences of music including classical music (Chornik, 2013; Cusick, 2006; John, 1991/2002; Moreno, 1999; Papaeti, 2013; Pieslak, 2009).

In this sense, self-reflection of what one is doing and participating is necessary for the ethics (Alanne, 2021; Henry, 1987/2012). Self-reflection means being in connection with the person's own feelings how things are felt that can help us to understand also others like refugees and traumatised: What is causing pain or pleasure? What is humiliating? We know this from our experiences of going through pain, being lost, confused, horrified, or crying sometimes in our lives. Therefore, self-reflection and reflexivity more broadly are meaning the understanding of the communicativeness and the culture of music through our own lived experiences and the body, the corporeality and auto-affectionality of being within music (Alanne, 2010, 2014, 2019, 2021, 2023; Trondalen, 2023; Zarate, 2022).

In their core, self-reflection and reflexivity are meaning the capacity for empathy towards other living beings and their situations that music can teach us. Like described in this book, sometimes they have been terribly lost and distanced from the life, feelings, and music. This opens the door for humiliation, traumatisation, and dehumanising practices of violence, torturing, and murdering in wars and societies—refugeeism—the darkness of soul.

References

Alanne, S. (2005). Music psychotherapy for torture survivors. *Music Therapy Today*, 6(4), 682–697. Special Issue: Proceedings of the 6th EMTC 2004 Conference, University of Jyväskylä. D. Aldridge & J. Fachner (Eds.), MusicTherapyWorld.net Witten: University Witten/Herdecke.

Alanne, S. (2010). *Music psychotherapy with refugee survivors of torture. Interpretations of three clinical case studies*. Sibelius Academy. Studia Musica.

Alanne, S. (2014). *Musiikkipsykoterapia*. Teoria ja käytäntö. [Music psychotherapy. Theory and practice.] Acta Universitatis Ouluensis D Medica 1248.

Alanne, S. (2019). Musiikki, vuorovaikutus ja sisäinen kokemus psykoterapiassa. [Music, interaction, and the inner experience in psychotherapy.]. *Psykoterapia, 38*(1), 39–49.

Alanne, S. (2020). Musiikin ja kielen suhteesta—sekä psykoterapeuttisesta arvosta. [About the relationship of music and language—And their psychotherapeutic value.]. *Psykoanalyyttinen Psykoterapia, 16*, 6–15.

Alanne, S. (2021). *Väärän tiedon puu*. Mallintava tieto ja kulttuurin elämästä vieraantuneisuus. [The three of ignorance. Modeling knowledge and the estrangement of culture from life.] BoD.

Alanne, S. (2023). *The theory and practice of psychodynamic music psychotherapy*. Barcelona Publishers.

Brauer, J. (2016). How can music be torturous?: Music in Nazi concentration and extermination camps. *Music & Politics, 10*(1). https://doi.org/10.3998/mp.9460447.0010.103

Chornik, K. (2013). Music and torture in Chilean detention centers: Conversations with an ex-agent of Pinochet's secret police. *The World of Music, New Series, 2*(1), 51–65.

Cloonan, M., & Johnson, B. (2002). Killing me softly with his song: An initial investigation into the use of popular music as a tool of oppression. *Popular Music, 21*, 27–39.

Cloonan, M., & Johnson, B. (2008). *Dark side of the tune. Popular music and violence.* Ashgate.

Cusick, S. G. (2006). Music as torture/music as weapon. *Transcultural Music Review, 10.* http://www.sibetrans.com/trans/article/152/music-as-torture-music-as-weapon

Cusick, S. G. (2008). Musicology, torture, repair. *Radical Musicology*, 3. http://www.radical-musicology.org.uk/2008/Cusick.htm.

Cusick, S. G. (2013). Towards an acoustemology of detention in the 'global war on terror'. In G. Born (Ed.), *Music, sound and space: Transformations of public and private experience.* Cambridge University Press.

Dixon, M. (2002). Music and human rights. In J. P. Sutton (Ed.), *Music, music therapy and trauma. International perspectives* (pp. 119–132). Jessica Kingsley.

Fisher, A., & Gilboa, A. (2016). The roles of music amongst Holocaust survivors before, during, and after the Holocaust. *Psychology of Music, 44*(6), 1221–1239.

Freud, S. (1930/1981). Civilizations and its discontents. In *Standard Ed.* (XXI, pp. 64–145). The Hogarth Press.

Gottesman, S. (2017). Hear and be heard: Learning with and through music as a dialogical space for co-creating youth led conflict transformation. *Voices: A World Forum for Music Therapy*, 17(1). https://doi.org/10.15845/voices.v17i1.857.

Grant, M. J. (2013). The illogical logic of music torture. *Torture, 23*(2), 4–13.

Henry, M. (1987/2012). *Barbarism* (S. Davidson, Trans.). Continuum.

John, E. (1991/2001). Music and concentration camps: An approximation (E. F. Livingstone, Trans.). *Journal of Musicological Research, 20*(4), 269–323.

Kohut, H. (1977/1980). *The restoration of the self.* International Universities Press.

Lehtonen, K. (2007). Musiikkia, rakas Sigmund! Sigmund Freudin musiikkisuhteen arvoitus. [Music, dear Sigmund! The enigma of Sigmund Freud's relationship to music.]. *Psykoterapia, 26*(3), 176–191.

Moreno, J. (1999). Orpheus in hell: Music and therapy in the holocaust. *The Arts in Psychotherapy, 26*(1), 3–14.

Papaeti, A. (2013). Music and 're-education' in Greek prison camps: From Makronisos (1947–1955) to Giaros (1967–1968). *Torture, 23*(2), 34–43.

Papaeti, A. (2020). On music, torture and detention: Reflections on issues of research and discipline. *Transposition* [Online], Hors-série 2 | 2020, http://journals.openedition.org/transposition/5289; https://doi.org/10.4000/transposition.5289.

Peltola, H.-R., & Vuoskoski, J. K. (2022). "I hate this part right here": Embodied, subjective experiences of listening to aversive music. *Psychology of Music, 50*(1), 159–174.

Pieslak, J. (2009). *Sound targets: American soldiers and Music in the Iraq war.* Indiana University Press.

Taipale, J. (2023). The modifying mirror: Binding one's experiences through music. In J. De Souza, B. Steege & J. Wiskus (Eds.), *The Oxford handbook of the phenomenology of music* (pp. C14S1–C14N65). Oxford Handbooks Online. https://doi.org/10.1093/oxfordhb/9780197577844.013.14.

Trondalen, G. (2023). *Ethical musicality.* Routledge.

Zarate, R. (2022). *Music psychotherapy and anxiety. Social, community, and clinical contexts.* Jessica Kingsley.

References

Abrams, B. (2021). Encountering transgenerational trauma through analytical music therapy. *Nordic Journal of Music Therapy, 30*(3), 197–218. https://doi.org/10.1080/08098131.2020.1853801

Ahonen, H., & Mongillo Desideri, A. (2014). Heroines' journey—Emerging story by refugee women during group analytic music therapy. *Voices: A World Forum for Music Therapy, 14*(1). https://doi.org/10.15845/voices.v14i1.686

Ahonen-Eerikäinen, H. (2007). *Group analytic music therapy*. Barcelona Publishers.

Akhtar, S. (1995). A third individuation: Immigration, identity, and the psychoanalytic process. *Journal of the American Psychoanalytic Association, 43*(4), 1051–1084.

Akhtar, S. (2009). *Comprehensive dictionary of psychoanalysis*. Karnac.

Akhtar, S. (2014). *Sources of suffering. Fear, greed, guilt, deception, betrayal, and revenge*. Karnac.

Akhtar, S. (2018). *Mind, culture, and global unrest. Psychoanalytic reflections*. Routledge.

Akombo, D. O. (2001). Reporting on music therapy in Kenya. *Voices: A World Forum for Music Therapy, 1*(1). https://doi.org/10.15845/voices.v1i1.45

Alanne, S. (2005). Music psychotherapy for torture survivors. *Music Therapy Today*, 6(4), 682–697. Special Issue: Proceedings of the 6th EMTC 2004 Conference, University of Jyväskylä. D. Aldridge & J. Fachner (Eds.), MusicTherapyWorld.net Witten: University Witten/Herdecke.

Alanne, S. (2010). *Music psychotherapy with refugee survivors of torture. Interpretations of three clinical case studies*. Sibelius Academy. Studia Musica.

Alanne, S. (2013). Psykodynaaminen musiikkipsykoterapia kidutuksesta traumatisoituneiden pakolaisten kanssa: Kliininen näkökulma. [Psychodynamic music psychotherapy with the refugees traumatised from the torture: A clinical point of view.]. *Psykoterapia, 32*(4), 264–276.

Alanne, S. (2014a). *Musiikkipsykoterapia*. Teoria ja käytäntö. [Music psychotherapy. Theory and practice.] Acta Universitatis Ouluensis D Medica 1248.

Alanne, S. (2014b). The ethnocultural and psychodynamic meaning of music for traumatised refugees. *Music Therapy Today*, 10(1), 48–49. Special issue: Proceedings of the 14th World Congress of Music Therapy Vienna/Krems, Austria, July 7–12, 2014.

Alanne, S. (2016a). Music as psychotherapy and the structure of personal identity. In M. Degli Stefani & F. Facchin (Eds.), *PerSona. Voce e identità. Opportunità musicali per la salute e il benessere* (pp. 131–137). CLEUP—Cooperativa Libraria Editrice Università di Padova.

Alanne, S. (2016b). Musiikki ja äänet tienä varhaislapsuuden kokemusmaailmaan—Kokemuksia mutismin psykoterapiasta. [Music and sounds as the road into the experience world of early childhood—Experiences of mutism's psychotherapy.]. *Psykoterapia, 35*(3), 186–195.

Alanne, S. (2017). Musiikillisen kokemuksen rajapinnat minuuden heijastajina. Milan Kunderan Naurun ja unohduksen kirjan avaamia näkökulmia. [The edges of musical experience as the

S. Alanne, *Music, Music Therapy and Refugees*,
https://doi.org/10.1007/978-3-031-94766-7

reflections of self. The points of view unfolded from The book of laughter and forgetting by Milan Kundera.]. *Psykoterapia, 36*(2), 116–126.

Alanne, S. (2018). *Transformations of fear in music, sounds, and therapy*. A paper presented 19th October 2018 at the XX International Forum of Psychoanalysis, Firenze, Italy. International Federation of Psychoanalytic Societies (IFPS).

Alanne, S. (2019a). Musiikki, vuorovaikutus ja sisäinen kokemus psykoterapiassa. [Music, interaction, and the inner experience in psychotherapy.]. *Psykoterapia, 38*(1), 39–49.

Alanne, S. (2019b). Musiikkipsykoterapia traumatisoituneiden pakolaisten ja maahanmuuttajien kuntoutuksessa. [Music psychotherapy in the rehabilitation of refugees and immigrants.]. *Psykoterapia, 38*(4), 306–318.

Alanne, S. (2020). Musiikin ja kielen suhteesta—sekä psykoterapeuttisesta arvosta. [About the relationship of music and language—And their psychotherapeutic value.]. *Psykoanalyyttinen Psykoterapia, 16*, 6–15.

Alanne, S. (2021). *Väärän tiedon puu*. Mallintava tieto ja kulttuurin elämästä vieraantuneisuus. [The three of ignorance. Modeling knowledge and the estrangement of culture from life.] BoD.

Alanne, S. (2023). *The theory and practice of psychodynamic music psychotherapy*. Barcelona Publishers.

Alayarian, A. (2024). *Group analysis for refugees experiencing trauma*. Routledge.

Allen, J. G., Fonagy, P., & Bateman, A. W. (2008). *Mentalizing in clinical practice*. American Psychiatric Publishing.

Alvin, J. (1965/1972). *Music for the handicapped child*. Oxford University Press.

Alvin, J. (1966/1975). *Music therapy*. Basic Books.

Alvin, J. (2001). Interview. VHS-Video. *Music Therapy in Europe in Occasion of the 5th European Music Therapy Congress*. Naples, April 2001. European Music Therapy Confederation (EMTC). Naples: ISFOM.

American Music Therapy Association (AMTA). (2014). *Music therapy and the military populations*. A Status Report and Recommendations on Music Therapy Treatment, Programs, Research, and Practice Policy. Silver Spring: American Music Therapy Association.

Austin, D. (1999). Vocal improvisation in analytically orientated music therapy with adults. In T. Wigram & J. De Backer (Eds.), *Clinical applications of music therapy in psychiatry* (pp. 141–157). Jessica Kingsley.

Austin, D. (2002). The wounded healer. The voice of trauma: A wounded healer's perspective. In J. P. Sutton (Ed.), *Music, music therapy, and trauma. International perspectives* (pp. 231–259). Jessica Kingsley.

Austin, D. (2009). *The theory and practice of vocal psychotherapy. Songs of the self*. Jessica Kingsley.

Baker, F., & Jones, C. (2005). Holding a steady beat: The effects of a music therapy program on stabilizing behaviours of newly arrived refugee students. *British Journal of Music Therapy, 19*(2), 67–74.

Barath, A. (1996). Creative therapies for war-traumatised children: 1991–95 Croatian experience. *Croatian Medical Journal, 37*(3), 174–184.

Barnard, L., & Jones, J. (2022). Bridging the gap: Developing a thinking space for refugees. In J. Stubley & L. Young (Eds.), *Complex trauma. The Tavistock model* (pp. 166–181). Routledge.

Beck, B. D. (2019). Music therapy for refugees. In S. Lindahl Jacobsen, I. Nygaard Pedersen, & L. O. Bonde (Eds.), *A comprehensive guide to music therapy. Theory, clinical practice, research and training* (2nd ed., pp. 342–352). Jessica Kingsley.

Beck, B. D., Messel, C., Lund Meyer, S., Cordtz, T. O., Søgaard, U., Simonsen, E., & Moe, T. (2018). Feasibility of trauma-focused guided imagery and music with adult refugees diagnosed with PTSD: A pilot study. *Nordic Journal of Music Therapy, 27*(1), 67–86.

Beck, B. D., Meyer, S. L., Simonsen, E., Søgaard, U., Petersen, I., Arnfred, S. M. H., Tellier, T., & Moe, T. (2021). Music therapy was noninferior to verbal standard treatment of traumatised refugees in mental healthcare: Results from a randomized clinical trial. *European Journal of Psychotraumatology, 12*(1), 1930960. https://doi.org/10.1080/20008198.2021.1930960

Bensimon, M. (2020). Perceptions of music therapists regarding their work with children living under continuous war threat: Experiential reframing of trauma through songs. *Nordic Journal of Music Therapy, 29*(4), 300–316. https://doi.org/10.1080/08098131.2019.1703210

Bensimon, M. (2023). Mechanisms of change in music therapy when treating adults coping with trauma. In L. E. Beer & J. C. Birnbaum (Eds.), *Trauma-informed music therapy. Theory and practice* (pp. 150–157). Routledge.

Bensimon, M., Amir, D., & Wolf, Y. (2008). Drumming through trauma: Music therapy with post-traumatic soldiers. *The Arts in Psychotherapy, 35*(1), 34–48.

Bernard, G., & Dvorak, A. L. (2022). Using music to address trauma with refugees: A systematic review and recommendations. *Music Therapy Perspectives, 41*(1), 30–43. https://doi.org/10.1093/mtp/miac013

Bernatzky, G., Strickner, S., Presch, M., Wendtner, F., & Kullich, W. (2013). Music as non-pharmacological pain management in clinics. In R. Macdonald, G. Kreutz, & L. Mitchell (Eds.), *Music, health, and wellbeing* (pp. 257–275). Oxford University Press.

Bettelheim, B. (1975/1994). *Satujen lumous.* Merkitys ja arvo. [The uses of enchantment. The meaning and importance of fairy tales.] (M. Rutanen, Trans.). WSOY.

Bion, W. R. (1959). Attacks on linking. *International Journal of Psycho-Analysis, 40*, 308–315.

Bion, W. R. (1961/2004). *Experiences in groups and other papers.* Routledge.

Bion, W. R. (1962a). A theory of thinking. In W. R. Bion (Ed.), *Second thoughts* (pp. 110–119). William Heinemann.

Bion, W. R. (1962b). *Learning from experience.* Karnac.

Bion, W. R. (1970/2018). *Attention and interpretation.* Routledge.

Blos, P. (1967). The second individuation process of adolescence. *Psychoanalytic Study of the Child, 22*, 162–186.

Blum, A., Goldberg, P., & Levin, M. (2023). *Here I'm alive. The spirit of music in psychoanalysis.* Columbia University Press.

Bonde, L. O. (2019a). Definitions of music therapy. In S. Lindahl Jacobsen, I. Nygaard Pedersen, & L.O. Bonde (Eds.), *A comprehensive guide to music therapy. Theory, clinical practice, research and training* (2nd ed., pp. 29–36). Jessica Kingsley.

Bonde, L. O. (2019b). Music therapy—A historical perspective. In S. Lindahl Jacobsen, I. Nygaard Pedersen & L.O. Bonde (Eds.), *A comprehensive guide to music therapy. Theory, clinical practice, research and training* (2nd ed., pp. 17–28). Jessica Kingsley.

Bonny, H. (2002). *Music and consciousness: The evolution of imagery and music.* Barcelona.

Bonny, H., & Pahnke, W. (1972). The use of music in psychedelic (LSD) psychotherapy. *Journal of Music Therapy, 9*(2), 64–83.

Boston Change Process Study Group (BCPSG). (2010). *Change in psychotherapy: A unifying paradigm.* Norton.

Braak, P. (2007). Musiktherapie mit kriegstraumatisierten Menschen. In H.-G. Wolf (Ed.), *Musiktherapie und Trauma* (pp. 89–96). Reichert Verlag.

Bracken, P. (2003). *Trauma. Culture, meaning and philosophy.* Whurr Publishers.

Brauer, J. (2016). How can music be torturous?: Music in Nazi concentration and extermination camps. *Music & Politics, 10*(1). https://doi.org/10.3998/mp.9460447.0010.103

Bruce, C. (2022). Performing normal: Restless reflections on music's dis/abling potential. *Music Therapy Perspectives, 40*(2), 125–131.

Brummer, M. (2005). Psykoterapeuttinen suhde ja prosessi. [Psychotherapeutic relationship and process.]. In M. Brummer & H. Enckell (Eds.), *Lasten ja nuorten psykoterapia* (Psychotherapy of children and adolescents) (pp. 109–142). WSOY.

Bruscia, K. E. (1987). *Improvisational models of Music therapy.* Charles C Thomas.

Bruscia, K. E. (1998). An introduction to music psychotherapy. In K. E. Bruscia (Ed.), *The dynamics of music psychotherapy* (pp. 1–15). Barcelona.

Bruscia, K. E. (2002). A psychodynamic orientation to the Bonny method. In K. E. Bruscia & D. E. Grocke (Eds.), *Guided imagery and music. The Bonny method and beyond* (pp. 225–243). Barcelona.

Bruscia, K. E. (2012). Introduction. In K. E. Bruscia (Comp.), *Case examples of music therapy for event trauma* (pp. 1–8). Barcelona.

Bruscia, K. E. (2014). *Defining music therapy* (3rd ed.). Barcelona.

Buis, J. S. (2013). Music and dance make me feel alive: From Mandela's prison songs and dances to public policy. *Torture, 23*(2), 55–67.

Cadesky, N. (2023). Group work with adults in short-term inpatient psychiatric treatment and recovery. In L. E. Beer & J. C. Birnbaum (Eds.), *Trauma-informed music therapy. Theory and practice* (pp. 96–103). Routledge.

Carr, C., d'Ardenne, P., Sloboda, A., Scott, C., Wang, D., & Priebe, S. (2012). Group music therapy for patients with persistent post-traumatic stress disorder—An exploratory randomized controlled trial with mixed methods evaluation. *Psychology and Psychotherapy: Theory, Research and Practice, 85*(2), 179–202. https://doi.org/10.1111/j.2044-8341.2011.02026x

Castaneda, A. E., Mäki-Opas, J., Jokela, S., Kivi, N., Lähteenmäki, M., Miettinen, T., Nieminen, S., Santalahti, P., & PALOMA Expert Group. (2018). *Pakolaisten mielenterveyden tukeminen Suomessa.* PALOMA käsikirja. [Supporting refugees' mental health in Finland. PALOMA handbook.] Guidance, May 2018. Publications of the National Institute for Health and Welfare.

Central Intelligence Agency (CIA). (1963). *KUBARK counterintelligence interrogation.*

Central Intelligence Agency (CIA). (1983/1988). *Human resource exploitation training manual.*

Chornik, K. (2013). Music and torture in Chilean detention centers: Conversations with an ex-agent of Pinochet's secret police. *The World of Music, New Series, 2*(1), 51–65.

Christensen, E. (2019). Music in body and brain. In S. Lindahl Jacobsen, I. Nygaard Pedersen, & L. O. Bonde (Eds.), *A comprehensive guide to music therapy: Theory, clinical practice, research and training* (2nd ed., pp. 51–64). Jessica Kingsley.

Cloonan, M., & Johnson, B. (2002). Killing me softly with his song: An initial investigation into the use of popular music as a tool of oppression. *Popular Music, 21*, 27–39.

Cloonan, M., & Johnson, B. (2008). *Dark side of the tune. Popular music and violence*. Ashgate.

Comte, R. (2016). Neo-colonialism in music therapy: A critical interpretive synthesis of the literature concerning music therapy practice with refugees. *Voices: A World Forum for Music Therapy, 16*(3). https://doi.org/10.15845/voices.v16i3.865

Convention on the Rights of the Child. (1989). United Nations. https://www.unicef.org/child-rights-convention/convention-text

Coombes, E. (2018). We all came from somewhere. *Voices: A World Forum for Music Therapy, 18*(1). https://doi.org/10.15845/voices.v18i1.915

Crenshaw, D. (2006). Neuroscience and trauma treatment. Implications for creative arts therapists. In L. Carey (Ed.), *Expressive and creative arts methods for trauma survivors* (pp. 21–37). Jessica Kingsley.

Cullberg, J., & Johannessen, J.-O. (2004). The dynamics of acute psychosis and the role of dynamic psychotherapy. In J. F. M. Gleeson & P. McGorry (Eds.), *Psychological interventions in early psychosis: A treatment handbook* (pp. 80–98). John Wiley & Sons.

Cusick, S. G. (2006). Music as torture/music as weapon. *Transcultural Music Review, 10.* http://www.sibetrans.com/trans/article/152/music-as-torture-music-as-weapon

Cusick, S. G. (2008). Musicology, torture, repair. *Radical Musicology*, 3. http://www.radical-musicology.org.uk/2008/Cusick.htm.

Cusick, S. G. (2013). Towards an acoustemology of detention in the 'global war on terror'. In G. Born (Ed.), *Music, sound and space: Transformations of public and private experience.* Cambridge University Press.

Davies, H. (2022). 'Autism is a way of being': An 'insider perspective' on neurodiversity, music therapy and social justice. *British Journal of Music Therapy, 36*(1), 16–26.

Davison, P. (2010, May 24). Paul Schäfer: Nazi colonel who established an anti-Semitic colony in Chile after the war. *The Independent.* https://www.independent.co.uk/news/obituaries/paul-schafer-nazi-colonel-who-established-an-antisemitic-colony-in-chile-after-the-war-1981014.html

De Backer, J., & Sutton, J. (2014a). Introduction. The music in music therapy: Writing without a pen. In J. De Backer & J. Sutton (Eds.), *The Music in Music therapy. Psychodynamic music therapy in Europe: Clinical, theoretical and research approaches* (pp. 14–22). Jessica Kingsley.

De Backer, J., & Sutton, J. (2014b). Theoretical perspectives of music therapy. The state of the art. In J. De Backer & J. Sutton (Eds.), *The music in music therapy. Psychodynamic music therapy in Europe: Clinical, theoretical and research approaches* (pp. 37–57). Jessica Kingsley.

De Backer, J., & Sutton, J. (2014c). Therapeutic interventions in psychodynamic music therapy: The music in music therapy. In J. De Backer & J. Sutton (Eds.), *The music in music therapy. Psychodynamic music therapy in Europe: Clinical, theoretical and research approaches* (pp. 338–349). Jessica Kingsley.

De Backer, J., & Van Camp, J. (2014). Music and psychosis: The answer from the patient to music therapy: Für Elise! In J. De Backer & J. Sutton (Eds.), *The music in music therapy. Psychodynamic music therapy in Europe: Clinical, theoretical and research approaches* (pp. 72–90). Jessica Kingsley.

Dimitrijević, A., & Buchholz, M. B. (2024). Introduction: Silencing the traumatised and hearing silencing. In M. B. Buchholz & A. Dimitrijević (Eds.), *Encountering silencing. Forms of oppression in individuals, families and communities* (pp. xv–xxxvii). Karnac.

Dixon, M. (2002). Music and human rights. In J. P. Sutton (Ed.), *Music, music therapy and trauma. International perspectives* (pp. 119–132). Jessica Kingsley.

Duey, C. J. (1991/1996). Group music therapy for women with multiple personalities. In K.E. Bruscia (Ed.), *Case studies in music therapy* (pp. 513–526). Barcelona.

Edwards, J. (2023). Cultural humility in music therapy practice. In L. E. Beer & J. C. Birnbaum (Eds.), *Trauma-informed music therapy. Theory and practice* (pp. 28–36). Routledge.

Einarsen, O. K., Krüger, V., Engebretsen, I. M. S., & Stige, B. (2024). Collaboration between social workers and music therapists in a child welfare context for unaccompanied refugee children: A focus group study. *Voices: A World Forum for Music Therapy, 24*(3). https://doi.org/10.15845/voices.v24i3.4071

Elliot, D. J., & Silverman, M. (2013). Why music matters: Philosophical and cultural foundations. In R. Macdonald, G. Kreutz, & L. Mitchell (Eds.), *Music, health, and wellbeing* (pp. 25–39). Oxford University Press.

Elman, S. J. (1998). Enactment, transference and analytic trust. In S. J. Elman & M. Moskowitch (Eds.), *Enactment: Toward a new approach to the therapeutic relationship* (pp. 183–203). Aronson.

Else, B. A., & González, M. (2023). Global trends in music therapy for disaster preparedness, response, and recovery. In L. E. Beer & J. C. Birnbaum (Eds.), *Trauma-informed music therapy. Theory and practice* (pp. 19–27). Routledge.

Enge, K. E. A., & Stige, B. (2021). Musical pathways to the peer community: A collective case study of refugee children's use of music therapy. *Nordic Journal of Music Therapy*. https://doi.org/10.1080/08098131.2021.1891130

Enge, K. E., Stige, B., & Øystein Nordanger, D. (2024). Refugee children's perspectives on participating in music therapy: A qualitative study. *Voices: A World Forum for Music Therapy, 24*(3). https://doi.org/10.15845/voices.v24i3.3998

Erel-Brodsky, H. (2016). I'm all ears—Thoughts on psychoanalysis: The musical reverie. *Contemporary Psychoanalysis, 52*(4), 578–601.

Erikson, E. H. (1950/1964). Toys and reasons. In M. R. Haworth (Ed.), *Child psychotherapy: Practice and theory* (pp. 3–11). Basic Books.

Erkkilä, J., Punkanen, M., Fachner, J., Ala-Ruona, E., Pöntiö, I., Tervaniemi, M., et al. (2011). Individual music therapy for depression: Randomised controlled trial. *The British Journal of Psychiatry, 199*, 132–139.

Ervamaa, T. (2002, April 6). Rapin tahdissa kansanmurhaan. [With the beat of rap to the genocide.] *Helsingin Sanomat*, p. B4.

Fancourt, D., & Saoirse, F. (2019). *What is the evidence on the role of the arts in improving health and well-being? A scoping review*. Health Evidence Network Synthesis Report 67. World Health Organization. Regional Office for Europe.

Feld, S. (2015). Acoustemology. In D. Novak & M. Sakakeeny (Eds.), *Keywords in sound* (pp. 12–21). Duke University Press.

Fisher, A., & Gilboa, A. (2016). The roles of music amongst Holocaust survivors before, during, and after the Holocaust. *Psychology of Music, 44*(6), 1221–1239.

Fonagy, P. (2004). *Attachment theory and psychoanalysis*. Karnac.

Fonagy, P., Gergely, G., Jurist, L. E., & Target, M. (2004). *Affect regulation, mentalization, and the development of the self*. Karnac.

Foucault, M. (1975/2001). *Tarkkailla ja rangaista*. [Surveiller et punir.] (E. Nivanka, Trans.). Otava.

Freud, S. (1900/1981). The interpretations of dreams. In *Standard Ed.* (IV–V). The Hogarth Press.

Freud, S. (1905a). Fragment of an analysis of a case of hysteria. In *Standard Ed.* (VII, pp. 7–122). The Hogarth Press.

Freud, S. (1905b). Three essays on the theory of sexuality. In *Standard Ed.* (Vol. VII, pp. 135–245). The Hogarth Press.

Freud, S. (1910/1981). The future prospects of psycho-analytic therapy. In *Standard Ed.* (XI, pp. 139–151). The Hogarth Press.

Freud, S. (1914a/1981). Remembering, repeating and working through (further recommendations on the technique of psychoanalysis II). In *Standard Ed.* (XII, pp. 147–156). The Hogarth Press.

Freud, S. (1914b/1981). The Moses of Michelangelo. In *Standard Ed.* (XIII, pp. 211–236). The Hogarth Press.

Freud, S. (1915/1981). The unconsciousness. In *Standard Ed.* (XIV, pp. 166–215). The Hogarth Press.

Freud, S. (1920/1981). Beyond the pleasure principle. In *Standard Ed.* (XVIII, pp. 7–64). The Hogarth Press.

Freud, S. (1923/1981). The ego and the id. In *Standard Ed.* (XIX, pp. 12–66). The Hogarth Press.

Freud, S. (1930/1981). Civilizations and its discontents. In *Standard Ed.* (XXI, pp. 64–145). The Hogarth Press.

Frith, S. (2004). Why does music make people so cross? *Nordic Journal of Music Therapy, 13*(1), 64–69.

Gallese, V. (2011). Intersubjektiivisuus neurotieteen näkökulmasta. Ruumiillinen jäljittely ja sen merkitys intersubjektiivisuudessa. [Intersubjectivity in the point of view of neuroscience. Bodily imitation and its meaning.] Trans. T. Välkki. *Psykoterapia*, 30(1), 4–17. (Original article: Embodied simulation and its role in intersubjectivity.)

Garland, C. (1998a). Action, identification and thoughts in post-traumatic states. In C. Garland (Ed.), *Understanding trauma. A psychoanalytic approach* (pp. 199–215). Second enlarged edition. The Tavistock Clinic Series. Karnac.

Garland, C. (1998b). Thinking about trauma. In C. Garland (Ed.), *Understanding trauma. A psychoanalytic approach* (pp. 9–31). Second enlarged edition. The Tavistock Clinic Series. Karnac.

Glaser, D. (2000). Child abuse and neglect and the brain—A review. *Journal of Child Psychology and Psychiatry, 41*(1), 97–116.

Gombert, D. J. (2022). Who is being silenced?: Sociocultural and privilege dynamics within music therapy education. *Music Therapy Perspectives, 40*(2), 164–173.

Gottesman, S. (2017). Hear and be heard: Learning with and through music as a dialogical space for co-creating youth led conflict transformation. *Voices: A World Forum for Music Therapy*, 17(1). https://doi.org/10.15845/voices.v17i1.857.

Grand, S. (2024). The wound and its social imperatives. In J. Salberg & S. Grand (Eds.), *Transgenerational trauma. A contemporary introduction* (pp. 45–59). Routledge.

Grant, M. J. (2013). The illogical logic of music torture. *Torture, 23*(2), 4–13.

Grassi, L. (2021). *The sound of the unconscious. Psychoanalysis as music*. Routledge.

Gratier, M., & Trevarthen, C. (2007). Voice, vitality, and meaning: On the shaping of the infant's utterances in willing engagement with culture. Comment on Bertau's "On the notion of voice". *International Journal for Dialogical Science, 2*(1), 169–181.

Gravestock, J. (2021). *Music therapy in adoption and trauma. Therapy that makes a difference after placement*. Jessica Kingsley.

Grocke, D., & Wigram, T. (2007). *Receptive methods in music therapy. Techniques and clinical applications for music therapy clinicians, educators and students*. Jessica Kingsley.

Grummitt, L., Baldwin, J. R., Lafoa, J., Keyes, K. M., & Barrett, E. L. (2024). Burden of mental disorders and suicide attributable to childhood maltreatment. *JAMA Psychiatry*. Published online May 8, 2024. https://doi.org/10.1001/jamapsychiatry.2024.0804.

Gulbay, S. (2021). Exploring the use of hip hop-based music therapy to address trauma in asylum seeker and unaccompanied minor migrant youth. *Voices: A World Forum for Music Therapy, 21*(3). https://doi.org/10.15845/voices.v21i3.3192

Hägg, V. (2020). Reverie-käsite ja sen soveltaminen kliiniseen käytäntöön. [The concept of reverie and its application in the clinical practice.]. *Psykoterapia, 39*(2), 91–103.

Handler Spitz, E. (1987). Separation-individuation in a cycle of songs. George crumb's ancient voices of children. *The Psychoanalytic Study of the Child, 42*, 531–543.

Hannibal, N. (2014). Implicit and explicit mentalisation in music therapy in the psychiatric treatment of people with borderline personality disorder. In J. De Backer & J. Sutton (Eds.), *The music in music therapy. Psychodynamic music therapy in Europe: Clinical, theoretical and research approaches* (pp. 211–223). Jessica Kingsley.

Hannibal, N. (2019). Mentalization-based treatment. In S. Lindahl Jacobsen, I. Nygaard Pedersen, & L. O. Bonde (Eds.), *A comprehensive guide to music therapy: Theory, clinical practice, research and training* (2nd ed., pp. 93–97). Jessica Kingsley.

Herman, J.L. (1992/2022). *Trauma and Recovery*. The Aftermath of Violence – From Domestic Abuse to Political Terror. New York: Basic Books.

Henry, M. (1987/2012). *Barbarism* (S. Davidson, Trans.). Continuum.

Herlihy, J., Ferstman, C., & Turner, S. W. (2004). Legal issues in work with asylum seekers. In J. P. Wilson & B. Drožđek (Eds.), *Broken spirits. The treatment of traumatised asylum seekers, refugees and torture victims* (pp. 641–658). Brunner–Routledge.

Herman, J. L. (1992/2022). *Trauma and Recovery*. The Aftermath of Violence – From Domestic Abuse to Political Terror. Basic Books.

Heynen, E., Bruls, V., van Goor, S., Pat-El, R., Schoot, T., & van Hooren, S. A. (2022). Music therapy intervention for refugee children and adolescents in schools: A process evaluation using a mixed method design. *Children, 9*(1434). https://doi.org/10.3390/children9101434

Hirch, L. E. (2007). Weaponizing classical music: Crime prevention and symbolic power in the age of repetition. *Journal of Popular Music Studies, 19*(4), 342–358.

Hoi Yan Fu, J. (2023). Finding one's voice: Working through developmental trauma with vocal psychotherapy. In L. E. Beer & J. C. Birnbaum (Eds.), *Trauma-informed music therapy. Theory and practice* (pp. 113–121). Routledge.

Hole, J., Hirsch, M., Ball, E., & Meads, C. (2015). Music as an aid for postoperative recovery in adults: A systematic review and meta-analysis. *Lancet, 386*, 1659–1671.

Holly, S. (2023). Changing the narrative: Exploring how music therapy can assist adolescents dealing with race-based traumatic stress. In L. E. Beer & J. C. Birnbaum (Eds.), *Trauma-informed music therapy. Theory and practice* (pp. 56–63). Routledge.

Hunt, M. (2005). Action research and music therapy: Group music therapy with young refugees in a school community. *Voices: A World Forum for Music Therapy, 5*(2). https://doi.org/10.15845/voices.v5i2.22

Ilmola-Sheppard, L., Rautiainen, P., Westerlund, H., Lehikoinen, K., Karttunen, S., Juntunen, M-L. & Anttila, E. (2021). *ArtsEqual*: Tasa-arvo taiteen ja taidekasvatuksen palveluiden suuntana. [ArtsEqual: Equality as the direction of the arts and the arts education services.]. University of the Arts Helsinki, CERADA.

International Committee of Red Cross (ICRC). (2014). *Rules of war (in a nutshell)*. Video, 22nd August 2014. https://www.icrc.org/en/document/rules-war-nutshell

John, E. (1991/2001). Music and concentration camps: An approximation (E. F. Livingstone, Trans.). *Journal of Musicological Research, 20*(4), 269–323.

Jones, C., & Baker, F. (2004). From healing rituals to music therapy: Bridging the cultural divide between therapist and young Sudanese refugees. *The Arts in Psychotherapy, 31*(2), 89–100.

Julkunen, E. (2024, February 24). Sodan erottama pari: Volodmyr jäi sotavangiksi, Inna pakeni Suomeen. [A couple separated by the war: Volodmyr was captured in war, Inna escaped to Finland.] *Ilta-Sanomat*. https://www.is.fi/ulkomaat/art-2000010246418.html

Keinänen, M. (2017). Mentalisaatiohoitomenetelmien teoreettiset perusteet ja toteutus. [Theoretical grounds and practice of mentalisation methods.] In I. Laitinen & S. Ollikainen (Eds.), *Mentalisaatio*. Teoriasta käytäntöön (pp. 82–104). [*Mentalisation*. From theory to practice.] Therapeia Foundation.

Kennedy, R. (2020). *The power of music. Psychoanalytic explorations*. Phoenix.

Kieseppä, V. (2022). *Mental health service use among immigrants living in Finland.* Doctoral Dissertation. Finnish Institute for Health and Welfare, University of Helsinki, Faculty of Medicine.

Kirves, J. (2008). "Päivittäinen myrkkyannoksemme"—sensuuria ja propagandaa jatkosodassa. ["Our daily portion of poison"—Censorship and propaganda in the continuing war.] In S. Näre & J. Kirves (Eds.), *Ruma sota.* Talvi- ja jatkosodan vaiettu historia (pp. 13–62). [*Ugly war. Silenced history of winter and continuing wars.*] Johnny Kniga.

Klafter, A. B. (2017). Mistrusting the analyst. In S. Akhtar (Ed.), *Mistrust. Developmental, cultural, and clinical realms* (pp. 165–177). Routledge.

Klause, I. (2013). Music and 're-education' in the Soviet Gulag. *Torture, 23*(2), 24–33.

Klein, M. (1946). Notes on some schizoid mechanisms. *International Journal of Psycho-Analysis, 27*, 99–110.

Klein, M. (1952). The origins of transference. *International Journal of Psycho-Analysis, 33*, 433–438.

Klein, M. (1955/1964). The psychoanalytic play technique. In M. R. Haworth (Ed.), *Child psychotherapy: Practice and theory* (pp. 277–286). Basic Books.

Knoblauch, S. H. (2000). *The musical edge of therapeutic dialogue*. The Analytic Press.

Kohut, H. (1977/1980). *The restoration of the self.* International Universities Press.

Kohut, H., & Levarie, S. (1950/1978). On the enjoyment of listening to music. In P.H. Ornstein (Ed.), *The search for the self. Selected writings of Heinz Kohut: 1950–1978. Vol. 1* (pp. 135–158). International Universities Press.

Koivisto, T-A. (2022). *The (un)settled space of healthcare musicians*. Hybrid Music Professionalism in the Finnish Healthcare System. The Sibelius Academy of the University of the Arts Helsinki. Studia Musica 89.

Kreutz, G., Quiroga Murcia, C., & Bongard, S. (2013). Psychoneuroendocrine research on music and health: An overview. In R. Macdonald, G. Kreutz, & L. Mitchell (Eds.), *Music, health, and wellbeing* (pp. 457–476). Oxford University Press.

Krüger, V., Nordanger, D. Ø., & Stige, B. (2018). Music therapy: Building bridges between a participatory approach and trauma-informed care in a child welfare setting. *Voices: A World Forum for Music Therapy, 18*(4). https://voices.no/index.php/voices/article/view/2593

Laitinen, I. (2017). Mentalisaatioon perustuvan terapian peruskäsitteet ja hoitotekniikat. [The basic concepts and treatment techniques of therapy based on mentalisation.] In I. Laitinen & S. Ollikainen (Eds.), *Mentalisaatio*. Teoriasta käytäntöön. [Mentalisation. From theory to practice.] (pp. 55–81). Therapeia Foundation.

Lansen, J., & Haans, T. (2004). Clinical supervision for trauma therapists. In J. P. Wilson & B. Drožđek (Eds.), *Broken spirits. The treatment of traumatised asylum seekers, refugees and torture victims* (pp. 317–353). Brunner–Routledge.

Leave No Marks. (2007, August). *Enhanced interrogation techniques and the risk of criminality.* Physicians for Human Rights and Human Rights First.

Lee, J. H. (2016). The effects of music on pain: A meta-analysis. *Journal of Music Therapy, 53*(4), 430–477.

Lefleur, J. (2022). *Music in the Holocaust: The roles of music in Nazi concentration camps*. MA Thesis. Hunter College, The City University of New York.

Lehtonen, K. (1996). *Musiikki, kieli ja kommunikaatio*. Mietteitä musiikista ja musiikkiterapiasta. [Music, language, and communication. Considerations of music and music therapy.] Jyväskylän yliopiston musiikkitieteen laitoksen julkaisusarja A: tutkielmia ja raportteja 17.

Lehtonen, K. (1997). Is there correspondence between the structures of music and the psyche? *Nordic Journal of Music Therapy, 6*(1), 43–52.

Lehtonen, K. (2007a). *Musiikin symboliset ulottuvuudet*. [Symbolic dimensions of music.] Finnish Society for Music Therapy.

Lehtonen, K. (2007b). Musiikkia, rakas Sigmund! Sigmund Freudin musiikkisuhteen arvoitus. [Music, dear Sigmund! The enigma of Sigmund Freud's relationship to music.]. *Psykoterapia, 26*(3), 176–191.

Lehtonen, K., & Heinonen, Y. (2007). Musiikki psyykkisen työn edistäjänä. Tapausseloste 8-vuotiaan tytön musiikkiterapiaistunnon analyyttisesta tulkinnasta. [Music as a promoter of psychic work. A case study of an 8-year-old girl's music therapy session and its analytic interpretation.] In M. Laitinen & H. Westerlund (Eds.), *Musikaalisuuden ytimessä*. Juhlakirja Kai Karmalle (pp. 165–181). [In the heart of musicality. Essays in honour of Kai Karma.] Sibelius Academy.

Lehtonen, K., Juvonen, A., & Ruismäki, H. (2016). Musiikkirajoitteisuus sukupolvien välisenä siirtotaakkana. [Music restrictiveness as a transfer between generations.] *The Finnish Journal of Music Education*, 19(1), 29–42.

Lemma, A. (2006). *Introduction to the practice of psychoanalytic psychotherapy*. Wiley.

LeVine, M. (2009). *Heavy metal Islam*—Vainoa, vastarintaa ja taistelua muslimisieluista. [Heavy metal Islam—Rock, resistance, and the struggle for the soul of Islam.] Johnny Kniga.

Levinge, A. (2015). *The music of being: Music therapy, Winnicott, and the school of object relations*. Jessica Kingsley.

Levitin, D. (2007). *This is your brain on music: Understanding a human obsession*. Atlantic Books.

Mahler, M., Pine, F., & Bergman, A. (1975/1991). *The psychological birth of the human infant: Symbiosis and individuation*. Karnac.

Mallon, T., & Hoog Antink, M. (2021). The sound of lost homes—Introducing the COVER model—Theoretical framework and practical insight into music therapy with refugees and asylum seekers. *Voices: A World Forum for Music Therapy, 21*(2). https://doi.org/10.15845/voices.v21i2.3124

McFerran, K. S., Lai, H. I. C., Chang, W.-H., Acquaro, D., Chin, T. C., Stokes, H., & Crooke, A. (2020). Music, rhythm, and trauma: A critical interpretive synthesis of research literature. *Frontiers in Psychology, 11*, 324. https://doi.org/10.3389/fpsyg.2020.00324

McWilliams, N. (2021). *Psychoanalytic supervision*. Guilford.

Mensfelt, J. (2017). *Auschwitz-Birkenaun muistopaikka*. Opas. [Auschwitz-Birkenau Memorial. Guide.] Auschwitz-Birkenau State Museum.

Miller, A. (1979/1984). *Lahjakkaan lapsen tragedia ja todellisen itseyden etsintä*. [The drama of the gifted child.] (T. Lahti, Trans.). WSOY, Finnish edition.

Miller, A. (1980/1985). *Alussa oli kasvatus*. Kätketty julmuus ja väkivallan juuret. [For your own good. Hidden cruelty in child-rearing and the roots of violence.] (M. Rutanen, Trans.). WSOY, Finnish edition.

Miranda, D., Gaudreau, P., Debrosse, R., Morizot, J., & Kirmayer, L. J. (2013). Music listening and mental health: Variations on internalizing psychopathology. In R. Macdonald, G. Kreutz, & L. Mitchell (Eds.), *Music, health, & wellbeing* (pp. 513–529). Oxford University Press.

Modvig, J., & Jaranson, J. M. (2004). A global perspective of torture, political violence and health. In J. P. Wilson & B. Drožđek (Eds.), *Broken spirits. The treatment of traumatised asylum seekers, refugees and torture victims* (pp. 33–52). Brunner–Routledge.

Monaci, M. G., Gratier, M., Trevarthen, C., Grandjean, D., Kuhn, P., & Filippa, M. (2021). Parental perception of vocal contact with preterm infants: Communicative musicality in the neonatal intensive care unit. *Children, 8*(6), 513. https://doi.org/10.3390/children8060513

Moreno, J. (1999). Orpheus in hell: Music and therapy in the holocaust. *The Arts in Psychotherapy, 26*(1), 3–14.

Mukamel, R., Ekstrom, A. D., Kaplan, J., Iacoboni, M., & Fried, I. (2010). Single-neuron responses in humans during execution and observations of actions. *Current Biology, 20*(8), 750–756.

Muriithi, B. A. K. (2020). Music as the medicine of trauma among refugees in Arizona. *Voices: A World Forum for Music Therapy, 20*(2). https://doi.org/10.15845/voices.v20i2.2891

Music, G. (2022). The body as the new royal road to the unconscious. In J. Stubley & L. Young (Eds.), *Complex trauma. The Tavistock model* (pp. 74–92). Routledge.

Myerscough, F., & Wong, D. (2022). (Un)learning from experience: An exposition of minoritized voices on music therapy training. *Music Therapy Perspectives, 40*, 132–142.

Naliwajek-Mazurek, K. (2013). Music and torture in Nazi sites of persecution and genocide in occupied Poland, 1939–1945. *The World of Music, New Series, 2*(1), 31–50.

Nathanson, A. (2022). Relational trauma and oppression: Clinical work with young men groomed and sexually abused as children. In J. Stubley & L. Young (Eds.), *Complex trauma. The Tavistock model* (pp. 130–142). Routledge.

Neustadt, R. (2004). Music as memory and torture: Sounds of repression and protest in Chile and Argentina. *Chasqui, 33*(1), 128–137.

O'Rourke, J. (2022). Therapeutic yoga and psychotherapy for facilitating posttraumatic growth. In J. Stubley & L. Young (Eds.), *Complex trauma. The Tavistock model* (pp. 226–239). Routledge.

O'Connell, A. (1990). Fifty years of music therapy at the University of the Pacific. *Music Therapy Perspectives, 8*, 90–92.

Ogden, T. H. (1999/2005). *Reverie and interpretation. Sensing something human*. Karnac.

Ortamo, S. (2024, January 6). Aigul pakeni Kiinan vankileiriltä—hän kertoo minkälainen kidutusvälinen on "tiikerituoli". [Aigul escaped from the prison camp of China—She tells what kind of torture equipment is a "Tiger Chair".] *YLE*. https://yle.fi/a/74-20065432?utm_source=social-media-share&utm_medium=social&utm_campaign=ylefiapp

Orth, J. (2005). Music therapy with traumatised refugees in a clinical setting. *Voices: A World Forum for Music Therapy*. http://www.voices.no/mainissues/mi40005000182.html

Orth, J., & Verburgt, J. (1998). One step beyond. Music therapy with traumatised refugees in a psychiatric clinic. In D. Dokter (Ed.), *Arts therapists, refugees and migrants. Reaching across borders* (pp. 80–93). Jessica Kingsley.

Orth, J., Doorschodt, L., Verburgt, J., & Drožđek, B. (2004). Sounds of trauma: An introduction to methodology in music therapy with traumatised refugees in clinical and outpatient settings. In J. P. Wilson & B. Drožđek (Eds.), *Broken spirits. The treatment of traumatised asylum seekers, refugees and torture victims* (pp. 443–480). Brunner–Routledge.

Papaeti, A. (2013a). Music and 're-education' in Greek prison camps: From Makronisos (1947–1955) to Giaros (1967–1968). *Torture, 23*(2), 34–43.

Papaeti, A. (2013b). Music, torture, testimony: Reopening the case of the Greek Junta (1967–1974). *The World of Music, New Series, 2*(1), 67–89.

Papaeti, A. (2020). On music, torture and detention: Reflections on issues of research and discipline. *Transposition* [Online], Hors-série 2 | 2020, http://journals.openedition.org/transposition/5289; https://doi.org/10.4000/transposition.5289.

Pavlicevic, M. (1997). *Music therapy in context. Music, meaning, and relationship*. Jessica Kingsley.

Peltola, H.-R., & Vuoskoski, J. K. (2022). "I hate this part right here": Embodied, subjective experiences of listening to aversive music. *Psychology of Music, 50*(1), 159–174.

Penn, M. L., & Kojo Clarke, P. (2008). Art, culture, and pediatric mental and behavioral health: An interdisciplinary, public health approach. In B. J. Koen (Ed.), *The Oxford handbook of medical ethnomusicology* (pp. 72–92). Oxford University Press.

Pérez-Martinez, C. (2023). Music therapy with children in the aftermath of a natural disaster. In L. E. Beer & J. C. Birnbaum (Eds.), *Trauma-informed music therapy. Theory and practice* (pp. 64–73). Routledge.

Pickard, B. (2022). Anti-oppressive pedagogy as an opportunity for consciousness raising in the music therapy profession: A critical disability studies perspective. *British Journal of Music Therapy, 36*(1), 5–15.

Pieslak, J. (2009). *Sound targets: American soldiers and Music in the Iraq war*. Indiana University Press.

Pitkäniemi, A., Sihvonen, A. J., Särkämö, T., & Soinila, S. (2020). Musiikki-interventiot kivun hoidon osana. [Music-based interventions in pain management.] *Lääkärilehti* [Finnish Medical Journal], 75(37), 1843–1848.

Plato. (2007). *Valtio*. [The state] (M. Itkonen-Kaila, Trans.). Otava.

Priestley, M. (1975). *Music therapy in action*. Constable.

Priestley, M. (1994). *Essays on analytical music therapy*. Barcelona.

Rechardt, E. (1987). *Experiencing music. The psychoanalytic study of the child, 42, 511–530*. Yale University Press.

Reik, T. (1948/1998). *Listening with the third ear. The inner experience of psychoanalyst*. Farrar, Straus and Giroux.

Reik, T. (1953/1960). *The haunting melody. Psychoanalytic experiences in life and music*. Grove Press.

Report of the Senate Select Committee on Intelligence Committee Study of the Central Intelligence Agency's Detention and Interrogation Program together with Foreword by Chairman Feinstein and Additional and Minority Views. (2014, December 9). 113th Congress 2d Session. S. Report 113–288.

Reuter, L., Grandke, V., Gumz, A., Tuinmann, G., & Bauer, S. (2021). Unbewusstes hörbar machen—psychodynamische Musiktherapie im klinischen Kontext. *Psychotherapeut, 66*, 545–558.

Reyes, A. (1999). *Songs of the caged, songs of the free: Music and the Vietnamese refugee experience*. University Press.

Robarts, J. Z. (2003). The healing function of improvised songs in music therapy with a child survivor of early trauma and sexual abuse. In S. Hadley (Ed.), *Psychodynamic music therapy: Case studies* (pp. 141–182). Barcelona.

Rose, G. J. (2004). *Between couch and piano. Psychoanalysis, music, art and neuroscience*. Brunner–Routledge.

Salberg, J. (2024a). Between silence and words: Attachment, trauma and the mode of transgenerational transmissions. In J. Salberg & S. Grand (Eds.), *Transgenerational trauma. A contemporary introduction* (pp. 27–44). Routledge.

Salberg, J. (2024b). Historical overview of theories of trauma and transgenerational transmissions. In J. Salberg & S. Grand (Eds.), *Transgenerational trauma. A contemporary introduction* (pp. 5–22). Routledge.

Salberg, J. (2024c). When wounds touch. Witnessing and enacting as embodied healing process. In J. Salberg & S. Grand (Eds.), *Transgenerational trauma. A contemporary introduction* (pp. 60–75). Routledge.

Salo, O. (2024). Negatiivinen kyvykkyys psykoanalyyttisen menetelmän läpäisevänä periaatteena. [Negative capability as the overall principle of psychoanalytic method.]. *Psykoterapia, 43*(4), 289–302.

Saraneva, K. (2002). Trauma ja pakolaisuus. Psykoanalyyttinen käsitys traumasta ja sen hoidosta pakolais- ja siirtolaiskohtaloissa. [Trauma and refugees. Psychoanalytic conception of trauma and its treatment in the destinies of refugees and immigrants.] In S. Haaramo & K. Palonen (Eds.), *Trauman monet kasvot*. Psyykkinen trauma sisäisenä kokemuksena (pp. 49–96). [Many faces of trauma. Psychic trauma as an inner experience.] Therapeia Foundation.

Saraneva, K. (2018). Vieraasta kulttuurista tulevan pakolaisen kohtaaminen ja hoitaminen—Haasteet terapeutille. [The encountering and treatment of refugee coming from foreign culture—Challenges for the therapist.] In A. Zonzi & N. Söderblom (Eds.), *Pakolaisuus*. Merkitykset ihmiselle ja yhteisölle (pp. 90–108). [Refugeeism. The meaning for individual and community.] Therapeia Foundation.

Schulman, G. (2002). Sietämisen kestämisestä eheytymiseen. Objektin sisällyttämiskyky ja trauman integrointi. [From bearing resilience to cohesiveness. The internalising of object and the integration of trauma] In S. Haaramo & K. Palonen (Eds.), *Trauman monet kasvot*. Psyykkinen trauma sisäisenä kokemuksena (pp. 162–187). [Many faces of trauma. Psychic trauma as an inner experience.] Therapeia Foundation.

Schwartz, E. K. (1956/1964). A psychoanalytical study of the fairy tale. In M. R. Haworth (Ed.), *Child psychotherapy: Practice and theory* (pp. 383–395). Basic Books.

Scrine, E., & Koike, A. (2023). Questioning the promise of safety in trauma-informed music therapy practice. In L. E. Beer & J. C. Birnbaum (Eds.), *Trauma-informed music therapy. Theory and practice* (pp. 37–44). Routledge.

Segal, H. (1957). Notes on symbol formation. *International Journal of Psycho-Analysis, 38*, 391–397.

Siirala, M. (1966/1969). *Medicine in metamorphosis. Speech, presence, and integration*. Tavistock.

Siirala, M. (1983). *From transfer to transference. Seven essays on the human predicament*. Therapeia Foundation.

Silove, D. (2004). The global challenge of asylum. In J. P. Wilson & B. Drožđek (Eds.), *Broken spirits. The treatment of traumatised asylum seekers, refugees and torture victims* (pp. 13–31). Brunner Routledge.

Siltala, P. (2014). Ydintietoisuuden muotoutuminen varhaisen vuorovaikutuksen tilassa. [The shaping of core-consciousness in the state of early interaction.]. *Psykoterapia, 33*(2), 83–92.

Sinkkonen, J. (1997). Musiikin merkitys lapsen kehityksessä. [The meaning of music in the development of child.] In M. Kaikkonen & S. Mattila (Eds.), *Musiikki ja mielen mahdollisuudet* [Music and the possibilities of the mind.] (pp. 41–54). Publication Series of Sibelius Academy Continuing Education 1.

Skinner, K., Kurkjian, A., & Ahonen, H. (2021). Bruscia's clinical techniques for improvisational music therapy in autism research: A scoping review. *Approaches: An Interdisciplinary Journal of Music Therapy, 13*(2), 162–177.

Slotoroff, C. (1994). Drumming technique for assertiveness and anger management in the short-term psychiatric setting for adult and adolescent survivors of trauma. *Music Therapy Perspectives, 12*(2), 111–116.

Smetana, M., & Storz, D. (2020). Psychotherapeutische Techniken in der Musiktherapie. In H. U. Schmidt, T. Stegemann, & C. Spitzer (Eds.), *Musiktherapie bei psychischen und psychosomatischen Störungen* (pp. 53–58). Elsevier.

Sokira, J., Allen, J., & Wagner, H. (2023). The resilience framework for trauma-informed music therapy. In L. E. Beer & J. C. Birnbaum (Eds.), *Trauma-informed music therapy. Theory and practice* (pp. 9–18). Routledge.

Solms, M. (2017/2019). Mikä "tiedostamaton" on ja missä se sijaitsee aivoissa? Neuropsykoanalyyttinen näkökulma. [What is "the unconscious," and where is it located in the brain? A neuropsychoanalytic perspective.] (A. von Schulman, Trans.). *Psykoterapia*, 38(1), 62–70.

Solms, M. (2018). Psykoanalyysin tieteellinen perusta. [The scientific ground of psychoanalysis.] (A. von Schulman, Trans.). Psykoterapia, 37(2), 136–140.

Solms, M. (2021). *The hidden spring: A journey to the source of consciousness*. Profile Books.

Solms, M., & Turnbull, O. (2002/2018). *The brain and the inner world. An introduction to the neuroscience of subjective experience*. Routledge.

Solomon, Z., Laor, N., & McFarlane, A.C. (1996/2007). Acute posttraumatic reactions in soldiers and civilians. In B.A. van der Kolk, A.C. McFarlane & L. Weisaeth (Eds.), *Traumatic stress. The effects of overwhelming experience on mind, body, and society* (pp. 102–114). Guilford.

Standley, J. (1996). Music as a therapeutic intervention in medical and dental treatment: Research and clinical applications. In T. Wigram, B. Saperston, & R. West (Eds.), *The art and science of music therapy: A handbook* (pp. 3–22). Harwood Academic Publishers.

Steel, Z., Mares, S., Newman, L., Bijou, B., & Dudley, M. (2004). The politics of asylum and immigration detention: Advocacy, ethics, and the professional role of the therapist. In J. P. Wilson & B. Drožđek (Eds.), *Broken spirits. The treatment of traumatised asylum seekers, refugees and torture victims* (pp. 659–687). Brunner–Routledge.

Stephens Langdon, G. (2023). Music therapy in the treatment of complex trauma in adult mental health. In L. E. Beer & J. C. Birnbaum (Eds.), *Trauma-informed music therapy. Theory and practice* (pp. 122–130). Routledge.

Stern, D. N. (1985/2004). *The interpersonal world of the infant. A view from psychoanalysis and developmental psychology*. Karnac.

Stern, D. N. (2004). *The present moment in psychotherapy and everyday life*. Norton.

Stern, D. N. (2010). *Forms of vitality. Exploring dynamic experience in psychology, arts, psychotherapy, and development*. Oxford University Press.

Storsve, V., Westbye, I. A., & Ruud, E. (2010). Hope and recognition: A music project among youth in a Palestinian refugee camp. *Voices: A World Forum for Music Therapy, 10*(1). https://doi.org/10.15845/voices.v10i1.158

Strachey, J. (1934/1969). The nature of the therapeutic action in psychoanalysis. *International Journal of Psychoanalysis, 50*, 275–295.

Strehlow, G. (2009). The use of music therapy in treating sexually abused children. *Nordic Journal of Music Therapy, 18*(2), 167–183.

Strehlow, G., & Hannibal, N. (2019). Mentalizing in improvisational music therapy. *Nordic Journal of Music Therapy, 28*(4), 333–346.

Strehlow, G., & Lindner, R. (2016). Music therapy interaction patterns in relation to borderline personality disorder (BPD) patients. *Nordic Journal of Music Therapy, 25*(2), 134–158.

Stubley, J. (2022a). Complex trauma: The initial consultation. In J. Stubley & L. Young (Eds.), *Complex trauma. The Tavistock model* (pp. 11–33). Routledge.

Stubley, J. (2022b). The Tavistock trauma service. In J. Stubley & L. Young (Eds.), *Complex trauma. The Tavistock model* (pp. 34–55). Routledge.

Sullivan, J. M. (2007). Music for the injured soldier: A contribution of American women's military bands during world war II. *Journal of Music Therapy, 44*, 282–305.

Sutton, J. (2002). Trauma. Trauma in context. In J. P. Sutton (Ed.), *Music, music therapy and trauma. International perspectives* (pp. 21–39). Jessica Kingsley.

Sutton, J., & De Backer, J. (2009). Music, trauma and silence: The state of the art. *The Arts in Psychotherapy, 36*(2), 75–83.

Sutton, J., & De Backer, J. (2014). Supervision in music therapy: The jumping-off point. In J. De Backer & J. Sutton (Eds.), *The music in music therapy. Psychodynamic music therapy in Europe: Clinical, theoretical and research approaches* (pp. 300–319). Jessica Kingsley.

Svedberg Yinger, O. (2023). I am safe and I am strong: Understanding adverse childhood experiences and building resilience through trauma-informed music therapy. In L. E. Beer & J. C. Birnbaum (Eds.), *Trauma-informed music therapy. Theory and practice* (pp. 47–55). Routledge.

Swallow, M. (2002). The brain—Its music and its emotion: The neurology of trauma. In J. P. Sutton (Ed.), *Music, music therapy and trauma. International perspectives* (pp. 41–53). Jessica Kingsley.

Swinburne, M. (2022). Helping the heroes: Psychoanalytic work with military veterans. In J. Stubley & L. Young (Eds.), *Complex trauma. The Tavistock model* (pp. 143–165). Routledge.

Tähkä, V. (1993/1997). *Mielen rakentuminen ja psykoanalyyttinen hoitaminen*. [Mind and its treatment: A psychoanalytic approach.] WSOY, Finnish edition.

Taipale, J. (2023). The modifying mirror: Binding one's experiences through music. In J. De Souza, B. Steege & J. Wiskus (Eds.), *The Oxford handbook of the phenomenology of music* (pp. C14S1–C14N65). Oxford Handbooks Online. https://doi.org/10.1093/oxfordhb/9780197577844.013.14.

Temple, N., & Waddell, M. (1998/2002). Series editors' preface (pp. viiii–x). In C. Garland (Ed.), *Understanding trauma. A psychoanalytic approach*. Second enlarged edition. The Tavistock Clinic Series. Karnac.

The BZFO reports. 2000–2002. *Meeting the music* (pp. 20–28). Centre for the Treatment of Torture Survivors.

Trevarthen, C. (2011). What is it like to be a person who knows nothing? Defining the active intersubjective mind of a newborn human being. *Infant and Child Development, 20*, 119–135.

Trevarthen, C., & Malloch, S. (2000). The dance of wellbeing: Defining the musical therapeutic effect. *Nordic Journal of Music Therapy, 9*(2), 3–17.

Trondalen, G. (2023). *Ethical musicality*. Routledge.

Trondalen, G., & Bonde, L. O. (2013). Music therapy: Models and interventions. In R. Macdonald, G. Kreutz, & L. Mitchell (Eds.), *Music, health, and wellbeing* (pp. 40–62). Oxford University Press.

Uurtimo, Y. (2000). *On puhuttava siitä mistä vaikenemme*. Martti Siiralan ajatuksia elämästä. [We must talk from what we are silent. Thoughts of Martti Siirala from life.] Tammi.

Välimäki, S. (2015). Musical representation of war, genocide, and torture: Treating cultural trauma with music. *Acta Translatogica* 3: Pax R. Hartama-Heinonen & P. Kukkonen (Eds.), (pp. 122–136). University of Helsinki, Nordica/Department of Finnish, Finno-Ugrian and Scandinavian Studies, Swedish Translation Studies.

van der Kolk, B. (1996/2007a). The complexity of adaptation to trauma. Self-regulation, stimulus discrimination, and characterological development. In B.A. van der Kolk, A.C. McFarlane & L. Weisaeth (Eds.), *Traumatic stress. The effects of overwhelming experience on mind, body, and society* (pp. 182–213). Guilford.

van der Kolk, B. (1996/2007b). Trauma and memory. In B.A. van der Kolk, A.C. McFarlane & L. Weisaeth (Eds.), *Traumatic stress. The effects of overwhelming experience on mind, body, and society* (pp. 279–302). Guilford.

van der Kolk, B. (2014). *The body keeps score. Mind, brain and body in the transformation of trauma*. Allen Lane.

van der Kolk, B.A., & McFarlane, A.C. (1996/2007). The black hole of trauma. In B.A. van der Kolk, A.C. McFarlane & L. Weisaeth (Eds.), *Traumatic stress. The effects of overwhelming experience on mind, body, and society* (pp. 3–23). Guilford.

van der Kolk, B.A., Weisaeth, L., & van der Hart, O. (1996/2007). History of trauma in psychiatry. In B.A. van der Kolk, A.C. McFarlane & L. Weisaeth (Eds.), *Traumatic stress. The effects of overwhelming experience on mind, body, and society* (pp. 47–74). Guilford.

van der Kolk, B. A., Burbridge, J. A., & Suzuki, J. (1997). The psychobiology of traumatic memory. Clinical implications of neuroimaging studies. *Annals of the New York Academy of Sciences, 821*, 99–111.

Vibe Jespersen, K., & Vuust, P. (2012). The effects of relaxation music listening on sleep quality in traumatized refugees: A pilot study. *Journal of Music Therapy, 49*(2), 205–229.

Volkan, V. D. (2004). From hope for a better life to broken spirits: An introduction. In J. P. Wilson & B. Drožđek (Eds.), *Broken spirits. The treatment of traumatised asylum seekers, refugees and torture victims* (pp. 7–12). Brunner–Routledge.

Volkan, V. D. (2018a). *Immigrants and refugees. Trauma, perennial mourning, prejudice, and border psychology*. Routledge.

Volkan, V.D. (2018b). Pakolaiskriisit, uhat ryhmäidentiteetille ja jaettu ennakkoluuloisuus. [Refugee crises, threats to the group identity, and the shared prejudice.] In A. Zonzi & N. Söderblom (Eds.), *Pakolaisuus*. Merkitykset ihmiselle ja yhteisölle (pp. 33–57). [Refugeeism. The meaning for individual and community.] Therapeia Foundation.

Volkman, S. (1993). Music therapy and the treatment of trauma. Induced dissociative disorders. *The Arts in Psychotherapy, 20*, 243–251.

Welten, R. (2002). I sing the body. On the corporeality of music. *Tijdschrift voor muziektheorie, 7*(3), 196–199.

Wigram, T. (2004). *Improvisation. Methods and techniques for music therapy clinicians, educators and students*. Jessica Kingsley.

Wigram, T. (2019). Free improvisation therapy—The Alvin model. In S. Lindahl Jacobsen, I. Nygaard Pedersen, & L.O. Bonde (Eds.), *A comprehensive guide to music therapy. Theory, clinical practice, research and training* (2nd ed., pp. 189–192). Jessica Kingsley.

Wilson, J. P. (2004). Empathy, trauma transmission, and countertransference in posttraumatic psychotherapy. In J. P. Wilson & B. Drožđek (Eds.), *Broken spirits. The treatment of traumatised asylum seekers, refugees and torture victims* (pp. 277–316). Brunner–Routledge.

Winnicott, D. W. (1971/1997). *Playing and reality*. Routledge.

Wolf, H.-G. (2007). Grundlagen der Psychotraumatologie und der Traumatherapie. In H.-G. Wolf (Ed.), *Musiktherapie und Trauma* (pp. 11–20). Reichert Verlag.

Yeomans, F. E., Clarking, J. F., & Kernberg, O. F. (2015). *Transference-focused psychotherapy for borderline personality disorder. A clinical guide*. American Psychiatric Publishing.

Young, L., & Stubley, J. (2022). Writing trauma: Literary representations of traumatic experience. In J. Stubley & L. Young (Eds.), *Complex trauma. The Tavistock model* (pp. 253–265). Routledge.

Zarate, R. (2022). *Music psychotherapy and anxiety. Social, community, and clinical contexts*. Jessica Kingsley.

Zharinova-Sanderson, O. (2004a). Can music help? Music therapy with traumatised refugees and torture survivors. In D. Aldridge & J. Fachner (Eds.), *Info CD ROM V*. Dialogue and Debate—Conference Proceedings of the 10th World Congress on Music Therapy (pp. 2049–2060). MusicTherapyWorld.net. University Witten Herdecke.

Zharinova-Sanderson, O. (2004b). Promoting integration and socio-cultural change: Community music therapy with traumatised refugees in Berlin. In M. Pavlicevic & G. Ansdell (Eds.), *Community music therapy* (pp. 233–248). Jessica Kingsley.

Index

S. Alanne, *Music, Music Therapy and Refugees*, https://doi.org/10.1007/978-3-031-94766-7

www.ingramcontent.com/pod-product-compliance
Lightning Source LLC
Chambersburg PA
CBHW052340040925
31950CB00065B/425
* 9 7 8 3 0 3 1 9 4 7 6 5 0 *